Singular Europe

Singular Europe

Economy and Polity of the European Community after 1992

Edited by

William James Adams

This volume is sponsored by the
Chicago Council on Foreign Relations

Ann Arbor

THE UNIVERSITY OF MICHIGAN PRESS

Copyright © by the University of Michigan 1992
All rights reserved
Published in the United States of America by
The University of Michigan Press
Manufactured in the United States of America

1995   1994   1993   1992   4   3   2   1

A CIP catalogue record for this book is available from the British Library.

Library of Congress Cataloging-in-Publication Data

Singular Europe : economy and polity of the European Community after
    1992 / edited by William James Adams.
        p.   cm.
    Includes bibliographical references and index.
    ISBN 0-472-09504-8 (alk. paper)
    1. European Economic Community.   2. Europe 1992.   3. European
Economic Community countries—Economic conditions.   4. European
Economic Community countries—Foreign economic relations.
    I. Adams, William James, 1947–   .
HC241.2.S5323   1992
341.24'22—dc20   92-22674
                                                                            CIP

For Richard E. Caves
Flawless mentor, faithful friend

Preface

During the past two years, it has been my pleasure to assist the Chicago Council on Foreign Relations in hosting a series of seminars on Europe after 1992. Featuring an exceptional cast of speakers, many of whom have shaped as well as studied European events, the series addressed a broad spectrum of issues associated with the economic, political, and legal futures of Europe.

In September, 1991, participants in the program assembled for two days at the University of Michigan to discuss the papers each had written for presentation in Chicago. Philip Allott and William Wallace were invited to serve as principal commentators, with help from Morris Bornstein, Greg Duncan, Mitsuo Matsushita, and Robert Stern. Following that convocation, each participant transformed his paper into the chapter that appears in this volume.

The seminar program in Chicago and the writing of the papers were supported by the Konrad Adenauer Program for European Policy Studies of the Chicago Council on Foreign Relations. The conference at the University of Michigan was supported primarily by a grant to the University of Michigan from the W. K. Kellogg Foundation and secondarily by the Adenauer program. I am deeply grateful to Harold Jacobson, Associate Vice-President for International Academic Affairs at Michigan, for his patronage. I wish also to acknowledge environmental assistance from the Cook Research Funds of the Michigan Law School and from the Committee on Comparative and Historical Research on Market Economies in the Michigan Department of Economics.

Several individuals deserve more than thanks for the energy they contributed to this enterprise. In Chicago: John Rielly, President of the Chicago Council, proposed the project and chaired the seminar session; Arthur Cyr, Vice-President of the Council, administered therapeutic doses of enthusiasm and tolerance to the entire venture; and Lotti Ross arranged each of the seminar evenings. In Ann Arbor: Irita Grierson deceived all present into thinking that a pleasant conference can be arranged without hitch or effort; she also kept me connected, during the project's long gestation period, with the authors, the Chicago Council, and my own wits; Wouter de Ploey and Ulrich Hommel preserved the conference proceedings; Rita Rendell, Christie Bonk,

viii   Preface

and Debbie Steinaway, with help orchestrated by Muray Taylor, processed
prodigious quantities of prose, in various languages and states of disrepair,
creating eventually the miraculous facsimile of a polished document. Finally,
at the University of Michigan Press: Colin Day, Director of the Press, assisted
actively and insightfully in shaping the final product, Deborah Evans and
Laurie Ham followed the project in detail, Liz Cunningham prepared the
index, and Chris Milton guaranteed the quick copyediting of which most
authors are doomed only to dream.

Contents

General Introduction

William James Adams

Not long ago, people referred to Europe as the Old Continent. This appellation served less to celebrate the longevity of Europe's contribution to civilization than to acknowledge the decline of its role in world affairs. In retrospect, it appears that those who trumpeted the finality of Europe's departure from center stage might have relied excessively on extrapolations from the period of material and psychological damage associated with two world wars. Today's perceptions of Europe's prospects and importance differ strikingly from those promenading at the end of World War II.

Europe now looks big. In terms of population, the United States is just 76 percent as large as the European Community (EC), 69 percent as large as Western Europe, and 50 percent as large as Europe (excluding the former USSR). In terms of GDP, the United States is 18 percent larger than the EC, but Western Europe as a whole is its equal.[1]

Europe also looks increasingly rich. Although the United States continues to best all European countries in income per capita, its margin of leadership has dwindled considerably. In 1955, after the cement had set on postwar "reconstruction," real income per capita in the United States was triple that in Italy, double that in France, 87 percent larger than in Germany, and 68 percent larger than in the United Kingdom. A mere quarter-century later, income per capita in the United States was 85 percent larger than in

---

1. The data in this paragraph relate to 1989. Data on population are taken from World Bank, *Social Indicators, 1990* (Baltimore: Johns Hopkins University Press for the World Bank, 1991). Data on GDP (measured at current prices and current purchasing-power-parity exchange rates) are taken from Organization for Economic Cooperation and Development, *National Accounts, 1960–1989*, vol. 1, *Main Aggregates* (Paris: OECD, 1991). The EC includes Belgium, Denmark, France, Federal Republic of Germany, Greece, Ireland, Italy, Luxembourg, the Netherlands, Portugal, Spain, and the United Kingdom. Western Europe is defined as the EC plus members of the European Free Trade Association (Austria, Finland, Iceland, Norway, Sweden, and Switzerland). Europe is defined as Western Europe plus Albania, Bulgaria, Czechoslovakia, German Democratic Republic, Hungary, Poland, Romania, and Yugoslavia.

Italy, 50 percent larger than in the United Kingdom, 20 percent larger than in France, and just 14 percent larger than in Germany. Moreover, many European countries now rank above the United States according to various social indicators. For example, the infant mortality rate is lower in all but two countries of Western Europe (Greece and Portugal) than it is in the United States.[2]

Most important, though, Europe is bubbling over with change. Between the conception and the completion of this study—a period of just three years—the Federal Republic of Germany absorbed the German Democratic Republic; Czechoslovakia, Hungary, and Poland dispatched communist rule; Yugoslavia and the Soviet Union lost their glue; and the Baltic states received recognition of their independence. Despite formidable traditions of neutrality, Sweden and Switzerland came to contemplate membership in the EC. Discussions of a European Economic Area recalled the pipedream of Charles de Gaulle: a semicohesive Europe stretching from the Atlantic Ocean to the Ural Mountains. If Europe is still old in the chronological sense, it is certainly experiencing the vitality of a second childhood.

Given the tumultuous course of its recent history, any attempt to predict the contours (let alone the details) of Europe's future must be considered brash; and no such attempt will be made here. Rather, this volume is designed to reveal Europe's pulse—to capture the excitement of the past decade's events and of the next decade's policy agenda. Written by people with extraordinary knowledge and experience of Europe, its chapters will help the reader to understand the economic and political forces behind tomorrow's headlines.

Central to an understanding of Europe as a whole is an understanding of the European Community. Most European countries already belong, covet membership, or recognize (however reluctantly) the need for close ties. Although unlikely ever to encompass all of Europe, the EC does and will shape decisively the futures of members and nonmembers alike. Accordingly, this book focuses on attitudes in and about the EC.

During the 1980s and the first part of the 1990s, the EC devoted its energy to removing artificial impediments to the free flow of goods, services, capital, and workers among its member states. More symbolically than expectantly, it set January 1, 1993, as the date for completing these efforts to create a single internal market. Project 1992 was not designed, however, to suppress all economic, political, and social variations among the twelve member coun-

---

2. Data on real gross domestic income per capita in 1955 and 1980 are taken from Irving B. Kravis, Alan Heston, and Robert Summers, *World Product and Income: International Comparisons of Real Gross Product* (Baltimore: Johns Hopkins University Press for the World Bank, 1982), table 8–3. Data on infant mortality are taken from World Bank, *Social Indicators*.

tries. Following its completion, then, what steps remained untaken along the path of European integration? This is the question addressed in part 1.

Ultimately, the authors of Project 1992 wished to modify the behavior and social performance of Europe's business enterprises. The proximate targets of their reforms, however, were governments rather than companies: the single internal market was to be created primarily by altering various laws, regulations, and administrative practices in the member states. The success of Project 1992 thus depended on the validity of two propositions: that EC policy would have the desired effect on national governments, and that the resulting changes in national-government behavior would have the desired effect on business. To what extent did Project 1992 have these effects? Did it alter the behavior of business enterprises and the structure of economically meaningful markets? These are the questions addressed in part 2.

Any attempt to strengthen the ties between some countries can be perceived as an attempt to weaken the ties of those countries to third parties. Americans are not alone in fearing that the EC constitutes a fortress in the making—a set of prosperous markets from which enterprises based in other nations will be excluded. The views of the outsiders are expressed and evaluated in part 3.

Part 1
A New European Community?

Introduction to Part 1

William James Adams

Nineteen ninety-two is not just a period of time; to many people, it is a deadline for and symbol of European economic integration. It acquired this status on June 14, 1985, when the EC Commission transmitted to the European Council a white paper proposing elimination of some 300 specific impediments to the free flow of goods, services, workers, and capital within the Community. Completion of the job was expected to take two full terms of effort on the part of the Commission. The second of these was scheduled to end on December 31, 1992. Hence the name, Project 1992.

As a deadline, 1992 can easily mislead. Even before publication of the white paper, the EC had achieved a great deal of economic integration. In the EEC, for example, by 1970, virtually all explicit tariffs and quotas had disappeared, a common external tariff had been established, ambitious rules of competition had been implemented, and the Common Agricultural Policy had been launched. During the subsequent decade, members of the EC inaugurated the European Monetary System and a comprehensive, Community-level industrial policy for steel. More generally, throughout the life of the Community, the European Court of Justice (ECJ) has fostered integration. Sometimes this took the simple if striking form of upholding the supremacy of Community law; at other times it amounted to treating Community-level legislative paralysis with tonic doses of judicial activism. In fact, the subtle interplay of legislative, administrative, and judicial initiative in the service of economic integration bears comparison to a parallel and contemporary dynamic, the racial integration of the United States. Neither process achieved steady and monotonic progress, but each advanced the relevant society incontestably toward its intended goal.

Just as the process of integration predated the white paper, so it outlived the deadline announced therein. To some extent, this occurred because Project 1992 fell behind schedule. More fundamentally, however, it occurred because Project 1992, properly construed, did not address all impediments to unification of the internal market; nor did it address the remaining requirements of a full customs union. Even if Project 1992 had been implemented on schedule, January 1, 1993, would not mark the exact moment at which twelve distinct national markets merged—let alone the moment at which twelve distinct governments and ways of life vanished. However optimistic they might have been, the authors of the white paper surely knew that the Europe of 1993 would be a region in which the borders of nation-states continued to matter. In this sense, 1992 was just another yearpost on the timepath to European unity.

Since 1992 was never destined to play the role of deliberate cataclysm, it is best cast as a symbol. During the Community's early years, most Europeans had direct experience of World War II. However much they differed in nationality, culture, or political ideology, they tended to share overriding beliefs in the importance of avoiding another war and the utility of economic integration as a means toward that end. The intensity and diffusion of these beliefs created a civic energy that was harnessed effectively in support of economic integration. Paradoxically perhaps, metaeconomic rationale made it possible to implement economic policies that cut painfully into muscular vested interests. Without such energy, it is doubtful whether the forces supporting continued insulation of national markets from foreign competition and complete preservation of sovereignty in the nation-states could have been overcome.[1]

As the fear and experience of war abated, the Community's interest in further integration required a new raison d'être. Given the nurturing prosperity experienced by the Community during its youth, it seemed natural to seek that purpose in economic welfare. As a result, Project 1992 was packaged and sold as an attempt to improve standards of living throughout the Community. It symbolized not only an explicit attempt to rally a new generation of Community citizens to the idea of integration but a change in the fundamental rationale for that integration. This, if anything, is what makes 1992 no ordinary yearpost.

Unfortunately, in the corridors of power if not in the graphs of textbooks, calculations of economic costs and benefits are easily manipulated by protectionist interests; such interests thrive in the slow-growth, high-unemployment setting of the period. As a result, on those matters that could be decided by qualified majority vote (thanks to the Single European Act of 1986), the EC was able to make reasonable headway in implementing Project 1992. On those matters that required unanimity (such as indirect taxes), however, Project 1992 fell well behind schedule. The prospect of economic benefit, it seems, was not the complete catalyst for integration that the prospect of peace had once been.

---

1. I develop this point further in William James Adams, *Restructuring the French Economy: Government and the Rise of Market Competition since World War II* (Washington: Brookings Institution, 1989).

Ironically, and perhaps fortunately for the integrationists, before Project 1992 could be implemented fully, German unification and Soviet disintegration revivified the security-based sentiment for European unity. As a result, the integrationists are back on the offensive. How will their energy be used? What is Europe's agenda after 1992?

1. *Political Union.* To accomplish so much institutional change has required reliance on a strong Commission and an activist ECJ. Neither body is elected directly by the citizens of Europe. As a result, believing that the Community's institutions show, on balance, a serious democratic deficit, many Europeans have argued that the legitimacy of Community action is at risk. Others have argued that economic integration has proceeded to the point where foreign and security policies should also be handled at the supranational level.

On December 15, 1990, the member states confronted these distinct but related issues by opening an intergovernmental conference on political union. The conference completed its work at Maastricht in December, 1991, and the resulting Treaty on European Union was signed on February 7, 1992. Joseph Weiler analyzes the problem of political legitimacy with which the conference had to deal.

2. *Economic and Monetary Union.* The internal market cannot be completed until a single currency is adopted by the EC. So argues Tommaso Padoa-Schioppa in his chapter on economic and monetary union. In keeping with this view, the member states opened another intergovernmental conference on December 15, 1990—this one to work out the details of such a union. It, too, ended at Maastricht in December, 1991, and its accomplishments were incorporated in the same Treaty on European Union. Padoa-Schioppa describes each of the fundamental issues addressed by the conference.

3. *Competition Policy.* Project 1992 was designed primarily to remove *governmental* impediments to the flow of goods and services between member countries. Insofar as *private* impediments remain—or grow to replace their departed governmental counterparts—Project 1992 will have been undertaken in vain.

Private impediments to trade are usually associated with the exercise of market power. Business enterprises often find it profitable to divide markets, creating a series of monopolies and tightly knit oligopolies where competition might otherwise prevail. Thus, an important feature of Europe after 1992 will be the degree to which the EC curbs socially noxious exercises of market power. The chapter by Frédéric Jenny describes the dilemmas Europe faces in the conduct of its competition policy.

4. *Social Policy.* Economic integration can intrude forcefully, and not necessarily desirably, on a country's social fabric. Although the gains from

trade can be distributed so as to raise the standard of living of all people, they are usually distributed such that some gain but others lose.

One important distributional effect of market integration is the pressure it might place on the welfare state. Countries offering generous public protection against the risks of old age, poor health, and unemployment, with tax burdens to match, worry that their largesse will induce local businesses to emigrate to member states offering fewer benefits and lower taxes. They also fear immigration of people likely to qualify for benefits but unlikely to contribute much in taxes. In other words, certain people in the EC's rich countries worry that market integration, without Community-level standards for social protection against major risks, contains a bias against the welfare state. In his chapter on European social policy, Stephan Leibfried considers several potential Community responses to this bias.

5. *Subsidiarity*. Some tasks of government are best handled at the supranational level, others at the municipal level, and the rest somewhere in between. *Subsidiarity* is the word used to convey the idea that a particular function of government should be assigned to the lowest level of government capable of performing it effectively.

The growing importance of decision making in Brussels has led some observers, not all of them British, to fear that what started as a benign integration of markets is being transformed into a pernicious centralization of power. The rise of Brussels, however, does not imply the fall of all other levels of government. Indeed, a convincing case could be made that a strong supranational government will result in strong regional and local governments. Those who fear excessive centralization are sometimes just lamenting the decline of the nation-state in relation to governments above *and* below it.

Germany is the European country that has been forced to think most immediately and practically about its national future. Ernst-J. Mestmäcker describes the content and implications of German reunification. His essay will inspire readers to contemplate the effects of national events on the dynamic of European integration and, reciprocally, the effects of European integration on the evolution of particular nations.

After Maastricht: Community Legitimacy in Post-1992 Europe

Joseph H. H. Weiler

This chapter was planned and executed in two distinct phases. The first phase, executed during the two intergovernmental conferences (IGCs) convened in 1990 to propose revisions to the Treaty of Rome with a view to establishing economic and monetary union and a political union, addresses long-term problems facing post-1992 Europe. These problems were defined on the basis of the Single European Act (SEA) heritage, the previous major revision of the treaties.[1] The problems were grouped around the concept of legitimacy, thus underscoring my interest in fundamentals rather than in the day-to-day mechanics of the institutional and constitutional architecture of the Community.

The chapter was then left in abeyance pending the outcome of the IGCs.[2] The second phase, executed in the weeks following the Maastricht summit of December, 1991, and superimposed on my original text, attempts to assess in

1. Of the immense literature on the 1992 program and the Single European Act, I have found the following particularly useful: De Ruyt, *L'Acte Unique Européen: Commentaire*, 2d ed. (1989); Bieber, Dehousse, Pinder, and Weiler, eds., *1992: One European Market?: A Critical Analysis of the Commission's Internal Market Strategy* (1988); Berman, "The Single European Act: A New Constitution for the Community?" 27 *Columbia Journal of Transnational Law* 529 (1989); Dehousse, "1992 and Beyond: The Institutional Dimension of the Internal Market Programme," [1989/1] *Legal Issues of European Integration* 109; Glaesner, "The Single European Act: Attempt at an Appraisal," 10 *Fordham International Law Journal* 446 (1987); Glaesner, "The Single European Act," 6 *Yearbook of European Law* 283 (1987); Glaesner, "L'Article 100A: Un Nouvel Instrument pour la Réalisation du Marché Commun," 5–6 *Cahiers de Droit Européen* 615 (1989); Ehlermann, "The Internal Market Following the Single European Act," 24 *Common Market Law Review* 361 (1987); Ehlermann, "The '1992 Project': Stages, Structures, Results and Prospects," 11 *Michigan Journal of International Law* 1097 (1990); Moravcsik, "Negotiating the Single European Act: National Interests and Conventional Statecraft in the European Community," 45 *International Organization* 19 (1991).

2. An earlier attempt of mine at this type of analysis, on which I am drawing, may be found in 46 *Swiss Review of International Economic Relations* 411 (1991).

preliminary fashion[3] the extent to which the new Treaty on European Union addresses these fundamental problems.

The focus on legitimacy may, at first blush, seem bizarre in this context. In particular, and unlike earlier steps in the process of European integration, it could be said that the current round of treaty revision enjoys a far greater measure of transparency, a wider level of public awareness, a more informed media discussion, and, consequently, a greater level of popular support. It would probably be the first major change in the architecture of the Community polity in relation to which general public legitimacy could be claimed. Is there any sense then in exploring "legitimacy problems" as a serious preoccupation for the post-1992 phase?

My view is that the legitimacy of the EC merits reflection for two reasons. First, despite the impressive public relations success of EC 92 (within Europe and even more so outside Europe), certain structural changes brought about by the SEA, coupled with some features of the 1992 program and its follow-up, may bring about problems whereby the very legitimacy of the polity—or at least some central features of it—may indeed be called into question. Second, the question of legitimacy of the European Community has not received adequate treatment, principally because it has always been conflated with the issue of the democratic deficit of the Community—the implicit, erroneous, assumption being that, if only the democracy deficit were addressed, there would be no issue of legitimacy. My view is that certain very real issues of legitimacy go well beyond the question of any democracy deficit.

To suggest that the legitimacy of the polity, or of some of its features, may be called into question is not to say that the polity is about to become illegitimate, either in the strict legal sense or in the court of public opinion. But it does mean that one may expect dislocations and destabilization problems that are novel in relation to the past of the Community. Thus, the purpose of this chapter will be to highlight the domains in which such legitimacy problems may arise.

Problems of Legitimacy I: Democratic Legitimacy

This is the most well-known issue in the legitimacy debate and, hence, can be discussed very briefly. The Community continues to suffer from a democratic deficit in its decision-making process. Despite the introduction, under the

---

3. I have based this assessment on the Draft Treaty on Political Union, issued immediately after the Summit (Doc. Conf-UP 1862/91 of December 13, 1991). This text is still subject to "legal editing" and hence is subject to changes. A final text has, at the time of my writing, not yet been signed, let alone ratified by the twelve member states. Needless to say, by virtue of the short time that has elapsed, my own thoughts are first impressions.

SEA, of the cooperation procedure and, in two limited areas, of the assent procedure, the voice of the European Parliament remains limited and its power to shape Community legislation indirect. The Council of Ministers, representing the executive branch in the member states, continues to enjoy primacy in the Community legislative process. This means, in the starkest terms, that, in the field of application of Community law and policy, there are still major public policy areas where the governments of the member states, which in their own countries may normally legislate only with (at least) the passive assent and scrutiny of the national parliaments, may, in the Community domain, legislate without meaningful control or even assent of the European Parliament. De facto, this often means that they can legislate without the meaningful control of any parliament.

This problem is, paradoxically, rendered more acute in the post-1992 era for two reasons.

a) The most important change brought about by the SEA was the resort to majority voting, first and foremost under Article 100a but then, following the change in the rules of procedure of the Council of Ministers,[4] in all areas where the treaty provides for such a majority vote. Although a proposal to abolish formally the legally dubious Luxembourg Accord was not accepted at the time of negotiating the SEA, the accord, for all practical intents and purposes, has expired. Majority voting has, of course, been a boon to the efficiency of the Community. But it does accentuate the democracy deficit. In the heyday of the Luxembourg Accord, most decision making of the Community, conducted under the shadow of the veto, was by consensus. No new norms and policy were adopted without the consent of all governments of member states. In theory, governments were answerable at least to their national chamber for their actions as Community legislators. In the post-SEA Community, this measure of indirect control by national parliaments is weakened. A member state government can no longer guarantee that a measure will not be passed by the Community (unless the treaty provides for unanimous decision mak-

---

4. See Amendment of the Council's Rules of Procedure adopted by the Council on 20 July 1987, on the basis of Article 5 of the Treaty of 8 April 1965 establishing a Single Council and a Single Commission of the European Communities, 87/508/Euratom, ECSC, EEC, OJ No. L 291/27 (October 15, 1987). The new Art. 5 provides:

1. The Council shall vote on the initiative of its President. The President shall, furthermore, be required to open voting proceedings on the invitation of a member of the Council or of the Commission provided that a majority of the Council's members so decide.

The new rules do not differentiate between votes ex Art. 100a and any other legal basis that provides for majority voting in the treaty.

ing) and, hence, answerability to a national parliament loses something of its efficacy and meaningfulness.

b) The creation of a Europe without frontiers, which is a centerpiece of the 1992 program, has brought in its wake the need, or at least the perception of a need, for a far greater measure of centralized regulation on behalf of the Community. The single market does not mean, as some believed for a while, a massive scheme of deregulation. It has come to mean, increasingly, a shift in the locus of regulation from the member states to the center, the new approach to harmonization notwithstanding. Delors's much touted claim that 80 percent of social legislation in Europe will be of Community origin may be exaggerated; but it certainly indicates the trend. This, in turn, accentuates the democracy deficit, since now it is not simply that European legislation continues to be adopted without adequate parliamentary control (at European or member state levels) but that this legislation has increased in scope and in social sensitivity.

The Maastricht Treaty on European Union (TEU) makes some notable advances in the powers of the European Parliament. Clearly it does not meet the demands of the European Parliament itself to become a veritable colegislator;[5] but ultimate evaluation will be conditioned by the levels of expectation and observational standpoint of the evaluator. From the outside, it seems that the Community has acted "true to form" in this sphere: It gives more than the pessimists had feared and less than the most outspoken had sought. If the issue of Parliamentary powers is to serve as the acid test of the entire TEU, the results of this test are clear enough: TEU does not represent a qualitative and transformative structural leap, but proceeds along the well-trodden path of cautious incrementalism.

The highlights of the proposed amendments to Parliamentary powers, especially in the legislative process, are as follows.

1. *The Assent Procedure*, whereby the entry into force of a Community measure depends on its receiving the assent of the European Parliament which shall act by an absolute majority of its component members, has been expanded. Hitherto, under the SEA, this procedure

---

5. The demands of Parliament are encapsulated in its Martin Report and Resolution of July, 1991, coupled with a detailed text of amended treaty articles submitted by Parliament to the IGCs. The essence of the Parliamentary demands is usefully summarized in Martin, "Progress towards European Union: EC Institutional Perspectives on the Intergovernmental Conferences— the View of the Parliament," 46 *Swiss Review of International Economic Relations* 281 (1991). For the complete texts of the Parliamentary resolutions, see *Les Nouveaux Traités—1993, Propositions du Parlement Européen* (1991).

existed only in relation to enlargement of the Community[6] and conclusion of association agreements.[7]

Parliamentary assent will now be required for all international agreements that (*a*) set up institutional frameworks and cooperation procedures as part of such agreements, (*b*) have important budgetary implications for the Community, and (*c*) require implementing legislation in relation to which the new "codecision"[8] is required.[9]

Parliamentary assent will also be required for some of the new provisions on citizenship,[10] structural funds,[11] adoption of a uniform electoral system for Parliament,[12] and also for changes to the proposed European System of Central Banks and to the European Central Bank itself.[13]

In the past, the assent procedure was a double-edged sword. On the one hand, it did not give Parliament a formal role in the legislative process itself, leaving it at the end with a "take-it-or-leave-it" option. On the other hand, the assent requirement as provided in the SEA meant that failure to overcome the high hurdle of obtaining a majority of all members of the European Parliament (MEPs), rather than a majority of those voting, results in the nonadoption of the measure. In other words, a minority of MEPs actually voting could defeat a measure. This knowledge will have conditioned consultation during the legislative (or negotiation in case of agreements) process.

Maastricht, as mentioned above, has extended assent to new areas. But it has also changed the voting requirements to obtain assent. Only in relation to enlargement and adoption of a uniform electoral procedure for Parliament is assent conditioned on obtaining an absolute majority of the component members of the Parliament. In the other areas (citizenship, international agreements—including association agreements—central bank, and structural funds) a simple majority of voting members will suffice for assent. If Parliament is to establish assent as a real power, it will have to exercise it once or twice (like a shot over the bows) even with the new voting rules.

---

6. Art. 237, EEC treaty. See also Art. O, Maastricht Treaty on European Union (hereafter, TEU). The version of TEU that was signed in Maastricht on February 7, 1992, appears in Agence Europe, *Europe Documents*, no. 1759/60 (February 7, 1992).

7. Art. 238, EEC treaty.

8. See text to note 18 et seq.

9. Art. 228, TEU. Note that time limits on receiving such assent are envisaged by agreement of the Council and Parliament.

10. Art. 8a(2), TEU.

11. Art. 130d, TEU.

12. Art. 138(3), TEU.

13. Art. 106(5), TEU.

Significantly, Maastricht did not extend the assent procedure to treaty revision, the provisions of Community-own resources, and to the "necessary and proper clause" of the Community (Art. 235). The exclusion of these provisions, especially the first, is more than symbolic. Requiring Parliamentary assent in future rounds of treaty revision would have given Parliament the power to hold up future IGCs for "ransom" and condition Parliamentary assent on a full acceptance of Parliament's demands for more power.[14]

In this context, one may add that Parliament will, under the Maastricht proposals, also be required to approve (or not) the new Commission—the term of office of which will coincide with the Parliamentary term.[15] This power, quite apart from its conferral of influence in the choice of president, will perhaps be more effective than is the existing power of dismissing the Commission. It will, however, primarily add to the legitimacy of the Commission and its president.

2. *The Cooperation Procedure* (Art. 149, EEC treaty, as amended by the SEA), whereby Parliament received a greater say in the legislative process (though final say was left to the Council), has been extended to seven new areas (including the problematic "opting in" area of social policy). This has also brought about some changes in those areas left to the old *consultation procedure.*[16] Apart from extension of this procedure to new areas, not much can be said. It will enjoy the advantages and suffer the difficulties of "cooperation."[17]

3. The new *Codecision Procedure.* This is the truly novel feature of the Maastricht Treaty.[18] Codecision will exist in fourteen areas, some of

---

14. This ability at horse-trading has always had a rhetorical allure to Parliament. In the immediate wake of Maastricht, a petition was circulated in Parliament threatening not to give assent to the critical treaty creating the European Economic Area unless more powers were given to the European Parliament.

15. Art. 158, TEU.

16. The following are the areas where "cooperation" is applied post-Maastricht: non-discrimination (Art. 16); transport (Art. 75(1)); social policy (Art. 118a(2), Special Protocol of the Eleven); social fund (Art. 125); vocational education (Art. 127, new competence); economic cohesion—implementation decisions (Art. 130e); research—implementation programs (Art. 130o, new competence); environment—implementation, trans-European networks—not policy (Arts. 130s(1) and 129d); development cooperation (Art. 130w, new competence). Regarding economic and monetary union, see Arts. 103(5), 104a(2), 104b(2), and 105a(2).

17. For a sober view of the advantages and weaknesses of "cooperation," see Corbett, "Testing the New Procedures: The European Parliament's First Experiences with its New 'Single Act' Powers," 27 *Journal of Common Market Studies* 359 (1989). See, too, "Draft Report on the Cooperation Procedure (Prag Report)," PE 144.081 of 21 August 1990.

18. Art. 189b, TEU.

which are quite important, notably legislation in the field of achieving the internal market ex Article 100a.[19]

The mechanics of the procedure are, on the whole, self-evident from the language of the treaty. Worth noting in this new proposal are the following elements. In the first place, unlike the assent procedure, the European Parliament is intimately connected with the actual legislative procedure in all its stages. Even on the formal level, it does not operate in a "take-it-or-leave-it" mode. Indeed, acts of this type are formally adopted over the signature of both the President of the Council and the Parliament.[20] Moreover, unlike the cooperation procedure, in the "third reading" of the proposed legislation on which Council and Parliament have not found a common accord, the possibility exists for *Parliament* to reject the measure and prevent its adoption.

However, the power of Parliament to have this final say is circumscribed by three intertwined elements. In the first place, for this to happen, Parliament must take an active step, namely the "third reading." Failing that, if the final text is confirmed by a qualified majority in Council, it is deemed to be adopted. Second, this positive act of Parliament must be taken within a relatively short period of six weeks. This is important, given the third circumscribing element, namely, the need for Parliament to act by absolute majority of all its members. If Parliament fails to reach that kind of majority, the measure will be deemed adopted, even if there is a simple majority of Parliament against it. The same "supermajority" is also needed if Parliament plans to reject the legislation totally without bothering to amend it.

As has been seen with the cooperation procedure, the ability of Parliament to mobilize the "supermajority" is not automatic and acts as a limitation on its powers. In some respects the new procedure is reminiscent of the kind of politicking in the U.S. Congress, where a "supermajority" (of a different kind) is needed to overturn a presidential veto. It is worth noting that the Council, on its part, only needs unanimous voting in order to overturn Parliamentary amendments on which the Commission has expressed a negative view. This undermines, even in the codecision context, the wish of the European Parliament to be seen as a totally equal colegislator with the Council. In cases of rift that cannot be resolved in conciliation, the dice are loaded somewhat in favor of the Council.

---

19. Free movement of workers (Art. 49); freedom of establishment (Arts. 54, 56(2), 57(1), and 57(2) second line); internal market (Arts. 100a and 100b); education (Art. 126(4), new competence); research (Art. 130i(1), new competence); environment (Art. 130s(3) partial); trans-European networks (Art. 129d, new competence); health (Art. 129(4), new competence); consumer protection (Art. 129a(2), new competence).

20. Art. 191, TEU.

It should also be noted that codecision does not apply in such important fields as agriculture and social policy. There can, however, be no doubt that codecision substantially increases the powers of the European Parliament. The importance of the measure should not be judged by the prospective pathological cases—that is, those cases where an unreconcilable rift develops and Parliament is unable to muster the required blocking majority. In most cases, one can expect an important say for Parliament at a level that it has not enjoyed so far. In particular, if Parliament is successful (in the first phases after Maastricht comes into force) in using its new power to the very full, the fear of success in all subsequent practice will act as a powerful incentive for Council (and Commission) to find compromises that are palatable to Parliament.

At the end of the day, even the combination of increased cooperation, codecision, and assent does not close the democracy deficit. Moreover, this deficit exists not merely because of the formal lack of accountability to Parliament but because of such deeper issues as transparency and remoteness. But compared to the original Community, and even to the post-SEA Community, the change is quite remarkable.

Problems of Legitimacy II: The Redefined Political Boundaries

Let us assume that, somehow, the problem of democratic legitimacy was solved by, say, making the European Parliament a full colegislator as it has demanded in the Martin Report and Resolution. Alas, this does not mean that legitimacy problems have been solved. There remains, at the center of the Community, the classical problem of legitimacy and integration.[21]

In order to understand this problem, I must burden the reader with a set of conceptual distinctions and relationships. I shall discuss, first, the difference between democracy, formal legitimacy, and social legitimacy. I shall then discuss the relationship between integration of polities and democracy.

Once these concepts and relationships are clarified, I shall try to show how they affect, in my view, some of our hitherto unquestioned assumptions about the Community and its governance.

Democracy and Legitimacy

Very frequently in discourse about Parliament and the Community, these concepts are presented interchangeably. In fact they do not necessarily coin-

---

21. I am drawing on my "Parlement Européen, Intégration Européenne, Démocratie et Légitimité," in Louis and Waelbroeck, eds., *Le Parlement Européen dans l'Evolution Institutionnelle* (1988).

cide. A stark example may drive the point home. During Weimar, Germany was democratic but its government enjoyed little legitimacy. During National Socialism, Germany ceased to be democratic (once A.H. rose to power) but government continued to enjoy widespread legitimacy well into the early 1940s.[22]

I think that, today, it would be difficult for a nondemocratic government structure or political system to attain or maintain legitimacy in the West, but it is still possible for a democratic structure not to enjoy legitimacy—either taken as a whole or over certain aspects of its operation. In other words while the existence of democratic structures surely influences the legitimacy of governance structure, it does not guarantee it.

Formal (Legal) Legitimacy and Social (Empirical) Legitimacy

So far I have treated legitimacy as a unitary concept. It will be helpful to break it down into formal (legal) and social (empirical) legitimacy.

Formal legitimacy as regards institutions or systems connotes that, in the creation of the institution or system, all requirements of the law are observed. (It is a concept akin to the juridical concept of formal validity.) Clearly, in Europe (and in the West generally) today, any notion of legitimacy must rest on some democratic foundation, loosely stated as the people's consent to power structures and process. But even so we can still speak of formal legitimacy if we can show that the power structure was created following democratic processes and with the people's consent. Thus, in our context, I would simply point out that the treaties establishing the EC, which gave such a limited role to the European Parliament, were approved by all of the national parliaments of the founding member states and, subsequently, by the parliaments of six acceding member states. Proposals for change that would give more power to the European Parliament have failed, for a variety of reasons, to complete the democratic process in the member states.

This definition of formal legitimacy distinguishes itself therefore from simple "legality." It is a legality understood, however, in the sense that law on which it is based (in our case the treaties) was created by democratic institutions and processes. Thus, in this formal sense, the existing structure and process could be said to rest on a formal approval by the democratically elected parliaments of the member states; and yet, undeniably, the Community process suffers, as explained above, from a clear democracy deficit.

Social legitimacy connotes a broad societal acceptance (empirically determined) of the system. Note that an institution or system may be socially

---

22. See, generally, Craig, *Germany 1866–1945* (1990), esp. chaps. 15 and 18.

legitimate even if broad sections of society do not favor its specific composition, program, or operation. Thus, in the last elections in Great Britain, only a minority of the electorate voted for the current Conservative government. But that government enjoys, beyond any doubt, social legitimacy because most people accept the systemic rules of the game according to which even a minority of the electorate may end up with a large Parliamentary majority. Many other factors contribute to social legitimacy.

Social legitimacy has an additional *substantive* component: Legitimacy is achieved when the government process displays a commitment to, and actively guarantees values that are part of, the general political culture—such as justice and freedom. The importance of this further refinement will be made clear subsequently.

Now we may explore the relationship between the two types of legitimacy. An institution or system or polity will, in most (but not all) cases, have to enjoy formal legitimacy in order to enjoy social legitimacy. This is most likely the case in Western democratic traditions. But a system that enjoys formal legitimacy will not necessarily enjoy social legitimacy. Most popular revolutions (from the French Revolution onward) took place in polities where government and the system were formally legitimate but that lost social legitimacy.

Integration and Democracy

Let us now turn to the even more delicate problem of the relationship between integration or unification of polities and democracy.[23] No modern polity aspiring to democracy can govern itself like the Greek Polis or the New England town. Representative (parliamentary) democracy has replaced direct participation. Nonetheless, one yardstick of democracy will be the closeness, responsiveness, representativeness, and accountability of the governors to the governed. Although this formula is vague, it is sufficient for present purposes.

Let us now consider three polities, each independent from the others, each enjoying a democratic and representative form of government. To simplify matters, let us assume that each of the three governments enjoys legislative and regulatory power in the following fields: education, taxation, foreign trade, and defense. This means that electors can directly influence their representatives as to the polity's education policy, the level of taxation, the type of

---

23. In this section I have been considerably helped by the following works: Dahl, "Federalism and the Democratic Process," in Pennock and Chapman, eds., "Liberal Democracy," 25 *Nomos* 95 (1983); Henkin, *Constitutionalism, Democracy, and Foreign Affairs* (1990); Franck, *The Power of Legitimacy among Nations* (1990); Brilmayer, *Justifying International Acts* (1989); Habermas, *Legitimation Crisis* (1975). My own synoptic presentation cannot do justice to the richness of these works.

foreign trade (protectionist or free), and the nature of the defense forces and policy.

Let us now assume that, for a variety of reasons, the three polities decide to integrate and to "share their sovereignty" in the fields of taxation, foreign trade, and defense. If within each of the three polities this decision was democratically reached the integrated polity will certainly enjoy formal legitimacy.

What about democracy? By definition, there will initially be a diminution of democracy in the new, integrated polity in respect of the three old polities. Why is this so? Because prior to the integration, the majority of electors in polity A would have a controlling influence over their level of taxation, the nature of their foreign trade policy, and the size and posture of their army. Under the integrated polity, the electors of polity A (even a huge majority) may be outvoted by the electors of polities B and C. This will even be the case if the new, integrated polity has a perfectly democratically elected "federal" legislature. The integrated polity will not be undemocratic, but it will be, in terms of the ability of citizens to influence policies affecting them, less democratic.

We see this idea, in reverse form, when a centralized state devolves power to regions. The division of sovereignty, and its bestowal on more or less autonomous regions (as has occurred recently in Italy, in Spain, and, to some extent, in France) is, in some respects, the opposite of integration. One of the prime motivations for regionalism is to enhance democracy in the sense of giving people more direct control of areas of public policy that affect their life.

To suggest, as I have, that, in the process of integration, there is a loss, at least in one sense, of democracy does not condemn the process of integration. There usually will have been formidable reasons that prompted the electors in polities A, B, and C to choose to integrate despite this loss of some direct control in the larger polity. Typically, the main reasons will be size and interdependence. By aggregating their resources, especially in the field of defense, their total welfare may be enhanced despite the loss of more immediate influence over their governments' policies. Similar advantages may accrue in the field of foreign trade and there may be entities such as multinational corporations that escape the control of any particular polity, so that only an integrated polity will be able, say, to tax them effectively. In other words, the independence and sovereignty of the single polities may be illusory in an interdependent world. Nonetheless, integration may diminish the ability of the citizens of the three polities directly to control and influence government policy.

It is true that, even within each polity, the minority had to accept majority decisions. So why am I claiming that, in the enlarged integrated polity (where an equally valid majoritarian rule applies) there is a loss of democracy? This is the toughest aspect of all democratic theory. What defines the boundary of the polity within which the majority principle should apply? There is no theoretical answer to this question. It is determined by long-term, very long-term, factors such as political continuity, social, cultural, and linguistic affinity, and a shared history. People accept the majoritarian principle of democracy within a polity to which they see themselves as belonging.

How convincing would it be to tell the Protestant majority electorate of Northern Ireland that, in a United Ireland, where it would suddenly be a minority within a Catholic majority, it will enjoy perfect democratic rights? The whole nature of the Protestants' polity would change despite their electoral rights.

The process of integration—even if decided upon democratically—brings about then, initially at least, a loss of democracy in its actual process of governance. What becomes crucial for the success of the integration process is the social legitimacy of the new, integrated polity despite this loss of total control over the integrated areas by each polity.

The next question is, how does one contribute to this increased social legitimacy? One way is to demonstrate visibly and tangibly that the total welfare of the citizenry is enhanced by integration. A second way is to ensure that the new, integrated polity will have democratic structures. A still more important way is to give, for a time at least, an enhanced voice to the separate polities. It is not an accident that some of the most successful federations that emerged from hitherto separate polities—the United States, Switzerland, Germany—experienced a period of confederation prior to unification in some form of federal state. This does not mean that one has to have a confederation prior to a federation. It simply suggests that, in a federation created by integration rather than by devolution, there will have to be a period of adjustment when the political boundaries of the new polity become socially accepted as appropriate for the larger democratic rules whereby the minority will accept a new majority.

From the political point of view (though not in its legal architecture),[24] the EC is in fact confederal in nature despite the important changes brought about by the SEA. The big debate is, therefore, whether the time is ripe for a radical change toward a more federal structure, or whether the process must allow itself to continue in a more evolutionary fashion.

Sadly, these methods of increasing social legitimacy can be at odds with each other. Giving an enhanced voice to each polity may impede the successful attainment of the goals of integration. Denying sufficient voice to the

---

24. See Weiler, "The Community System: The Dual Character of Supranationalism," 1 *Yearbook of European Law* 267 (1981).

constituent polities (allowing the minority to be overridden by the majority) may bring about a decline in the social legitimacy of the polity with consequent dysfunctions and even disintegration. Here is an example to demonstrate the difficulty of balancing these two interests. The American confederal structure, which gave a large amount of voice to each individual state (not unlike the Council of Ministers in the Community) debilitated itself so much that it failed to exploit the benefits of size. Hence the drive that resulted in the constitutional convention (200 years ago) that adopted the new federal constitution.

Be this as it may, in terms of democratic theory, the final objective of a unifying polity is to recoup the loss of democracy initiated by the process of integration. This "loss" is recouped when the social fabric and discourse is such that the electorate accepts the new boundary as defining the polity and then totally accepts the legitimacy of being subjected to majority rule in a much larger system comprising the integrated polities.[25]

But this process can take a long time. The social legitimacy of the federal government in the United States was not consolidated until well into the nineteenth century and saw, in the process, a very bloody Civil War that was triggered by the slavery issue but was really fought over the rejection (by the old South) of the federal discipline. They simply could not accept as legitimate democratic decisions made in a Congress dominated by a Northern majority.

Obviously there is no risk today that the member states of the Community would resort to armed force to solve any problems they have among themselves. The greatest success of the EC in a long-term, historical perspective has been, indeed, making war not only impossible but unthinkable. But it is less clear whether a radical change in the political architecture of the Community would not introduce serious destabilizing forces.

Even today, after adoption of the SEA, it can be argued plausibly that the electorate in most member states accepts only grudgingly the notion that crucial areas of public life should be governed by a decision process in which their national voice becomes a minority that may be overridden by a majority of representatives from other European countries. In theoretical terms, there is still no legitimacy to the notion that the boundaries within which a minority will accept (as democratically legitimate) a majority decision must now be European instead of national.

At its starkest, one could claim that, in terms of social legitimacy, there is no difference between a decision made in the Council of Ministers and a decision made in the European Parliament. To the electorate, both present themselves as legislative chambers with representatives of the member states.

---

25. See Brilmayer, *Justifying International Acts*, esp. chaps. 1 and 3.

In both cases, until this dimension of legitimacy is resolved by time and other factors, the electorate of a minority member state may find it hard to swallow and could consider it socially illegitimate that they have to abide by a majority decision of a redefined polity.

On this premise, the single most legitimating element (from a social point of view) was the Luxembourg Accord and the veto power. To be sure, one paid a huge cost in terms of efficient decision making and progress. But it was this device that enabled the Community to legitimate its program and its legislation, for it provided both an ex-ante "insurance policy" to the national electorates that nothing could get through without their voice having a controlling say and it presented an ex-post legitimation as well. Everything that the Community did, however unpopular it might have been, was passed with the assent of national ministers. To the extent that the output of the Community decision process was legitimate, it was so at least partially because of the knowledge that it is controllable in this way.

I do not wish to be misunderstood here. I am not suggesting that, based on my analysis, the restoration of majority voting in the Community was a negative development. But I am saying that this course of action may exacerbate legitimacy problems and that even a beefed up European Parliament (which also operates on a majority principle) will not necessarily solve that legitimacy problem. In my analysis, the legitimacy crisis does not derive principally from the accountability issue at the European level, but from the very redefinition of the European polity.

Where is the evidence for these contentions? There are no decisive empirical measures for legitimacy.[26] I am rather skeptical about public opinion polls that show that, in the abstract, the European electorate is in favor of more European integration. These things can only be tested in the crucible of real life. The Community is now in a phase of transition whereby it is difficult to get clear indications. On the one hand, there are still instances of considerable political capital gained in some member states by national politicians "standing up to the Community." This is particularly so in states such as Britain, Denmark, and Greece. But it is also in strong evidence in many of the older member states. Even after conclusion of the SEA (championed by France), assurances had to be given that the abhorrent Luxembourg Accord remained intact. Indeed, it would appear to me that both the British foreign minister and his French counterpart knowingly misled their Parliaments in claiming that the Luxembourg Accord retained all its guarantees post SEA.[27]

---

26. Cf. Hyde, "The Concept of Legitimation in the Sociology of Law," *Wisconsin Law Review* 379 (1983).

27. See, e.g., statements by the French and British Foreign Ministers before their respective parliaments on presentation of the SEA. *Hansard*, 5th ser., vol. 96 (1986), European Communities (amendment) Bill, at 320; *Journal Officiel de la République Française*, 1986 No. 109 [1] A.N. (C.R.), 21 November 1986 at 6611 (debate of November 20th).

On the other hand, strong arguments have been put forward that the effect of the new "information society" has been to break down national boundaries and diminish the member state as the principal referent for political legitimacy.[28] The Community might even be in the peculiar situation where the member states can no longer fulfil that legitimating function but neither can the Community—suggesting an enquiry into such other loci as regions and corporations.[29]

Finally, let me go back to the notion of substantive legitimacy alluded to previously. Our principal objections to the regimes in Greece (under the colonels), Spain, and Portugal (prior to democracy) was not simply an abstract objection to a nondemocratic process—important as that may have been. Objection was critically tied to the content of those regimes characterized by an oppression of individual rights, by a fundamental lack of liberty and due process of law.

By contrast, if we were to observe, by way of example, the British model of democracy, many of its structural features would leave us perplexed. Britain has an electoral system (regional, first by the post) that regularly gives large majorities in the House of Commons to parties for which only a minority of the voting electorate cast their vote. The millions who vote for the Liberal party (and more recently for the Social Democrats) have been practically disenfranchised. The upper house (the House of Lords) has a majority of members who are there by hereditary right. The highest judge in the realm, the Lord Chancellor, who not infrequently sits in judgment as a member of the highest court, is an active member of the government. And, finally, there is no bill of rights to protect individuals and minorities (or indeed, in the British case, majorities) from any dictate of Parliament.

As a textbook model, the British system would fail many of our basic notions of democratic legitimacy. And yet we rightly, despite discrete criticism, continue to regard Britain as a bastion of democracy. We do so for two principal reasons. First, despite the structural defects, the operation of the system is respectful of minorities and individuals, there are changes of government, and fundamental liberty is usually protected de facto; second, the rule of law is truly respected in Britain.[30]

Why this is important emerges from the following consideration regarding the European Community. It is true of course that structurally the EC suffers from a democracy deficit (as I have explained). But in truth there are only a few cases to which we can point where, in terms of *content*, the Council has, in what it adopts, taken advantage of its nonaccountability and

---

28. See Østrom Moller, *Technology and Culture in a European Context* (1991).

29. Id.

30. See, generally, Dahrendorf, "A Confusion of Powers: Politics and the Rule of Law," 40 *Modern Law Review* 1 (1977).

subverted basic values. And the rule of law in the Community, though not perfect (where is it perfect?), has reached, thanks to the Court of Justice, a level that is enviable in any other transnational venture.

Usually, though not always, complaints about the democracy deficit amount in practice to complaints that the Council is not proceeding vigorously enough in the process of European integration—contrary to the wishes of the electorate as expressed through the European Parliament. If I am right in this last contention, two points emerge. First, it shows that the outcry about the democracy deficit is fueled at least in part by a different agenda— furtherance of European integration. Second, more important, one can at least query whether the current position of the European Parliament favoring a stronger process of integration is self-evidently an expression of the people's will.

I am not suggesting that the European Parliament has not gotten a mandate for its call. But in nonunitary systems, electorates quite happily give conflicting mandates to differently elected organs. In the United States, the House of Representatives, the Senate, and the president are all popularly elected by universal franchise and all claim to have a mandate from the people. Yet frequently these mandates conflict. We see similar phenomena in France and, on occasion, in Germany. It is at least arguable that the collective wish of national parliaments that, at least by inaction, are content to leave the Community structure as it is, is an equally authentic expression of a popular mandate.

Where does all this lead in practical terms? My prediction is that conflicts of authority between the European institutions and national parliaments will increase as it becomes more and more evident that "Europe" can override the elusive national interest, especially that of the larger member states such as France, Britain, and even Germany. Much will depend on the wisdom of the Commission and other Euro-institutions in diffusing these conflicts. At what point European citizens will accept the newly defined boundaries is impossible to say.

There is little in the Maastricht Treaty that addresses this issue directly. On the one hand it is well known that any attempt to insert the word *federal* into the aspirational parts of the treaty was rejected. At the symbolic level, this may simply constitute another piece of evidence of the problem under discussion. Likewise, in those areas such as foreign affairs and defense, the three-pillar approach adopted by the Maastricht text, whereby these areas were decidedly not incorporated into the Community structure *simpliciter* but were included in the two "intergovernmental" pillars, may have been a disappointment to those aspiring to a comprehensive Community. In the optic of the legitimacy problem highlighted here, however, it may also be seen as a clever way of easing the transition to a polity with redefined political boundaries. This optic is even more useful when considering the third pillar, justice and home affairs, touching directly on the question of boundaries and policies toward non-Community migration.

Problems of Legitimacy III: The Issue of Community Competences

The student of comparative federalism discovers a constant feature in practically all federative experiences: a tendency, which differs only in degree, toward controversial concentration of legislative and executive power in the center at the expense of constituent units.[31] This is apparently so independent of the mechanism for allocation of jurisdiction, competences, or powers between the center and "periphery." Differences, where they occur, depend more on the ethos and political culture of polities than on mechanical devices.

The Community has both shared in and differed from this general experience. It has *shared* it in that the Community, especially in the 1970s, saw a weakening of any workable and enforceable mechanism for the allocation of jurisdiction, competences, and powers between the Community and its member states. It has become impossible to define the limits of Community competences with any measure of certainty. This has occurred through a combination of two factors.

a) Profligate legislative practices, especially in the usage of Article 235. It would appear that other than in relation to organic changes, there was no field of activity that could be excluded from the reach of Community legislation, be it educational measures or emergency food aid to foreign countries.[32] Thus we find the authoritative conclusion of Lenaerts claiming, *à titre juste*, that in today's Community, "[t]here simply is no nucleus of sovereignty that the member states can invoke, as such, against the Community."[33]

b) A bifurcated jurisprudence of the Court that, on the one hand, extensively interpreted the reach of the jurisdiction, competences, and powers granted the Community and, on the other hand, has taken a self-limiting approach toward the expansion of Community jurisdic-

---

31. I am drawing here from Jacqué and Weiler, "On the Road to European Union—A New Judicial Architecture," 27 *Common Market Law Review* 185 (1990).

32. For a detailed analysis of the breakdown of the principle of enumeration in the Community during the 1970s, with extensive reference to practice, case law, and commentary, see Weiler, "The Transformation of Europe," 100 *Yale Law Journal* 2403 (1991), esp. pt. 2.

33. Lenaerts, "Constitutionalism and the Many Faces of Federalism," 38 *American Journal of Comparative Law* 205 (1990).

tion, competence, and powers when exercised by the political organs, especially under Article 235.[34]

To make these statements is not tantamount to criticizing the Community, its political organs, and the Court. This is a question of values. It is a sustainable thesis that this process was generally beneficial, in its historical context, to the evolution and well-being of the Community, its member states, and their citizens and residents. But this process also constitutes a ticking constitutional time bomb that one day might threaten the evolution and stability of the Community. Sooner or later, "supreme" courts in the member states would realize that the "sociolegal contract" announced by the Court in its major constitutionalizing decisions (namely that "the Community constitutes a new legal order . . . for the benefit of which the states have limited their sovereign rights, *albeit within limited fields,*" Van Gend & Loos v. Nederlandse Administratie der Belastingen, Case 26/62, 1963 ECR 1, italics added) has been shattered—that although they (the "supreme" courts) have accepted the principles of the new legal order (supremacy and direct effect)

---

34. Broadly speaking, there are two principal conditions that must be fulfilled for invoking Art. 235 of the EEC treaty. The measure must be "necessary" to attain one of the objectives of the treaty. In addition, Art. 235 may be used when the treaty does not provide the "necessary" powers. In the leading case of that period (Hauptzollamt Bremerhaven v. Massey Ferguson, Case 8/73, 1973 ECR 897), the Court addressed both conditions liberally. As regards the second, it was explicit. In an action for annulment of the regulation adopting the Community customs valuation regime, the Court had to decide whether reliance on Art. 235 as an exclusive basis was justified. While acknowledging that a proper interpretation of the alternative legal bases in the treaty (Arts. 9, 27, 28, 111, and 113) would provide an adequate legal basis, and thus, under a strict construction, render Art. 235 not "necessary," the Court, departing from an earlier statement, nonetheless considered that the Council's use of Art. 235 would be "justified in the interest of legal certainty." Legally, this might have been an unfortunate formulation, since almost ipso facto an aura of uncertainty attaches to a decision to make recourse to Art. 235. Politically, it may have been wise, since a more rigid interpretation could have thwarted the desire of the member states, consonant with the treaty objectives, to expand greatly the areas of activity of the Community, even if by dubious use of Art. 235. Practically speaking, in that period, recourse to Art. 235 made little difference in the content of measures adopted, because virtually all measures were adopted under the penumbra of de facto unanimity. Taking their cue from this case, Community institutions henceforth made liberal use of Art. 235 without exhaustively considering whether other legal bases existed. As regards the first requirement, that the measure be "necessary" to attain one of the objectives of the treaty, in a whole range of cases not directly concerned with Art. 235, but also in *Massey-Ferguson* itself, the Court showed itself willing to construe Community legal reach and the notion of objectives very widely. Since member states had the ability to control the usage of Art. 235, disagreements on the proper scope to be given to the first condition—often acrimonious—were resolved within the Council and not brought before the Court. Since the entry into force of the SEA, the Court has changed its jurisprudence and now disallows the usage of Art. 235 when an alternative legal basis exists. This no doubt has occurred because many of the alternative legal bases, unlike Art. 235, provide for majority voting.

the fields do not seem any more to be limited, and that in the absence of Community legislative or legal checks it will fall on them to draw the jurisdictional lines of the Community and its member states.

The interesting thing about the Community experience, and this is where it does not share the experience of other federative polities, is that, despite the massive *legislative* expansion of Community jurisdiction, competences, and powers there has not been any political challenge or crisis on this issue from the member states. The challenges and dissatisfaction occurred on some of the occasions when competences mutated as a result of a Court decision, as in *ERTA* or *Rubber*. How so?

The answer is simple and obvious and resides in the pre-SEA decision-making process. Unlike federal states, the governments of the member states themselves (jointly and severally) could control absolutely the *legislative* expansion of jurisdiction, competences, and powers. Nothing that was done could be done without the assent of all national capitals. This fact diffused any sense of threat and crisis on the part of governments. This era has now passed with the shift to majority voting, and the seeds—indeed the buds—of crisis are with us. Not only is there imminent danger that one of the national courts will take the position predicted (and this might happen sooner rather than later with the decision now pending before the Federal Constitutional Court in Germany concerning the directive on television without frontiers), but the member states have become aware that, in a process that does not give them a de jure or de facto veto, the question of jurisdictional lines has become crucial.

The problem for legitimacy is clear. I already noted that, in and of itself, majority voting creates a legitimacy challenge even in those areas where the jurisdiction of the Community is clear. The problem is exacerbated in a constitutional climate whereby the limits to Community competences are vague and no clear constitutional limit appears readily available.

At face value it would seem that the Maastricht Treaty on European Union exacerbates this problem. After all, apart from economic and monetary union, it expands Community competences proper in fields such as culture, education, health, and consumer protection as well as bringing foreign policy and security into the union structure, albeit under the "intergovernmental" pillars. And yet, there are a few highly interesting features in the Maastricht Treaty that illustrate a renewed sensitivity to this issue and possibly the beginning of a strategy for its containment.

In the first place the treaty contains a new general subsidiarity clause applicable to all operations of the Community.[35] New Article 3b provides:

---

35. The SEA contained the subsidiarity principle in the operation of aspects of the Community's environmental policy. See, for example, Art. 130r(4), EEC treaty.

The Community shall act within the limits of the powers conferred upon it by this Treaty and of the objectives assigned to it therein.

In areas which do not fall within its exclusive competence, the Community shall take action, in accordance with the principle of subsidiarity, only if and in so far as the objectives of the proposed action cannot be sufficiently achieved by the member states and can therefore, by reason of the scale or effects of the proposed action, be better achieved by the Community.

Any action by the Community shall not go beyond what is necessary to achieve the objectives of this Treaty.

It must first be noted that, in the Maastricht Treaty, subsidiarity is used entirely as a device for setting limits on Community competences. In the past, subsidiarity was also evoked as a principle that allows expansion of Community competences rather than their containment. In the Treaty of Rome, the limiting clauses on Community competences rested in the more indirect allusions in Articles 4 and 164 and, of course, in Article 173. There is an important symbolic innovation in stating clearly that the Community is a system of limited competences.

But the importance of subsidiarity goes beyond symbolism. By inserting subsidiarity into the operative part of the treaty, and not, say, in the preamble alone, the principle becomes a mechanism for review that could be pleaded before the Court of Justice and used as a ground for annulment ex Article 173 and 177b. There is, of course, an ongoing debate whether such a principle is in fact justiciable. This is not the place to canvass the arguments in this context. I have argued elsewhere that nothing impedes the Court's use of this principle in its judicial review.[36] In the face of a subsidiarity challenge, the Court would have to evaluate evidence put before it on both sides of the challenged measure—much in the same way as it does when there is a challenge that the Community legislator violated the principle of proportionality. It may then adopt one of two principal standards of review. The more severe review would be one in which the Court would actually weigh the arguments in each case and decide whether, on the balance of evidence submitted to it, the principle of subsidiarity was satisfied or not. One could imagine that, in the face of legislation already enacted, the presumption would be in favor of legality and it would be up to the challenger to prove that subsidiarity had been violated. Of course, if this were the standard of review, the Court would, in cases where it annulled a measure, be preferring its judgment to the judgment of a majority of member states (and, in relevant cases, the European Parliament). A less severe test, and one with which the Court may feel more comfortable in that it would not involve such an egregious preference

---

36. Jacqué and Weiler, supra n. 31.

of its wisdom over that of the Community legislator, would be one in which the Court would simply review the challenged act for "reasonableness"—in which it would ask whether it was unreasonable for the Community legislator to take the view that the conditions of subsidiarity were satisfied. Either way, there would be judicial control, and the threat of judicial control, over competences based on subsidiarity.

The inclusion of the subsidiarity clause may have another effect relevant to our discussion. It may send a message to the Court that, on issues of competences, the member states and the Community generally expect a more vigilant process of judicial review.

A second feature of the Maastricht Treaty in this context may be found in the areas of "new competences." These are often crafted in a way that actually seems to limit the competence, even compared to preexisting law. Title 10 on public health is indicative. Whereas, on the one hand, Article 129 begins by stating that "the Community shall contribute towards ensuring a high level of human health protection . . . ," it becomes clear from the remainder of the Article that the Community competence is to be highly circumscribed as subsidiary to that of the member states. The Community must encourage cooperation among the member states, lend support to their actions, and promote research (though presumably not conduct it), education, and information. All this is far short of true legislative competence.

And whereas Article 129 goes on to provide that "health protection requirements shall form a constituent part of the Community's other policies," this again is clawed back when the article specifies that this may not include harmonization of the laws and regulations of the member states, something that arguably was permitted hitherto under Article 100a.

Rather than rely on implicit competences, the limits to which seem out of control, the Maastricht Treaty opted for an explicit grant that circumscribes the modes of action and the reach of such policies. It remains to be seen how the Commission, Council, and Court will act in the face of such circumscribed language.

Problems of Legitimacy IV: The Ideology, Ethos, and Political Culture of European Integration

By way of conclusion I would like to examine, far more tentatively, another potential challenge to the legitimacy of the European Community: that which concerns the ideology, ethos, and political culture of European integration, particularly in relation to Project 1992.[37]

Ideological discourse within the Community, especially in the pre-1992

---

37. I am drawing here from my "Transformation of Europe," 100 *Yale Law Journal* 2403 (1991).

period, has been characterized by two peculiar features. On the one hand, despite the growing centrality of Community activity to important issues of social choice, there has been, for reasons that will emerge, a near absence of overt debate on the Left-Right spectrum. As a code for the overall set of changes, Project 1992 represents a break from this pattern that merits some analysis. On the other hand, there has been plentiful discourse on the politics and choices of the model of integration itself. But this discourse has been fragmented. In specialized political constituencies, especially those concerned with Community governance, public discourse was typically cast as a dichotomy between those who favored the Community and further European integration and those set to defend "national sovereignty" and the prerogatives of the member state. The outcome of the debate was curious. In the visible realm of political power, from the 1960s onwards, it did seem that the "national interest" was on the ascendancy. In contrast, the "high moral ground" seemed to be occupied fairly safely by the "integrationists."

But as far as the general public was concerned, the characterizing feature was a relatively high level of indifference, disturbed only on rare occasions when Community issues caught the public imagination. Although opinion polls always showed a broad support for the Community, it was, as I argued earlier, still possible to gain political points by defending the national interest against the faceless Brussels Eurocracy.

Here, the importance of Project 1992 has been not only in modifying the political process of the Community, but also in an altogether fascinating mobilization of very wide sections of general public opinion behind the "new" Europe. The significance of this mobilization cannot be overestimated. It fueled the momentum generated by the White Paper and the Single European Act and made the ground auspicious for Community institutions to push toward the next step beyond 1992: the opening in December, 1990, of the two new IGCs designed to fix the time table and modalities of economic and monetary union as well as the much more elusive task of political union. Although, as noted, no one has a clear picture of what is meant by political union,[38] it is worth noting that, with open talk about Community government, federalist solutions, and other such codes,[39] in the "battle" between state and

---

38. The term has no fixed meaning and is used to connote a wide variety of models from most federalist to intergovernmentalist. See, generally, Mayne and Pinder, eds., *Federal Union: The Pioneers* (1990); Lodge, ed., *European Union: The European Community in Search of a Future* (1986).

39. See President Delors's speech of January 17, 1990, to the European Parliament: "Cet exécutif [of the future Community on which Delors was speculating—the Commission according to the logic of the founders] devra être responsable, bien entendu, devant les institutions démocratiques de la future *fédération* . . ." (*Europe Documents*, no. 1592 [January 24, 1990], 7, emphasis added); likewise, when speaking approvingly of Mitterrand's idea of an all-European Confederation, Delors adds: "Mais ma conviction est qu'une telle confédération ne pourra voir le jour qu'une fois réalisée l'Union politique de la Communauté!" (id. at 4).

Community, it may appear that the old nationalist voice has become
ingly marginalized and that the integrationist ethos has risen to full
dancy. The demise of Mrs. Thatcher symbolizes this change.

The impact of 1992 goes, however, well beyond these obvious fa⌐ɪ⌐ of
mobilization and "European ascendancy." Just below the surface lurk some
questions, choices, perhaps even forces that touch on the very ethos of European integration, on its underlying ideology, and on the emergent political
culture associated with this new mobilization. And in some respects the very
success of 1992 highlights some inherent (or at least potential) contradictions
in the very objectives of European integration and in its legitimacy as a viable
political force. I shall deal first with the break from (the supposed) ideological
neutrality of the Community and then turn to the question of the ethos of
European integration in public discourse.

1992 and the "Ideological Neutrality"
of the Community

The idea of the single market has been presented in the White Paper as an
ideologically neutral program around which the entire European polity could
coalesce in order to achieve the goals of European integration. In this respect,
one was tapping into an interesting feature of the pre-1992 Community—the
relative absence of ideological discourse and debate on the Left-Right spectrum. The chill on Left-Right ideological debate derived from the governance
structure of the Community.[40]

Since in Council at any given time there would be representatives of
national governments from both Left and Right, the much sought after consensus had to be one that would be acceptable to all major political forces in
Europe. Thus, policies verged toward centrist, pragmatic choices, and issues
involving sharp Left-Right division were either shelved or mediated so as
to conceal or mitigate the choice involved.[41] The tendency toward the lowest common denominator also applied to the lowest common ideological
denominator.

Likewise, although the political structure of the European Parliament
replicates the major political parties in Europe, and although members of
Parliament sit by political group rather than by country, the politics of integration itself (especially on the issues of the power of the European Parliament
and the future destiny of the Community) were for a long time far more
important than differences between Left and Right. The clearest example

---

40. Of course, I am not suggesting that choices with ideological implications were not
made; but they were rarely perceived as such. For further discussion of this point, see Leibfried in
this volume.

41. Thus, the proposed European Company Statute was shelved for many years because of
the inability to agree, especially on the role of labor in the governance structure of the company.

of this was the coalescing of Parliament with a large majority behind the Independent-Communist Spinelli and his Draft Treaty for European Union.[42]

Most interesting in this perspective is the perception of the Commission. It is an article of faith of European integration that the Commission is not meant to be a mere secretariat but an autonomous political force shaping the agenda and brokering the decision making of the Community. And yet, at the same time, as broker, it must be ideologically neutral—not favoring Christian Democrats, Social Democrats, or others.

This neutralization of ideology has conditioned, in its turn, the belief that an agenda could be set for the Community, and the Community could be led toward an ever closer union among its peoples without having to face the normal political cleavages present in the member states. Thus, the Community political culture that developed in the 1960s and 1970s saw an habituation of the political class in Europe to the idea of European integration as ideologically neutral regarding, or ideologically transcendent over, normal debates on the Left-Right spectrum. It is easy to understand how this served the process of integration by allowing a nonpartisan coalition to emerge around its overall objectives. Project 1992 changes this in two ways.

The first is a direct derivation from the turn to majority voting. It is now possible for policies to be adopted within the Council that run counter not simply to the perceived interests of a member state but, more specifically, to the ideology of a government in power. The debates about the European Social Charter, the shrill cries of "socialism through the backdoor," and the emerging debates about Community adherence to the European Convention on Human Rights and abortion rights are harbingers of things to come. In many respects, this is a healthy development since the real change from the past rests in the ability to make difficult social choices and, particularly, in the increased transparency of the implications of the choice. But it does represent a transformation from earlier patterns, with obvious dysfunctional tensions.

The second impact of Project 1992 on ideological neutrality is more subtle. The entire program rests on two pivots: the single market plan encapsulated in the White Paper and its operationalization through the new instrumentalities of the Single European Act. Endorsing the former and adopting the latter by the Community and its member states—and more generally by the political class in Europe—was a most remarkable expression of the process of habituation alluded to previously. People were called, successfully, to rally behind and identify with a new, bold step toward a higher degree of integration. A *single European* market is a concept that still has the power to stir. But it is also a single European *market*. The single market is not simply a

---

42. Typically, the Left and Right did differ sharply in Parliament on issues of foreign affairs and extra-Community policies.

technocratic program to remove the remaining obstacles to the free movement of all factors of production. It is, at the same time, a highly politicized choice of ethos, of ideology, and of political culture: the culture of the market. It is a philosophy, at least one version of which—the predominant version—seeks to remove barriers to the free movement of factors of production and remove distortions to competition as a means for the maximization of utility and is premised on the assumption of formal equality of individuals.[43] It is an ideology the contours of which have been the subject of intense debate within the member states in terms of their own political choices. This is not the place to explicate these. Two slogans—the one-dimensional market and big market as big brother—have been used elsewhere to emphasize the fallacy of ideological neutrality.[44] Thus, for example, open access, the cornerstone of the single market and the condition for effective nonprotectionist competition, will also put pressure on local consumer products in local markets as an expression of cultural diversity. Such pressure will be especially strong in the case of such explicit "cultural products" as television and cinema. The advent of Euro-brands has implications, for better or for worse, that extend beyond the bottom line of national and Community economies. Likewise, the indispensable need for the success of the single market to engage in widespread harmonization of standards of consumer, environmental, and employee protection is bound not only to accentuate the pressure for uniformity but also to manifest a social (and hence ideological) choice that prizes market efficiency and Europe-wide neutrality of competition above other competing values. It is not impossible that consensus may be found on these issues and, indeed, that this choice enjoys broad legitimacy. From my perspective, it is simply important to highlight that it does involve a powerful pressure in shaping the political culture of the Community and, as such, is an important element of the transforming of Europe.

The Ethos of European Integration: Europe as Unity and Europe as Community

As I have indicated, Project 1992 also brings to the fore questions, choices, and contradictions in the very ethos of European integration. I shall explore these questions, choices, and contradictions by construing two competing

---

43. There is an alternative construction of the community political ideology also present in the European debate, which recognizes "inequalities but deploring their inequities, considers the market to be just one of several basic means of governing society" (Snyder, *New Directions in European Community Law* [1990], at 89).

44. "Back to the Future: Policy, Strategy and Tactics of the White Paper on the Creation of a Single European Market," in Bieber, Dehousse, Pinder, and Weiler, eds., *1992: One European Market?* (1988), at 18–20.

visions of the promised land to which the Community is being led in 1992 and beyond; the two visions are a synthetic construct distilled from the discourse and praxis of European integration.

Europe as Unity and Europe as Community

Both unitarian and communitarian visions share a similar departure point. If we go back to the 1950 Schuman Declaration and the consequent 1951 Treaty of Paris establishing the European Coal and Steel Community (ECSC), despite their economic content, they must first and foremost be seen as a long-term and transformative strategy for peace among the states of Western Europe and principally France and Germany.[45] The "mischiefs" that this strategy tried to address were the excesses of the modern nation-state and the traditional model of intercourse among them. Premised on full *sovereignty, autonomy*, and *independence*, this intercourse amounted to a relentless defense and maximization of the national interest. This model was opposed not simply because it had displayed a propensity to degenerate into violent clashes but also because it appeared unattractive for the task of reconstruction in times of peace.[46] The European Community was to be an antidote to those negative features of states and of intercourse between them; and establishment of the ECSC in 1951 was seen as the beginning of a process,[47] the realization of which would bring about their elimination. It is at this point that the two visions depart.

According to the unity vision, the process that started in 1951 was to go through the steps of establishing a common market and approximation of economic policies,[48] proceed to ever tighter economic integration (economic and monetary union), and finally result in full political union—in some version of a federal United States of Europe. If we were to link this vision to governance processes and constitutional structures, the ultimate model of the Community and the constitutionalized treaties would stand as the equivalent

---

45. "The gathering of the nations of Europe requires the elimination of the age-old opposition of France and the Federal Republic of Germany" (Schuman Declaration of May 9, 1950); "Considering that world peace can be safeguarded only by creative efforts commensurate with the dangers that threaten it . . ." (Preamble to the Treaty of Paris, 1951).

46. This does not mean that states and statesmen were engulfed in some teary-eyed sentimentalism. Signing on to the Community idea was, no doubt, a result of cool calculation of the national interest. See Milward, *The Reconstruction of Western Europe 1945–51* (1984). But this does not diminish the utility of seeking the overall ethos of the enterprise that they were joining.

47. On the one hand: "In taking upon herself for more than 20 years the role of champion of a united Europe, France has always had as her essential aim the service of peace." On the other hand: "Europe will not be made all at once or according to a single plan . . ." (Schuman Declaration).

48. Art. 2, EEC treaty.

in the European context to the utopian model of "world government" in relation to classical international law. Tomorrow's Europe in this form would indeed constitute the final demise of member state nationalism and, thus, the ultimate realization of the original objectives through political union in the form of a federalist system of governance.[49]

The community vision of integration also rejects the classical model of international law, which celebrates statal sovereignty, independence, and autonomy. Fundamentally, it sees international legal regulation as providing a "neutral" arena for states to pursue their own goals premised on power and self-interest.[50] The community vision is, instead, premised on limiting (or sharing) sovereignty in a select (albeit growing) number of fields—on recognizing, and even celebrating, the reality of interdependence and of counterpoising to the exclusivist ethos of statal autonomy a notion of a *community* of states and peoples sharing values and aspirations.

Most recently, it has been shown convincingly (and not for the first time) how the classical model of international law is a replication, at the international level, of the liberal theory of the state.[51] The state is implicitly treated as the analogue on the international level to the individual within a domestic situation with international legal notions such as self-determination, sovereignty, independence, and consent having their obvious analogy in theories of the individual within the state. The idea of community is, thus, posited in juxtaposition to the international version of pure liberalism and substitutes, in its stead, a modified communitarian vision.

Since the idea of "community" is currently in vogue and has become many things to many people, I would like to explain the meaning I attach to it in this transnational, European context.[52] The importance of the EEC intersta-

---

49. Of course, even in this vision, one is not positing a centrist, unified Europe but a federal structure of sorts in which, as is the case to differing degrees in other federations, local interests and diversity would be maintained. Thus, although Delors speaks in his January 17, 1990, speech of Europe as a federation, he is—in good faith—always careful to maintain respect for "pluralism." See his speech of October 17, 1989, at Bruges, *Europe Documents*, no. 1576 (October 21, 1989), esp. at 5.

50. This, of course, is the classical model of international law. It is not monolithic. There are, in international law, voices—both from within and outside—calling for an alternative vision expressed in such notions as the common heritage of humankind. See, e.g., Sand, *Lessons Learned in Global Environmental Governance* (1990).

51. Koskenniemi, *From Apology to Utopia: The Structure of International Legal Argument* (1989), at, e.g., xvi and passim.

52. I certainly do not find it useful to try to make an explicit analogy to the theories of community of domestic society reflected in the writings of, say, Sandel (e.g., *Liberalism and the Limits of Justice* [1982]) or Walzer (*Spheres of Justice: A Defense of Pluralism and Equality* [1983]), and in the fierce debates about these (see, e.g., Dworkin, "To Each His Own," *New York Review of Books*, April 14, 1983; "Spheres of Justice: An Exchange," *New York Review of Books*, July 21, 1983).

tal notion of *community* rests on the very fact that it does not involve a negation of the state. It is not state *or* Community. The idea of community seeks to dictate a different type of intercourse among the actors belonging to it, of self-limitation in their self-perception, of a redefined self-interest and, hence, redefined policy goals. To the interest of the state must be added the interest of the Community. But, crucially, it does not extinguish the separate actors who are fated to live in an uneasy tension with two competing senses of the polity's self—the autonomous self and the self as part of a larger community—and committed to a search, destined to be elusive, of an optimal balance of goals and behavior as between the community and its actors.

I say it is crucial because, in this view, the unique contribution of the European Community to the civilization of international relations—indeed, its civilizing effect on intra-European statal intercourse—derives from that very fact of tension of the state actors among themselves and with their community and their need to reconcile the reflexes and ethos of the "sovereign" national state with new modes of discourse and a new discipline of solidarity.[53] Civilization is thus perceived not in the conquering of Eros but in its taming.[54]

Moreover, the idea of Europe as community not only conditions discourse among states but also spills over to the peoples of these states, and it at least seeks to influence relations among individuals. The treaty provisions prohibiting, for example, discrimination on grounds of nationality, allowing the free movement of workers and their families, and generally supporting a rich network of transnational social transactions are not intended (on my reading) simply to create the optimal conditions for the free movement of factors of production in the common market. They also serve to remove nationality and state affiliation of the individual, so divisive in the past, as the principal referent for transnational human intercourse.

The unity vision of the promised land sees, then, as its "ideal type" a European polity that finally and decisively replaces its hitherto warring member states in a political union of federal governance. The community vision sees as its "ideal type" a political union in which Community and member state continue their uneasy coexistence, although with an ever-increasing embrace. It is important also to understand that the voice of, say, Thatcher is not an expression of this community vision. Thatcherism is one pole of the first

---

53. Cf. Art. 5, EEC treaty.

54. This tension between actor and community finds an evocative expression in the Preamble and opening articles of the EEC treaty. The Preamble speaks of "an ever closer union among the *peoples*" of Europe, whereas Art. 2 speaks of "closer relations between the *states* belonging to it." Note, too, that the Preamble speaks about the peoples of Europe, rejecting any notion of melting pot and nation building. And, finally, note the "ever closer union"; something that goes on for "ever" incorporates, of course, the "never."

vision, whereby Community membership continues to be assessed and re-evaluated in terms of its costs and benefits to Great Britain, which remains the ultimate referent for its desirability. The Community is conceived, in this way of thinking, not as a redefinition of the national self but as an arrangement, elaborate and sophisticated, of achieving long-term maximization of the national interest in an interdependent world. Its value is measured ultimately and exclusively with the coin of national utility and not Community solidarity.

I do not think that Project 1992 can be seen as representing a clear preference and choice for one vision over the other. But there are manifestations, both explicit and implicit, suggesting an unprecedented and triumphal resurgence and ascendancy of the unity vision of Europe over the competing vision of community—part and parcel of the Project 1992 momentum. If, indeed, the road to European Union will be paved on this vision, at the very moment of its ascendancy, the Community may be endangering something noble at its very core and, like other great empires, with the arrival of success may be sewn the seeds of self-destruction. Why such foreboding? Whence the peril in the unitary vision?

At an abstract, logical level, it is perhaps easy to question the unitary vision that sets up a fully united Europe as the pinnacle of the process of European integration. It would be more than ironic if a polity and political process set up to counter the excesses of statism ended up by coming around full circle and transforming itself into a (super-) state, and it would be equally ironic if an ethos that rejected the nationalism of the member states gave birth to a new European nation and nationalism. The problem with the unity vision is that its very realization entails its negation.

But the life of the Community (like some other things) is not logic, but experience. And experience suggests that with all the lofty talk of political union and federalism, we are not about to see the demise of the member states, not at least for a long time. The Maastricht Treaty on European Union is clear proof of this.

Even that being so does not remove the unease with the unitary vision. For if the unity ethos becomes the principal mobilizing force of the polity, it may, combined with the praxis and rhetoric of Project 1992's single market, compromise the deeper values inherent in the community vision, even if the EC's basic structure does not change for years to come.

I have suggested above that these values operated both at the interstate level, by conditioning a new type of statal discourse and self-perception, and at the societal and individual levels, by diminishing the importance of nationality in transnational human intercourse. How then would the unity vision and the 1992 praxis and rhetoric corrode these values?

The successful elimination of internal frontiers will, of course, accentuate in both symbolic and real senses the external frontiers of the Community.

The privileges of Community membership for states and of Community citizenship for individuals are becoming increasingly pronounced. This is manifest in such phenomena as the diffidence of the Community to further enlargement (packaged in the notion of the concentric circles),[55] in the inevitable harmonization of external border controls, immigration, and asylum policies, and in policies such as local European content of television broadcasting. It takes picaresque character with the enhanced visibility of the statal symbols already adopted by the Community: flag, anthem, Community passport. The potential corrosive effect on the values of the community vision of European integration are self-evident. Nationality as referent for interpersonal relations, and the human alienating effect of *Us* and *Them* are brought back again, simply transferred from their previous intra-Community context to the new inter-community one. We have made little progress if the Us becomes European (instead of German or French or British) and the Them becomes those outside the Community.

There is a second, slightly more subtle, potentially negative influence in this realm. A centerpiece of the agenda for further integration has been the need of Europe to develop the appropriate structures for a common foreign and defense policy to which Maastricht has given but a partial response. It has, indeed, been anomalous that, despite the repeated calls since the early 1970s for a Europe that will speak with one voice, the Community has never successfully translated its internal economic might into commensurate outside influence. The potential corrosive element of this inevitable development rests in the suspicion that some of the desire for a common foreign policy is the appeal of strength and the vision of Europe as a new, global superpower. Europe *is* a political and economic superpower and often fails to see this and discharge its responsibilities appropriately. But the ethos of strength and power, even if transferred from the member state to the European level, is closer to the unity than to the community notion of Europe; and, as such, it partakes of the inherent contradiction of that vision.

All these images and my previous questions are not intended as indictments of Project 1992 and the future road of European integration. Both in its structure and process and in a part of its ethos, the Community has been more than simply a successful venture in transnational cooperation and economic integration. It has been a unique model for reshaping transnational discourse among states, peoples, and individuals that barely a generation ago emerged from the nadir of Western civilization. It is a model the relevance of which is acute to other regions in the world with bleak histories or an even bleaker present.

Today's Community is impelled forward by the dysfunctioning of its

---

55. See Delors, supra, n. 39.

original architecture. The transformation now taking place has immense promise that is widely discussed. If I have given some emphasis to the dangers, it is not simply to redress a lacuna in the literature. It is to alert the observer that in this movement forward are embedded serious ideological choices on which European citizens and residents differ. A choice that simply happens—no choice at all—may sow the seeds of deep legitimacy problems in the future. To this problem, the Maastricht Treaty has no response at all, because it leaves the fundamental elements conditioning the problem unaffected. Only time will tell how real the problem is, and how creative the solutions will be.

The New Germany in the New Europe

Ernst-J. Mestmäcker

The European Context

In addressing the implications of 1992 for Germany, we should keep in mind that the unification of Germany is part of the truly revolutionary developments in Eastern Europe. The "German question" has finally come to be a European question with respect to both European integration and the process of returning to Eastern Europe its own European traditions. There are some important similarities of the problems encountered in German unification and the transition of other societies from communist dictatorships to democracy, the rule of law, and the market economy. That is not to neglect obvious differences that result from the accession of the former German Democratic Republic to the Federal Republic of Germany—a country with a strong market economy and stable currency.

The decision of Chancellor Adenauer's government after World War II to lead West Germany into European integration and into NATO was, at that time, frequently criticized as an implied decision against German reunification. Adenauer turned this argument around by insisting that the only way to achieve reunification was through West Germany's firm commitment to the free world. The slogans that won an absolute majority at the polls in 1953 for the Christian Democrats summarize major tenets of German policies to this day. They referred to Adenauer's foreign policy as reestablishing Germany's position in the network of free nations ("Er knüpfte die Fäden zur freien Welt") and Ludwig Erhard's economic policies for a social market economy as "affluence for everybody" (Wohlstand für alle). It should be noted, however, that the implementation of these policies with respect to European integration was not without conflict. Ludwig Erhard was critical of institutionalized economic integration. He felt that the regulatory powers of a supranational agency would interfere with international free trade. In the end, the objectives of political integration by means of economic integration prevailed over these objections.[1]

In the communist countries of Eastern Europe, European integration was looked upon, from the very beginning, as a capitalist plot that was incompatible with peace in Europe, public international law, and, of course, with German reunification. The supranational character of the European Community was said to amount to an interference with the internal affairs of member states. This background may explain why the unification of Germany in 1990 was seen by many observers in East Germany and in Eastern Europe as an almost miraculous vindication of Adenauer's policies. At the same time, the EC has come to be regarded as a possible model for constitutional reform in such countries as Czechoslovakia, Yugoslavia, and even the former USSR. When I visited with the then newly established Constitutional Council in Moscow, conflicts between the Union and the Republics claiming sovereignty for themselves was the main topic of discussion. My question about what the future constitution of the union might be like was answered by a reference to the EC. There was, however, no analysis of the implications of such a policy. In this context, it is probably the supranational structure of the EC and the supremacy of Community law over national law in cases of conflict that explains its attraction. In the republics, however, people will point to the sovereignty of the Community's member states in such matters as foreign policy and defense.

In those countries that look to the Community in the expectation of future membership, there appears to be a certain hesitation concerning the future integration and unification of Europe. They are afraid that the barriers to entry are going to become even higher than they are already. And with the COMECON experience behind them, they are opposed to centralization anyway.

The Community's apparent economic and institutional success in moving toward a single internal market by 1992 has added to the pressures for full membership in Central Europe. Austria and Sweden have applied for membership; Switzerland agonizes over the compatibility of membership with her status of neutrality. In the EEC treaty's preamble, the present member states "call upon the other people of Europe who share their ideal to join their efforts." Article 237 of the treaty provides for the procedure to be observed if and when a European state applies for membership. There is, however, no obligation under the treaty to act positively on those applications.

---

1. For a comprehensive account of the negotiations leading to the European Community, see Hanns Jürgen Küsters, *Die Gründung der Europäischen Wirtschaftsgemeinschaft*. Baden-Baden: Nomos, 1982.

The Legal Framework of Unification

German unification and the accession of the former German Democratic Republic to the EC has been brought about by a single legal act: the unilateral declaration of the German Democratic Republic that it wanted to join the Federal Republic. This road to unification is provided for in Article 23 of the Federal Republic's constitution, which reads: "For the time being, this basic law shall apply in the territory of the Länder. . . . In other parts of Germany it shall be put into force on their accession." With the accession of the German Democratic Republic, the Treaty of Rome and all other rules of Community law became applicable in the new territory of the Federal Republic. Consequently, no negotiations and no adjustments to the treaty were necessary. Even before the accession of the German Democratic Republic to the Federal Republic, the Community treated German unification as a "special case" that did not depend on adjustments to the treaty under Article 237. The Community adopted, of course, a number of measures providing for temporary exemptions from the general rules of the treaty in favor of the East German territory. Most important were certain exemptions from the Common Agricultural Policy and the rules governing subsidies.[2] The internal implementation of unification is provided for in a treaty between the Federal Republic and the German Democratic Republic that was entered into before the accession under Article 23.[3] As far as the general legal framework is concerned, the principle is that the law of the Federal Republic shall apply in the new territory. There are, however, important exceptions to this rule. They concern measures and regulations adopted in the treaty concerning the gradual restructuring of East Germany's institutions as well as the partial preservation of the legal status quo. In looking at the political and economic implications of 1992 for Germany, I propose to discuss, first, some of the major economic challenges that bear simultaneously on German economic policies and upon the completion of the internal market. This will be followed by a look at the major policy options before the Community in light of the completion of the internal market. In trying to relate these issues to each other, one must realize that it becomes ever more difficult—maybe even impossible—to distinguish the implications of German unification for Germany as such from those for the EC as a whole. I propose to discuss these questions in light of the present

---

2. For details see *The European Communities and German Unification, Bulletin of the European Communities*, Supplement no. 4, 1980.

3. Vertrag zwischen der Bundesrepublik Deutschland und der Deutschen Demokratischen Republik über die Herstellung der Einheit Deutschlands - Einigungsvertrag -, *Bulletin der Bundesregierung*, no. 104, September 6, 1990.

constitutional structure of the Community without dealing with the reforms contained in the Treaty on European Union signed in Maastricht on February 7, 1992.

Rebuilding the Institutions of a Free Society

The basic task before the German people is to rebuild the institutions of a free society in East Germany. The transfer of the legal order of West Germany to East Germany and the establishment of five new Länder in the new territory are important steps in this direction. They tend, however, to obscure the true dimension of the problems that have to be addressed. The laws on the books do not recreate the institutions that are taken for granted in developed industrial countries. These institutions and organizations develop in a democracy on the basis of a highly complex interaction of society with the legislative, executive, and judicial branches of government, but they have been dismantled by the communist party and government. All ways of life were shaped by a system that relied on command and obedience as well as on a perfect system of surveillance and control. There was no independent judiciary. The access to and the substance of legal education were subservient to party control and ideology. The system of state ownership of all economic resources destroyed private property, private enterprise, and the skill and know-how needed to operate a market economy. Some of the more serious economic and legal problems of German unification derive from this heritage.

Privatization and Competition in the Transformation of a Socialized Economy to a Market Economy

The administration of the state-owned enterprises of East Germany had been transferred, even before German unification, to a public corporation. With the accession of East Germany to the Federal Republic, ownership passed to the federal government. The treaty of unification confirms the statute governing the privatization and reorganization of state property through a public corporation (*Treuhandanstalt*). The corporation's statutory purpose is to restructure the state-owned enterprises in accordance with the principles of competition and to privatize them. We are dealing with approximately 8,000 enterprises representing 90 percent of the economic and industrial resources of East Germany. As far as EC rules are concerned, there are no serious obstacles to public ownership as such. Article 220 of the EEC treaty provides that "this Treaty shall in no way prejudice the rules of member states concerning the system of property ownership." There are, however, special rules that require reporting of financial relations and transactions between member states and undertakings controlled by the member states. The purpose of these rules is to prevent subsidies that distort or tend to distort competition.

Privatization must be distinguished from the dissolution of the monopolistic organization of industry and trade. In order to implement central economic planning, the economy of East Germany had been organized on the basis of industrywide monopolies. As markets were opened and entry occurred, many of these industries were immediately exposed to competition. If there is, nevertheless, a probability that privatization may create a dominant market position, German or European merger control does apply. Under present circumstances, the priority goal is to encourage investment and to facilitate the acquisition of East German economic units by German or foreign investors. It follows that, in cases of doubt, privatization will take precedence over traditional concerns of the antitrust laws. But even if antitrust standards were to prevail, application of the failing company doctrine would justify tolerance of most reorganizations.

The task of privatization is a formidable one. It is both a prerequisite to and an instrument of private investment in East Germany. Uncertainties surrounding title to property are among the most serious impediments to investment. The treaty of unification provides that private property taken by the communist government or the Communist party has to be returned to its rightful owners. There are, however, exceptions to the rule. Where restitution is impossible, the owner is entitled to compensation. Where title has been acquired bona fide by private persons or where those in possession have other legitimate interests, a solution shall be sought on the basis of equity. There is no restitution for real property expropriated under the authority of the Soviet Military Government until 1949. In many cases, it will take years until the conflicting claims to specific pieces of property are resolved.

There are further difficulties facing potential investors. Generally, these are due to the uncertainty over the future viability of enterprises with their present work forces, machinery, and product lines. Balance sheets and profit and loss statements are not very informative if they relate to enterprises that have not stood the test of the market. Frequently, managements remain unchanged from the days of the former regime. These people are not eager to give up their positions and to lose the protection they associate with government ownership.

Pollution of soil, air, and water to an almost unimaginable degree poses no less fundamental problems. Add to this a nonexistent infrastructure for a modern economy. There is no modern communication system; even phone calls from and to East Germany are next to impossible at the moment.

These are some of the reasons economic recovery in general and privatization in particular have proved much more difficult than expected. The delay has triggered controversy over the priorities and methods of privatization. The opposing views concern the priorities in the sequence of privatization and reorganization of firms. Should privatization be the instrument of reorganization or should modernization go before privatization? These alternatives— even though they are obviously not mutually exclusive—indicate policy choices with far-reaching consequences. Those who argue for giving priority to privatization are afraid that the federal government may find itself burdened with enterprises dependent upon subsidies in the expectation of an illusory future recovery. Those who argue for giving priority to reorganization warn against giving away public property.

These issues indicate the greatest economic and social challenge now facing government, the trade unions, and employers: the necessity of relocating a substantial portion of the work force. This task is all the more difficult because real wages continue to differ considerably between West and East Germany. An East German worker earns not quite 50 percent of his or her western colleague. In a market economy, structural changes necessarily involve temporary unemployment. The estimates of the degree and the duration of future unemployment differ widely, but there is no doubt that it will be substantial. The social hardships of unemployment will cause considerable unrest and political difficulties. These difficulties will be all the more serious because socialist propaganda relied upon the absence of open unemployment as proof of the superiority of the planned economy over capitalism. It will take a considerable effort to convince workers in East Germany that today's unemployment has been caused by a policy that favored the appearance of full employment over the demands of economic efficiency. As unemployment in East Germany is rising, the economy of West Germany is booming because of the additional demand from customers in East Germany. It is one of the primary objectives of the present economic policies to encourage West German industry to invest in, rather than just sell to, East Germany.

The campaign for the election to the first all-German Parliament was dominated by a controversy over whether the immediate and total exposure of the East German economy to national and international competition was a wise and responsible decision. The introduction of the West German Deutsche Mark as the official currency even before political unification and the accession of East Germany to the European Community amounted to a "Big Bang" policy. It is my considered opinion that this decision was the right one for both political and economic reasons. It was the only way to generate the information needed to judge the competitiveness and viability of East German industry. Now that judgment can be based on facts rather than on political speculation, and the wishful thinking and wishful lying that obscured the true state of the East German economy for decades can be brought to an end. Only in this

way has it been possible to achieve German unity in accordance with the open
market standards of the Community.

Political Impact of the Transition Process

So far the transition process in the formerly separate parts of Germany has
strengthened and reinforced traditional political affiliations, priorities, and
preferences. In the former Federal Republic, the heavy financial burdens of
reunification are contributing to conflicts characteristic of a welfare state.
Affluence does not mean that voters are prepared to forego traditional benefits
or to accept with equanimity higher taxes or higher social security contributions. In the Länder where elections have been held since reunification, the
Social Democrats have won control of the governments, usually in coalition
with the environmentalists (the Greens). In the former German Democratic
Republic, there appears to be widespread disappointment with unification in
general and the market economy in particular. Very high unemployment is the
most obvious cause. More fundamental reasons are probably the dramatic
institutional and structural changes that touch upon and transform literally all
aspects of everyday life. Among the more pervasive and enduring teachings
of socialism is the belief in social and economic equality as the cornerstone of
justice. However, the transition process itself produces even more hardships
and inequalities than are normally associated with market processes. Spokes-
men for the new Länder keep reminding "The West" to be more sensitive to
social values. This attitude cuts across party lines and religious affiliations. It
is reflected in proposals for constitutional amendments to incorporate the right
to work and the right to adequate housing into the constitution.

It is not without irony that, in the face of the bankruptcy of a planned
socialist economy, there are strong forces at work to move the market economy toward more social obligations and, consequently, more state intervention than before.

To what extent these attitudes will translate themselves into actual politics is impossible to foresee. It is even more difficult to know in what way
changing political interests and attitudes are going to influence Germany's
position in the EC. At present, there are no discernable effects on the more
important fields of European integration. East Germany's agriculture is not
basically different from West Germany's as far as products are concerned. The
additional production capacity in combination with its relatively low productivity may, however, add to the difficulties that have prevented fundamental
changes in the wasteful common agricultural policy.

As far as the accession of East European countries to the EC is concerned, Germany has a more receptive attitude than most other member

countries. The reason for this is not difficult to understand. Poverty and social unrest in these countries is expected to cause uncontrollable immigration, primarily into Germany. It is, therefore, in Germany's self-interest to assist her eastern neighbors in their economic recovery. Definite prospects of membership in the EC on the basis of a binding timetable could enlist both the Community as a whole and its member countries in common efforts to rebuild gradually the economies of future members. Membership in the Community depends, of course, upon national economies that accept open markets and effective transborder competition. The German experience does not prove that these conditions can and must be created in one irrevocable step. In Germany, monetary union was the first step toward unification, preceding even the step of political unity. The countries in Eastern Europe have their own monetary systems, and, therefore, they are in a better position to prepare gradually for membership in the EC.

The accession of East European countries would probably retard the development of a more political European union. It has been one of the revolutionary effects of European integration to overcome the nation-state as the final arbiter of collective self-interest. In countries that have lived under communist dictatorships, which were reinforced by a communist superpower, liberation has been achieved in the name of national identity. These countries cherish their newly won sovereignty, and they are critical of any integration that implies Community powers that take precedence over national powers.

German and European Monetary Union

In a widely quoted and controversial statement before the European Parliament, a former president of the German Bundesbank argued that German monetary union contains important lessons for European monetary union. Most important among these (according to his view) is the prospect that the region-specific structural changes triggered by monetary union cannot be controlled or mitigated by monetary policies. A minimum of harmonization with respect to both economic development and economic and financial policy is needed before taking the irrevocable step toward monetary union with a single currency and a European central bank. The underlying controversy is as old as the EC itself. Should monetary union be an instrument of integration, forcing monetary discipline as well as necessary structural changes upon member states? Or should an economic union, based upon integration and harmonization of national policies, go before monetary union? If there are lessons to be learned from the present German experience, they concern the far-reaching implications of monetary union when the union contains an economically backward region. The necessary and inevitable structural changes are such that, for both economic and political reasons, they cannot be left to work themselves out through private initiative and market forces alone. Regional unemployment, poor infrastructure, and different standards of environmental protection create irresistible pressures for financial burden sharing. The Community's present constitutional structure is ill-equipped to cope with those demands. It is highly doubtful whether the member states are prepared to confer the power to tax upon the Community or to participate, on a meaningful scale, in the necessary financial equalization among themselves. Even the West German Länder are extremely reluctant to let their East German counterparts participate in the established system of financial equalization.

Under those circumstances, a European central bank would have a formidable task in adhering to a policy of tight money. This applies even if we assume a European central bank to be endowed with full political independence—an assumption that can hardly be taken for granted. There are quite different traditions and attitudes among the member states with respect to the uses of monetary policies and the acceptable degree of inflation. A European central bank, its independence notwithstanding, could not isolate itself from economic and political processes and expectations in the member states. It would be unrealistic to expect the European central bank to have the kind of public support that has made it possible for the German Bundesbank to be steadfast during these difficult times in the implementation of its mandate to preserve price stability.

The Community after 1992

There is a veritable stream of directives, regulations, decisions, and blueprints for Community action pouring out of Brussels these days. The Commission is addressing such diverse fields as energy and broadcasting, R&D by industry and academic institutions, industrial and intellectual property rights, merger control and industrial policy, data protection, and a social charter for Europe. It is the Community's very effectiveness in implementing the Single European Act that poses the question whether the present legal structure of the Community is a sufficient constitutional basis for these far-reaching activities. This question should be distinguished from proposals for monetary and political union. Such unions raise far-reaching constitutional issues of their own. On the other hand, our question cannot be distinguished from the creation of the single internal market; it is the conflicts brought about by implementation of the Single European Act that have put the new activities on the EC's agenda. These conflicts are in the background of the present constitutional debate. The treaty's system of enumerated powers has been eroded. There is no readily apparent alternative principle for the future federal structure of the Community. This issue is closely related, and, indeed, partially identical, to the controversy over the Community's economic order. Those who argue for a decentralized federal system will, as a rule, favor an economic order that guarantees open markets and limits central regulation to essential concerns of the public interest that cannot be dealt with effectively by the member states. Further issues are the democratic legitimacy of the Community and the protection of human rights against legislative and administrative measures of the Community's institutions.

A case that highlights these problems is the Community's directive providing for free transborder television within the EC. It is representative of the constitutional issues associated with many of the recent policies adopted by the Community. Under Germany's federal structure, broadcasting is under the exclusive jurisdiction of the Länder. The principles that govern the structure of the electronic media derive from the case law of the constitutional court. They are derived from an interpretation of the guarantee of free speech as a basic right. The Länder appealed to the German constitutional court, arguing that the EC directive was incompatible with Germany's federal structure. This raises the question of the German court's jurisdiction over Community measures. The German constitutional court has decided that, as a rule, it will defer to the rulings of the European Court of Justice. This is predicated upon the effective protection of human rights by the European Court. There is no ruling, thus far, on whether this principle will also prevail where it is argued that Germany's federal structure as such is at stake. A similar issue concerns the directive's controversial provision for the reservation of a majority proportion of broadcasting time for "European works." The United States has complained to GATT about this part of the directive. This provision raises difficult questions under the Treaty of Rome as well.

This case shows, as does the constitutional debate, that the EC is confronted with far-reaching questions concerning the proper exercise of its powers under the treaty as it stands today. However, these questions are by no means specific to Germany; as Joseph Weiler demonstrates in his contribution to this volume, they concern the Community as a whole. I have no doubt that the present German government as well as its successors will participate in the development of the EC, just as German governments have done in the past. There is no indication that the united Germany will adopt European policies that are different in principle from those of the past. That is not to say that our fellow citizens in East Germany will not influence the political course of the country. But I am confident that there will be no deviation from the traditional dedication to the cause of Europe. The changes that have occurred in Eastern Europe and that have made German unification possible will further strengthen the European commitment of German foreign policies. The most cogent among them is the impossibility for any European country to cope alone with the new challenges that arise as the regional communist predominance has come to an end. The demands upon Europe and the Atlantic community will differ from the demands of the cold war. But they will be no less important or difficult to answer.

Key Questions on
Economic and Monetary Union

Tommaso Padoa-Schioppa

At a certain point, the renewed vigor of economic integration among the EC countries in the mid-1980s put the issue of economic and monetary union (EMU) back at the top of the Community agenda. The mandate that the European Council, meeting in Hannover in June, 1988, gave to the Delors Committee to study the realization of EMU set a wide-ranging process in motion. While academic debates continue, the Community has taken practical steps toward EMU by launching phase one of the Delors Committee plan and, more important, by calling an intergovernmental conference to amend the EEC treaty to allow for EMU. The conference completed its work in December, 1991, and the new treaty is expected to be ratified by member countries in 1992.

This chapter treats the subject of EMU by dealing with the three key questions that an observer of the process might wish to raise: (1) can there be a single market without a monetary union, (2) can there be monetary union without fiscal union, and (3) can there be monetary union without political union. Each is addressed in a separate section.

The order of the arguments addressed in the three sections reflects the fact that monetary union represents the key issue in the evolution from the single market to the EMU project. Therefore I focus mainly on the monetary leg of EMU and its interaction with the two aspects of the economic leg, the single market program, already adopted, and fiscal union, which was brought into the picture as a complement to monetary union.

The three questions deal with economics, but each is deeply political and constitutional in character. As a result, satisfactory answers to all three require a blend of economic analysis and judgment. Economic theory, in identifying constraints on policy, may help the policymaker to avoid mistakes, but it cannot, in itself, produce unambiguous policy recommendations for particular historical situations. In this chapter, on the basis of my judgment as well as my economic expertise, I argue in support of particular answers to each of the three questions.

Can there Be a Single Market without Monetary Union?

My answer is negative: a single market can last and yield all its expected benefits only if it is complemented by monetary union, that is, if a single currency circulates within it.

The EC's single market is something very different from a free-trade area. In the single market, nationality can no longer be the basis for distinctions between economic agents, products, and services: any transaction that can be made between residents of one country should also be possible, under the same conditions, between residents of two different countries.[1] The EC's rules on the free circulation of goods, services, capital, and persons have constitutional status for member states; they thus have priority over national legislation.

The Community follows the minimal government principle of *subsidiarity*, according to which the transfer of powers should be strictly confined to the areas in which collective decision making is necessary to make the system work. All policy functions that can be carried out at national level without adverse repercussions on the functioning of the Community should remain within the competence of the member countries.[2]

Given this definition, the issue of what monetary order is required by a single market can be tackled in two steps. The first is to clarify whether, in an internal market, there is room for different monetary policies by individual countries, exchange rates being allowed to vary. The second is to identify the appropriate institutional framework to ensure the desired monetary regime. The answer the EC has given to the first question is that a single market cannot be effective and durable if exchange rates between the currencies of member countries are allowed to fluctuate. This answer, with which I concur, is based on both microeconomic and policy considerations.

From the microeconomic standpoint, exchange rate stability is the condition for reaping all the benefits of the single market.[3] Even where national currencies are fully convertible, uncertainty concerning rates of exchange imposes a cost on operations between residents of different countries and reduces the mobility of factors.[4] Even with the most solemn commitment that

---

1. See Padoa-Schioppa 1987.
2. Committee for the Study of Economic and Monetary Union 1989, paragraph 20.
3. See Commission of the European Communities 1990.
4. See Bertola 1989.

exchange rates will always stay fixed, a multiplicity of currencies and central banks cannot but prompt doubts about such a commitment and leave room for risk premiums linked to fears of parity changes. And even if such doubts were reduced to zero, transaction and information costs would still be significantly higher than with one currency. Only when the entire area uses a single currency does the advantage of intraborder over cross-border trading disappear.

From a policy perspective, the exchange rate can be considered as a threefold instrument of commercial policy, of tax policy, and of adjustment to real economic disturbances.[5] As an instrument of commercial policy, the exchange rate affects the relative prices of goods produced in different countries: its use for this purpose runs counter to the elimination of trade barriers and the conduct of a single commercial policy in the Community. As an instrument of tax policy, the exchange rate reflects the different inflation tax rates involved in holding different currencies. But in an area with full capital mobility, money cannot earn different rates of interest (except for differences due to differentials in creditworthiness) in the various regions without leading to large-scale currency substitution. Such substitution undermines the ability of national authorities to control domestic liquidity and, hence, to use the exchange rate as a fiscal instrument.[6] Community countries have increasingly recognized that, in a fully integrated area, the exchange rate should not be used for commercial purposes and that its use for fiscal purposes is necessarily short-lived. This is the rationale for the European Monetary System (EMS).[7]

Finally, the exchange rate can be used as a policy instrument in adjusting to differentiated real shocks.[8] Whether or not the Community is an optimal currency area is a question to which a conclusive, "scientific" answer can hardly be given.[9] This is ultimately a matter of judgment, and, in forming a judgment, a relevant consideration is that, through the single market program, the Community aims to develop precisely those mechanisms of adjustment, in particular enhanced market flexibility, that will bring it closer to the conditions defining a currency area. Further, it should be noted that EMS members have long abandoned the exchange rate as an instrument for adjustment to real disturbances: there has been no realignment since 1987 despite fluctuations in the price of oil of up to 100 percent in six months—fluctuations that could have spurred alterations in member countries' exchange rates to compensate for differences in energy dependence.[10] Similarly, the unification of Germany,

5. See Bini Smaghi 1990.
6. See Padoa-Schioppa and Papadia 1984; Woodford 1990.
7. See Padoa-Schioppa 1992.
8. Cf. Mundell 1969, chap. 12.
9. See Bini Smaghi 1990; Eichengreen 1990; International Monetary Fund 1991.
10. See Giavazzi and Giovannini 1989.

which has represented a major real disturbance for the Community, has not been accompanied by any adjustment of exchange rates.[11]

Concluding, then, that exchange rate stability is a natural complement to the internal market, the issue is, what institutional setting can best ensure it. Conceptually, this could involve either a fixed exchange rate regime or the creation of a single center for monetary policy decisions.

A fixed exchange rate regime by itself does not solve the problem of monetary management, because it does not establish who is to decide the overall policy stance of the system, the so-called nth country problem. Fixed exchange rate regimes presuppose that one country's central bank (the U.S. Federal Reserve System under Bretton Woods) sets monetary policy for the whole area.

On both economic and political grounds, this hegemonic model would not be appropriate to a fixed rate regime in the EC. From an economic point of view, in an area with perfect capital mobility and a high degree of currency substitution, it would be extremely difficult for any one national authority to retain the great control over domestic monetary conditions required to play the role of anchor for the whole area. It is no accident that the Deutsche Mark is currently one of the currencies whose use by foreign holders is subject to restrictions. Moreover, as experience shows, fixed rate regimes with large numbers of central banks are bound to develop internal tensions and, eventually, to break down.

More fundamentally, the adoption of one national central bank and currency for the whole union could never be considered politically acceptable. The essence of the Community is to be a constitutional system of equals, in which a long (and bloody) history of failed attempts by one nation to dominate the others is supplanted by a common rule of law, in which sovereignty is shared. This is why the alternative solution has been chosen, namely, conferring the monetary policy powers now exercised by national monetary authorities on a Community institution.

The indeterminacy inherent in a fixed rate system is resolved by a single monetary policy that ensures full convertibility of currencies at par rates. As long as national currencies subsist, they operate as fractions of a single currency. Eventually they will be replaced by a single currency. Such replacement facilitates economic calculations and reinforces the irreversibility of unification.

To sum up, a single market cannot be fully realized if exchange rates are allowed to vary. Success depends on the creation of a single authority charged

---

11. See Centre for Economic Policy Research 1990; International Monetary Fund 1990.

with conducting the single monetary policy. The market can be truly unified only if there is a single currency.[12]

Can there Be Monetary Union without Fiscal Union?

My answer is positive, with the following qualification: while monetary union does not require the centralization of fiscal policy, it would benefit from some degree of "federal" discipline in the conduct of national fiscal policies.

Since *fiscal union* is an elusive term, let me specify that what I mean thereby is any arrangement by which the Community has the authority to condition the overall fiscal policy of the area. This can be done through the Community budget or by influencing national budgetary policies. Rules constraining national budgetary policies, fiscal transfers through the Community budget, and a large Community budget with a macroeconomic impact are all forms of fiscal union.

In most constitutional systems, monetary powers are exercised at the same level of government as most of the fiscal powers. This has led some to doubt whether monetary union is compatible with a completely decentralized budget system.

The main argument in support of the thesis that monetary union requires fiscal union runs as follows. Since monetary union precludes the use of the exchange rate as an instrument of economic policy, a fiscal instrument might be needed at the Community level to ease adjustment to shocks that affect the member countries differently. Otherwise, it is said, undue pressures would develop for monetary policy to tackle country-specific shocks. This argument is the basis of proposals that the Community partly finance national unemployment insurance schemes and receive a commensurate portion of the contributions.[13]

To my mind, this line of argument is not convincing. Most country-specific shocks are caused by the policies of the country's government or by the behavior of its private economic agents, and one wonders whether such shocks should entitle the country concerned to compensation. It could be argued that each country should pay for its own errors.

Moreover, there are important examples of federal states with very limited provisions for interregional transfers. A notable case is the United States. Before 1929, the federal budget was substantially smaller than the state bud-

---

12. See Emerson 1991. In Hannover, the heads of state and government stated that, "in adopting the Single Act, the member states of the Community confirmed the objective of progressive realization of economic and monetary union."

13. See Bean 1990; Eichengreen 1990.

gets, a situation similar to that in the Community today. Even today, recent studies suggest that, with a much larger federal budget, interstate transfers to cope with uneven, short-term economic developments are very small in scale.[14] In the United States, budgetary transfers seem rather to be determined by persistent differences in income levels or economic trends. They seem designed to reduce longstanding inequalities between states and to stimulate growth in poorer regions. These transfers cannot be considered a substitute for the exchange rate. The fundamental point is that devaluation is not an instrument for promoting economic development; indeed, the experience of the major industrial countries since World War II suggests that the currencies of fast-growing countries tend to appreciate.[15]

It should also be emphasized that, when regions are affected by uneven shocks, adjustment-inducing resources do not have to be transferred through the budget but can be transferred through market mechanisms.[16] Residents of regions where growth is slower than expected will tend to smooth their consumption plans by borrowing from the residents of faster-growing regions whose savings increase.

In summary, the claim that a fiscal union in the form of fiscal transfers through the Community budget is the *necessary* complement to monetary union, because such transfers replace the exchange rate in coping with country-specific shocks, is built on weak ground. Let me stress that this conclusion does not apply to similar but different issues, such as the desirability (as opposed to necessity) of fiscal transfers or the role of fiscal instruments in dealing with regional (as opposed to national) backwardness (as opposed to adverse shocks).

While fiscal union in the form of fiscal transfers should not be considered a prerequisite for EMU, it can be argued that fiscal union in the form of a "federal" discipline on national budgetary policies would enhance the efficiency of the economic policy of the union. The main argument for this thesis is that monetary union might reduce the incentive for governments to conduct

---

14. Von Hagen 1991 shows that the U.S. fiscal system does not represent a buffer for transitory regional differences in economic performance. Unemployment insurance, in particular, is financed almost entirely by the individual states. Such a system bars any significant redistribution of resources between states. Further, he finds that the relationship between income and net transfers from and to the federal government, discussed in Sachs and Sala-i-Martin 1989, holds only for levels, but not for first differences, implying that these transfers are related to the level of income, or to permanent changes therein, rather than to its fluctuations.

15. The exchange rate can be regarded as an efficient instrument for easing adjustment in the face of nonrecurring permanent shocks; see Cohen and Wyplosz 1988. The argument that interregional budgetary stabilizers, which are typically aimed at temporary disturbances, should be used as a substitute for the loss of the exchange rate instrument does not seem theoretically valid.

16. See Gros 1991.

prudent budgetary policies. In particular, the fact that the interest rate response to any one country's fiscal expansion is not borne by the country of origin alone but spread throughout the area and is therefore smaller in size reduces the restraints on fiscal laxity.[17] This issue is relevant because of the relative size of some of the member countries. A deficit of 10 percent of the GDP of one of the larger countries can correspond to as much as 2 percent of GDP and 10 percent of savings in the Community as a whole.

There is no lack of counterarguments. In a monetary union without fiscal union, a properly chartered central bank would be able to resist pressures to bail the lax fiscal authority out of its debt. Moreover, in the single market, national governments will have no possibility of facilitating their borrowing through regulation. Even if the evidence in support of either argument is inconclusive, one may favor complementing monetary union with some general rules of fiscal discipline on the ground that such rules are desirable per se, that is, for any kind of constitutional system, not just for the particular case of EMU.

Budgetary discipline can be promoted by three main rules that, it is now widely agreed, will be written into the treaty. The first rule bans direct government access to central bank financing in forms such as overdraft facilities or the direct purchase of government paper on the primary market. It is worth noting that this rule is stricter than the comparable ones now in force in all the member countries, including Germany. The second rule is that governments have full and exclusive responsibility for their own debts and cannot be rescued by other governments or the Community. These two rules are intended to enhance the discipline the market exerts on governments. The third rule sets upper limits to government deficits by stating that "excessive deficits" should be avoided. Its rationale is the consideration that market discipline may have a rather limited effect. For instance, in Canada, where the divergence in provincial budgetary stances and indebtedness is wider than in other federal countries, the maximum difference between borrowing rates is less than 50 basis points.

Setting limits on budget deficits poses problems of definition and enforcement. Since it is hard to identify clear-cut, universally applicable criteria to determine when a deficit is excessive, the assessment must rely on judgment and be based on some simple indicator. Moreover, the scope for ensuring compliance with Community rules by national Parliaments is limited. At this stage, it is hard to predict whether the mix of rules and procedures for judgment and enforcement (mainly through peer pressure) that the treaty is

---

17. This result is derived from the traditional literature on the efficacy of monetary and fiscal policy under flexible or fixed exchange rates (Mundell 1969). See Buiter and Kletzer 1989; Casella 1989.

likely to adopt with regard to the "no excessive deficit" rule will constitute a sufficient basis to institute the practice of effective Community supervision of national budgetary policies.

Can there Be Monetary Union without Political Union?

My answer is that it all depends on what is meant by "political union." The Community is already a kind of political union, and it will continue to be so with EMU. On the other hand, EMU does not require that the Community evolve as did our highly centralized member states over the centuries.

On the same day of April, 1989, that the report of the Delors Committee was made public, the British chancellor of the exchequer, Nigel Lawson, declared that "monetary unity would require political union, which is not on the agenda." In a way, he was right. There is no doubt that the links between the economic and the political dimensions of the Community to which he was pointing are critical. However, the concept of political union he had in mind was probably one for which his statement would not be valid.

There are two ways to validate Lawson's proposition. The first is to say that the EC is *already* a kind of political union. The second is to say that the Community will experience even greater political union if the single market is supplemented with EMU.

Many elements substantiate the contention that, in several respects, the EC is already a political union. How could it be denied that establishing joint, supranational management of coal and steel, the two fundamental natural resources of the nineteenth and early twentieth centuries, over which France, Germany, and the rest of Europe fought cruel wars, was a highly political project? And the protracted battles over majority voting that were fought in the preparation of the Treaty of Rome, in the De Gaulle-Hallstein crisis of 1965, and on many subsequent occasions, were eminently political. Similarly, the firm desire of Greece, Spain, and Portugal to link the restoration of democracy to participation in the EC is a clear expression of the political, not just economic, value of the Community.

"Political" is what "affects the state or its government" (Concise Oxford Dictionary). The present Community is about matters that deeply affect the state and its government. Abolishing barriers to trade, setting agricultural prices, deregulating the banking sector, stipulating association treaties with third countries, harmonizing indirect taxes, and prosecuting and sanctioning state aid to industry all impinge on acts of government. The fact that their content is economic does not deprive them of a strong political character. Such acts involve choices among different, often conflicting, interests.

The present EC is a political union not only because of the political character of the matters falling under its jurisdiction but also in its institutional structure, which has much closer similarities to a "national" constitutional system than to international forums for consultation and cooperation. The Community has effective decision-making authority in the areas covered by the treaty, an authority organized in the classic, threefold division into a legislative, executive, and judicial branch. Drawing an analogy to the U.S. institutional system, it has a House of Representatives (the European Parliament), a Senate (the Council of Ministers), an Administration (the European Commission), and a Supreme Court (the Court of Justice). The supremacy of Community law over national legislation is well established; it is applied in national as well as Community courts. In many situations, Community law can be directly invoked by firms and individuals.

Thus, Mr. Lawson's remarks were right but untimely. From its birth, the EC has been a political union—that is why the United Kingdom decided not to join in the 1950s. It was still a political union in 1989.

Monetary union would add substantively to this political construction. Monetary policy has always been the prerogative of the state, and so the transfer of responsibility for monetary policy from sovereign states to a supranational entity has profound political content. This is recognized both by the proponents and by the opponents of EMU.

Monetary policy has more or less political content depending on the type of monetary regime and the role assigned to monetary policy within the general conduct of economic policy. At one extreme is a fiat money regime with a highly politicized central bank. In this case, monetary policy constitutes one of the many instruments of economic policy to be used in combination or alternation. At the other extreme are metal standards with strong central banks. In this case, de facto, the supply of money is largely determined outside the direct control of the "prince." Monetary history shows frequent shifts, from one extreme to the other, depending on the institutional setting, the intellectual and political climate, and the ability of the ruling authority to extract seignorage from the use of money. It is interesting to note that international monetary regimes have generally been developed around metal standards, in which the political content of monetary policy is relatively low. In contrast, monetary isolationism developed when countries decided to use the monetary lever actively as an instrument of economic policy management.

Both recent economic research and the experience with the long inflation of the 1970s have led to a consensus that it is suboptimal to harness monetary policy to multiple objectives. With sophisticated financial markets and forward-looking economic agents, monetary policy has only a temporary effect on real economic activity, while it primarily affects the overall level of prices.[18] Attempts to use monetary policy to stimulate growth are, in the end,

---

18. See Friedman 1968; Phelps 1972. For more recent developments, see Lucas and Sargent 1981.

unsuccessful and only lead to higher inflation. The current prevailing view is that, in a fiat money system, the supply of money should be regulated with the primary objective of promoting price stability.

Another crucial concept emanating from both experience and theory is credibility. The achievement of price stability will be greatly facilitated if economic agents are convinced that the central bank will not, even temporarily, sacrifice the objective of price stability for faster economic growth.[19] The credibility of the commitment can be established by showing the market that any such temptation will be resisted.[20] One way to bolster such credibility is to assign the responsibility for monetary policy to an institution that is not subject to political influence.[21] In countries where monetary policy is traditionally the responsibility of the government, credibility has been sought through membership of the EMS and linkage to the Deutsche Mark.[22] Independence of the central bank might not be a sufficient safeguard, however. The agreement of public opinion that price stability is a priority objective is equally important in ensuring lasting, low inflation. The experience of the last ten years suggests that such a consensus has spread to most countries in the Community.

Those considerations suggest, and explain the fact, that the present historical circumstances are propitious for making the politically crucial decision to create a monetary union without, or before, attributing to the Community other important public functions, ranging from fiscal policy to internal and external security. Not only are the national governments more inclined than in the past to accept an independent, stability-oriented central bank; but the Community is a most favorable institutional environment in which to perform central banking functions in an independent, stability-oriented fashion.

In the preparation of the EMU treaty, a consensus was reached at an early stage that the single monetary policy of the Community would be conducted by a European Central Bank (ECB) that is independent of Community institutions and national authorities alike. The overriding objective of the ECB would be price stability, with support for the general economic policy of the Community to play a secondary role. In effect, then, it was agreed that the political dimension of Community monetary policy would be relatively small.

Another important political aspect of monetary union is the legitimacy of the ECB. In any democracy, the decisions of government must be legitimated, directly or indirectly, by elected representatives of the citizenry. This must also hold true for the central bank.

19. See Barro and Gordon 1983.
20. See Barro 1984.
21. See Rogoff 1985.
22. See Giavazzi and Pagano 1988.

In the EMU, the legitimacy of the ECB will be defined in four ways. First, the treaty and the statute of the ECB (the latter taking the form of a protocol attached to the treaty) are to be approved by all of the national parliaments (i.e., by the elected representatives of the member states). The Court of Justice will be directly responsible for ensuring compliance with the law in the interpretation and implementation of the treaty and its protocols. Second, members of the ECB Council, in their capacity as national central bank governors, will be appointed via national procedures, while the remaining members will be appointed by the European Council, acting on a proposal from the EC Council of Ministers. Third, the president of the Council of Finance Ministers will attend meetings of the ECB Council as an observer, and the president of the ECB Council can attend meetings of the Council of Finance Ministers when matters relating to the system's objectives and tasks are discussed. Fourth, the ECB will present an annual report on the activities of the system to the European Council, the Council of Ministers, the European Parliament, and the European Commission; and the members of the ECB Board may be asked to attend meetings of the European Parliament's specialized committees.

By means of these provisions, though independent in the exercise of its tasks, the ECB will clearly fit into the political structure of the Community and interact directly with the other institutions.

The link between the single market and the EMU on the one hand and political union on the other is also substantiated in a forward-looking perspective. Economic and monetary union is part of an evolutionary process that started in the early 1950s and went through many stages: the European Coal and Steel Community, the common market, various enlargements from the original six to the twelve member countries, repeated changes in procedures and institutions. In 1988–89, when the EMU project was relaunched and the decision was made to call an intergovernmental conference to negotiate an EMU treaty, the heads of state and government did not foresee, perhaps, that their initiative would soon be followed by others, outside the economic and monetary field. Partly as a response to the need to define a new order in Europe following the fall of the Berlin Wall and of the regimes in Central and Eastern European countries,[23] European political union (EPU) came on the agenda, providing an additional validation to Mr. Lawson's declarations.

Indeed the heads of state and government have now decided to proceed with two treaties (EMU and EPU), following similar timetables. To dwell upon the content and problems of EPU is beyond the scope of this chapter.[24] The only point that needs to be stressed is that—like that of fiscal union—the

---

23. See Mestmäcker in this volume.
24. See Weiler in this volume.

concept of political union is much less clear-cut, much more elusive than it might first appear. Only for highly centralized and tightly organized European nation-states, whose cultural and constitutional identity and structure have been built up over centuries, is political union a comprehensive reality in which "the state" tends to monopolize all the functions of government. But even in Europe, not to say in the world, very few nation-states conform to this particular model. For the others, the functions "affecting the state or its government" are divided among many agencies, levels of government, and institutions. If EPU is taken to mean that the Community should give itself a governmental structure similar to France or Britain, this is clearly not on the agenda and will not be in any foreseeable future. With *this* particular type of EPU, the single market and the EMU have no necessary link. Subsidiarity, not Leviathan, is the essence of European political union.

Conclusion

At the end of 1991, the curtain fell on the intergovernmental conference forging the legal framework for EMU. This is not the final act. Economic and political developments inside and outside the Community in the next few years could require further modifications of the final project or a change in the speed of its implementation. Ultimately, the completion of EMU hinges on the political will of the member countries to continue moving forward toward ever-closer economic and political union.

REFERENCES

Baer, G., and T. Padoa-Schioppa. 1989. "The Werner Report Revisited." In *Report on Economic and Monetary Union in the European Community: Collection of Papers Submitted to the Committee for the Study of Economic and Monetary Union.* Luxembourg: Office for Official Publications of the European Communities.
Barro, R. 1984. "Rules vs. Discretion." NBER Working Paper no. 1473. National Bureau of Economic Research. Photocopy.
Barro, R., and R. Gordon. 1983. "Rules, Discretion and Reputation in a Model of Monetary Policy." *Journal of Monetary Economics* 12:101–21.
Bean, C. 1990. "Policies for 1992: The Transition and After." In *The Macroeconomics of 1992.* CEPS Paper no. 42. Brussels: Centre for Economic Policy Studies.
Bertola, G. 1989. "Factor Flexibility, Uncertainty, and Exchange Rate Regimes." Princeton University. Photocopy.
Bini Smaghi, L. 1990. "Progressing towards EMU: Selected Issues and Proposals." *Temi di Discussione*, no. 133. Rome: Banca d'Italia.
Bishop, G. 1990. *Separating Fiscal from Monetary Sovereignty.* New York: Salomon Brothers.

Buiter, W., and K. Kletzer. 1989. "Fiscal Policy, Interdependence, and Efficiency." Yale University. Photocopy.

Casella, A. 1989. "Letter to the Editor." *Economist*, July 22–28, 1989.

Centre for Economic Policy Research. 1990. *Monitoring European Integration*. London: CEPR.

Cohen, D., and C. Wyplosz. 1988. "The European Monetary Union: An Agnostic Evaluation." National Bureau of Economic Research. Photocopy.

Commission of the European Communities. 1977. *Report of the Study Group on the Role of Public Finance in European Integration* (McDougal Report). Luxembourg: Office for Official Publications of the European Communities.

Commission of the European Communities, Directorate-General for Economic and Financial Affairs. 1990. "One Market, One Money: An Evaluation of the Potential Benefits and Costs of Forming an Economic and Monetary Union." *European Economy*, no. 4 (October): 7–347.

Committee for the Study of Economic and Monetary Union. 1989. *Report on Economic and Monetary Union in the European Community*. Luxembourg: Office for Official Publications of the European Communities.

Eichengreen, B. 1990. "Is Europe an Optimum Currency Area?" CEPR Working Paper no. 478. Centre for Economic Policy Research. Photocopy.

Emerson, M. 1991. *The Economics of EMU*. Oxford: Oxford University Press.

Friedman, M. 1968. "The Role of Monetary Policy." *American Economic Review* 58:1–17.

Giavazzi, F., and A. Giovannini. 1989. *Limiting Exchange Rate Flexibility: The European Monetary System*. Cambridge, Mass.: MIT Press.

Giavazzi, F., and M. Pagano. 1988. "The Advantage of Tying One's Hands: EMS Discipline and Central Bank Credibility." *European Economic Review* 32:1055–82.

Giovannini, A., and L. Spaventa. 1990. "Fiscal Rules in the European Monetary Union: A No Entry Clause." CEPR Discussion Paper no. 516. Centre for Economic Policy Research. Photocopy.

Gros, D. 1991. "Fiscal Issues in EMU." *Moneda y Credito*. Forthcoming.

International Monetary Fund. 1990. *German Unification: Economic Issues*. Washington, D.C.: IMF.

International Monetary Fund. 1991. "Issues in the Operation of Monetary Unions and Common Currency Areas." Paper SM/91/110. IMF. Photocopy.

Kehoe, P. J. 1986. "Coordination of Fiscal Policies in a World Economy." Staff Report no. 98. Federal Reserve Bank of Minneapolis.

Lucas, R., and T. Sargent. 1981. *Rational Expectations and Econometric Practice*. Minneapolis: University of Minnesota Press.

Mundell, R. 1969. *International Economics*. New York: Macmillan.

Padoa-Schioppa, T. 1987. *Efficiency, Stability, and Equity: A Strategy for the Evolution of the Economic System of the European Community*. Oxford: Oxford University Press.

Padoa-Schioppa, T. 1990. "Towards a European Central Bank: Fiscal Compatibility and Monetary Constitution." Paper presented at the Conference on Aspects of Central Bank Policy-making, Tel Aviv.

Padoa-Schioppa, T. 1992. "The Exchange Rate Mechanism of the EMS." In *The New Palgrave Dictionary of Money and Finance*. New York: Macmillan.

Padoa-Schioppa, T., and F. Papadia. 1984. "Competing Currencies and Monetary Stability." In *Europe's Money, Problems of European Monetary Coordination and Integration*, ed. R. S. Masera and R. Triffin, 79–110. Oxford: Clarendon Press.

Phelps, E. 1972. *Inflation Policy and Unemployment Theory: The Cost Benefit Approach to Monetary Planning*. New York: Norton.

Pöhl, K. 1990. "Prospects for the European Monetary Union." Paper presented at the Conference on Britain and the EMS.

Rogoff, K. 1985. "The Optimal Degree of Commitment to an Intermediate Monetary Target." *Quarterly Journal of Economics* 100:1169–90.

Sachs, J., and X. Sala-i-Martin. 1989. "Federal Fiscal Policy and Optimum Currency Areas." Harvard University. Photocopy.

Von Hagen, J. 1991. "Fiscal Arrangements in a Monetary Union: Evidence from the U.S." Indiana University. Photocopy.

Woodford, M. 1990. "Does Competition between Currencies Lead to Price Level and Exchange Rate Stability?" Photocopy.

Competition and Competition Policy

Frédéric Jenny

The completion of Project 1992 will significantly change the environment of European firms. This transformation will benefit European industry in two main ways. First, as impediments to intra-EC trade are lifted, the costs of such trade will decline, enhancing efficiency directly. Second, as the geographic size of markets increases, competition among European firms will intensify, leading indirectly to increased efficiency. No wonder that completion of Europe's internal market is viewed primarily as a means of improving the allocation of resources within the EC, increasing the competitiveness of European industry vis-à-vis the rest of the world and significantly increasing the real income of Europeans.

Serious questions can be raised about whether or not the lifting of barriers to trade within the EC will ever lead to benefits commensurate with the optimistic estimates put forth by the Commission, based on its assumption of a truly unified market. Indeed, the lifting of barriers to trade between the member states does not necessarily mean that the various markets will be totally unified and that all firms in an industry, no matter where they are located, will necessarily compete with all the other firms in the same industry. What it means is that they will not be prevented from competing with each other or that consumers will not be prevented from making them compete if the firms wish to do so. Observation of what goes on within the various member states suggests that, even in the context of such smaller geographic areas as France or Germany, markets are not completely unified because of differentiation of products, regional preferences of buyers, and so forth. What is more, even in sectors where it is likely that intra-EC trade will develop, one should remember that a significant part of this trade may have little to do with increased competition; it may simply reflect the fact that some firms have shifted the location of their productive facilities to countries other than those where their traditional markets are located.

If one should be careful to avoid unrealistic expectations about the completion of the European market, in terms of its time frame and magnitude of effects, it remains true that the institutional changes that will facilitate trade within the EC are likely to lead to increased competitive pressures in a number of industries.

Firms will, thus, have an incentive to anticipate the likely changes in their environment and to modify their strategies accordingly. The range of possible reactions to the expected changes in market conditions may vary widely depending on the particular circumstances of the firms considered and the specific features of the sectors or the countries in which they operate.

At the European level, there is concern that some of the strategic responses of firms might be aimed at preventing the development of competitive pressures accruing from the completion of the unified market. Thus, strict enforcement of Articles 85 and 86 is seen as a necessary complement to the unification of the internal market. Beyond this, the fear that large firms belonging to the same sector but based in different countries may engage in international mergers in order to acquire a dominant position at the European level and avoid having to compete with each other after 1992 was an important factor that prompted the EC authorities to establish a merger control procedure. The design and the enforcement of this merger regulation will have important consequences for the competitive environment of firms after 1992.

In section 1, I survey the changes that will take place in connection with the 1992 Program and discuss the estimates of their potential long-run effects. In section 2, I examine EC competition law and comment on the new merger regulation that is expected to play a leading role in preventing large European firms from resisting the competitive pressure resulting from the completion of the internal market.

The Completion of the Internal Market

The history of the EC can be roughly divided into three phases.[1] First, during the 1960s, rapid progress was made toward the unification of the internal market. By the end of the decade, the elimination of customs duties and quantitative restrictions to intra-EC trade led to a considerable increase in intra-EC trade and a restructuring of industries. Second, during the 1970s, in spite of the fact that optimistic observers at the beginning of the decade had forecasted the achievement of the internal market by 1981, several events led to a slowdown in the process. The combination of international monetary crisis and oil shocks led to protectionism through the development of nontariff barriers to international trade. These barriers frequently grew from the adop-

---

1. See B. Aliouat, "Comprendre l'Acte Unique pour Préparer 1993: L'Apprentissage d'une Liberté pour les Entreprises Européennes," *Les Petites Affiches*, no. 89 (July 25, 1990): 47–55, and no. 90 (July 27, 1990): 44–49.

tion of different national norms that prevented manufacturers in one country from selling their products in other EC countries or through the multiplication or increase in complexity of customs formalities that artificially increased the cost of importing goods. Third, at the beginning of the 1980s, after the European economies had absorbed most of the effects of the oil shocks of the mid-1970s, European policymakers started to worry again about the long-term effects of the fragmentation of the European market. Such fragmentation was seen as preventing European firms from increasing their competitiveness through the exploitation of economies of scale and scope. The poor R&D performances of European firms, compared to both American and Japanese firms, largely attributed to a lack of concentration of industry due to the fragmentation of markets, was seen as particularly worrisome. A well-known study sponsored by the European Parliament in 1983 was instrumental in popularizing the concept of "the cost of non-Europe" and estimated this cost at ECU 50 billion (roughly 2 percent of EC GNP).[2] This set the stage for a new effort to dismantle physical, technical, and fiscal barriers to trade within the EC.

In 1986, this new frame of mind led to the adoption of the Single European Act (SEA), which came into effect on July 1, 1987, and states that "the Community shall adopt measures with the aim of progressively establishing the internal market over a period expiring on 31 December 1992. . . . The internal market shall comprise an area without internal frontiers in which the free movement of goods, persons and capital is ensured in accordance with the provisions of the Treaty." By 1992, the EC Commission intended, member states would agree on the abolition of barriers to trade of all kinds, the harmonization of legislation and tax structures, the strengthening of monetary cooperation, and the adoption of the measures necessary to encourage European firms to work together. Agreement would be facilitated by the SEA's introduction of qualified majority voting in the Council on several matters, the most notable exceptions being fiscal harmonization and free movement of people, which still require unanimity.

While Article 8(2) of the EEC treaty now declares that the common market should be completed by December 31, 1992, failure to achieve that goal entails no legal consequences. Although it is likely that the European market will not be completely unified by this date, it is equally likely that Europe will have significantly accelerated the movement toward unification.

The effort to complete the internal market will affect many different areas and is expected to bring wide-ranging direct and indirect benefits.[3]

---

2. M. Albert and R. J. Ball, *Toward European Economic Recovery in the 1980s: Report to the European Parliament* (New York: Praeger, 1984).

3. M. Catinat, "Les Conditions de Réussite du Grand Marché Intérieur: Concrétiser les Opportunités," *Economie et Statistique*, no. 217–18 (January-February 1989): 97–115.

The Elimination of Nontariff Barriers

The suppression of a number of nontariff barriers (NTBs) will directly decrease transaction costs within the EC. These NTBs fall into four categories.

1. Costs associated with compliance with customs formalities will disappear. Customs controls imply the filling out of numerous administrative forms, which is costly for the firms involved in import or export whether they choose to handle the customs formalities themselves or to pay a specialized shipping agent to do so. Besides the direct cost involved, firms face delays associated with the approval of imports and exports and, therefore, bear the opportunity cost of the personnel and equipment idled at borders. To these costs borne directly by the firms must be added the costs of administering customs controls borne by national government agencies and the opportunity costs of lost trade.[4]

2. It is estimated that there are over 100,000 different technical industrial standards or specific national regulations pertaining to the commercialization of products within the EC.

   National technical standards regarding product forms, functioning, quality, compatibility, and/or interchangeability are not legally binding. However, they can hinder trade in a variety of ways. First, customers of a particular country tend to see the national standard as an indicator of quality and shy away from imported goods that do not meet the standard. Second, and more important, the existence of national standards may impose costs on users of imported products and, therefore, limit trade. As an example, in the case of certain building materials, French insurance companies will only pay for damages caused by a product if it meets the national standard. Thus, architects, who can be held liable for damages in France, are reluctant

---

4. In a survey of 11,000 European industrialists in 1988, Gernot Nerb found that the administrative cost associated with importing and exporting within the EC was considered the highest NTB in most countries and the second highest in Denmark, France, Germany, and the United Kingdom. In addition, the administrative cost associated with customs controls was considered to be a particularly severe impediment to trade by small- and middle-sized firms, which represent about 95 percent of all EC firms and account for two-thirds of total employment in Europe. Indeed, for those small- and middle-sized firms, the fixed administrative costs associated with customs formalities cannot be spread over a large volume of shipments. See G. Nerb, *The Completion of the Internal Market: A Survey of European Industry's Perception of the Likely Effects*, vol. 3 of *Research on the "Cost of Non-Europe" : Basic Findings* (Luxembourg: Office for Official Publications of the European Communities, 1988).

to use foreign products meeting different standards, even if their level of safety is the same.

Beyond national standards, there are also legally binding regulations, theoretically justified by domestic considerations of health, safety, or environmental protection, that often prevent the commercialization of foreign products in a given country. A particularly telling example of such a regulation relates to the pasta purity laws in France, Italy, and Greece.[5] These laws specify that "pasta" must be composed of durham wheat only and, thus, preclude export to those countries of British-made pasta, which is a combination of durham and soft wheat.

Finally, trade barriers also result from testing and certification procedures that are designed to ensure the conformity of imported products to existing regulations or standards of the country into which they are imported. Thus, exporters have to incur R&D costs as well as production, distribution, and administrative costs in order to adapt their products to the different standards or regulations of the countries in which they want to sell them and to obtain certificates of conformity.[6]

The completion of the internal market will involve a significant decrease in the NTBs associated with different national standards or regulations for the same products. This will be made possible by the adoption of the principle of mutual recognition in certain sectors (according to which a good lawfully produced and commercialized in one member country can be transported to and sold in another member country without having to be modified, tested, certified, or renamed) and, in other sectors, through harmonization of national regulations in the form of binding EC directives that will apply to all member states and will define the conditions that a particular product should meet to be lawfully commercialized in any member state.

3. National public authorities will be required to make public purchasing procedures transparent and open to all qualified EC suppliers. Public

---

5. Groupe MAC, *Technical Barriers in the EEC: Illustrations in Six Industries*, vol. 6 of *Research on the "Cost of Non-Europe" : Basic Findings* (Luxembourg: Office for Official Publications of the European Communities, 1988); see also John Jackson in this volume.

6. According to Nerb, *Completion of the Internal Market*, industrialists in six of twelve EC countries considered international differences in standards and regulations to be the highest or the second highest NTB to intra-EC trade. Significantly, exporters in France, Germany, and the United Kingdom—the three EC countries that sell the most industrial products outside their own borders—considered such differences to be the most important NTB. So did EC firms with more than a thousand employees.

procurement markets account for roughly 8 percent of EC GNP and only a marginal share of those markets is awarded to foreign firms.[7] Indeed, member states have widely used public purchasing to support national or regional firms or industries for strategic reasons (e.g., in the defense, telecommunications, and aerospace industries), for employment reasons (e.g., in the shipbuilding and automobile industries), or for high-technology reasons (e.g., lasers or telecommunications systems). Such behavior leads to suboptimal size of plants and R&D efforts, lack of incentive to invest in new technology to confront competition from non-EC firms, and a lack of product specialization, so that even large EC firms have uneconomically wide product ranges and short production runs.

4. Nontariff barriers also exist in the capital market. Services such as banking, insurance, and brokerage are regulated in most countries. In the banking sector, there are, in principle, no overt barriers to the establishment of foreign banks in any country. However, in most countries, the acquisition of domestic banks by foreign entities is subject to control. As of 1986 in all countries except the United Kingdom, branches of banks were required to maintain their own minimum endowment capital, and some countries also imposed solvency ratios. In addition, there were restrictions on the services that could be offered by a branch or subsidiary of a foreign bank. As far as brokerage was concerned, the main obstacle to trade resulted from regulations that prevented foreigners from being licensed as brokers. The lack of harmonization of regulations in this area was considered by the banking community to be an important barrier to trade.

Benefits from the Completion of the Internal Market

The removal of NTBs within the EC and the integration of national markets is expected to have positive effects on the competitiveness of European firms.

The most immediate effect will be the ability of European firms to better exploit the various economies of scale and scope.[8] The overall importance in

---

7. W. S. Atkins Management Consultants, *The "Cost of Non-Europe" in Public Sector Procurement*, vol. 5, pts. A and B, of *Research on the "Cost of Non-Europe": Basic Findings* (Luxembourg: Office for Official Publications of the European Communities, 1988).

8. C. Pratten, "A Survey of Economies of Scale," chap. 2 in *Studies on the Economics of Integration*, vol. 2 of *Research on the "Cost of Non-Europe": Basic Findings* (Luxembourg: Office for Official Publications of the European Communities, 1988).

each sector of scale and scope economies, not to speak of the relative importance of each type of scale economy, is a subject of considerable debate because these economies are difficult to measure. If economies of scale in a given industry relate to the size of the firms (or, to a lesser extent, to the size of plants) and are significant, it is likely that the completion of the internal market will lead to an increase in concentration in the sector considered. This increase in concentration could derive from the initial intensification of competition among the firms of different countries, because smaller firms will have higher unit costs than their larger counterparts and are likely to be driven out of the market. To avoid being driven out of the market, smaller firms may be tempted to abandon certain product lines and increase their specialization, to merge in order to benefit from the economies of scale associated with firm size, or to carve out market niches for themselves by differentiating their products from those of their competitors. In all such cases, however, concentration will increase. In contrast, in industries in which economies of scale are mostly related to the length of production runs, reorganization of production does not *necessarily* mean an increase in concentration at the firm level.

The fact that the main efficiency benefit from the completion of the internal market lies in the exploitation of economies of scale and that this benefit will, in all likelihood, result from and in an increase in concentration creates a dilemma for the EC Commission. Indeed, these benefits will be transmitted to the consumer only to the extent that competition remains strong. But the increase in market concentration brought about by the initial intensification of competition on the enlarged European market may, itself, lead to decreasing competition and increasing barriers to entry.

Thus, in many important sectors, market structure will undergo major changes after 1992 and edge toward oligopoly. This possibility then raises important questions from the point of view of competition policy. Should the EC prevent large firms from engaging in mergers that are likely to increase the efficiency of the firms involved, simply because they are also substantially likely to increase seller concentration? Alternatively, should the EC take a more relaxed attitude toward mergers (by prohibiting only mergers that increase concentration substantially without bringing about any efficiency gains) and rely mostly on Articles 85 and 86 of the EEC treaty to ensure that powerful firms pass the efficiency benefits associated with their large sizes on to consumers?

Before examining the way in which the EC authorities plan to answer these questions, it is useful to examine specific industries so as to identify those that are most likely to be affected by the completion of the European market.

Consequences of the Completion of the Internal Market
for Various Industries

It may be best to concentrate on a small number of key sectors in which the direct effects of the completion of the internal market are most likely to be important, even in the short run, and on the sectors for which scale economies are the greatest.

The direct effects of the removal of intra-EC barriers to trade are expected to be particularly important for manufacturers of office and data-processing equipment, telecommunications equipment, transportation equipment other than motor vehicles, building materials, and chemicals (where differences in national standards have limited international competition with respect to pharmaceuticals, detergents, and fertilizers). The motor vehicles sector should also be affected.

Pratten's study of scale economies in major industries is particularly thorough and provides useful insight into the potential consequences of the completion of the internal market for most industries or groups of industries. It provides both a ranking of major manufacturing industry groups according to the overall importance of scale economies and some details on the main source of economies for each group—details that are important for predicting the potential effects of the completion of the internal market.

Economies of scale appear most important in the following ten industry groups (presented in decreasing order of importance): motor vehicles, other transportation equipment, chemicals, artificial and synthetic fibers, metals, office machinery, mechanical engineering, electrical engineering, instruments, and paper products.

Four of these ten sectors (office machinery, electrical engineering, chemicals, and transportation equipment other than motor vehicles) are also on the list of sectors most likely to be directly affected by the removal of barriers to intra-EC trade. The combination of declining artificial impediments to EC trade and very large economies of scale generates an expectation of rather rapid structural changes in those sectors.

The overall picture that emerges from the studies undertaken by the EC is that the benefits from the completion of the European market are expected to result, to a large extent, from restructuring enabling firms in several high-technology sectors to achieve economies of scale (sometimes by sharing R&D and distribution costs). This restructuring will result from increased competitive pressures brought about by the elimination of NTBs and, it is estimated, will account for nearly half of the total expected benefits. To cite a few examples of particular industries that will be directly affected by the elimination of NTBs, mergers and plant closures are expected in the boiler industry (in which there are 12 EC firms and only 6 U.S. firms) and in the locomotive industry (in which there are 16 EC firms and only 2 U.S. firms), while mergers and rationalization of production are expected in the turbine generator industry (in which there are 10 EC firms and only 2 U.S. firms) and in the public switching industry (in which there are 11 EC firms and only 4 U.S. firms).

The preoccupation with economic efficiency that is implicit in the goal of the completion of the single European market also surfaces in the new title, "Research and Technological Development," that has been added to the EEC treaty by the SEA. As Manfred Caspari remarked, "Under Article 130f, an unambiguous industrial policy terminology has for the first time been introduced into the EEC Treaty, albeit within a clearly restricted framework."[9] Indeed, Article 130f now states that "the Community's aim shall be to strengthen the scientific and technological basis of European industry and to encourage it to become more competitive at international level." In order to achieve this goal, the Community is to encourage research and technological development and to support the efforts of undertakings to cooperate with one another (Art. 130f(2)).

The question that must be raised at this point is what type of competition policy would be best suited to accompany the completion of the European market. Indeed, a conflict may arise between the goal of allowing mergers and agreements among firms (at the risk of creating individual or collective dominant positions) in the industries that need to be restructured to become more technically efficient and the goal of maintaining competition (at the risk of preventing or, in some cases, deferring efficiency-enhancing reorganizations of firms) that will have the advantage of keeping price-cost margins low. To see where the EC is heading, it is, therefore, important to consider the provisions of the EEC treaty dealing with cartels and abuses of dominant position as well as the newly introduced merger control regulation.

EC Competition Policy and the Completion
of the Internal Market

Since the inception of the EC, competition policy has been one of the foundations of the construction of Europe. The most notable exception to this general rule concerns the agricultural sector. Article 42 of the EEC treaty provides

---

9. M. Caspari, "1992—EEC Competition Law and Industrial Policy," in *1992 and EEC/US Competition and Trade Law* (New York: Fordham University School of Law, 1989), 163–80.

that competition rules shall apply to production and trade in agricultural products only to the extent determined by the Council, taking into account the objectives of the Common Agricultural Policy.

Up to 1989, EEC competition rules prohibited anticompetitive behavior but did not encompass structural control. Thus, EEC law in this area reflected the benign neglect approach with which mergers were considered by most member states. The main change in these rules, linked to the completion of the internal market, occurred with the establishment of merger control in 1989.[10] This does not mean, however, that mergers had been totally unregulated beforehand. As a matter of fact, as we shall see later, European authorities did use the prohibition of abuse of dominant position to block some mergers and some thought was given to the idea of using the prohibition against anticompetitive agreements to prevent some forms of mergers (in particular, the acquisition of minority shareholdings).

The Prohibition of Anticompetitive Practices

The prohibition of anticompetitive practices at the EC level is embodied in Articles 85 and 86 of the EEC treaty.[11]

Substantive Content of Articles 85 and 86
Under Article 85, efficiency can, to a certain extent, be taken into consideration when appraising anticompetitive agreements. Indeed, under certain conditions, agreements or practices that are held to contribute to improving the production or distribution of goods or to promoting technical or economic progress can be exempted from the prohibition of anticompetitive practices through the application of Article 85(3).

Although the EC Commission has been reluctant to allow anticompeti-

---

10. Council Regulation (EEC) no. 4064/89 of 21 December 1989 on the control of concentrations between undertakings, OJ No. L 395/1 (December 30, 1989).

11. Art. 85(1) prohibits "as incompatible with the common market: all agreements between undertakings, decisions by associations of undertakings and concerted practices which may affect trade between Member States and which have as their object or effect the prevention, restriction or distortion of competition within the common market." Cooperative behavior may be exempted from the prohibition if it satisfies the four conditions specified in Art. 85(3): (1) it "contributes to improving the production or distribution of goods or to promoting technical or economic progress," (2) it allows "consumers a fair share of the resulting benefit," (3) it does not impose "restrictions which are not indispensable to the attainment of" its legitimizing objectives, and (4) it does not afford "the possibility of eliminating competition in respect of a substantial part of the products in question." Art. 86 states that "any abuse by one or more undertakings of a dominant position within the common market or in a substantial part of it shall be prohibited as incompatible with the common market in so far as it may affect trade between Member States."

tive practices, even those that contribute to economic efficiency, examples of such authorization can be found.[12] Thus, toward the end of the 1970s, the Commission allowed capacity closure agreements between the main EC producers of artificial and synthetic fibers in light of the fact that the industry had developed massive surplus capacity due to misjudgment by the firms of market-growth and expansionary policies pursued by public firms in various member states. Similarly, at the beginning of the 1980s, the Commission approved a series of bilateral transfers, specialization agreements, and joint ventures in the petrochemical industry under Article 85(3).

Along the same lines, in a review of the application of Article 85 to telecommunications, two officials of the Commission (expressing their own personal views), Colin Overbury and Piero Ravaioli, made the following statement.

> In any area where industry is involved with technology, there can be a high incentive to share the risks involved. Research and development, access to the technology of others or specialisation in exploitation may require cooperation between competitors if the advantages of quick results, cost reduction or economies of scale are to be achieved. The Commission has declared itself in favour of such cooperation as an essential element in the process of completing the internal market and improving the competitiveness of Europe. Such cooperation does have its limit and a line has to be drawn in the arrangements between competitors at the point where, on an objective assessment, the restrictive objects or effects become greater than the economic advantage.[13]

This comment clearly suggests that, when it comes to applying Article 85 to a sector in which there is a considerable amount of uncertainty due to rapidly changing technological, economic, and regulatory context, the Commission finds it appropriate to adopt an approach in which agreements with undesirable anticompetitive effects are not prohibited per se but may be allowed if they have sufficiently positive effects on static or dynamic efficiency.

In contrast with Article 85, Article 86, which prohibits abuse of dominant position, does not allow for an efficiency defense. This is particularly noteworthy since, as we shall see, the European Court of Justice (ECJ) has

---

12. See comments on this point in Caspari, "1992—EEC Competition Law and Industrial Policy."

13. C. Overbury and P. Ravaioli, "The Application of EEC Law to Telecommunications," in *1992 and EEC/US Competition and Trade Law* (New York: Fordham University School of Law, 1989), 271–312.

interpreted Article 86 in a manner permitting its use to block certain mergers. (In the past, the EC Commission was the principal beneficiary of this interpretation; in the future, national authorities might use it to prevent mergers that do not meet the size criterion found in the EEC merger control regulation.) The discrepancy resulting from the impossibility of using an efficiency defense in relation to the Article 86 prohibition of abuse of dominant position and the possibility of using such a defense (within limits) in relation to the Article 85 prohibition of anticompetitive agreements is somewhat difficult to justify on economic or legal grounds. The discrepancy is particularly troubling following *Alsatel*, in which the Commission expressed its desire to have the ECJ hold that parallel behavior can place a set of independent firms in a collective dominant position.[14] Such a holding would effectively deny to cooperating firms the opportunity to seek the derogation of Article 85(3).

There is little doubt that the wording of Article 86 partly reflects a general distrust, going beyond a mere concern for competition, of large firms holding substantial economic, financial, and, possibly, political power.

The Scope of Application of Articles 85 and 86 after 1992
In the past, the ECJ gave an extensive definition of the kind of practices affecting trade.

> In prohibiting agreements which may affect trade between Member States and which have as their object or effect the restriction of competition, Article 85(1) of the Treaty does not require proof that such agreements have in fact appreciably affected such trade, which would moreover be difficult in the majority of cases to establish for legal purposes, but merely requires that it be established that such agreements are capable of having that effect.[15]

With the completion of the European market, it is likely that a larger number of restrictive agreements involving firms based in different countries and covering a sizeable part of the EC will emerge. Thus, in a unified market, the concept of anticompetitive practices affecting trade between member states will lose much of its significance because it will encompass most, if not all, anticompetitive practices. Some authors have, therefore, called for an adaptation of the criterion defining the practices that come within the jurisdiction of EC legislation.

---

14. Alsatel v. Novasam, Case 247/86, 1988 ECR 5987, at 6011. The ECJ dismissed the request on procedural grounds but invited the Commission to test its theory in a proceeding of its own.

15. Miller International Schallplatten v. Commission, Case 19/77, 1978 ECR 131.

The Enforcement of Articles 85 and 86 after 1992
Under the current interpretation of Articles 85 and 86, the scope of their application will be enlarged. However, this does not mean that the scope of application of national competition laws will be reduced, because the anti-competitive practices of firms situated in different countries will have the effect of reducing competition in each of the countries in which these firms sell their products and, therefore, are likely to be attacked by each of the relevant national competition authorities. What it does mean is that there will be more cases of anticompetitive practices prohibited both by the EEC treaty and by one or more national laws.

This prospect raises two interrelated questions. The first question relates to the compatibility of the various national competition laws with EC law and to possible conflicts that may arise. The second question relates to who will be responsible for applying European competition law to practices prohibited by the EC.

As far as the first question is concerned, it seems that the move toward harmonization of national competition laws and EC law, which is already perceptible, will become inevitable. Indeed, when both national and EC rules apply to a particular sector, parallel jurisdiction emerges. However, the ECJ has ruled that the application of national law "may not prejudice the full and uniform application of EEC law or the effects of measures taken or to be taken to implement it."[16] Thus, conflicts between EC rules and national rules must be resolved by giving precedence to EC law. In fact, this means that a practice prohibited under EC antitrust law cannot be exempted under national antitrust law. Conversely, it means that a practice falling under Article 85(1) but that has been granted an exemption by application of Article 85(3) cannot be prohibited by national law. However, the ECJ has stated that "the fact that a practice has been held by the Commission not to fall within the ambits of the prohibition contained in Article 85(1) and 85(2), the scope of which is limited to agreements capable of affecting trade between Member States, in no way prevents that practice from being considered by the national authorities from the point of view of the restrictive effects it may produce nationally."[17]

To answer the question of who will be responsible for applying EC competition law, one must examine the jurisdictional rules contained in Article 9 of Council Regulation 17/62 (the basic procedural regulation for the implementation of Articles 85 and 86). Only the Commission can grant exemptions under Article 85(3), but member state authorities can apply Articles 85(1) and 86 as long as the Commission has not initiated a procedure with a

---

16. Wilhelm v. Bundeskartellamt, Case 14/68, 1969 ECR 1.
17. Procureur de la République v. Giry and Guerlain, Joined Cases 253/78 and 1 to 3/79, 1980 ECR 2327, at 2375.

view to granting an exemption or issuing a prohibition. These provisions do not preclude the possibility that, after 1992, different national authorities may have jurisdiction over the same practice (if it affects more than one national market) and entertain different views of whether or not the practice is prohibited by Article 85(1) or Article 86. This state of affairs has prompted some authors to argue in favor of a revision of jurisdictional rules in the area of anticompetitive practices along the lines adopted for the merger regulation.

The problems associated with enforcement of Articles 85 and 86 would, in any case, be less severe if member states were to adopt national competition laws similar to EC law. As an official of the EC Commission (expressing his personal view) put it recently: "If the Member States develop comprehensive systems of competition law enforcement similar to the EEC regime, a decentralised system of multiple administration of a single policy is conceivable, within a legal system under the aegis of the Court of Justice. EEC law contains the requisite mechanisms in the Article 177 procedures for preliminary rulings and the doctrine of direct effect and supremacy."[18]

It is thus interesting to review briefly the competition laws of the three main countries (the United Kingdom, Germany, and France) and outline some of their main differences and similarities.

In the United Kingdom, horizontal agreements, franchising agreements, and exclusive dealing agreements are treated under the Restrictive Trade Practices Act of 1976. Unless they fall under one of the exempted categories, agreements that deal with prices to be charged, conditions on which goods are to be supplied or acquired, process of manufacture to be applied, persons to or from whom goods are to be supplied or acquired, and areas to or from which goods are to be supplied or acquired are presumed to be against the public interest. However, if the director general of fair trading refers a particular agreement to the Restrictive Practices Court, the parties to the agreement may satisfy the court that each of the restrictions involved has beneficial effects outweighing its negative impact. The beneficial effects that the firms can claim are very broadly drawn and can fall in one of eight categories.

a) The restriction is necessary to protect the public against injury.
b) Removal would deny the public other benefits or advantages arising from the restriction.
c) The restriction is necessary to counteract measures taken by a nonparty to prevent or restrict competition.

---

18. J. Faull, "Effects on Trade between Member States and Community-Member State Jurisdiction," in *1992 and EEC/US Competition and Trade Law* (New York: Fordham University School of Law, 1989), 485–505.

d) The restriction is necessary to negotiate fair terms with a nonparty who controls a preponderant part of the trade in such goods.

e) Removal of the restriction would have a serious and adverse effect on employment in an area in which a substantial part of the trade in question is situated.

f) Removal of the restriction would cause a reduction in exports.

g) The restriction is required for the maintenance of any other restriction found by the court not to be contrary to the public interest.

h) The restriction does not directly or indirectly restrict or discourage competition to any material degree in any relevant trade or industry and is not likely to do so.

In a 1988 green paper, the British government announced its intention to move toward a general prohibition of all agreements having the "object or effect of preventing or restricting or distorting competition." Such a prohibition would apply to vertical as well as horizontal agreements and to tacit as well as overt agreements. The green paper stated that "the effects based prohibition which the government proposes has the added benefit of alignment with the existing EC law for the sake of consistency and simplicity. Increasingly U.K. companies must have close regard to EC competition rules. Much greater compatibility between EC and U.K. law than the present system affords will make the latter more easily comprehensible and workable for the business community."

British control of monopolies and market power is based on both the Fair Trading Act of 1973 and the Competition Act of 1980. A statutory monopoly exists when one firm has more than 25 percent of the market for a good or service. When two or more companies have more than 25 percent of a market and act in a way that prevents, restricts, or distorts competition, the situation can be considered to be that of a "complex monopoly." The director general of fair trading may refer monopolies to the Monopolies and Mergers Commission (MMC) unless such a reference is vetoed by the secretary of state for trade and industry. The MMC must then assess whether or not the monopoly situation operates or may be expected to operate against the public interest. The 1973 act states that the commission "shall have regard to the desirability of maintaining and promoting effective competition" but also instructs the commission to "take into account all matters which appear to them in the particular circumstances to be relevant." Recommendations may be made by the MMC to the secretary of state as to possible remedies.

In the Federal Republic of Germany, Article 1 of the Act against Restraints of Competition (enacted in 1957 and amended five times since) prohibits all agreements between firms or groups of firms that are likely to influence the production or commercialization of goods and services through a restriction of competition on a market. However, Article 1 does not apply to certain agreements (e.g., general sales conditions or rebates) or to certain sectors. Additionally the Bundeskartellamt can give an exemption to standardization, rationalization, or specialization agreements and to crisis cartels if those agreements significantly contribute to economic progress and do not reduce competition beyond what is necessary to obtain the positive results expected. Export cartels and import cartels can also be exempted under certain conditions. These exemptions are given for a limited time and are subject to review. The Act against Restraints of Competition also contains various provisions designed both to protect small- and medium-sized firms from the anticompetitive practices of their large competitors, suppliers, or customers and to relax the rules against anticompetitive agreements initiated by such firms.

Market domination is defined in the act as a situation where a firm is not exposed to competitors or has "a superior market position" vis-à-vis its competitors or where there is no substantial competition within a group of firms (tight oligopoly).

A single firm is presumed to have a dominant position if it controls one-third of the relevant market, and a group of firms is presumed to have a dominant position if three or fewer enterprises have a combined market share of 50 percent or more, or if five or fewer enterprises have a combined market share of two-thirds or more. Abuses of dominant positions (e.g., impairing the competitive possibilities of other enterprises without justification or making demands that deviate from those that would result if competition existed) can be prohibited by the Bundeskartellamt, but the agency must first allow the firm or firms involved to discontinue the practice.

Finally, in France, Articles 7 and 8 of the December, 1986, Ordinance on Freedom of Price and Competition prohibit agreements, whether tacit or explicit, vertical or horizontal, among independent firms, and the abusive exploitation by a firm or a group of firms of a dominant position in the domestic market, or in a substantial part of the market, when they are designed for or may have the effect of curbing, restraining, or distorting competition.

Practices that fall under Articles 7 or 8 can be exempted from the prohibition if the firms involved demonstrate that the practice contributed to economic progress, reserved an equitable share of the resulting benefits for the buyers, and did not enable the sellers to eliminate competition in a substantial portion of the markets involved. The Conseil de la Concurrence, the independent administrative body charged with enforcement of French antitrust law, requires firms to show, first, that the alleged economic progress was the direct consequence of the practice examined and, second, that it could not have been achieved by any means other than adoption of the practice.

In France, there is no compulsory notification of agreements or statutory definition of dominant position. Charges of anticompetitive agreement or abuse of dominant position can be referred to the Conseil de la Concurrence by any firm, registered business or consumer organization, or local authority as well as by the minister in charge of economic affairs.

As should be clear from this brief review, substantial differences still exist among these countries. First, whereas the concept of "public interest" exists in British law, it does not exist in the EC, French, and German laws. Second, whereas an efficiency defense for all anticompetitive agreements is admissible, although rarely successful, under Article 85 of the EEC treaty and under Article 10 of the French ordinance, the German Act against Restraints of Competition narrowly defines the cases in which anticompetitive agreements can be exempted. Third, whereas an efficiency defense is not admissible in cases of abuse of dominant position under Article 86 of the EEC treaty and under Article 22 of the German act, such a defense is admissible under Article 10 of the French ordinance. Finally, whereas the British and German laws give statutory definitions of a dominant position, no such definition exists in French or EEC law.

Those differences should not obscure the fact that the competition laws of these three European countries are being amended in ways that bring them closer to the wording of Articles 85 and 86 and hence closer to each other. This is shown by the discussion of the British law referred to earlier, the adoption of the 1986 French Ordinance on Freedom of Price and Competition, and the amendment of the German act at the beginning of the 1990s.

Merger Control

As should be clear from the first part of this review (and from the chapter of Alexis Jacquemin in this volume), the completion of the internal market will entail major changes in the concentration of various European industries. These changes may come in different forms, varying from outright mergers to the acquisition of minority interests, the creation of joint ventures, or the internal growth of some firms to the detriment of their competitors.

Reorganization of European industry has already begun in the form of a merger wave.[19] Since 1988, the predominant motives announced by firms engaging in mergers have been the reinforcement of market position and the expansion of sales, followed by the desire to exploit complementarities and to achieve product diversification. Up to 1990, the predominant motive for joint ventures was R&D; in 1990, the predominant motive for joint ventures

---

19. Information on the external growth of the EC's largest firms appears in Alexis Jacquemin's chapter in this volume.

became expansion and reinforcement of market position, with R&D rated second.

Merger Control at the National Level

Not all member states regulate mergers, and existing national laws differ considerably. In Germany, the Bundeskartellamt is required to prevent proposed or completed mergers "if it is to be anticipated that a merger will result in or reinforce a market dominating position . . . unless the participating firms demonstrate that, as a result of the merger improvements in the conditions for competition will also occur and that these improvements will outweigh the disadvantages of the market domination." The German economics minister has the power to overrule, on public policy grounds, formal prohibition decisions by the Bundeskartellamt. However, Kurt Markert points out that

> as the burden for proving sufficiently strong competitive effects is fully on participating firms, the chances of persuading the Cartel Office or the Courts to accept a market dominating merger by application of the "balance-clause" are minimal. The same may be safely said with respect to the ministerial exemption clause. Since 1973 only six such exemptions were granted.[20]

Overall, the statutory standard clearly favors structural criteria, because a decision regarding whether or not a merger results in or reinforces a dominant position "is to be determined primarily on the basis of market or firm-related structural criteria such as market shares and financial and other firm resources."

In the United Kingdom, merger control was established in 1965 and applies only to large mergers (combined market shares larger than 25 percent or assets taken over greater than £30 million). The secretary of state for trade and industry opposes a merger only if the Monopolies and Mergers Commission (MMC) has found that it is expected to work against the public interest. The public interest concept is not defined in the U. K. legislation, but the MMC must consider mergers in light of five specific criteria: maintaining and promoting effective competition between suppliers of goods and services in the United Kingdom; promoting the interest of consumers of goods and services in the United Kingdom; promoting competition through cost reductions and the development of new techniques and products and facilitating the entry of new competitors; maintaining and promoting the balanced distribution of industry and employment in the United Kingdom; and maintaining and pro-

---

20. K. E. Markert, "Merger Control in Germany," in *International Mergers and Joint Ventures* (New York: Fordham Corporate Law Institute, 1991), 149–60.

moting competitive activity in markets outside the United Kingdom on the part of suppliers in the United Kingdom. According to Sidney Lipworth, the current chairman of the MMC,

> It is . . . in practice fairly rare for the MMC to go beyond competition matters in reaching its conclusions, but the breadth of the public interest definition in the Act does mean that the MMC has to consider the possible effects of mergers over a very wide range, and is therefore likely to debate—at least from time to time—such matters as defence and national security, reciprocity, the financial situation of the bidder, employment and regional issues. . . . There is also the possibility that the MMC might consider that potentially detrimental effects under the competition criterion would be more than offset by beneficial effects under other criteria although such cases are unusual; British Airways/British Caledonia is an example: some detriments to competition were considered to be more than offset by benefits of synergy for the merged company, the strengthening of British Airways's competitive position worldwide and the removal of the risk of British Caledonia's liquidation.[21]

In France, as in the United Kingdom, the minister in charge of economic affairs has the power to block or to impose conditions on large mergers (i.e., when the combined market share of the firms involved is larger than 25 percent or when their aggregate turnover is over FF 7 billion with two of the merging parties having a turnover of at least FF 2 billion), after having sought the opinion of an independent body (the Conseil de la Concurrence). The Conseil de la Concurrence must, in formulating its opinion, establish whether or not "the concentration makes a great enough contribution to economic progress to offset the damage to competition." It must also take into account "the competitiveness of the businesses in question with regard to international competition." Although few merger cases were referred to the Conseil de la Concurrence before 1988, the trend has shifted recently toward a more determined effort to prohibit anticompetitive mergers. The efficiency defense for anticompetitive mergers, which was frequently accepted in the past, is less likely to be easily accepted in the future because the Conseil de la Concurrence has stated that firms must now prove that the economic progress alleged must be the direct consequence of the merger and that those benefits cannot have been obtained by other means.

For example, in 1989, when the Conseil examined the proposed takeover of Spontex (a French manufacturer of synthetic sponges for household use) by

---

21. S. Lipworth, "Merger Control in the United Kingdom," in *International Mergers and Joint Ventures* (New York: Fordham Corporate Law Institute, 1991), 205–19.

3M (a French subsidiary of Minnesota Mining and Manufacturing Co.),[22] it considered that the merger should be allowed to proceed despite the fact that it reduced competition on the declining synthetic sponge market because it contributed to economic progress through combining the two firms' R&D efforts to invent new products. However, the Conseil failed to consider whether there would have been ways other than a full merger (damaging to competition) to achieve this result (such as, for example, a joint R&D venture). In contrast, in 1990, when it examined the proposed merger between Eurocom and Carat (respectively, the largest advertising agency in France and the largest French-based firm specializing in the buying and reselling of advertising space), the Conseil proposed that the merger be allowed only on the condition that the advertising-space-buying activities of the two firms remain separate in France. In this instance, the Conseil reasoned that if the merger was likely to decrease competition in the domestic buying of advertising space while improving efficiency somewhat in the international operations of the firms involved, it was not established that grouping of advertising space purchases in France by the two firms was necessary for their economic development abroad. Thus, the Conseil (for the first time) restricted the use of the efficiency defense in merger cases to instances where the expected economic progress could not be obtained if the (anticompetitive) merger did not take place.[23]

European Merger Control
If the EEC treaty did not include a specific provision for merger control, the ECJ established, in *Continental Can*, that the strengthening, by merger, of a dominant position to such an extent that "the degree of dominance substantially fettered competition" so that "only undertakings remain on the market whose behavior depends on the dominant one," constituted an abuse of dominant position contrary to Article 86.[24] Yet, from the point of view of merger control, the scope of this ruling was rather limited in that it only applied to mergers and acquisitions that strengthened a preexisting dominant position (and not to the creation of a dominant position). Also, in *Philip Morris*,[25] the

---

22. "Avis no. 89-A-05 du Conseil de la concurrence relatif au projet de concentration entre les sociétés Spontex (du groupe Chargeurs S.A.) et 3M France (filiale de Minnesota Mining and Manufacturing Co) dans le secteur des 'outils d'entretien ménager,'" Conseil de la Concurrence, *Troisième Rapport d'Activité* (Paris: Direction des Journaux Officiels, 1989), 203–04.

23. "Avis no. 90-A-10 du Conseil de la concurrence relatif au projet de concentration entre les groupes Eurocom, WCRS Group Plc, Carat Espace dans le secteur de la communication publicitaire," *Rapport Annuel du Conseil de la Concurrence pour l'Année 1990*, Annexe 80: 180.

24. Europemballage and Continental Can v. Commission, Case 6/72, 1973 ECR 215.

25. British American Tobacco and Reynolds Industries v. Commission, Joined Cases 142 and 156/84, 1987 ECR 4487.

ECJ opened the possibility of applying Article 85 to agreements through which firms acquired shares in other firms, stating that if the acquisition by one company of an equity interest in a competitor does not in itself constitute conduct restricting competition, such an acquisition may nevertheless serve as an instrument for influencing the commercial conduct of the companies in question so as to restrict or distort competition in the market where they carry on business. It was not entirely clear, however, whether Article 85 applied in cases in which a firm acquired 100 percent of the shares of another firm.

Articles 85 and 86 were both considered by the EC Commission to be rather clumsy instruments for controlling mergers, if only because they could not be used to establish preventive control. Thus, it considered that merger control was a necessary addition to Articles 85 and 86 of the EEC treaty in order to maintain competitive structures in the unified market.

The adoption, at the end of 1989, of Council Regulation 4064/89 on the control of concentrations between undertakings, which ended nearly fifteen years of negotiations among the member states, was intended to put a stop to the use of Articles 85 and 86 by the Commission to control concentration, and it represented "a victory for the Commission in its efforts to strengthen and centralize merger control in the Community."[26] Indeed, it established a preventive mandatory control for large European mergers and a system of compulsory premerger notification.[27]

For a variety of reasons, the EC merger regulation is likely to have far-reaching consequences for competition policy after the internal market is completed. First, it delineates the jurisdiction of the EC Commission and of the national competition authorities by distinguishing concentrations of Community dimension from other concentrations and by establishing a one-stop review for the former. Even if this attempt at clarification leaves some room for dual jurisdiction, it does reduce the amount of that room. A similar system could be used in the future for anticompetitive practices and, thereby, solve some of the problems raised previously in my discussion of Articles 85 and 86.

Second, since there is reason to believe that, at least in a transitional period, completion of the internal market will lead to structural reorganizations among firms established in different countries and operating over large segments of the European market, the adoption of the merger regulation vests considerable power in the EC Commission for monitoring competition and shifts the balance of power, as far as control of market structures is concerned,

---

26. B. Hawk, "The EEC Merger Regulation: The First Step Toward One-Stop Merger Control," *Antitrust Law Journal* 59 (1990): 195–235.

27. See Council Regulation (EEC) no. 4064/89 of 21 December 1989 on the control of concentrations between undertakings, OJ No. L 395/1 (December 30, 1989).

further away from the national laws which, with the possible exception of those of the Federal Republic of Germany, were not enforced strictly.

However, the merger regulation also raises some questions about the future of European competition policy. The initial question it raises concerns the boundary between a concentration (which falls under the regulation if it meets the turnover standards) and an anticompetitive agreement (which falls under Article 85). This question is important for two reasons. First, an efficiency defense exists for agreements falling under Article 85, but not for concentrations falling under the merger regulation. Second, substantial fines may be imposed on firms that fail to notify the Commission of concentrations falling within the merger regulation. In August, 1990, the Commission issued a notice regarding the definition of concentrative and cooperative operations under the merger regulation.[28] In general terms, cooperative joint ventures are defined as those that have as their object the coordination of competitive behavior of undertakings that remain independent, whereas concentrative joint ventures are defined as those that perform, on a lasting basis, all the functions of an autonomous economic entity and do not give rise to coordination between parents or between parents and the joint venture.

An additional and more general question concerns the adequacy of the merger control regulation and its consistency with the objectives underlying integration of European markets. As I said in the first part of this chapter, an important benefit to be expected from market unification is the increased efficiency due to changes in firm scale. If there is no doubt that changes in efficiency can be effected via increased competition and internal growth of efficient firms, what about the impact of mergers on efficiency?

The most comprehensive study of mergers to date, which covered Belgium, France, Germany, the Netherlands, Sweden, the United Kingdom, and the United States, dealt with the determinants and the effects of mergers from the point of view of static efficiency.

> [N]o consistent pattern of either improved or deteriorated profitability can therefore be claimed across the seven countries. Mergers would appear to result in a slight improvement here, a slight worsening there. If a generalization is to be drawn, it would have to be that mergers have but modest effects, up or down, on the profitability of the merging firms in the three to five years following merger. Any economic efficiency gain from the mergers would appear to be small, judging from these statistics, as would any market power increases.[29]

---

28. Commission Notice no. 90/C 203/6 regarding the concentrative and cooperative operations under Council Regulation (EEC) No. 4064/89 of 21 December 1989 on the control of concentrations between undertakings, OJ No. C 203/10 (August 14, 1990).

29. D. C. Mueller, ed., *The Determinants and Effects of Mergers: An International Comparison* (Cambridge, Mass.: Oelgeschlager, Gunn and Hain, 1980).

The results of this study are somewhat troubling because they suggest that, in the various countries surveyed, there is very little difference (on average) between the performances of merging firms before and after their mergers or between the merging firms and matched firms belonging to the same industry and the same size-class that have not merged. Commenting on these results, F. M. Scherer states that

> the weight of the postmerger profitability evidence for an assortment of nations suggests that on average, the private gains from mergers were either negative or insignificantly different from zero. Since social benefits are seldom large, and since firms would be free alternatively to expand through internal building and market development, the net balance of benefits versus costs under a strict policy is hardly apt to be decisively unfavorable and it seems more likely to be favorable. . . . [I]t is much easier to nip the growth of market concentration in the bud through a hard line against mergers than it is to correct abuses or atomize market structures once monopoly or tight oligopoly has emerged. . . . For these reasons and perhaps also for sociopolitical reasons, there is much to be said for a policy that errs on the side of a hard line against mergers, accepting the risks that occasionally mergers offering substantial efficiency benefits will be barred because the judicial system is such an imperfect screen.[30]

Neither the evidence presented by Mueller nor the comment by Scherer precludes the possibility that some mergers will lead simultaneously to increased market power and increased static (and possibly dynamic) efficiencies. According to a study by Jacquemin, Buigues, and Ilzkovitz, such cases are likely to present themselves in two types of industries.

> [T]hose heavily dependent on the public sector and parts of the food and drink industry. The industries mainly serving public-sector markets are boilermaking, heavy electrical plants, railway equipment and shipbuilding. In these sheltered industries each member state has hitherto been able to support its "national champion." Consequently, intra-EEC trade has remained at a very low level and the number of European producers is much higher than in the USA. The result is that EEC firms have excess capacity and are less efficient. As the industries show substantial economies of scale and require large scale units, . . . rationalization and the attendant reduction in the number of producers should allow the firms that remain to lower their costs. . . . Thus the industries in this group

---

30. F.M. Scherer, *Industrial Market Structure and Economic Performance*, 2d ed. (Chicago: Rand McNally, 1980), 546.

benefit considerably from greater concentration but also present a real
danger of monopolization. . . . In . . . parts of the food and drinks
industry (pasta, flour milling, chocolate, and beer) the prospect of 1992
is already producing a wave of mergers designed to lead to groups of
world scale. . . . [T]hese mergers have some benefits because they allow
greater exploitation of economies of scale but they could also reduce
competition.[31]

Thus, the crucial question is what one should do when confronted with
a merger that is likely simultaneously to reduce competition and increase
efficiency.

The question is all the more important because, as Williamson has shown
under simplifying assumptions, "modest unit cost savings tend rather quickly
to outweigh appreciable price effects."[32] As an example, he calculates that
with a market demand elasticity of unity, a unit cost reduction of less than 0.5
percent would be sufficient to offset the allocative inefficiency resulting from a
5.0 percent price increase. Williamson then adds that "whether the delayed
realization of economies is more than offset by the rivalry gains from prohibiting the merger requires an examination of the time stream of benefits and
costs associated with the merger versus nonmerger options."

This leads to the idea that merger control should include the possibility of
an efficiency defense, both on theoretical grounds and on empirical grounds.
At the theoretical level, if merger control is designed to increase economic
welfare, one cannot just assume that productive (or dynamic) efficiency gains
can never result from a merger and one also cannot assume that such gains, if
they exist, are irrelevant. As Williamson puts it when referring to merger
control in the United States: "If neither the courts nor the enforcement agencies are sensitive to these considerations, the system fails to meet a basic test
of economic rationality. And without this the whole enforcement system lacks
for defensible standards and becomes suspect." At the empirical level, Scherer
points out that

requiring the leaders of large merging enterprises to think through their
postmerger rationalization plans sufficiently carefully that they can be
explained to a skeptical Commission staff would help prevent many a

31. A. Jacquemin, P. Buigues, and F. Ilzkovitz, "Horizontal Mergers and Competition
Policy in the European Communities," *European Economy*, no. 40 (May 1989): 3–95.
32. O. E. Williamson, "Economies as an Antitrust Defense: The Welfare Tradeoffs,"
American Economic Review 58 (1968): 18; Williamson, "Economies as an Antitrust Defense
Revisited," in *Welfare Aspects of Industrial Markets*, ed. A. P. Jacquemin and H. W. de Jong
(Leiden: Nijhoff, 1977), 237–71.

mistake. And that might be benefit enough to warrant European Community intervention into the merger process.[33]

However, the European merger regulation does not allow for an efficiency defense of mergers.

> [G]iven that the criterion of technical and economic progress (included in Article 2-1-b of the regulation) can be used only if it is perfectly compatible with competition and consumer's interests, it is difficult to see how an operation which creates or reinforces a dominant position could be accepted because the negative anticompetitive effects are outweighed by the positive effects of such a progress. The wording also implies that only consumer's surplus and not producer's surplus is retained: apparently some sacrifice of consumer interest for the sake of higher profits is not accepted. If this is so, the role of the efficiency criteria in the regulation is empty.[34]

Sir Leon Brittan, the commissioner responsible for competition, has also rejected the idea of a possible efficiency defense in the European merger regulation by stating that "once a dominant position which significantly impedes competition has been found, there is no way around a declaration of incompatibility."[35]

Some observers have argued that, over time, the interpretation of the EEC merger regulation will soften and that efficiency considerations will be allowed to play a more important role in the adjudication of cases. However, it seems that the wording of the regulation, as it stands today, will remain a significant obstacle to a balanced appraisal of the social costs and benefits of a merger. Indeed, if the Commission wants to allow a merger on the basis of productive (or dynamic) efficiency benefits that outweigh the loss of consumer surplus, it will have to declare that the merger "does not create or strengthen a dominant position as a result of which competition would be significantly impeded in the Common Market" even if the market share of the merging firms is high and barriers to entry are quite significant.

Existing case law, although quite limited, is rather ambiguous on the issue of the handling of mergers that increase efficiency. During the first year

33. F. M. Scherer, "European Community Merger Policy: Why? Why Not?," in *European/American Antitrust and Trade Law* (New York: Fordham Corporate Law Institute, 1988), 24–1 to 24–16.

34. A. Jacquemin, "Horizontal Concentration and European Merger Policy," *European Economic Review* 34 (1990): 539–50.

35. Sir Leon Brittan, "The Principles and Practice of Merger Policy in the European Community" (Address to the Centre for European Policy Studies, Brussels, 1990).

of enforcement of the merger regulation, efficiency considerations have rarely come into play, and there is even some evidence that increased efficiency can make a merger more objectionable because it reinforces the position of the merging firms on the market.

A good example of this rather dubious approach is the January, 1991, Commission decision on the acquisition of NCR (a manufacturer of computers, in particular of financial and retail workstations) by AT&T (specialized in telecommunications equipment and communications networks). In its decision, the Commission noted, among other things, that "there is a potential complementarity in the technical field and the marketing of workstations and communication products, and these synergies may give AT&T/NCR the chance of developing more advanced communications features at lower cost." This possibility for technical progress was, however, seen as a threat to competition by the Commission when it stated: "It is not excluded that potential advantages flowing from synergies may create or strengthen a dominant position." In order to come to the conclusion that these potential benefits to AT&T/NCR do not lead to the creation or strengthening of a dominant position, the Commission took into consideration the fact that similar attempts to combine computer and telecommunications businesses have so far failed. It also mentioned that, should AT&T/NCR be successful, it would have to face important competitors (although by its own admission these competitors have apparently not been able to develop the synergies in question). In the end, the Commission stated that it was only because "the potential advantages which AT&T hopes to gain from this concentration are for the moment theoretical and have yet to be proved in a future market place" that it did not object to the merger. One may then venture that if the Commission had believed that the merger between AT&T and NCR was likely to contribute to economic progress (by allowing the merged firm to develop "more advanced communication features at lower cost") it might have considered opposing it on the ground that it would have created or strengthened a dominant position for the merging firms.

If the AT&T/NCR decision clearly suggests that, during the first few months of 1990, the Commission was following a misguided economic approach to the merger problem, the decision it made in October, 1991, declaring the proposed merger between Aérospatiale-Alenia and De Havilland incompatible with the Common Market, although worded with extreme caution and not entirely convincing, seems to indicate that the Commission may be more willing to balance possible productive efficiency gains and expected consumer surplus losses when examining mergers in the future. Indeed, in this decision, the Commission stated that

the parties argue that one of their objectives in acquiring de Havilland is to reduce costs. . . . Without prejudice as to whether such considerations are relevant for assessment under Article 2 of the Merger Regulation, such cost savings would have a negligible impact on the overall operation of ATR/de Havilland, amounting to around 0.5 percent of the combined turnover. The parties have identified (although not quantified) cost savings which could be made by better management of certain aspects of de Havilland's internal operation. These cost savings would not arise as a consequence of the concentration *per se,* but are cost savings which could be achieved by de Havilland's existing owner or by any other potential acquirer. . . . For the above reasons, the Commission does not consider that the proposed concentration would contribute to the development of technical and economic progress within the meaning of Article 2(1)(b) of the Merger Regulation. Even if there was such progress, this would not be to the consumers' advantage.[36]

This decision offers some solace to the economists in that, although the Commission refuses to say explicitly whether productive efficiency gains are relevant for considering whether or not a merger is compatible with the common market, it nevertheless does discuss the importance of the manufacturing cost reductions alleged by the parties in a way that, at least implicitly, suggests that productive efficiency gains must be compared to the potential losses of consumer surplus due to the increase in concentration brought about by the merger.

---

36. Commission Decision no. 91/619/EEC of 2 October 1991 declaring the incompatibility with the common market of a concentration (Aérospatiale-Alenia/de Havilland), OJ No. L 334/42 (December 5, 1991), at 60.

Europe's Could-Be Social State: Social Policy in European Integration after 1992

Stephan Leibfried

Will the single market process eventually result in a European welfare state, with comprehensive social rights addressed to or standardized by Brussels? To answer this question, we must enter uncharted, ideological, and controversial terrain. Our journey is bound to be speculative, but it affords a view of one of the European Community's most prominent black holes: the social dimension of Project 1992.

Before setting out in search of social Europe, let us understand that what some presently perceive as EC "neutrality" on social policy is not so neutral at all: the ongoing integration process necessarily affects national social policies. As integration deepens, these effects become pervasive. Whether or not the EC moves toward "Social Europe," it shed its ideological neutrality in this sphere when it grew from EC 6 to EC 12. Touching contentious terrain, therefore, is unavoidable.

I shall begin by outlining the general state of EC social policy (see also Henningsen 1989, Lange 1992, and Mosley 1990). Though the EC may be characterized as a *fragmented* welfare state, already delivering *some* welfare to *some* groups, it does not presently rest on an entitlement base: European citizens do not generally have social rights vis-à-vis the EC. The EC has no direct social state capability.[1] It lacks a strong social rights foundation. Cur-

My title builds on Lindberg and Scheingold 1970. I am grateful to William James Adams, Jutta Allmendinger, Greg Duncan, Claus Offe, Elmar Rieger, Barbara Schmitter-Heisler, Bernd Schulte, and two anonymous reviewers for comments, advice, and prompt help; to Gitta Stender for help with the many revisions of the manuscript; and to Mark Ebers, Sylvia Korupp, Paul Pierson, Jutta Mester, and Torsten Schaak for help with the literature.

1. In Anglo-American societies, *welfare state* is the common term; on the continent, especially in Germany, *Sozialstaat* is the better label. In its *Sozialstaat* version, the entitlement element is stressed—it is a public and constitutional law category with great normative meaning (Ogus 1990). In contrast, students of the welfare state focus on outcomes and employ the analytical techniques of the social sciences to evaluate its desirability. Legally, *largesse* (Reich 1964) seems to complement *welfare* but contrast with *entitlement*.

rently, the primary impact of the EC on social policy involves the protection of the social rights of intra-EC migrants vis-à-vis the member states.

Next I shall discuss how a more developed welfare state, possibly combined with a social rights base, might come about at the EC level. I explore four grand options for post-1992 Community social policy; the first two options involve incremental adjustments to existing EC institutions and tendencies, and the other two build on two academic proposals for major reform.

All options are informed by the controversial premise that the EC must—rather sooner than later—transcend the integration of markets. A people's Europe is more than a common market for goods and services. It is also more than attending to the employed of Europe through social security. "The people" is a more inclusive category than "the employed": the latter comprise less than half of all "citizens" of Europe.

The term *social policy*, as used here, refers to public transfers and public services. It encompasses only those public interventions that are connected to social risks as historically defined: sickness, disability, old age, unemployment, poverty, and parenthood.[2] In continental Europe, social policy is based on an entitlement approach to absorbing social risks: the welfare state is not largesse but, rather, a social state's response to social rights. It provides the focus for social policy and colors its definition. Labor market policy provides a frame for social policy, but the genuine territory for social policy lies before, after, and beyond the operative labor market.[3]

Social Policy in Europe Today: Europe's Non-Social State

As yet there exists no European social state to speak of; most social policy is conducted at the national level.[4] An important exception to this rule involves

---

2. The EC includes education in its definition of social policy (Sieveking 1990). It thus deviates from some continental traditions, including that of Germany. In Germany, a strict line has traditionally been drawn between social security and education. By reaching out to education, the EC conforms to the American view of the welfare state. Heidenheimer (1981) compares the German and U.S. approaches.

3. As a rule, labor market policy is not based on social rights and is not particularly close in spirit to the social state. It relies on macro and microeconomic policies (pump priming and infrastructure, respectively) and on integrating the major social actors (employer and employee organizations) into a collective bargaining system.

4. An exception to national preemption is social policy for civil servants of the EC itself (Plantey 1981). An indirect exception is exemptions from national social security granted by the EC to "Eurocompanies." Such an exemption allows a company to contract out for insurance against all risks in a uniform way throughout the EC. Such an exemption was made for Airbus (Langendonck 1991; Leibfried and Allmendinger 1991, 20 ff.). These two aspects of European social policy are not yet well researched. Since much of European national social policy evolution

the effects of national social policies on workers migrating between member states:[5] For EC migrants,[6] national social security systems are coordinated.[7] The other exception involves the EC's guarantee of gender equality throughout the Community.

Social and cultural policies may turn out to be the last national prerogatives of the member states.[8] For this reason, social policy has been called a stepchild of European integration (Bellers 1984, 246). This status has been

---

in the nineteenth century began with public servants and company welfare, these twentieth-century examples from the EC might provide especially interesting, and maybe contrasting, cases.

5. Quite a few articles of the EEC treaty touch upon social policy. Art. 51 empowers the Council to implement the free movement of employed persons within the EC. Toward that end, Council Regulation (EEC) no. 1408/71 of 14 June 1971, JO No. L 149 (July 5, 1971), and Council Regulation (EEC) no. 574/72 of 21 March 1972, JO No. L 74 (March 27, 1972), coordinate social security for migrant workers. Art. 117 is about improving living standards, improving conditions of work, and making both progressively uniform (leveling up). Art. 118 makes the Commission responsible for supporting cooperation among member states in social issues. (Neither article confers much of a legal mandate.) Art. 119 creates a strong legal basis for gender equality in the labor market. Art. 120 guarantees national minimums on paid vacations. Art. 121 allows the Council to delegate responsibility to the Commission for migrant workers. Art. 122 obliges the Commission to include a chapter on the development of social conditions in its yearly report to the Parliament. Arts. 123–28 provide for the European Social Fund (ESF). Art. 130a (added via the Single European Act) is about the harmonious development of the EC as a whole, about diminishing welfare disparities between regions, and about the improvement of the least favored regions.

6. Migrant workers from EC member states are a minority of all migrants in the EC 12. Today, they number about 2 million (5 million when families are included), as compared to 140 million employed people and 340 million inhabitants (Schulte 1991b). The Community's coordination of social policy—the major area of EC regulatory activity in this field—thus addresses only 1.4 percent of the employed and 0.5 percent of the total population of the EC.

In addition there are more than 5 million non-EC citizens, with more than 3 million dependents, on Community territory (Soysal 1991). These are mostly from northern Africa, Turkey, or Yugoslavia. Many citizens of "third countries" belong to the real poor of Western Europe—an issue the EC could and should also take up, maybe as part of a common European immigration policy. "Coordination" does not currently apply to "third country citizens," only to EC citizens.

7. Coordination should be contrasted with "harmonization," i.e., with establishing a basically common social policy structure in 12 national systems. Harmonization has always been a slogan, never a successfully implemented policy. The only area where harmonization of social policy in the EC has been achieved until now is equality of gender in the labor market, under Art. 119 of the EEC treaty (Hoskyns 1986; Mazey 1988; Raasch 1990).

8. Nevertheless, Norbert Reich (1988, 7) notes a "social statification" [*Versozialstaat-lichung*] of the Community, as the EC develops such fields as consumer protection, ecology, equal opportunities, health protection, and industrial safety—embodying a "general protection policy," as opposed to just a "social security" policy. Such policies are marginal to the core of traditional social policy ("income transfers"), but they are more strongly juridified at the Community level than is EC social policy itself.

reaffirmed by the Single European Act (SEA) of 1986.[9] The focus of integration has been the citizen of the marketplace (the *Marktbürger*, see Grabitz 1970) and market freedom (*Europäische Marktfreiheit*, see Oppermann 1987, 57ff.).[10]

EC activity in the social policy arena has mainly centered on the free movement of persons (Art. 51 of the EEC treaty). Employed and employable citizens of the member states—with their families—may move within the Community, may cumulate their respective social security rights, and are not to be discriminated against.[11] The treaty presumes that social policy is for the member states to decide. National differences are to be respected; they are to be "coordinated" only when there is overlap due to intra-EC mobility.

The other major prong of EC social policy is the structural funds. The Treaty of Rome (Arts. 123–28) provided for a European Social Fund (ESF).[12] The ESF finances measures to retrain and relocate the European unemployed. In the context of EC 6, it was meant to address the problems of the *Mezzo-*

---

9. More than 300 "1992" measures were agreed on at the European summit in Milan in July, 1985. None of them pertained to social policy. In the second half of the 1980s, the reactions to the glaring absence of any welfare state issues—and the polemics about "social dumping"— have made "social cohesion" and the "social dimension" a European issue again (see Keohane and Hoffmann 1991).

The Single European Act excepted all "Single Market" measures from unanimity and allowed for majority rule in the Council. It left social policy issues—other than essential health and safety requirements—under the old regime of unanimous rule, thus giving veto politics full reign. Interestingly enough, Germany, which, together with the United Kingdom, has blocked supranationalization of social policy throughout the 1980s, has recently made overtures for majority rule in this area (Clever 1991; Schulz 1991). If this were to become official EC policy, it would free the Commission's hand in social policy considerably.

10. See also Pieters 1989a, 1990a, 1990b. There is a broader debate on the "constitutionalization" of social rights at the national and EC levels, which would broaden the competence of the European Court of Justice (ECJ) substantially. It may suffice to indicate that mostly only "minimal protection" is thought to be wisely constitutionalized at the Community level. There also remains the discussion on the nature of the 1961 Social Charter of the Council of Europe, especially on whether it legally binds the Community as such.

11. In terms of class, the growth of the Community's social policy has been from the "bottom up," not from the "top down." Art. 51 EEC aimed at the untrained southern workers migrating north to Germany. In their own setting in the South, though, these people would not be considered at the "bottom" but rather as "labor aristocrats." This was the typical situation in the 1950s and 1960s. Today, white-collar or well-trained blue-collar employees and the self-employed are typical—and they migrate from any member state to any other member state (Pieters 1991a, 75). As yet, changes in the patterns of mobility have not been reflected in EC regulation. The emergent regulation of private pension benefits signals that the social policy priorities of the EC are being updated and reordered.

12. The European Coal and Steel Community (ECSC) of 1951 had already developed similar programs. It also funded social housing for workers in the coal and steel industries. On the ECSC's social policy, see Collins 1975, vol. 1.

giorno.[13] It is important to recognize, however, that individuals hold no entitlements against it. Thus, the ESF does not operate like a social state. Rather, it finances national governments and their national programs (Anderson 1991). As a result, the ESF does not substantially weaken national hegemony over social policy. The ESF amounted to about ECU 3.6 billion in 1987, roughly 6 percent of the EC budget (Schulte 1990, 85).[14] In addition, there is the somewhat larger European Regional Development Fund (ERDF),[15] financing infrastructural measures weighted toward the EC 12's periphery.[16] Under the reforms of 1988, both funds were to increase twofold by 1993. The 1992 budget request of the Commission includes roughly ECU 19 billion for the structural funds (29 percent of the EC budget); in comparison, it contains some ECU 37 billion for agriculture (56 percent of the EC budget).[17]

Large welfare disparities exist—and are perceived to exist—between the EC's core (the rich, northern welfare states) and its periphery (the Latin countries, Ireland, and the northern United Kingdom). The core's perspective for development is: "coordination instead of harmonization. Neither today nor in the foreseeable future may national social security systems be harmonized. The reason for this is the great differences between these national systems, which have historical, political and economic causes" (Schulte 1991a, 282,

---

13. The EC 6 was homogeneously northern in the expression of its welfare statism. The exception that proved the rule was the *Mezzogiorno*.

Thus, northern welfare statism at the national level was taken for granted in the EEC treaty; only at the margin (the ESF, the *Mezzogiorno*) did action at the EC level seem to be required. The enlargements of the EC, especially the one leading to EC 12, have undone this homogeneity. Welfare state issues have become forcing mechanisms at the EC level, attracting institutional and (tentative) regulatory attention (Leibfried 1992b).

14. This is less than Germany spent for child allowances. Nevertheless, the structural funds (ESF and ERDF) spend significant amounts in terms of the GNP of peripheral EC countries: 3.8 percent of Portugal's GNP, 2.6 percent of Ireland's GNP, and 1.6 percent of Greece's GNP, for example (Ermer et al. 1990, 99). On the Canadian example of a national welfare state strongly oriented toward regional redistribution, see Banting 1982.

15. The ERDF is a 1972 spin-off from the European Agricultural Guidance and Guarantee Fund (EAGGF), gaining its independent standing in 1975 (cf. Konegen 1984a and Konegen 1984b, 235). The EAGGF was created with two missions in mind: implementation of price supports (EAGGF-Guarantee) and finance of structural reforms (EAGGF-Guidance). The EC's agricultural funds go mainly to EAGGF-Guarantee, which benefits the better-to-do (central and northern) farmers on relatively efficient farms. The guidance section, which attends to straight income transfers to the less well-to-do farmers (on the periphery and in the south), is concerned with macroeconomic and social policy and has been systematically underfunded (Benedictis, Fillipis, and Salvati 1990; Rosenblatt 1988). In 1988, ERDF spent ECU 4.19 billion, which amounted to 7.4 percent of that year's EC budget (Schulte 1990, 84f.).

16. The ESF and the ERDF together received ECU 7.75 billion in 1988, or 13.7 percent of the EC budget (Schulte 1990, 84f.).

17. *Frankfurter Allgemeine Zeitung*, July 24, 1991, and February 13, 1992.

citing the German National Association of Insurance Science and Social Security Policy).[18]

If we try to establish a framework within which to classify EC social policy, it is notable that Brussels does not deal equally earnestly with all problems. It is concerned in a major way with only one group (farmers) and only one risk (insufficiently high prices). To be sure, the EC addresses the problems of Europe's periphery and of its regions lacking infrastructure, but it does so haphazardly. Few risks are attended to; these are handled only experimentally in "projects" of the structural funds. Present EC practice—dealing with few risks and few social groups—might therefore be characterized as a *fragmented welfare state* (see matrix 1). Thus, the EC still falls far short of the social state capability existing in most of its member states.

With respect to coordination by the EC, where its competence pertains to "migrant workers" only, the Community's prorating and other regulatory outcomes have a broad reach: for these mobile employees, Community regulation potentially deals with (almost) all risks covered by national legislation.[19] Thus, the EC takes potential, indirect responsibility for *all* risks of *one* group—which I characterize as a *segmented welfare state* approach in matrix 1. But since the EC also actually provides social security directly and comprehensively for its own employees—including more than 10,000 professionals (Plantey 1981, 331ff.)—the EC is also involved in a *fully developed* case of a segmented welfare state approach at the supranational level. In both cases we can actually speak of a segmented *social* state, since both rest on a strong and nearly encompassing entitlement base.

At present, no EC program covers at least one risk for all citizens. As a result, the EC is not a *partial welfare state* (as outlined in matrix 1). A fortiori, the EC does not deal with all risks for all citizens—or even with most risks for most groups—as in a comprehensive welfare state. At the national level, though, most of the northern countries would be placed in this last category.[20]

Could the post-1992 Community move from its present position in cell 1 of matrix 1 to cells 2, 3, or 4? I want to explore the Community's institutional potential for different welfare state trajectories along these corridors: each cell

---

18. Gesellschaft für Versicherungswissenschaft und -gestaltung e.V. (GVG). The quotation is from "GVG-Leitlinien für ein soziales Europa" (Köln 1990). Schmähl (1989, 1990, and 1992) and Maydell (1989) present a typical extended argument for this position.

19. All but dire poverty (Leibfried 1992a, 236ff.; Pieters 1991a, 77; Steinmeyer 1990).

20. Extensive comparisons of European poverty regimes, together with reviews of the literature, appear in Leibfried 1992a and Flora 1986f. When, during the New Deal, the United States federalized its social policy, it moved from cell 1 (post–Civil War military and agriculture) toward cell 2 (Skocpol and Ikenberry 1983). Due to the lack of health insurance and categorically restrained income transfers, the United States should be classified as a partial welfare state (Schmitter-Heisler 1991, 463).

MATRIX 1. The EC Welfare State and Possible Future Welfare States

Coverage of Risks	Coverage of People	
	Few Groups (Categorical)	Most Groups (Universal)
Few risks	*(1) Fragmented*	*(2) Partial*
	1. CAP now	1. CAP decoupled once
	2. Structural funds	2. *M2:* Guaranteed Basic Income or
	3. *M1:* Compensate integration losers	Welfare
Most risks	*(3) Segmented*	*(4) Comprehensive*
	1. Migrant workers	1. *M4:* European Social Policy Band
	2. EC civil servants	(ESPB); ESSS insofar as it serves
	3. Gender equality	as a "target system"
	4. *M3:* European Social Security System (ESSS; the "Thirteenth State")	

contains examples of current EC practices or perspectives and of four models of development (*M1-M4*) to be discussed as Europe's could-be states of welfare.[21] First, I explore expansions of the structural funds to their utmost: a compensation regime for all losers in the 1992 and post-1992 processes, designated *M1*. Then I focus on the Common Agricultural Policy (CAP), wondering whether its reform points us in the direction of *M2*, a guaranteed basic income. Finally, I explore two academic visions of the future. The first, designated *M3*, is the EC as a thirteenth state—a state in which a genuine social code, providing an entering wedge for a Communitarian welfare state, would be developed. The second, designated *M4*, is a European Social Policy Band (ESPB), designed with the snake of the European Monetary System in mind. The ESPB amounts to a comprehensive European welfare state. I shall discuss each of these options within the framework of matrix 1.

Post-1992 Social Policy: Europe's Could-Be Welfare States

Going Bismarck: The Compensatory Model (The Structural Funds as a "Second Leg")

The EC's two structural funds (ESF, ERDF) have been described as "ridiculously underfinanced in relation to the problems they are supposed to attack"

---

21. I shall focus on monetary transfers, not on services, even though services are central to a welfare state's potential. For an exploration of the educational dimension, see Leibfried and Allmendinger 1991.

(Scharpf 1988, 241). In 1987, Germany alone devoted more resources to child allowances than the Community devoted to either fund. Nevertheless, since the mid-1980s both funds have developed into a second leg of the 1992 integration process. The second leg draws additional strength from the European Court of Justice (ECJ),[22] which has systematically increased legal pressures pointing toward European standards in educational and social policy.[23]

The rebuilding of the two structural funds into a second leg of the 1992 process symbolizes that horizontal fiscal equity (revenue sharing) and social redistribution between member states have become forcing mechanisms at the European level. Since firms located in the core nations are expected to gain most from market integration, these nations are to compensate peripheral states for granting them untrammeled access to their markets.[24] As market integration in Western Europe has intensified, the funds have provided an important bargaining arena between the center and the periphery. As homogeneity in economic policy increases, especially in fiscal and monetary policy, the traditional national options for coping with domestic social needs by building up nationally tailored compensating welfare state programs will also wither away. This will put additional pressure on Brussels and provide another impetus for a European welfare state.

The funds compensate, albeit mostly symbolically, the peripheral regions of Europe and routinely supplement national programs.[25] The structural funds often become prisoners of national dilemmas and do not allow for a truly European, independent policy focus. Structurally, they are incompatible with a welfare state built on entitlements. Instead of direct and standardized rela-

---

22. If the United States at the turn of the century was "a state of courts and parties" (Skowronek 1982), then the EC today is "a state of the European Court and EC technocrats." The most comprehensive U.S.-EC comparison has been undertaken in a series of publications sponsored by the European University Institute (Florence), edited by Mauro Cappelletti, Monica Secombe, and Joseph Weiler, and titled "Integration through Law: Europe and the American Federal Experience" (1986). The idea that the most natural comparative material for the EC process is found in the United States seems to be held most strongly by lawyers—i.e., by students of the ECJ.

23. The mechanisms used by the Court have included broad definition of "employed," broad interpretation of "social benefits," and broad interpretation of Arts. 128 and 135 EEC (on education); see Zuleeg 1991. The Court may also seize upon the still-born social charter (Addison and Siebert 1991; Silvia 1991) to extend its social rights interpretation.

24. As Keeton 1963 and Henderson 1939 show, on a smaller scale, such a redistributive regime, financed by Prussia and compensating for lost customs income, already was part of the German *Zoll Verein* structure in the nineteenth century.

25. The Commission has shortened the policy circuit by dealing with regions and other subnational authorities. Further shortening, via direct-dealing with citizens, is still a long way off (cf. Anderson 1991). In education, by contrast, such programs as ERASMUS show that short circuiting existed from the start (cf. Sieveking 1990; Witte 1989).

tionships with clients, the funds cultivate relationships with staffs and with provider groups—most of them at the national level.

If one were to radicalize the present fund approach, the EC welfare state could become a regime of comprehensive compensation for "integration damages." The funds could expand in many directions; they could move from delivering services, incomes, and infrastructure in an experimental, haphazard way (i.e., away from projects) to systematic and standardized delivery across Europe. The funds could address other types of damage (new risks), such as cultural and social deprivation or general spatial imbalance. They could advance such new forms of compensation as establishing public education as a systematic and broader path of mobility from the periphery to the center,[26] a European version of equal access and affirmative action programs. Finally, the funds could become more comprehensive, addressing all European citizens damaged by the integration process (new groups).

If European welfare state activity evolved further in this direction, it would basically extend the German compensatory welfare state model to the Community level.[27] The German model is compensatory because it focuses (ex post) on payments for damages and not (ex ante) on preventive intervention or on delivering social services. Unlike the Scandinavian model (Leibfried 1992a, 233), the German approach is not built around comprehensive labor market participation but simply around comprehensive *Versorgung* ['provision of livelihood']. This variant of a European welfare state would not address all European citizens but only the losers in European integration, residing mostly on the European periphery. It would resonate best with the fragmented welfare state approach (cell 1 of matrix 1). It might also be addressed to those merely tolerating European integration without gaining much from it.

But, to continue this line of speculation, such a European welfare state could not address all social risks of these persons, only those attributable to further European integration. Since such borderlines are hard to police (if they are not considered to be altogether artificial), this particular compensation regime might evolve into a general compensation regime for peripheral location and backwardness, a segmented welfare state for the periphery (cell 3 of matrix 1).[28] But a case could also be made for a development in the opposite

---

26. Here, the Community would follow the U.S. model and break out of the Bismarck model; see Heidenheimer 1981.

27. For a comparison of this model with other European approaches, cf. Leibfried 1992a, 232.

28. This may also be an unintended consequence of a particular compensation regime. Just as disability pensions in the *Mezzogiorno* have come to fulfill a basic income function for the region, particular European compensation regimes might be converted into general regimes if the social and policy environment were suitable.

direction. The present system of revenue sharing might shed its particular welfare mantle—the structural funds approach—and might be turned into a novel system of general European revenue sharing (Franzmeyer and Seydel 1976). Such a move toward a general European welfare state, operating through intergovernmental fiscal redistribution, would delegate all the specification of welfare components to member states.

Going Anglo: The Residual Model ("Decoupling" the Community's Agricultural Policy)

The Common Agricultural Policy (CAP) is the only large component of social policy to be conducted for several decades in nearly federal fashion at the EC level. In 1992, CAP still accounted for roughly 50 percent of the EC budget. Only here do we find an independent policy sphere, comparable, for example, to important federal policies in Germany or the United States. Only here do we find an autonomous Community tax base, a partial emancipation from national dues—from the captive structure that characterizes the EC in all other domains and tends to immobilize it.

The structural arm of CAP (EAGGF-Guidance) has not been nearly as important as its price stabilization arm (EAGGF-Guarantee). As the official Green Book (Commission of the European Communities 1985) reveals, however, the EC is now attempting to contain the growth of stabilization expenses. It has proposed the "decoupling" of income maintenance and price stabilization via increased reliance on structural reform and a return to the market.[29] For example, the Green Book

> called for a reduction in price supports and a realignment with world prices, together with direct support to farmers' income partially and selectively decoupled from the quantity of products generated. (Benedictis, Fillipis, and Salvatici 1990, 175)[30]

---

29. Also, the North-South divide after the last enlargement of the EC is significant in this regard. It sharpened the division between a North that did benefit from agricultural stabilization and a South that did not—leading the South to embrace decoupling. This implied "a diversification of the instruments of intervention, which were increasingly divorced from the achievement of common objectives and increasingly related to a more equitable distribution of financial resources among member states" (Benedictis, Fillipis, and Salvatici 1990, 173). Redistributive welfare conflict is thus a basic premise for agricultural reform (Rieger 1991).

30. This process goes hand in hand with a slow erosion of the Community "interest triangle" that had its base in the "food industrial complex." During the last decade, new groups have politicized the CAP scene: "consumers, environmentalists, countries with which the EC has relations in GATT, and groups interested in the development of sectors other than agriculture" (Benedictis, Fillipis, and Salvatici 1990, 175).

But when income transfers are decoupled—transformed from price supports into direct income grants—agricultural policy turns into straightforward social policy, albeit a policy limited to one sector and one status group (cell 1 of matrix 1). A guaranteed basic income for European farmers is at the moment—and this is notable—thought to be a general remedy also in the quarters of continental liberal market orthodoxy. In the struggle against agricultural sclerosis, the end seems to justify any means. This discussion presently is separated strictly from another, rarer debate on an EC-wide basic income.[31]

Once the transformation of agricultural policy from stabilization policy to income policy occurs, it will be harder to insulate this policy domain from claims by other European interest groups, however fluid their organizational state may be.[32] Sectoral logrolling among member states in agriculture might be eroded and replaced by cross-sectoral, class-style bargaining. This could lead to continuous EC-wide controversies about, and bargaining over, turning the new agricultural policy into an increasingly comprehensive EC social policy. The first decoupling (from price support) would turn into a second decoupling (from agriculture itself). Since the southern extension of the Community brought states with more substantial farming populations into the EC, a basic minimum income for farmers in these nations is closer to a general basic income for all citizens. In contrast, in the original EC, agricultural employment has already withered away, depriving it of its structural political importance for social policy.

If a European social state perspective were applied to this transformation of agricultural policy, one would imagine a net of individual entitlements similar to a regime of comprehensive citizenship benefits. Contrasted with the German compensatory regime, this would entail quite a different trajectory for a European social state. Thomas Humphrey Marshall's hopes for social citizenship in post-World War II England would resurface on the Community level. All European citizens would be entitled to such benefits, either independent of their means (basic income) or means tested (welfare).[33] Although it might relate to all social groups, such a net would not address all or most

---

31. The BIEN (Basic Income European Network) network of researchers functions as an academic "lobby equivalent" for a general basic income. It spans the Community and is funded by it.

32. Transforming farmers into nature wardens and paying them for this public service (Hrubesch 1987, 47) will not suffice to distinguish farmers from other social groups.

33. For over a decade now, Hauser (1980, 1983, 1987) has been advocating a European welfare policy based on the U.S. experience. He proposes not just a harmonization of European welfare law, but also an AFDC-like scheme of supranational revenue sharing for the Community. It could especially compensate the poorer regions of Europe. For a similar U.S. plea, see Peterson and Rom 1990.

risks, but only the risk of having no income. Within the framework of matrix 1, I would classify it as a partial welfare state approach. Again, a border is hard to draw, and an extension of the net to other risks might not be too unlikely a development.

The EC has achieved its most important gains in labor market policy with such postindustrial topics as gender equality and ecology (Streeck 1991). A guaranteed basic income, if it builds on EC citizenship rather than on labor market attachment, would accord well with the postindustrial perspective.

Going European: Two Supranational Models
(EC 13 and the Social Policy Band)

With the history of legal integration in the United States as precedent (Zweigert 1963; see also the Cappelletti, Secombe, and Weiler series referenced in note 22), the European Commission might develop a Community model, or a uniform code for social security, for implementation by the 12 member states. Such a code, leaving some room for choice at the national level, might seem a sensible approach to European social policy. To many members of the Community, however, such a proposal is not attractive.[34] In contrast to the United States, many Western European countries developed welfare states at the national level some time ago.

Danny Pieters, a Belgian lawyer from Leuven's Catholic University, has given a different spin to a trajectory of this sort. He has proposed that the EC, itself, begin to function as if it were the thirteenth member state of the Community (Pieters 1989b and 1991a, 85ff.): EC 13 would be a social security state. The Community would go beyond coordination and create an autonomous, comprehensive,[35] contribution-based, and unitary European Social Security System (ESSS).[36] It would be aimed primarily at migrant workers. Membership could be optional (migrants could choose to remain in the present national framework of coordination) or mandatory (migrants would be transferred automatically from national systems to ESSS). If ESSS offered benefits on a par with French, German, and British social security, it would already improve upon most EC 12 systems. Should it offer even more benefits than do the three major member states, it would promote intra-

---

34. In 1971, an official initiative within the EC (the Marjolin plan) aimed to supranationalize unemployment insurance. The Commission formally proposed such a program, but it foundered in 1978 because major governmental actors resisted in the Council.

35. That is, it would cover all risks. It should be kept in mind that the migrant workers of the last decade in the EC 12 are highly skilled and well paid. The proposed ESSS would, thus, start European social insurance at the top of the social pyramid. It could offer good insurance contributions.

36. The acronym is mine.

European mobility (Pieters 1991a, 83).[37] Contributions already made by a migrant to a national system would be transferred to ESSS. The system could be subsidized by the EC, as national systems are subsidized by the member states.

ESSS would lift the Community from a fragmented welfare state to the segmented social state plateau. Since the ESSS for migrant workers[38] could become the benchmark for a harmonization of the remaining national social security systems (Langendonck 1991),[39] it could also orient employers and employees toward a European wage bargaining system and point toward a comprehensive European social state.[40] None of this should be expected to occur soon. Nevertheless, EC 13 is useful as an analytical device. It illustrates what it really means to Europeanize Europe through social policy (Henningsen 1989).

The European Social Policy Band (ESPB)[41] is a model that points directly toward going comprehensively European in social policy. It is proposed by Michel Dispersyn (1990) and his collaborators (Dispersyn et al. 1990; see also Pieters 1991a, 87; Pieters, Palm, and Vansteenkiste, 1990), a group of Belgian researchers. They modeled their proposal on the European Monetary System.[42] The ESPB attempts to level up social benefits by providing an automatic instrument of fiscal redistribution. Resources would be transferred from richer to poorer member states without lowering benefits in the richer states. Instead of general revenue sharing, ESPB involves social budget sharing in EC 12.

The ESPB would rely on some uniformly calculated statistical indicators of coverage and benefit levels in each national system of social security. From

---

37. The ESSS would exacerbate intrafirm inequality of remuneration, because two sorts of social protection would coexist in one work setting. Such inequality already exists, however, in border regions.

38. Pieters points out that the system could be extended to the upper grades of white-collar employees of companies operating under a European charter or operating in more than one member state. It could also be opened to any EC citizen who wanted to join. Access might be controlled through collective bargaining. Whichever strategy is chosen, the danger exists that Europe would assume some of the good risks and leave the rest to the national systems.

39. In Germany, introduction of the white-collar insurance scheme (1911) had similar functions.

40. The system would give rise to competitive upgrading between the supranational and the national systems. In Germany, such competition already occurs between the white-collar and blue-collar sick funds.

41. The acronym is mine.

42. Note that Dispersyn, Pieters, and collaborators are all Belgian. Belgium seems to produce most models of integration for the EC, even if it has difficulty doing the same for itself. The European Monetary System stabilizes exchange rates between European currencies. Created formally in March, 1979, it owes its origins to the collapse of the Bretton Woods system. See Padoa-Schioppa in this volume.

these measures, a score would be assigned to each member state, and the EC average could be calculated. This average would serve as the initial norm. Maximal acceptable departure from the norm could be specified, as could a (positive) rate of change in the norm.[43] If a member state lowered its social protection (as measured by these parameters), consultation and action (against social dumping) would be triggered at the EC level. If a member state were substantially below the protection average to begin with, ESPB would intervene and level up protection to some predetermined standard of adequacy. Countries with above-average protection would consult within ESPB on how to upgrade protection in their below-average counterparts. Unlike ESSS, ESPB would operate primarily at the fiscal level. This would expose ESPB to a much higher level of resistance than would confront ESSS.

The ESPB would lead almost directly to a comprehensive European welfare state (cell 4 of matrix 1), though not to a European social state. It is certainly a radical view of Europe's welfare state future. On the other hand, ESPB is also just an analogy to the European Monetary System, which itself is a radical response to transformation of the European economy and of its national monetary systems. If EC 12 can bring its exchange rates into line, why can it not do the same for social policy?

Summary: Europe's Could-Be States of Welfare

I introduced several prototypes of social Europe in matrix 1. Although Europe is the continent on which the comprehensive welfare and social states originated, and although the social state is well entrenched in the north at the national level, a comprehensive version of either type of state will be difficult to realize at the European level.

Expansion of the structural funds or decoupling income maintenance from price supports in agriculture (depending on implementation) would also fit the trajectory of a bifurcated European welfare state (Leibfried 1992a, 236). Supranational authorities would deal exclusively with the poor of Europe, while national programs would continue to serve middle-class social policy and social security for the employed (Schulte 1991c). Such a bifurcation could only be overcome by forceful movement toward a comprehensive welfare state (cell 4 of matrix 1). The opposite bifurcation would occur under ESSS. Although the thirteenth state is meant to be more comprehensive in the long run, it would initially privilege Europe's well-to-do employees.[44] The

---

43. Dispersyn et al. 1990 propose a detailed ESPB model for some areas.

44. Such a growth pattern of social policy would find some precedents in the evolution of the German welfare state. It trickled down from the top: starting from (1) the public servant model of social protection, it was expanded (2) to the blue-collar labor aristocracy, as well as (3) white-

ESPB has little potential for welfare state bifurcation. On the contrary, a goal of such a European budgetary system for all national social policy is to level up social protection within EC 12 through solid policy engineering.

Insofar as these trajectories lead to stronger EC involvement—especially in directives, but also, perhaps, in finance and personnel—they will add welfare state components to the post-1992 Community. Only the path of a thirteenth state would unambiguously lead to a social state. In all other cases, the threshold between welfare and social states would not necessarily be crossed at the Community level. At the national level, these programs would arrive preintegrated by the EC. They might or might not be incorporated into the social state, depending entirely on the member state's legal tradition and political culture.

Prospects for Social Europe: Going Dutch Post-1992?

Economic competition with the United States and Japan is what triggered the 1992 process (Moravcsik 1991). In the long run, it might bring Europe's would-be polity to supranational ideological differentiation vis-à-vis the United States and Japan, giving a truly singular European face to the welfare state and recasting the European compact anew. On its own, the economy cannot drive political integration beyond the 1992 process. According to Tommaso Padoa-Schioppa (1987, 25), "The cement of a political Community is provided by indivisible public goods such as 'defense and security,'" whereas "the cement of an economic Community inevitably lies in the economic benefits it confers upon its members." Is not social security part and parcel of the security element of political union? If so, the Community will not thrive if it is viewed only as a commercial venture. It will have to become an adventure also in communitarian social policy. Otherwise, the present logic of negative integration—removing barriers only—might consume its own base.

Going Dutch in European social policy—integrating markets only and otherwise practicing "to each nation according to its wealth"—damages the indivisible public good of social protection. As integration proceeds, such damages intensify. Eurocrats have sensed this strategic omission in the Single European Act. Since the second half of the 1980s, they have made an issue of a people's Europe. To go Dutch with respect to social policy (includ-

---

collar social security, and then (4) to other employed people before penetrating (in the end) even into (5) the citizen's domain of universal welfare rights. The growth of the English welfare state reverses this order by starting from step 4 and moving upward, downward, and sideways (gender). The Community's initial welfare policies, dating from the 1950s and based on Art. 51 EEC (coordination of migrant workers) and Arts. 123ff. EEC (dealing with the ESF), look more like the English growth pattern.

ing education) would probably, in the long run, erode other features of the Community as well. The EC might be reshaped incrementally in the image of EFTA (the European Free Trade Association), a form of organization that the Community presumably outcompeted with a better model of integration.

Argued from the extremes, diversity in social security in the post-1992 single market may be decreased in either of two ways.

> The economic import of national systems is decreased so much that the differences cease to be relevant factors in intra-Community competition. Then these systems would not hinder integration, since they have been demoted to subsidiary levels—schemes of last resort—which may as well remain a national prerogative. Or . . . the present diversity of national systems is diminished in such a way that the existing relatively high level of protection is harmonized and no longer interferes in the competitive situation between EC member states. (Pieters 1991a, 83)

Nobody seems to propose or to bank on Pieters's first alternative. But not much is being done to implement his second alternative, either. The current social situation, together with the Community's current approach, supports inaction at best and an ongoing, slow process of leveling-down or erosion of the universalist elements of the welfare state.[45] The great challenge, then, is to actively develop the Community's welfare and social state capacities.

The prospects for social Europe depend on the future spillovers of economic integration (Leibfried and Pierson 1991, 21ff.). Such spillovers may increasingly force the EC 12 to face the social consequences of intensified market integration and to invade the national social domains. In the last decade, harmonization of monetary, fiscal, and environmental policies has come to be seen as a logical by-product of the integration process. Some already see social policy progressing on this trajectory (Berghman 1990; Langendonck 1991; Pieters 1991a). The intensifying integration process is bolstered by a leveling down—real or perceived—of social benefits (social dumping). Leveling down has been an issue at the national level for some years and will politicize national policy landscapes even more as mobility in, and especially to, Europe increases.

Also, consider institutional spillover in the division of competency between the Community and its member states. It has been dawning on national governments and parliaments slowly that their ability to absorb social conflict

---

45. This is supported by some of the features of coordination described in detail in Leibfried 1992a. Coordination also enforces the export of many social citizenship benefits (including child allowances and welfare payments, but not so much housing allowances), which tends to freeze or shrink universal benefits first.

through social policy reforms has dwindled. Benefits may not be restricted to national citizens anymore; most benefits may not even be confined to the national territory.[46] If reforms, such as the German initiative to establish an SSI program, are aborted because the majority of benefits will flow not to resident German citizens but rather to EC citizens who have worked temporarily in Germany, have acquired a right to an insufficient pension increment, and now reside somewhere else in the Community, the only alternatives are to move toward a European solution or to stall such national reforms.

But cultural and ideological pressures must also be considered. The EC 12 is not likely to tolerate as much inequality (visible and growing urban poverty, for example) as have such other countries as the United States. Shared traditions (welfare and religion), as well as higher levels of population density and inescapability, point more toward social citizenship than toward condoning a downward spiraling of national citizenship benefits. European citizenship has already become a major issue in defining the "outs" of eastern and southern Europe. The more important it becomes to define who is "in," the more pressing it will be to establish what "in" means. Social citizenship would seem to be an emergent issue in this respect as well.

The possible pathways to a European welfare or social state are, as outlined here, neat and logical trajectories. Real developments in the Community may not be as tidy. Movement will not just be in one direction, but it will combine different approaches or move in several directions at once (disjointed incrementalism). The first two models are the most likely depictions of post-1992 reality. Here, large existing institutions are already under continuing reform pressure, and the field is open for more radical change. In both models, member states, especially those on the periphery, are actors forcing systematic change. Also, strong traditional interest groups (farmers, unions, employers), as well as newer social movements, have joined the struggle.

At the Maastricht summit of December, 1991, the member states decided to achieve monetary union by the end of the 1990s. In so doing, they substantially increased the pressure to expand the redistributive function, and to build the welfare state, of the EC. Indeed, it is difficult to see how such construction can now be avoided. Monetary unification will dissolve the last buffers (such as devaluation, special interest rate policies, capital controls, and differences in factor prices) that permit "deviant" social policy cultures to survive at the

---

46. The conflict over child allowances in Germany is quite telling. EC rules allow EC citizens to claim child allowances in the country of residence, even when children are residents of another EC country. German political debate has focused on the proverbial Portuguese construction worker with three children: the worker moves to Germany, leaving his family in Portugal. By claiming child allowances in Germany, he is said to be able to remit to Portugal as much money as he had earned there as an average construction worker.

national level. A look at U.S. experience (Eichengreen 1990) confirms the
plausibility of a radically increased redistributive potential, and of a singular welfare state (however limited its scope), in Europe at the turn of the
millenium.

REFERENCES

Addison, John T., and Stanley Siebert. 1991. "The Social Charter of the European
    Community: Evolution and Controversies." *Industrial and Labor Relations Re-
    view* 44 (July): 597–625.
Anderson, Jeffrey J. 1991. "Skeptical Reflections on a Europe of Regions: Britain,
    Germany and the ERDF." *Journal of Public Policy* 10:417–47.
Banting, Keith G. 1982. *The Welfare State and Canadian Federalism*. Kingston, Ont.:
    McGill-Queen's University Press.
Bellers, Jürgen. 1984. "Europäische Sozialpolitik." In *Europäische Gemeinschaft:
    Problemfelder-Institutionen-Politik*, ed. Wichard Woyke, 246–53. Vol. 3, *Wörter-
    buch zur Politik*, ed. Dieter Nohlen. Munich: Piper.
Benedictis, Michele de, Fabrizio de Fillipis, and Luca Salvatici. 1990. "Social and
    Economic Consequences of the EC Agricultural Policy." In *Agrarian Policies and
    Agricultural Systems*, ed. Alessandro Bonano, 151–79. Boulder, Colo.: West-
    view Press.
Berghman, Jos. 1990. "European Integration and Social Security." In *EISS Yearbook*
    (European Institute for Social Security), 1–10. Leuven: Acco.
Clever, Peter. 1991. "Die EG auf dem Weg zur politischen Union—Sozialpolitische
    Perspektiven." *Zeitschrift für Sozialhilfe und Sozialgesetzbuch* 29:124–32.
Collins, Doreen. 1975. *The European Communities: The Social Policy of the First
    Phase*. 2 vols. London: Martin Robertson.
Commission of the European Communities. 1985. *Perspective for the Common Agri-
    cultural Policy* (Green Book), COM (85) 333. Luxembourg: Office for Official
    Publications of the European Communities.
Dispersyn, Michel. 1990. "Le Serpent Social Européen." In (European Institute for
    Social Security), *EISS Yearbook* 185–90. Leuven: Acco.
Dispersyn, Michel, Pierre van der Vorst, M. de Falleur, Y. Guillaume, and D.
    Meulders. 1990. "La Construction du Serpent Social Européen." *Revue Belge de
    Sécurité Sociale* 32 (December): 889–978.
Eichengreen, Barry. 1990. "One Money for Europe? Lessons from the U.S. Currency
    Union." *Economic Policy* 10:117–87.
Ermer, Peter, Thomas Schulze, Frank Schulz-Nieswandt, and Werner Sesselmeier.
    1990. *Soziale Politik im EG-Binnenmarkt: Bisherige Entwicklung und zukünftige
    Entwicklungschancen*. Regensburg: Transfer Verlag.
Flora, Peter, ed. 1986f. *Growth to Limits. The Western European Welfare States since
    World War II*. 5 vols. Berlin: Walter de Gruyter.
Franzmeyer, Fritz, and Bernhard Seydel. 1976. *Überstaatlicher Finanzausgleich und
    Europäische Integration*. Bonn: Europa Union Verlag.

Grabitz, Eberhard. 1970. *Europäisches Bürgerrecht zwischen Marktbürgerschaft und Staatsbürgerschaft.* Cologne: Europa Union Verlag.

Hauser, Richard. 1980. "Probleme und Ansatzpunkte einer gemeinsamen Politik zur Bekämpfung der Armut in der Europäischen Gemeinschaft." In *Theorie und Politik der internationalen Wirtschaftsbeziehungen: Hans Möller zum 65. Geburtstag*, ed. Knut Borchardt and Franz Holzheu, 229–51. Stuttgart: Fischer.

Hauser, Richard. 1983. "Problems of Harmonization of Minimum Income Regulations among EC Member Countries." Working Paper no. 118, sfb 3, J. W. Goethe University.

Hauser, Richard. 1987. "Möglichkeiten und Probleme der Sicherung eines Mindesteinkommens in den Mitgliedsländern der Europäischen Gemeinschaft." Working Paper no. 246, sfb 3, J. W. Goethe University.

Heidenheimer, Arnold. 1981. "Education and Social Security Entitlements in Europe and America." In *The Development of Welfare States in Europe and America*, ed. Peter Flora and Arnold J. Heidenheimer, 269–304. New Brunswick, N.J.: Transaction Press.

Henderson, William O. 1939. *The Zollverein.* Cambridge: Cambridge University Press.

Henningsen, Bernd. 1989. "Europäisierung Europas durch eine europäische Sozialpolitik?" In *Europäisierung Europas*, ed. Peter Haugs, 55–80. Baden-Baden: Nomos.

Hoskyns, Catherine. 1986. "Women, European Law and Transnational Politics." *International Journal of the Sociology of Law* 14:299–315.

Hrubesch, Peter. 1987. "30 Jahre EG Agrarmarktsystem Entstehungsgeschichte-Funktionsweise-Ergebnisse." In *Aus Politik und Zeitgeschichte*, B 18/37: 34–47.

Keeton, George W. 1963. "The Zoll Verein and the Common Market." In *English Law and the Common Market*, ed. George W. Keeton and Georg Schwarzenberger, 1–16. London: Stevens and Sons.

Keohane, Robert O., and Stanley Hoffmann. 1991. "Institutional Change in Europe in the 1980s." In *The New European Community: Decision Making and Institutional Change*, ed. Robert O. Keohane and Stanley Hoffmann, 1–39. Boulder, Colo.: Westview Press.

Konegen, Norbert. 1984a. "Europäischer Fonds für Regionale Entwicklung." In *Europäische Gemeinschaft: Problemfelder-Institutionen-Politik*, ed. Wichard Woyke, 315–19. Vol. 3, *Wörterbuch zur Politik*, ed. Dieter Nohlen. Munich: Piper.

Konegen, Norbert. 1984b. "Europäische Regionalpolitik." In *Europäische Gemeinschaft: Problemfelder-Institutionen-Politik*, ed. Wichard Woyke, 234–40. Vol. 3, *Wörterbuch zur Politik*, ed. Dieter Nohlen. Munich: Piper.

Lange, Peter. 1992. "The Politics of the Social Dimension." In *Europolitics: Institutions and Policymaking in the "New" European Community*, ed. Alberta M. Sbragia, 225–56. Washington, D.C.: Brookings Institution.

Langendonck, Jeff van. 1991. "The Role of the Social-Security Systems in the Completion of the European Market." *Acta Hospitalia*, no. 1: 35–57.

Leibfried, Stephan. 1992a. "Towards a European Welfare State? On Integrating Poverty Regimes into the European Community." In *Social Policy in a Changing*

116   Singular Europe

Europe, ed. Zsuzsa Ferge and Jon Eivind Kolberg, 227–59. Frankfurt am Main: Campus Verlag.

Leibfried, Stephan. 1992b. "Welfare State Europe?" In *Status Passages, Institutions and Gatekeeping*, ed. Walter Heinz. Weinheim: Deutscher Studienverlag. In press.

Leibfried, Stephan, and Jutta Allmendinger. 1991. "Regimes of Labor Market Entry and Marginalization—A Comment." Paper presented at the Conference on Poverty and Social Marginality, Paris.

Leibfried, Stephan, and Paul Pierson. 1991. "The Prospects for Social Europe." Working Paper no. 34, Center for European Studies, Harvard University.

Lindberg, Leon N., and Stuart A. Scheingold. 1970. *Europe's Would-Be Polity*. Englewood Cliffs, N.J.: Prentice-Hall.

Maydell, Bernd von. 1989. "Das Recht der Europäischen Gemeinschaften und die Sozialversicherung—Supranationales Sozialversicherungsrecht und Auswirkungen des EG-Rechts auf die nationale Sozialversicherung." *Zeitschrift für die gesamte Staatswissenschaft*, nos. 1–2: 1–28.

Mazey, Sonia. 1988. "European Community Action on Behalf of Women: The Limits of Legislation." *Journal of Common Market Studies* 27 (September): 63–84.

Moravcsik, Andrew. 1991. "Negotiating the Single European Act: National Interests and Conventional Statecraft in the European Community." *International Organization* 45 (Winter): 19–56.

Mosley, Hugh G. 1990. "The Social Dimension of European Integration." *International Labour Review* 129:147–64.

Ogus, Anthony. 1990. "The Federal Republic of Germany as Sozialstaat: A British Perspective." Working Paper no. 3, Department of Law, University of Manchester.

Oppermann, Thomas. 1987. "Europäische Wirtschaftsverfassung nach der Einheitlichen Europäischen Akte." In *Staat und Wirtschaft in der EG: Kolloqium zum 65. Geburtstag von Prof. Dr. Bodo Börner*, ed. Peter Christian Müller-Graff and Manfred Zuleeg, 53–71. Baden-Baden: Nomos.

Padoa-Schioppa, Tommaso, with Michael Emerson. 1987. *Efficiency, Stability, and Equity: A Strategy for the Evolution of the Economic System of the European Community*. Oxford: Oxford University Press.

Peterson, Paul E., and Mark C. Rom. 1990. *Welfare Magnets: A New Case for a National Standard*. Washington, D.C.: Brookings Institution.

Pieters, Danny. 1989a. "Fundamental Social Rights in the Member States of the European Community (E.C.)." In *Law, Social Welfare, Social Development*, 142–45. Frankfurt am Main: Deutscher Verein für öffentliche und private Fürsorge.

Pieters, Danny. 1989b. "Sociale Zekerheid na 1992: Één over Twaalf." Tilburg: Katholieke Universiteit Brabant/Studierichting Social Zekerheidswetenshap. Typescript.

Pieters, Danny. 1990a. "Soziale Grundrechte in den Mitgliedstaaten der EG." In *Soziale Rechte in der EG: Bausteine einer zukünftigen europäischen Sozialunion*, ed. Bernd von Maydell, 21–30. Berlin: E. Schmidt.

Pieters, Danny. 1990b. "Soziale Grundrechte—Rechte auf soziale Leistungen für die Bürger der Europäischen Gemeinschaft." In *Zur sozialen Dimension des EG-*

Binnenmarktes, ed. Claus Reis and Manfred Wienand, 19–31. Frankfurt am Main: Deutscher Verein für öffentliche und private Fürsorge.

Pieters, Danny. 1991a. "Europäisches und nationales Recht der Sozialen Sicherheit—Zukunftsperspektiven." *Zeitschrift für ausländisches und internationales Arbeits- und Sozialrecht*, no. 1: 72–94.

Pieters, Danny. 1991b. "Centralism, Decentralisation and Federalism in Social Security: Towards a Typology." In Pieters 1991c, 277–95.

Pieters, Danny, ed. 1991c. *Social Security in Europe: Miscellanea of the Erasmus-Programme Social Security in the EC*. Antwerp and Brussels: MAKLU Uitgevers/ Bruylandt.

Pieters, Danny, Willy Palm, and Steven Vansteenkiste. 1990. "De Dertiende Staat." *Belgisch Tijdschrift voor Sociale Zekerheid* 32 (December): 861–92.

Plantey, Alain. 1981. *The International Civil Service: Law and Management*. New York: Masson.

Raasch, Sibylle. 1990. "Perspektiven für die Gleichberechtigung der Frau im EG-Binnenmarkt '92." *Kritische Justiz* 23:62–78.

Reich, Charles. 1964. "The New Property." *Yale Law Journal* 73:733–87.

Reich, Norbert. 1988. *Schutzpolitik in der Europäischen Gemeinschaft im Spannungsfeld von Rechtsschutznormen und institutioneller Integration*. Hannover: Hennies und Zinkeisen.

Rieger, Elmar. 1991. "Der Wandel der Landwirtschaft in der Europäischen Gemeinschaft." *Kölner Zeitschrift für Soziologie und Sozialpsychologie*. Forthcoming.

Rosenblatt, Julius. 1988. *The Common Agricultural Policy of the European Community: Principles and Consequences*. Washington, D.C.: International Monetary Fund.

Scharpf, Fritz J. 1988. "The Joint-Decision Trap: Lessons from German Federalism and European Integration." *Public Administration* 66 (Autumn): 239–78.

Schmähl, Winfried. 1989. "Europäischer Binnenmarkt und soziale Sicherung—einige Aufgaben und Fragen aus ökonomischer Sicht." *Zeitschrift für die gesamte Versicherungswirtschaft*, nos. 1–2: 29–50.

Schmähl, Winfried. 1990. "Soziale Sicherung in Deutschland und der EG-Binnenmarkt: Anmerkungen aus ökonomischer Sicht." In *Soziale Sicherung im EG-Binnenmarkt*, ed. Winfried Schmähl, 11–38. Baden-Baden: Nomos.

Schmähl, Winfried. 1992. "Harmonization of Pension Schemes in Europe? A Controversial Issue in the Light of Economics." In *Age, Work and Social Security*, ed. Martin Rein and Anthony Atkinson. London: Macmillan. Forthcoming.

Schmitter-Heisler, Barbara. 1991. "A Comparative Perspective on the Underclass: Questions of Urban Poverty, Race and Citizenship." *Theory and Society* 20:455–83.

Schulte, Bernd. 1990. "'. . . und für den Arbeitnehmer wenig oder nichts?' Sozialpolitik und Sozialrecht in den Europäischen Gemeinschaften." *Kritische Justiz* 23:79–97.

Schulte, Bernd. 1991a. "Abstimmung der Ziele der Politiken des Sozialschutzes in den Mitgliedstaaten der Europäischen Gemeinschaften—Ein weiterer Schritt auf dem Weg zur Sozialgemeinschaft." *Zeitschrift für Sozialhilfe und Sozialgesetzbuch* 30 (June): 281–99.

Schulte, Bernd. 1991b. "Die Folgen der EG-Integration für die wohlfahrtsstaatlichen Regimes." *Zeitschrift für Sozialreform* 37 (September): 548–80.

Schulte, Bernd. 1991c. "Das Recht auf ein Mindesteinkommen in der Europäischen Gemeinschaft—Nationaler Status Quo und supranationale Initiativen." *Sozialer Fortschritt* 40:7–21.

Schulz, Otto. 1991. "Grundsätze, Inhalt und institutionelle Verankerung im EWG-Vertrag." *Sozialer Fortschritt* 40 (June-July): 135–40.

Sieveking, Klaus. 1990. "Bildung im Europäischen Gemeinschaftsrecht." *Kritische Vierteljahresschrift für Gesetzgebung und Rechtswissenschaft* 73:344–73.

Silvia, Stephen J. 1991. "The Social Charter of the European Community: A Defeat for European Labor." *Industrial and Labor Relations Review* 44 (July): 626–43.

Skocpol, Theda, and John Ikenberry. 1983. "The Political Formation of the American Welfare State in Historical and Comparative Perspective." In *The Welfare State, 1883–1983*, ed. Richard F. Thomasson, 87–148. Greenwich, Conn.: JAI Press.

Skowronek, Stephen. 1982. *Building a New American State: The Expansion of National Administrative Capacities, 1877–1920*. Cambridge: Cambridge University Press.

Soysal, Yasemin Nuhoglu. 1991. "Limits of Citizenship: Guestworkers in the Contemporary Nation-State System." Ph.D. diss., Department of Sociology, Stanford University.

Steinmeyer, Heinz-Dietrich. 1990. "Freizügigkeit und soziale Rechte in einem Europa der Bürger." In *Das Europa der Bürger in einer Gemeinschaft ohne Binnengrenzen*, ed. Siegfried Magiera, 63–80. Baden-Baden: Nomos.

Streeck, Wolfgang. 1991. "More Uncertainties: German Unions Facing 1992." *Industrial Relations* 30 (Fall): 317–49.

Witte, Bruno de, ed. 1989. *European Community Law of Education*. Baden-Baden: Nomos.

Zuleeg, Manfred. 1991. "Die Europäische Gemeinschaft auf dem Weg zur Sozialgemeinschaft." *Nachrichtendienst des Deutschen Vereins für öffentliche und private Fürsorge* 71:20–29.

Zweigert, Konrad. 1963. "Grundsatzfragen der europäischen Rechtsangleichung, ihrer Schöpfung und Sicherung." In *Vom deutschen zum Europäischen Recht, Festschrift für Hans Dölle*, ed. Ernst von Caemmerer, Arthur Nikisch, and Konrad Zweigert, 2:401–18. Tübingen: J. C. B. Mohr.

Part 2
A New European Economy?

Introduction to Part 2

William James Adams

Pursuant to the Single European Act, the EC Commission reports periodically on the degree to which Project 1992 has been implemented.[1] Specifically, it describes which issues raised in the white paper have generated formal legislative proposals from the Commission, which of these proposals have been adopted by the Council, and which Council directives have been transposed into national law by which member states. To students of law or politics, these documents feed delectable morsels on the pace and course of formal integration. To students of economics, however, they merely whet the appetite.

Tantalizingly absent from the Commission's tallies are indications of whether and how the new legislation, regulations, and administrative practices have affected market outcomes. Have business enterprises "transposed" the Community's new rules into their market behavior? If so, have they accepted the new order and responded to the exigencies of a pan-European, quasi-competitive market, or have they sought to sterilize Community initiatives, whether or not in collaboration with member states, by devising new ways to reach preexisting equilibria?

To the extent that all member states support the Community's work enthusiastically, that the Community enjoys both the authority and the budget to enforce its new rules, and that violators can be punished painfully for their infringements, institutional innovation is likely to be followed by sympathetic economic response. Needless to say, however, none of these preconditions is satisfied completely. Not infrequently, the European Court of Justice (ECJ) has heard the Commission accuse a member state of failure to fulfill the member's obligations under an EC treaty. Virtually never is the ECJ empowered to impose financial penalties on offending member states. Hardly surprisingly, therefore, the Commission has had to bring some member states

---

1. See, for example, Commission of the European Communities, *Fifth Report of the Commission to the Council and the European Parliament Concerning the Implementation of the White Paper on Completion of the Internal Market*, COM(90) 90 final (Luxembourg: Office for Official Publications of the European Communities, 1990).

back to court for failure to implement a prior ECJ decision.[2] With regard to private behavior, the Commission does have the power to fine those who contravene the Community's rules; even so, it continues to detect business strategies tantamount to a division of the Community's market along national lines.[3] In sum, a priori, the economic impact of Project 1992 must be considered an open question. The chapters in this section are designed to address it.

The impact in question might well differ by size of company. On the one hand, it could be argued that most large industrial enterprises of the Community are already constructed on multinational foundations; completion of the internal market will impinge less on their behavior than on that of their smaller cousins. On the other hand, it could be argued that multinationals are precisely the companies that will benefit most from removal of remaining impediments to trade and establishment.

Alexis Jacquemin and Bo Carlsson discuss the futures of big and small business in the EC.[4] Jacquemin identifies specialization (via shedding of peripheral activities) and horizontal mergers (expansions of primary activity) as two prevalent features of current business strategy. Recalling Adam Smith's dictum that the division of labor is limited by the extent of the market, one might consider such behavior consistent with the proposition that Project 1992 is succeeding in increasing the economic size of European markets. In contrast, Carlsson discusses the vitality and growing importance of small business. Questioning the conventional wisdom, entrenched especially deeply in Europe, that bigger is better, Carlsson argues that technological change has reduced appreciably the efficient scale of operation in many industries, so that the competition arising from market integration will stimulate, not eliminate, small businesses.

The impact of Project 1992 might differ not only by size of company but also by type of industry. After all, industries differ in the degree to which nature itself limits the geographic extent of a market and also in the degree to which, in effect as well as design, Project 1992 dealt with the artificial obstacles to geographic expansion of a market. Many believe that Project 1992 was especially likely to deal with barriers to trade and establishment affecting finance, telecommunications, and transport. The chapters by Gunter Dufey, Reinhard Ellger, and Severin Borenstein focus on recent developments in these sectors.

---

2. See Commission of the European Communities, *Fifth Report of the Commission to the Council and the European Parliament Concerning the Implementation of the White Paper on Completion of the Internal Market*, annex 4.

3. The Commission publishes an annual summary of the Community's antitrust activity. See, for example, Commission of the European Communities, *Nineteenth Report on Competition Policy* (Luxembourg: Office for Official Publications of the European Communities, 1990).

4. See also Frédéric Jenny in this volume.

Ellger describes the prodigious amount of legislation associated with the effort to deregulate the telecommunications sector. In so doing, he provides a rare discussion of how a member state incorporates Community policy into its own rules for an industry.

Dufey reminds us that market developments outside the EC altered European banking well before the rules of Project 1992 took effect. His account might tempt one to ask whether changes in market behavior occasioned changes in market regulations rather than vice versa. In either event, Dufey also points to segments of the banking market where Project 1992 did affect market outcomes.

Finally, Borenstein suggests that a paucity of infrastructure (in the form of airports and air traffic-control facilities) constitutes the principal obstacle to increased competition in European markets for air transport services. Neither Project 1992 nor other Community-level legislation of the period fostered expansion of such infrastructure. As a result, even if the battle to deregulate and privatize is won, competition is unlikely to increase and market outcomes are unlikely to change dramatically.

Corporate Strategy and Competition Policy in the Post-1992 Single Market

Alexis Jacquemin

The challenges and opportunities associated with the single internal market affect business enterprises most of all. Indeed, over the last few years, the workings of the European economies have come to depend more and more on company strategies linked to anticipation of the post-1992 single market.

The name of the game is to cooperate with one's competitors over common components, yet maintain keen competition at the final product stage; to erect credible barriers against new players likely to enter the market; to merge in order to control products likely to act as substitutes for one's own activity or to speed up the learning process; to modify one's bargaining power vis-à-vis suppliers and purchasers or to increase the cost of inputs for rivals by means of long-term contracts or control of upstream operations; and to influence the balance of forces by making strategic moves and anticipating change. Viewed from this angle, competition is not based on a series of simultaneous interactions between passive agents who consider comparative advantages, the structures of markets, and the behavior of others as givens. It is a sequential game in which the application of new forms of organization, the opening up of new markets, and the introduction of new products and production methods continually undermine the possible equilibria and modify the rules of the game (Jacquemin 1987; Stiglitz and Matnewson 1986).

Thus, although Project 1992 will contribute to static and dynamic efficiency (Baldwin 1989; Emerson et al. 1989), spontaneous market forces are unlikely to achieve Pareto-optimality in the post-1992 European Community: economic activities in the EC will still be affected by nonconvexities in production, extensive product differentiation, incomplete information, and various forms of oligopolistic behavior. Ultimately, such proximate sources of imperfect competition result from exogenous characteristics of the demand and cost functions, as well as from the strategies adopted by various private and public actors.

In this chapter, I will first examine the strategies adopted by large corporations, including cooperative agreements, mergers, and acquisitions, and then analyze the policies adopted by the European Community to oversee such strategies.

Internal and External Corporate Strategies

In 1989, the staff of the European Commission surveyed European industrialists concerning the impact of 1992 on their restructuring plans. The survey revealed that the internal market's effect is clearest in the area of product adaptation and restructuring of production plants (see table 1). It also revealed considerable differences in answers from one member state to another. Despite these differences, however, the strategies of large European corporations display two main tendencies: a trimming of product lines, coupled with a broadening of geographical coverage; and an increasing role for external growth through cooperation, mergers, and acquisitions.

During the past few years, many large corporations have attempted to increase their brand strength and to extend their geographic reach. On the product side, the strategy is to concentrate on the main product lines and withdraw from other activities.

This specialization is understandable in the light of economic studies showing that profitability is far greater in a firm's main activity than in its other activities. No wonder that, in the agriculture and food industry, BSN progressively abandoned other activities before establishing itself in Italy and Spain in the mineral water business (it was the leader for this type of product in France). Ferruzzi, the leading Italian sugar manufacturer, extended its empire to other member states (France, Germany, and the United Kingdom); it is pursuing the same kind of strategy for all starch products. In other industries, corporations such as Volvo, Unilever, and Philips are trying to reinforce their specialization in the activities in which they are best and to dispose of assets related to activities in which their competitive position is weak.

More generally, large firms are transforming themselves into pan-European operations. The convergence of consumption patterns and technological developments combine with more flexible and less costly transportation and distribution to compel firms to devise transnational strategies. In many cases, corporations are concentrating their production of particular products in a smaller number of locations. For example, in 1973, Unilever ran nine production units for detergents in nine different countries of the EC. In 1989, there were just four facilities left (one each in Italy, Portugal, Germany, and the United Kingdom). Although production volume did not increase, productivity rose sharply (over 200 percent) between 1978 and 1987. Needless to say, this type of business behavior does not generalize to all activities. Some products are still characterized by highly divergent national prefer-

TABLE 1. Influence of the Completion of the Internal Market on the Strategies of Industrial Firms (in percentages of firms polled)

Area Affected	Belgium[a]	Denmark	Spain[a]	France	Italy[b]	Netherlands	Portugal[b]	United Kingdom	All EC Members
Production Plant									
Effect	50	82	25	73	62	36	52	43	61
No answer	1	3	6	14	—	3	—	10	6
Products									
Effect	70	64	61	77	55	45	18	66	63
No answer	1	3	8	—	—	5	—	7	3
Distribution									
Effect	57	64	53	58	53	42	28	53	56
No answer	3	0	10	—	—	6	—	10	5
R&D									
Effect	53	50	56	73	49	36	18	61	55
No answer	5	6	9	—	—	3	—	7	4

[a]Due to differences in question wording, results for Belgium and Spain are not comparable to results for other countries.
[b]In the results for Italy and Portugal, nonrespondents were eliminated from the sample and the percentages were calculated on the basis of only those firms that replied.

ences, requiring a different approach for each national market. In such cases, enterprises will prefer to grant their national subsidiaries greater autonomy to adopt strategies with a national emphasis (Buigues, Ilzkovitz, and Lebrun 1990).

Concerning marketing and distribution, the example of Colgate-Palmolive is revealing. Until 1988, this American multinational managed each national market independently. Colgate-Palmolive's subsidiary in each member state was vertically integrated and self-sufficient, and distribution and marketing were independent for each national market. In September, 1988, "in order to be better prepared for 1992," the group announced the creation of a board of management in Brussels for all European operations.

Minnesota Mining and Manufacturing (3M) provides a somewhat different example of the same phenomenon. It restructured its European production long ago (one or two factories for all of Europe). Thus, the current phase of European integration offered it few possibilities for realizing further economies of scale in production. On the other hand, the company set up a pan-European team charged with reevaluating the structure of its distribution network. The aim is to replace existing national networks with an integrated European network.

Some European manufacturers are already applying a global marketing strategy at the European level. This is true, for example, of the Italian confectionery company Ferrero, which sells its products (Nutella, Tic Tac) all over Europe in the same way. L'Oréal adopts the same approach for certain of its hair care products in all Community markets. Nevertheless, the brand images of identical products may also differ substantially depending on the member state: Barilla noodles are considered of high quality in certain markets and of average quality in others. Advertising campaigns and sales strategies must, therefore, differ depending on the market (Buigues, Ilzkovitz, and Lebrun 1990).

The current popularity of privatization is inducing strategic adjustments to the post-1992 environment in Europe's public corporations (past and present) as well. In countries such as France and Italy, the state sector still produces a large fraction of GNP. In 1988, public enterprises accounted for close to 12 percent of value added in the EC. But various factors, such as national budgetary constraints and the need to participate fully in the wave of transnational mergers, acquisitions, and joint ventures, have favored partial or total privatization.[1]

---

1. Note that privatization is not a prerequisite for mergers and joint ventures. There is a growing number of cross-shareholdings between public and private enterprises. A well-known example, which led to important restructuring, is the share exchange between Renault and Volvo. In this context, it is also useful to note that a recent directive of the EC Commission requires fuller disclosure of financial dealings between governments and state-owned manufacturing enterprises. The intention is to identify possible sources of subsidy, such as cheap loans.

A complementary move concerning foreign direct investments is also expected. The single market will be an integrated system based on trans-European networks in transportation, transmission of information, transfer of technologies, and norms and standards. Non-EC firms will then have a growing interest in being located within the system. This suggests a tendency for complementing (or replacing) exports by direct investments (even in the absence of tariff barriers) because such direct investments allow a more complete exploitation of the benefits of the system; furthermore, the specificity and sunk cost character of these investments create a more irreversible commitment to the European market than do exports (Jacquemin 1989). Recent evidence confirms this prediction. For example, as a destination for U.S. manufacturing exports, the EC has been relatively stable; but as a destination for U.S. direct investment, the EC has grown rapidly in relative importance. In 1988, the Community received roughly 50 percent of foreign U.S. operations. In the case of Japan, the proportion of exports going to the Community has been growing sharply; recently, however, the relatively low proportion of Japanese industrial direct investment located in the EC (10 percent in 1988) has also begun to increase rapidly—and become more sophisticated in the process.

Cooperative agreements, mergers, and acquisitions play a growing role in the restructuring attributable to increased competition. The number of cooperative agreements, especially in the form of joint ventures, has increased importantly in recent years (see table 2). These joint ventures are concentrated in industries characterized by important research activities, and partners from nonmember countries (mainly the United States and Japan) are especially prized.

Coalitions permit the combination of skills and resources in ways that may allow firms to reconfigure and redefine their activities. According to various business surveys (Camagni 1988; Lemettre 1990), cooperative behavior can accelerate entry into new markets while reducing the associated risk. On the one hand, the speed with which firms can deploy resources and enter new markets affects their ability to develop first-mover advantages; on the other hand, joint actions permit risk spreading (that is, sharing the costs and benefits of a project among a number of firms) and risk pooling (that is, pursuing multiple independent projects).

Furthermore, the pooling of various complementary resources can provide financial capital on advantageous terms (if capital markets are imperfect), spread the high fixed and generally sunk costs of development, and produce synergy by combining research information, technological and marketing know-how, or the like.

Finally, a proliferation of strategic alliances among firms of different nationalities reduces the likelihood of protectionism—not only because it heightens the degree of global interdependence but also because it compli-

TABLE 2. Number of Joint Ventures in the EC: Manufacturing and Construction

Sector	National[a]				Community[b]				International[c]				Total			
	1986–87	1987–88	1988–89	1989–90	1986–87	1987–88	1988–89	1989–90	1986–87	1987–88	1988–89	1989–90	1986–87	1987–88	1988–89	1989–90
Food	—	6	4	5	1	3	2	2	4	1	3	4	5	10	9	11
Chem.	3	7	8	12	1	5	9	9	10	12	11	16	14	24	28	37
Elec.	4	8	8	2	3	5	7	8	14	7	14	13	21	20	29	23
Mech.	9	4	6	5	—	—	2	3	8	3	2	4	17	7	10	12
Comp.	1	2	—	0	1	1	2	0	3	2	3	0	5	5	5	0
Meta.	1	2	9	6	1	6	3	6	1	2	3	4	3	10	15	16
Trans.	1	1	4	5	3	4	2	12	—	1	1	5	4	6	7	22
Pap.	3	7	4	3	1	1	5	6	2	1	—	5	6	9	9	14
Extra.	—	3	2	1	1	1	—	0	—	1	—	0	1	5	2	1
Text.	—	—	3	0	—	2	—	2	—	1	—	2	—	3	3	4
Cons.	3	1	4	2	2	2	3	2	—	3	—	1	5	6	7	5
Other	4	4	4	0	2	1	1	5	3	1	—	6	9	6	5	11
Total	29	45	56	41	16	31	36	55	45	35	37	60	90	111	129	156

Source: Commission of the European Communities, *Twentieth Report on Competition Policy* (Luxembourg: Office for Official Publications of the European Communities, 1991).

Note:

Food:	Food and drink	Trans.:	Vehicles and transport equipment
Chem.:	Chemicals, fibers, glass, ceramic wares, rubber	Pap.:	Wood, furniture, and paper (including printing and publishing)
Elec.:	Electrical and electronic engineering, office machinery	Extra.:	Extractive industries
Mech.:	Mechanical and instrument engineering, machine tools	Text.:	Textiles, clothing, leather, and footwear
Comp.:	Computers and data-processing equipment	Cons.:	Construction
Meta.:	Production and preliminary processing of metals, metal goods	Other:	Other manufacturing industry

[a]All firms from the same member state.

[b]Firms from different member states.

[c]Some firms from inside, others from outside, the EC; effects inside the EC.

cates identification of national and European origin (for example, in terms of local content). Despite their virtues, however, cooperative agreements are often fragile and unstable, especially in Europe. Confronted with various difficulties, they generally lead to early breakups, buyouts, or mergers.

Partial cooperation, especially cooperation limited to R&D, is particularly difficult, given that the results of the joint efforts are not easily incorporated and that the speed of incorporation will vary from one firm to another. Full exploitation of the results of cooperative research often requires cooperation in manufacturing and marketing. Development of first-mover advantages in research requires an ability quickly to bring new products and techniques to the market where the greatest potential payoffs result. Limiting cooperation to pure R&D, or to the so-called precompetitive level, could then deter the emergence of socially desirable agreements. On the other hand, cooperation between competitors, especially between market leaders, can induce defensive attitudes, price control, and protectionism.

The European computer industry illustrates these problems well. Today, the three largest manufacturers (Olivetti, Bull, and Siemens-Nixdorf) are all losing money. The immediate cause is heavy pressure on profitability due to the falling cost of basic technology and greatly increased competition. But the fundamental problem has been the inability of the three to overcome the limits of small national markets, and hence the diseconomies of small scale; the three have also followed a narrow, "national champion" approach that has hampered European collaboration and cooperation. Hopes of establishing pan-European companies capable of competing with the dominant U.S. and Japanese groups evaporated with Fujitsu's purchase of Britain's ICL. One of the few remaining options is to join one of the world's new groupings of computer companies, in which firms work together in some areas but compete in others. This is what U.S. and Japanese companies have been doing for some time and what European companies are doing today (as evidenced by the recent agreement between IBM and Bull).

Mergers and acquisitions are also important means of restructuring. They have been occurring with increasing frequency recently in Europe: in telecommunications, CGE has acquired ITT's European operations for $1.5 billion, and, in cars, Volkswagen has acquired 75 percent of Seat for $0.7 billion; in the United Kingdom, Thomson has acquired EMI's leisure electronics business. These acquisitions, in the form of asset mergers, occurred in a high-volume environment, in which economies of scale and capacity utilization rates can be important and in which fragmented national markets breed inefficiency. This is especially true of industries supplying the public sector, in which the number of European producers is very high by comparison with the United States. For example, there are 12 producers of boilers for electric power plants in the EC against only 6 in the United States; there are 10 producers of turbine generators in the EC compared with 2 in the United States; and there are 16 makers of electric locomotives in the EC but just 2 in the United States. The opening up of government and public utility procurement should eventually lead to mergers in these industries also. In the railway equipment industries, mergers are already under way. After buying up the railway equipment business of Jeumont-Schneider, for example, Alsthom has acquired a majority stake in ACEC, a firm with railway equipment and energy interests.

More generally, there has been an impressive wave of mergers and acquisitions involving the EC's top 1,000 firms (see table 3). For a long time, these mergers had been mainly horizontal, with purely national operations in the majority. These often embodied efforts to strengthen the positions of national champions. In recent years, however, the level and percentage of cross-border European transactions have been increasing. There has also been a large number of operations involving firms from outside the EC; more specifically, in the industrial sector, mergers, acquisitions, and joint ventures were initiated by U.S. purchasers in a third of the cases.

Mergers and takeovers offer one possible route to efficient restructuring, especially in sectors characterized by important economies of scale, scope, and learning. The corresponding reallocation of capital among firms might generate important gains in three distinct ways: an increase in industry output, a new distribution of output among firms in favor of the most efficient ones, and a reallocation of productive assets (physical capital, patents, management skills, and so forth) in favor of the best users.

In fact, confirming the tendency mentioned earlier, EC companies have consolidated by focusing on core activities instead of following the U.S. mode of conglomerate operations and diversification into new business. This is reflected in the high proportion of mergers between companies in the same sector (see table 4). By purchasing local competitors or by undertaking cross-border acquisitions, firms build upon their existing expertise and increase their market shares.

However, a strong caveat is required. Given the frequent failure of horizontal mergers and conglomerate diversifications, we should mistrust amalgamations based exclusively on financial or personal links. These do not lead to any genuine integration or overall strategy. Some mergers ultimately produce combinations with no internal coherence. They can represent a desperate attempt at survival on the part of an ailing company unable to make any new investments. Studies by management consultants come to similar conclusions.

Thus Coley and Reinton (1988) look at U.S. and British companies on the *Fortune* 250 and *Financial Times* 500 lists that had entered new markets in the past via acquisitions. They conclude that only 23 percent of the 116 firms

TABLE 3. Number of Mergers and Acquisitions of Majority Holdings in the EC: Manufacturing and Construction

Sector	National[a] 1986–87	1987–88	1988–89	1989–90	Community[b] 1986–87	1987–88	1988–89	1989–90	International[c] 1986–87	1987–88	1988–89	1989–90	Total 1986–87	1987–88	1988–89	1989–90
Food	39	25	35	41	11	18	27	44	2	8	14	17	52	51	76	102
Chem.	38	32	37	38	27	38	56	75	6	15	14	35	71	85	107	148
Elec.	33	25	23	20	6	4	18	16	2	7	8	10	41	36	49	46
Mech.	21	24	31	25	8	5	17	13	2	9	7	14	31	38	55	52
Comp.	2	2	3	1	—	1	—	1	—	—	1	0	2	3	4	2
Meta.	15	28	16	29	4	9	13	28	—	3	6	7	19	40	35	64
Trans.	15	3	7	11	6	9	6	13	—	3	1	8	21	15	14	32
Pap.	17	24	32	28	7	6	26	30	1	4	7	21	25	34	61	79
Extra.	8	9	11	10	1	2	5	8	—	1	3	1	9	12	19	19
Text.	4	11	11	4	2	2	7	8	—	1	2	1	6	14	20	13
Cons.	13	21	20	19	3	12	19	17	3	—	—	3	19	33	39	39
Other	6	10	7	15	—	5	3	4	1	7	3	7	7	22	13	26
Total	211	214	233	241	75	111	197	257	17	58	62	124	303	383	492	622

Source: See table 2.

Note: See table 2.

[a] All firms from the same member state.

[b] Firms from different member states.

[c] Some firms from inside, others from outside, the EC; effects inside the EC.

TABLE 4. Merger Targets by Sector of Bidder (in percentages of total transactions of target industry)

Target Industry	Bidder Industry							
	Energy	Engineering	Manufacturing	Chemicals	Construction	Distribution	Transportation	Finance
Energy	89	1	0	1	1	0	1	6
Engineering/autos	1	65	1	4	1	0	0	21
Manufacturing, other	0	1	62	1	1	1	0	33
Chemicals/minerals	4	2	2	56	0	0	0	35
Construction	1	10	0	1	54	0	0	35
Distribution	3	2	5	2	0	57	0	29
Transportation/communications	0	2	4	0	0	0	75	17
Finance	0	3	4	1	1	1	1	87

Source: Morgan Stanley, Acquisitions Monthly, March 1991.

analyzed were able to recover the cost of their capital or, better still, the funds invested in the acquisition program. It also appears that the greater the degree of diversification, the smaller the likelihood of success. For horizontal mergers in which the acquired firm is not large, however, the success rate is around 45 percent. The main reasons for failure appear to be too high a price paid for the acquisition, overestimation of the potential of the acquired business in terms of synergies and market position, and inadequate management of the process of integration after the acquisition. Concerning shareholders, it appears that there is a striking contrast between ex-ante event studies of the potential gains from corporate mergers and ex-post evaluations of the effective results. Mueller (1989) concludes that, prior to merger, the shares of an acquiring firm tend to outperform the market. At the time of the announcement, there is little change in the acquiring firm's share price. The post-acquisition performance of acquiring company share prices is below the corresponding premerger performance and, in some studies, below that of the market. This postmerger performance matches the constant or declining performance of the acquired units, as measured by profitability, market share, or productivity. This pattern appears to be characteristic of mergers in the United States over the last 60 years, and probably over the last century. It also appears characteristic of mergers in Europe and Japan. Hence, despite their sometime utility, mergers are far from being a panacea for a lack of competitiveness.

Finally, by permitting an integrated use of previously independent productive assets and facilitating collusion between fewer independent firms, mergers and acquisitions are also a way of acquiring unilateral or shared market power (Adams and Brock 1986).

Concentration, Cooperation, and European Competition Policy

The expected welfare effects of corporate strategies anticipating the single market are ambiguous. On the one hand, these strategies entail healthy restructuring and rationalization, leading to true competitive advantages for Europe that are compatible with increased actual and potential competition in product and capital markets. On the other hand, whether or not by design, through various forms of concentration and cooperative behavior, such strategies can permit powerful incumbents to maintain control of industry dynamics after 1992. In this respect, two EC policies, competition policy and industrial policy (including technology policy), are likely to play important roles in determining which effect prevails.

Competition policy could play a privileged role, given that it is the most impersonal and least discriminatory means of exercising social control over an economy. As the Economic Council of Canada (1969) stated, "Where competition is such as to promote the efficient use of manpower, capital and natural resources, it obviates or lessens the need for other forms of control such as more or less detailed public regulation or public ownership of industry."

Today, there is a broad consensus in Europe that market competition exerts a positive influence on social welfare. Such influence justifies an effective competition policy. Nevertheless, citing various types of "market failures," most legislation tolerates some behavior restricting competition, even when the restriction is not minor in nature. The more weight that is given to such an "efficiency defense" or, more broadly, to the "public interest criterion," the larger is the discretionary power of the antitrust authorities, and the greater is the danger of confusion between competition policy and industrial policy. It is in this context that I shall briefly examine the policy adopted by the EC with respect to cooperative agreements in R&D and to mergers and acquisitions (see also George and Jacquemin 1990; Jenny in this volume).

Article 85 of the Treaty of Rome contains a broad prohibition of explicit and tacit collusion. In contrast to section 1 of the Sherman Act, however, Article 85 also contains an exemption from this prohibition for collusive behavior generating sufficiently beneficial effects. An important illustration is cooperation qualifying for the block exemption on R&D agreements, which came into force in March, 1985.[2] To appreciate its content, it is necessary to examine cooperative R&D in some depth.

The main argument for permitting cooperative research is based on a problem of market failure associated with appropriability of the benefits of R&D. The crux of the argument is that the amount of research performed by private firms and the diffusion of the knowledge generated by them may be socially inefficient over a broad range of market structures, including competition. The reason is simple. On the one hand, a firm will conduct R&D only if it can appropriate a sufficient amount of the benefits; such appropriation requires limited diffusion of R&D output. On the other hand, nearly perfect appropriability impedes socially costless spillovers of R&D results to other firms (Arrow 1962). Cooperative R&D can then be viewed as a means of internalizing the externalities created by significant R&D spillovers while providing a more efficient sharing of information among firms.

Katz (1986) and d'Aspremont and Jacquemin (1988) have established conditions under which a cooperative agreement could raise social welfare through its effects on the equilibrium level of R&D and the cost of achieving a given R&D level. In the presence of sufficient spillovers of R&D benefits,

---

2. Commission Regulation (EEC) no. 418/85 of 19 December 1984, OJ No. L 53/5 (February 22, 1985).

firms cooperating in R&D but not in output spend more on R&D than do noncooperative firms; they also produce more output, arriving closer, thereby, to the socially optimal level. Concerning the collection and sharing of information in research consortia, Vives (1990) suggests, on the basis of a simple model, that information pooling creates competitive advantages and that active promotion by government of information collection and dissemination can be socially valuable.

Although cooperative R&D has potential advantages from society's standpoint, it can also lead to a socially harmful reduction of competition (Jacquemin 1988). Even if it is feasible to limit agreements solely to R&D, thereby excluding coordination at the level of the final product, cooperative R&D could permit a dominant firm to avoid competition through innovation, by co-opting innovative rivals and controlling the innovation race. Cooperative R&D might also create barriers to entry downstream, and foreclose firms not party to the agreement from some segment of the market. Furthermore, coordinating the R&D process to avoid duplication can reduce initiative and lead to inflexible or dead-end research when multiple, imperfectly correlated research strategies might have been selected by noncooperating firms.

The text of Regulation 418/85 expresses a compromise between cooperation and competition in research. It covers not only joint R&D but also joint exploitation of the results of that R&D.[3] Underpinning the regulation is the belief that cooperation in R&D should not always be limited to R&D, narrowly defined: joint exploitation of the results may be needed to stabilize an agreement and to solve the appropriability problem. Moreover the regulation gives priority to basic research and tends to secure an efficient sharing of information. Finally, it rejects arrangements conducive to market monopolization.

After reviewing EC policy toward cooperative R&D, Adams concludes that, despite the impression left by Henkel/Colgate[4] and VW/Man,[5] and by the texts of relevant regulations and notices, "careful examination of EC practices does not reveal wanton tolerance of cooperation" (1991, 248). Adams also suggests that "moderately kindly antitrust treatment of cooperative research may not suffice to stimulate research appreciably" (241). This raises the issue of industrial policy—an issue I shall now examine briefly.

No article in the Treaty of Rome deals explicitly with mergers and acquisitions. This explains why the Commission proposed, as far back as

---

3. Art. 1(2)(d) specifies that "exploitation of the results" means the manufacture of the joint venture product or the licensing of intellectual property rights to third parties, but joint marketing is not covered.

4. Commission Decision no. 72/41/EEC, JO No. L 14/14 (January 18, 1972).

5. Commission Decision no. 83/668/EEC, OJ No. L 376/1 (December 31, 1983).

1973, a specific regulation for merger control. In the 1992 perspective, with its wave of mergers and takeovers, the urgency of this regulation has increased.

Finally adopted in December 1989, and now in force, the merger regulation is founded upon two main principles.[6] First, a regime of premerger notification is applicable to mergers of truly EC dimension (combined worldwide sales exceeding ECU 5 billion). Second, a merger of Community dimension must be vetted purely on the basis of its effect on competition (i.e., on creation and enlargement of dominant market positions); an "efficiency defense" is not available.

Let us examine this second principle more closely; it will impinge decisively on the post-1992 relationship between the competition and industrial policies of Europe. As I have suggested, some efficiency gains can be expected from mergers, especially in the context of the restructuring required to achieve the internal market: static and dynamic scale economies as well as the discipline imposed by a "market for corporate control" can increase producers' and consumers' surplus. On the other hand, the empirical evidence does not justify a general presumption that mergers improve the productivity of business assets. Furthermore, the negative effects of an increase in monopoly power must be taken into account.

Despite the complexity inhering in such analyses and trade-offs, the regulation that came into force on September 21, 1990, adopts a straightforward position: it leaves no room for the Commission to authorize an anticompetitive merger simply because there is some other public benefit to be gained. Contrary to what has been argued by some commentators (e.g., Hölzler 1990), there is no ambiguity in the text; on the contrary, the European merger control system is probably the least ambiguous of all existing regulations in this domain, including those of the United States, Canada, the United Kingdom, and Germany.

In fact, the nearly final drafts of the regulation did contain an "efficiency defense." For example, provisionally, recital 16 had stated that "authorization should be available in respect of concentrations which, although they impede effective competition, contribute to the attainment of the basic objectives of the Treaty in such a way that, on balance, their economic benefits prevail over the damage they cause to competition." This language does not appear in the regulation as adopted. Similarly, in Article 2 of the draft regulation, we read that "concentrations which create or strengthen a position as a result of which the maintenance or development of effective competition is impeded in the

---

6. Council Regulation (EEC) no. 4064/89 of 21 December 1989, OJ No. L 395/1 (December 30, 1989).

common market or in a substantial part thereof shall be declared incompatible with the common market unless authorized on the ground that their contribution to improving production and distribution, to promoting technical or economic progress or to improving the competitive structure within the common market outweighs the damage to competition."

As adopted, the regulation contains no such language. What is left is a reference to technical and economic progress in Article 2, paragraph 1. Among the criteria for determining whether a merger creates or strengthens a dominant position is "the development of technical and economic progress provided that it is to the consumers' advantage and does not form an obstacle to competition." This wording confirms that the regulation contains no "efficiency defense" at all, and that effective competition is the only reference. Indeed, the criterion of technical and economic progress can be used only if it is perfectly compatible with effective competition and consumers' interests. Therefore, it is difficult to see how an operation that creates or reinforces a dominant position (by definition affecting competition) could be accepted *even if* its negative anticompetitive effects are outweighed by its positive effects on economic progress. Although producers' surplus and consumers' surplus should receive equal weights when calculating the effects of a merger on economic welfare, the wording of the regulation also implies that some sacrifice of consumers' surplus for the sake of higher profits is not accepted.

During the first year it held the power to vet large takeovers, the Commission approved all 52 of the mergers it considered (in 5 of these, it attached conditions demanding divestments or restructuring). Recently, however, it actually blocked a takeover. It did so in the acquisition of de Havilland, a Canadian subsidiary of Boeing, by Aérospatiale of France and Alenia of Italy. The Commission argued mainly that the merger would have given de Havilland and ATR (the Franco-Italian joint venture) 50 percent of the world market and 67 percent of the EC market for commuter aircraft with 20 to 70 seats. This would have created a dominant position, affecting even the largest producers (such as British Aerospace and Fokker), with no competition from the United States or Japan. Whatever its specific merits and problems (especially the definition of the relevant market), it can be argued that this first negative decision by the Commission is important: even in a "special" sector such as aerospace, the Commission stuck to the principle that mergers and takeovers should be judged purely on competitive grounds.

Of course, there will always be dangers of surreptitious compromises in the application of the regulation, but the main message carried by the new law is that the goal of preserving a free market system in the post-1992 era remains the central concern of European antitrust authorities.

This leads us to consider briefly the conception and the role of a European industrial policy. Until the 1970s, European industrial policy, insofar as it existed at all, complemented competition policy in favoring the realization of an integrated market. In most cases, the actions of the Commission were "counterinterventionist" in the sense that they were designed to prevent excessive industrial policy-making by the member states.

More recently, there has been a debate within the Community about the possible role of a more deliberate strategy. One approach leads to picking winners and implementing various forms of protectionism. Another is to provide the right integrated business environment around, and adequate balance between, the following key elements.

—Lay down stable and long-term conditions for an efficiently functioning market economy by ensuring high levels of educational attainment and social cohesion to complement the competitive market environment.
—Provide the main catalysts for structural adjustment. In this respect, completion of the internal market plays a strategic role. The principles on which the internal market program is based (harmonization of the essentials, mutual recognition of national policies for the rest) also provide optimal opportunities for industrial development.
—Develop instruments to accelerate structural adjustment and to enhance competitiveness.

Concerning this last element, the Commission has made a clear choice in its communication to the Council and to the European Parliament (*Industrial Policy in an Open and Competitive Environment*, COM(90) 556 final, Luxembourg: Office for Official Publications of the European Communities, 1990). The European authorities have officially decided to concentrate on the creation of a supportive business environment. Four measures are emphasized.

—Strengthening the size and cooperative nature of precompetitive research efforts. If the efforts of public authorities are to bear fruit, firms must remedy the low level of their own investments in technological research, development, and innovation. The creation of an appropriate fiscal environment would be helpful here.
—Promoting an active innovation policy, based on the rapid transfer of know-how from basic research through industrial application by ensuring that small- and medium-sized enterprises in particular have access to this know-how and the ability to make best use of it. This policy should, as a result, focus on the circulation of information, including that from abroad.

—Recognizing the positive effects on demand that can flow from introducing high product standards, from implementing technologically advanced trans-European networks, and from opening public procurement to the most sophisticated technologies.

—Strengthening training, in particular through specialized centers of higher education.

Despite the pressures exercised by some "champions" in "strategic" sectors, this choice has been supported by a large segment of the European business community. In a recent report (September 16, 1991), from the European Round Table of Industrialists, grouping the representatives of the most important European corporations, it is stated that "European business views industrial policy as a set of measures designed to ensure that industry has the environment it requires to develop in an orderly fashion in the face of competition. The central aspect of this environment must be an open market based on free and vigorous competition, with a minimum of government interferences. If government intervention cannot yet be abolished, business demands that it be judged on a European scale and controlled by Community authorities."[7]

Although markets often work well, they can also be affected by a range of "market failures," such as externalities and imperfect information, arising from problems of coordination between highly interdependent economic agents and nations. This suggests important roles for a European industrial policy that is not protectionist but, nevertheless, goes further than opening up markets: they are the roles of arbiter, referee, and coordinator. This is the basis of the EC's science and technology policy, an essential part of industrial policy. A well-known example is ESPRIT, a joint effort of the Community and the private sector in the domain of information technology (microelectronics, information processing, software, and so forth). The amount of money spent has been fairly modest (most in basic R&D); much effort has been expended in promoting precompetitive alliances among European firms and in adopting standards that will help induce an efficient division of labor within the Community.

One must conclude, however, that, to date, the Commission has stimulated restructuring more successfully at the national than at the European level, even though the latter was (and remains) the more important of the two.

---

7. The report adds that "European businessmen see a close and friendly transatlantic partnership as the best guarantee for political and economic freedom throughout the world. They hope that Japan will take its place as a member of the same partnership, once a condition of mutual trust has been established."

Conclusion

Anticipating completion of the internal market, European firms are implementing strategies intended to create or consolidate their competitive advantages after 1992. They have improved their core competencies, their geographic diversification, their R&D capacity, and their human capital. They have done so through internal restructuring, selloffs, acquisitions, and alliances. Many of these corporate strategies are leading to structural efficiency gains that are sustainable even in an economic slowdown.

Nevertheless, alliances, mergers, and acquisitions can also lead to the creation of dominant positions, barriers to the entry of new firms, market sharing, predatory pricing, and disguised forms of protectionism. These activities are often transnational, but they can also involve national competitors attempting to protect their domestic positions and exercise their market power internationally. This leads to market failures at a supranational level, with national governments being tempted to ignore the costs imposed on other countries. The frequency of such situations justifies a European policy that regulates important transnational operations, prevents strategic national actions that lead to an international Prisoner's Dilemma, and takes full account of the problems characterizing many second-best solutions.

In fact, European authorities have followed this road in the case of cooperation and mergers. On the one hand, they have obtained delegation of national regulatory powers; in a context of incomplete information, such a transfer of power is desirable given the requirements of coordination and credibility (Gatsios and Seabright 1989). On the other hand, the adopted regulations, although far from perfect, have avoided the dangers of a rigid approach: they seem well adapted to implementing a pragmatic competition policy that is clearly distinct from industrial policy. Despite its limited power and resources relative to national governments, the Commission has also been able to implement a distinctive industrial policy designed to stimulate and coordinate pan-European efforts in fields such as information technology, energy, and the environment, whose economic boundaries exceed those of nations. This is a far cry from promoting "global leadership" or from creating the mythical "fortress Europe."

REFERENCES

Adams, W., and J. Brock. 1986. *The Bigness Complex*. New York: Pantheon.
Adams, W. J. 1991. "Antitrust Treatment of Cooperative Research: How Reasonable Is the Rule of Reason?" In *Competition in Europe*, ed. P. de Wolf, 229–63. Dordrecht: Kluwer.

Arrow, K. 1962. "Economic Welfare and the Allocation of Resources for Invention." In *The Rate and Direction of Inventive Activity: Economic and Social Factors*, 609–26. Princeton: Princeton University Press.

Aspremont, C. d', and A. Jacquemin. 1988. "Cooperative and Noncooperative R&D in Duopoly." *American Economic Review* 78:133–37.

Baldwin, R. 1989. "The Growth Effect of 1992." *Economic Policy* 9:243–70.

Buigues, P., F. Ilzkovitz, and J.-F. Lebrun. 1990. "The Impact of the Internal Market by Industrial Sector: The Challenge for the Member States." *European Economy* (special edition): 1–340.

Camagni, R. 1988. "Cooperation Agreements and New Forms for External Development of Companies." Moduli-IBM. Mimeo.

Coley, S., and S. Reinton. 1988. "The Hunt of Value." *McKinsey Quarterly* (Spring): 23–34.

Economic Council of Canada. 1969. *Interim Report on Competition Policy*. Ottawa: Queen's Printer.

Emerson, M., M. Aujean, M. Catinat, P. Goybet, and A. Jacquemin. 1988. *The Economics of 1992: The E.C. Commission's Assessment of the Economic Effects of Completing the Internal Market*. Oxford: Oxford University Press.

Farrell, J., and C. Shapiro. 1990. "Horizontal Mergers: An Equilibrium Analysis." *American Economic Review* 80:107–26.

Flaherty, M. T. 1980. "Business and Technology History of Silicon Wafers for Integrated Circuits." Harvard University. Mimeo.

Gatsios, K., and P. Seabright. 1989. "Regulation in the European Community." *Oxford Review of Economic Policy* 2:37–60.

George, K., and A. Jacquemin. 1990. "Competition Policy in the European Community." In *Competition Policy in Europe and North America: Economic Issues and Institutions*, ed. A. Jacquemin, 206–45. Chur: Harwood Academic Publishers.

Geroski, P. 1987. "Competition and Innovation." In *Research on the "Cost of Non-Europe": Basic Findings*. Vol. 2, *Studies on the Economics of Integration*. Luxembourg: Office for Official Publications of the European Communities.

Hölzler, H. 1990. "Merger Control." In *European Competition Policy*, ed. P. Montagnon, 9–30. London: Pinter for the Royal Institute of International Affairs.

Jacquemin, A. 1987. *The New Industrial Organization*. Oxford: Oxford University Press.

Jacquemin, A. 1988. "Cooperative Agreements in R&D and European Antitrust Policy." *European Economic Review* 32:551–60.

Jacquemin, A. 1989. "International and Multinational Strategic Behavior." *Kyklos* 42:495–513.

Jacquemin, A. 1990. "Horizontal Concentration and European Merger Policy." *European Economic Review* 34:539–50.

Katz, M. 1986. "An Analysis of Cooperative Research and Development." *Rand Journal of Economics* 17:527–43.

Lemettre, J. F. 1990. "Accords entre Firmes: Collusion ou Compétition dans les Oligopoles." Aix-en-Provence. Mimeo.

Mueller, D. 1989. "Mergers: Causes, Effects and Policies." *International Journal of Industrial Organization* 7:1–10.

Neumann, M., I. Böbel, and A. Haid. 1982. "Innovations and Market Structure in West German Industries." *Managerial and Decision Economics* 3:131–39.

Onida, F. 1990. "Technological Competition, Structural Change and International Integration of the European Single Market." University Bocconi, Milan. Mimeo.

Ordover, J. W., and W. J. Baumol. 1988. "Antitrust Policy and High Technology Industries." *Oxford Review of Economic Policy* 4:90–100.

Stiglitz, J., and F. Mathewson, eds. 1986. *New Developments in the Analysis of Market Structure.* Cambridge, Mass.: MIT Press.

Vives, X. 1990. "Information and Competitive Advantage." *International Journal of Industrial Organization* 8:17–35.

Von Hippel, E. 1982. "Appropriability of Innovation Benefits as a Predictor of the Source of Innovation." *Research Policy* 2:95–115.

The Rise of Small Business:
Causes and Consequences

Bo Carlsson

There is now substantial evidence that the share of small firms and plants in industrial output and employment has increased in most industrial countries during the last two decades. To the extent that this evidence is an accurate reflection of reality, it represents a reversal of the trend during several previous decades. This is of interest for its own sake, but it is particularly interesting in the context of the completion of the European internal market in 1992. Does the new trend toward small business mean that economies of scale are weakening and that, therefore, one of the fundamental arguments for further European integration is no longer valid?

The claim that the role of small business is increasing is surrounded by considerable controversy. Because different indicators yield different results, there is justifiable doubt about the robustness of the findings. But even if a convincing case can be made, there is reluctance on the part of many people to accept it, because such evidence flies in the face of much conventional wisdom concerning the importance and pervasiveness of economies of scale.

The purpose of this chapter is to examine the evidence supporting the claim that there has been a shift toward small business in recent years both in Europe and elsewhere, to consider what the causes of this shift might be, and to discuss the consequences for industrial structure and competitiveness as well as the implications for public policy, particularly in the context of further European integration after 1992.

Several measures of small business activity are used in the literature.[1]

The author would like to thank the editor of this volume as well as Alan Hughes and two anonymous referees for insightful comments and suggestions. All remaining errors and omissions are the sole responsibility of the author.

1. The role of small business has been investigated in several recent studies. Acs and Audretsch (1990a and 1990b) and Loveman and Sengenberger (1991) provide excellent surveys. For analyses of particular issues or countries, *Small Business Economics* (a new journal, first published in 1989) is a good source.

145

Most studies have focused on the manufacturing sector (due mainly to the existence of relatively accessible data), although some have examined broader segments of the economy. In a few countries, data are available on both firms and establishments (plants); in most, however, data are available for only one or the other. Since the overwhelming majority of firms are quite small and operate only a single establishment, measures of average establishment size and average firm size tend to be highly correlated. Nevertheless, it is quite possible for plants to get smaller while companies (through multiplant operations) get larger. I will return to this point subsequently.

The most commonly used indicators of firm and plant size are based on employment data; others utilize output data (in the form of sales, shipments, or value added). Whenever output data are used, the difficulties of evaluating output may cause problems with respect to comparisons over time and/or across countries.

Due to the limited availability of other kinds of data on internationally comparable bases, I shall focus on employment in manufacturing plants. When possible, I report evidence based on output as well.

The chapter is organized as follows. In the next section, international data are presented on the changing shares of small plants in manufacturing employment and on the development of plant size in manufacturing industry. In the third section, several hypotheses concerning the causes of these changes are considered. In the fourth section, the most persuasive of these hypotheses, namely that pertaining to flexible specialization, is set out in detail. Implications for the future, particularly in the European context, for further research, and for public policy are discussed in the final section.

International Evidence on the Rise of Small Business

Share of Employment in Manufacturing

Figure 1 summarizes some of the best international data available on long-term changes in the share of manufacturing employment in plants of smallish size. It shows, on the whole, that the share of such plants (those with fewer than 200 employees) declined in the largest European countries, the United States, and Japan between the end of World War II and 1970 or so. (Among the countries represented in fig. 1, the only exception is Italy, where the overall trend has been increasing, although with some fluctuations.) Around 1970, however, the trend reversed, and the share of small plants has tended to increase—except possibly in Germany, where the share of the smallest plants has fluctuated around the 1970 share. Thus, over the postwar period as a whole, the small-plant share of manufacturing employment has exhibited a V-shaped pattern—first falling and then rising—with the turning point occur-

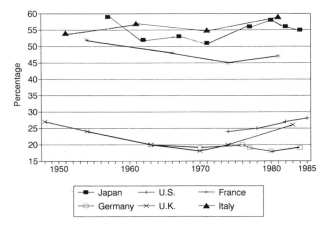

Fig. 1. Share of manufacturing employment in small plants, 1948–85. (Data from Loveman and Sengenberger 1991.)

ring somewhere around 1970. It is not an isolated event, but is characteristic of all the world's largest industrial countries.[2]

Figure 1 also shows that the share of smallish-sized plants varies considerably from country to country. In Italy, Japan, and France, small plants represent 45–60 percent of manufacturing employment, while in the United Kingdom, Germany, and the United States their share is between 18 and 28 percent. These differences seem to persist over time; there seems to be a kind of bifurcation with no tendency toward a narrowing of the differences. The dichotomy is not between large economies on the one hand and smaller economies on the other; instead, there are large and small countries in both groups, with Japan and Italy at one extreme and the United States, the United Kingdom, and Germany at the other. Whatever the determinants of the small-business share, size of the economy is not apparently among them. This makes the universality of the observed V-shaped pattern all the more remarkable—and intriguing.[3]

---

2. For further evidence to this effect, see Acs and Audretsch 1990a, 3–4 on the United States; Thurik 1990 on the Netherlands.

3. The persistence of international differences in the importance of small business is a topic worthy of separate study. Several hypotheses come to mind. The composition of industrial output differs among countries; if small business units are strongly associated with certain industries, such differences may result in persistent differences in the role played by small businesses. However, differences in the role of small units seem to remain even at very disaggregated levels. History probably plays a role, in the form of different institutional arrangements (regulation, guilds, financial markets, and so on) leading to differences in how economic activity is structured. Also, the relationships that exist between business units of various sizes (e.g., whether they cooperate or compete, how supplier-customer relationships are organized, and so on) are proba-

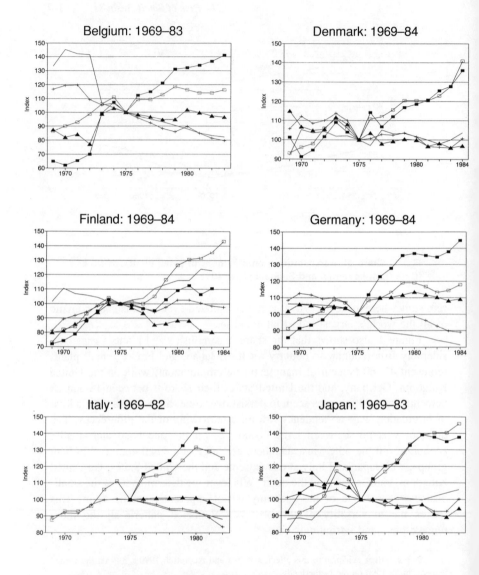

Fig. 2. Output, employment, number of plants, and average plant size in manufacturing. (Data from United Nations, *Industrial Statistics Yearbook*, vol. 1, *General Industrial Statistics*, various issues.)

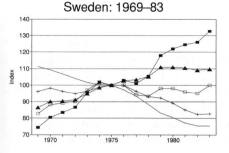

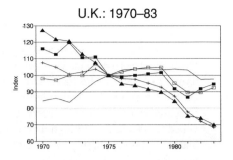

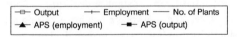

Average Plant Size

The results presented in the previous section require data on individual plants or firms. Such data are available for only a few countries. Can corroborating, if cruder, evidence be found for a larger set of countries?

If economic activity has been shifting toward smaller plants, then average plant size (APS) should be falling. Since APS can be computed from aggregate data, it is available for many countries. Changes in APS in nine countries (during the 1970s and the first half of the 1980s) are reported in figure 2. Figure 2 contains data on output,[4] employment, number of establish-

---

bly also important. The degree to which firms in various countries perceive themselves as competing in international or even global markets, as distinct from local or regional markets, may also play a role.

4. The output measure used is the index of production for manufacturing.

ments, and average plant size in manufacturing, reported in index form (1975 = 100).[5]

Even a cursory examination of figure 2 reveals substantial differences in most countries between changes in APS_e (APS measured in employment terms) and APS_o (APS measured in output terms). In all countries except the United Kingdom, but particularly in Belgium, Sweden, and Germany, APS_o increased over the period observed. APS_e shows more mixed results. It declined fairly steadily throughout the period in Denmark, Japan, and the United States, and quite sharply in the United Kingdom, while it first increased and then fell in Belgium and Finland. It rose over the period as a whole in Germany and Sweden. (Data on the number of establishments are not available for Italy prior to 1975; after that, APS_o increased rapidly, while APS_e remained constant until 1980. Thereafter, there have been slight declines in both measures.)

Thus, the picture we see is rather complicated. In most of the countries shown in figure 2, manufacturing employment peaked some time during the early 1970s; the only exceptions are the United States and Finland, where the peak occurred around 1980. Manufacturing output increased over the period as a whole except in the United Kingdom, where it declined slightly; the increase was quite modest in Sweden. Thus, the differences between the two plant-size measures largely reflect changes in labor productivity: plants have generally increased their output more than their labor force. In fact, for the most part, employment has been constant or declining. In other words, for the average industrial worker, the workplace has been getting smaller in employment terms; productivity has increased in small plants and firms, with the result that their share of economic activity has increased.

In the countries where the number of plants stayed relatively constant (Denmark, Italy, the United Kingdom, and the United States), APS_o tracked output and APS_e tracked employment, for obvious reasons. In that sense, the change in the number of plants is the most interesting variable to analyze. Where the number of plants declined most sharply (Belgium, Sweden, and Germany), APS increased in terms of both output and employment. Where it increased, APS stagnated or declined (the United Kingdom and Japan prior to 1975, Finland after 1975).

Summing up, we can draw the following conclusions.

1. The share of small businesses in manufacturing employment and output has increased since the early 1970s in most industrialized coun-

---

5. No establishment data are available for France and the Netherlands, hence their absence here.

tries, reversing the previous trend. This reversal has occurred regardless of whether the country is large or small or has relatively large or relatively small plants.

2. Differences among countries in the share of small business persist; there does not seem to be any tendency toward convergence of APS or small business share.
3. Consistent with the increasing share of small plants in manufacturing employment and output, there has been a decline (since 1975) in most countries in the average plant size as measured by employment. After 1980, the decline has been universal in the countries studied here.
4. However, average plant size in terms of output has continued to increase in all countries (except the United Kingdom), reflecting increasing labor productivity. Thus, the average manufacturing workplace has fewer workers but a larger output now than it did a decade or two ago.

Does the divergence of the two APS measures make it impossible to claim unequivocally that the importance of small business is increasing? Not really. In a growing economy, units that do not grow have difficulty surviving; it is relative performance that counts. A unit that doubles its output over a certain time period may still be small if other units grow at the same (or a greater) rate. Moreover, most people think of the size of their workplace in terms of the number of people working there. The finding that output has tended to increase in all plants, large and small, cannot obscure the fact that the share of small businesses in total output (and employment) has been rising.

From a more purely European perspective, it is noteworthy that there seems to be no distinctive European profile or pattern as far as these developments are concerned. For example, in figure 1, the United States and Japan are in the middle of the figure, while European countries are at both the extremes: Italy and France have very large shares of their employment in small plants, and Germany and the United Kingdom have the opposite. Similarly, it is difficult to find any distinctive European or EC pattern in figure 2. There is no reason to believe that these intra-European differences will fail to persist.

Possible Causes of the Observed Changes

What explains the increasing share of small businesses reported in the preceding section? Have large units been decomposed into smaller ones? Has labor productivity in large plants increased so much that such plants have shed enough workers to drop into smaller size classes? Or has labor productivity in smaller plants increased so much that such plants have become more competitive vis-à-vis their larger rivals? If so, is the increase in productivity attributable to the formation of new relationships (networks) among small units?

The evolution of APS (and of small business generally) depends not only on what happens to surviving units but also on entry and exit. Unfortunately, changes in the aggregate number of plants are *net* measures: they combine the effects of gross entries and exits. In fact, our data reveal none of the dynamics of the transformation processes taking place within the aggregates. Behind the aggregate changes may be numerous types of changes. For example, the same decline in average plant size (or rise in the employment share of small enterprises) may be achieved in several different ways. It may result from exits of large firms while small firms remain constant in number and size, from births of small firms and stable size in large firms, from growth among existing small firms at a rate exceeding that among large firms, from declines in size among the large enterprises, and so forth (Loveman and Sengenberger 1991, 11). In order to analyze such underlying factors more systematically, it is necessary to have more detailed and disaggregated data than are currently available.[6]

However, several more macro-type hypotheses have been put forward in the literature concerning the possible causes of the increasing share of small businesses. In a useful survey, Loveman and Sengenberger (1991) discuss five different explanations. The first is that there has been no real shift to smaller units and that the observed changes are merely a *statistical illusion* due to sectoral recomposition (changes in the mix of output toward industries where the operating units are traditionally smaller while the operating units in each sector remain constant in size). The primary counterarguments to this "explanation" are (1) the shift to smaller units can be observed over a long period of time in many countries with different institutional environments and different initial APSs; and (2) where the sectoral recomposition argument can be tested, structural evolution accounts for only a portion, at most, of the observed change.[7]

The second hypothesis is that the increasing share of small businesses is

---

6. An international study of industry dynamics and small firms, with EC funding and participation by researchers in twelve European countries, the United States, and Japan, is addressing these very issues and is currently under way.

7. For example, based on data available to the author, it can be demonstrated that the large difference in plant size between Japan and the United States can not be attributed to differences in the sectoral composition of manufacturing. In fact, if in 1987 U.S. manufacturing had had the same structure of employment at the two-digit level as had Japan, its APS would have been even larger (slightly) than the actual level. Thus, average plant size seems to be generally and genuinely smaller in Japan than elsewhere, regardless of industry.

due to *transitory changes* in connection with the business cycle.[8] While there is certainly an element of truth in this, again, the observed change occurs in enough countries and over a long enough period to render the hypothesis largely unsupported by the evidence.

A third potential explanation is that *wage costs are lower* in small units, making it profitable to shift production to them. Such differences do indeed exist—but they have existed for a long time. Why should they suddenly lead to a shift in production toward smaller units? To make the argument persuasive, one would have to show either that the cost differential has increased in recent years, or that preexisting impediments to such a shift have recently been removed. Also, the size of the differential appears to bear no relation to the growth of small unit employment shares. Italy, for example, has relatively small wage differentials, yet shows relatively large employment share gains by small units (Loveman and Sengenberger 1991, 26).[9]

A fourth hypothesis is that *liberalization,* in the form of tax reductions and deregulation, has lifted restrictions that historically impeded small businesses. Related to this, management has attempted to reduce the power of labor unions. Loveman and Sengenberger (1991, 27) find that existing research on these hypotheses does not support their acceptance.

The argument that Loveman and Sengenberger find most convincing—and in this I concur—is that the shift to smaller units results from technological change permitting replacement of mass production by *flexible specialization.* This argument will be spelled out in detail in the following section. It is based upon some recent findings concerning the use of flexible technology in the form of numerically controlled machine tools (NCMTs) in U.S. manufacturing industry (Carlsson and Taymaz 1991). That study reveals a significant and increasing concentration of machine tools in small plants and an increase in the use of flexible automation equipment (represented by NCMTs) in plants of all sizes, but particularly (during the 1980s) in small plants. As a result, the number of NCMTs per employee in small plants increased from 2 to 1 relative to that in large plants in 1983 to nearly 5 to 1 in 1989. Thus, it appears that small plants have been the main beneficiaries of the changes in flexible technology.

---

8. For example, if a business downturn has a severely negative impact on economic activity in heavy industries with large operating units, while smaller units in other industries are less sensitive to cyclical variation, one might get the impression that the role of small business in the economy is rising. But this would be only a temporary phenomenon, one that would presumably be reversed in the next business upturn.

9. Nonwage labor-cost differences among small and large units—having to do with, e.g., the greater flexibility of small units in hiring/firing decisions and in deploying labor—are subsumed under the flexible specialization argument.

Unfortunately, similar data on the distribution of flexible technology by plant size are unavailable for other countries. As we shall see, however, the use of NCMTs is not unique to U.S. manufacturers—in fact, it is very similar to that in several European economies. Thus, developments in the United States should shed light on developments elsewhere.

The fact that my analysis is confined to the engineering (metalworking) industries may limit the applicability of its results to other sectors. I focus on the engineering industries because they are heavy users of metal-cutting machine tools. Nevertheless, flexible technology similar to that embodied in NCMTs is used in other industries; hence, the analysis conducted here might have more general relevance to the evolution of APS.

The Link between Flexible Technology and Plant Size

There are many possible reasons to link the 1980s shift in output toward smaller plants (on the one hand) to increased use of NCMTs (on the other). The technological change taking place with respect to machine tools and other components of flexible automation came about quite independently of the changes occurring in the global economic environment, but once both were set in motion, they tended to reinforce each other.

During the past two decades, the world economy experienced three major changes that are relevant here: (1) intensified *global competition,* caused by technological changes in transportation, information, and communication, that resulted in increased integration of the world economy; (2) a high degree of *uncertainty* in all industrial countries, triggered by the oil price shocks in the 1970s, exacerbated by volatility of exchange rates, and reflected in high rates of interest, inflation, and unemployment; and (3) intensified *fragmentation,* due to growing consumer demand for distinctive products, inducing firms to increase their emphasis on product differentiation.

Each of these changes has engendered microlevel responses by business enterprises. Increased global competition tends to lead to increased specialization ("back to basics"), while uncertainty and fragmentation force firms to increase their flexibility and search for new ways to differentiate their products. Each of these responses, in turn, has been facilitated by the changes in flexible technology and has also involved a shift in output toward smaller units.

Specialization

Specialization (meaning both vertical disintegration and horizontal "deglomeration"—see Carlsson 1989a and Jacquemin in this volume) has increasingly been regarded as (1) a way to cut overhead and fixed costs, (2) a mechanism to transfer uncertainty, (3) a means of accessing cheap labor sources,[10] and (4) a way to obtain new sources of high-quality, specialized inputs. Various forms of specialization and vertical disintegration have been observed.

1. *Decentralization:* ownership of single large plants declines, but ownership of multiple new and small plants flourishes.
2. *Subcontracting:* parts and components are obtained from specialized plants by forming semipermanent relationships (not involving ownership).
3. *Other out-sourcing:* parts and components are no longer manufactured in-house but are purchased from the market without any long-term relationship with the producer.

Firms are becoming smaller and less vertically integrated. Thus, for example, the largest 500 industrial companies in the United States ("The *Fortune* 500") have lost some of their share of manufacturing employment as well as output during the 1980s (Carlsson 1989a, 28). The trend toward specialization and vertical disintegration in the United States is also shown by the rapid growth of the business services industry. This sector (SIC 73) had the highest rate of employment growth (1969–1984) of any two-digit SIC sector (Kutscher and Personick 1988, 9).

In many cases, the purpose of vertical disintegration is to achieve a flexible network of firms. Individual firms in this network may become highly specialized, while the network as a whole is flexible (Carlsson and Stankiewicz 1990). Networks of specialized firms have long been developing in Japan (Imai 1989). Small- and medium-sized enterprises account for 94.4 percent of all enterprises and 81.4 percent of all employment in Japan.[11] Some 65.5 percent of all small- and medium-sized manufacturers are subcontractors; they account for 35.5 percent of total shipments by small- and medium-sized manufacturers (Keiei Joho Shuppan 1988, v). Given the importance of subcontracting in Japan, the country's low value of APS is hardly surprising.

The Japanese system of industrial networks has many peculiarities that stem from the historical development of Japanese industry and business firms;

---

10. In the United States, the average wage rate in plants with fewer than twenty employees is around 25 percent lower than the rate in plants with more than 500 employees. The corresponding wage disparity is more than 50 percent in Japan.

11. In Japan, small- and medium-sized enterprises are defined as business establishments with fewer than 300 employees (fewer than 100 in wholesaling, and fewer than 50 in retail and service businesses).

therefore, it may not be replicable in any other industrial country. However, the trend toward vertical disintegration, subcontracting, and networks of specialized plants is obvious in many countries.[12]

The data needed to determine which form of vertical disintegration is the most important does not exist. However, data on multiunit and single-unit companies can shed light on this issue. The share of multiunit companies in U.S. manufacturing employment increased throughout the postwar period until the late 1970s, rising from 60 percent in 1954 to 76 percent in 1977. But after 1977, the share of multiunit companies declined for the first time; it was 74 percent in 1982 (U.S. Bureau of the Census, *Census of Manufactures*, various issues). This suggests that subcontracting and out-sourcing may have become more important forms of disintegration in recent years. The recent literature on subcontracting and supplier-customer relationships provides growing support for this hypothesis (see Nishiguchi 1990 for an excellent literature survey; see also Helper 1987, 1990, and 1991 and the references therein). There is also anecdotal evidence in trade journals to support this argument.

Increased Flexibility

The conventional response to increased uncertainty is diversification. Why would increased flexibility be an appropriate response?

In discussing flexibility, it is useful to distinguish between risk and uncertainty. Following Knight (1921, 223), it is customary to use the term *risk* to refer to homogeneous, repetitive events whose relative frequencies can be calculated or measured, and the term *uncertainty* to refer to events that cannot be assigned numerical probabilities. Given that risks are calculable, it is possible, at least in principle, to guard against them via insurance, often in the

---

12. For example, a survey of U.K. manufacturing concludes that there is a "fundamental shift in manufacturing industry away from the all-purpose, we-can-tackle-anything approach of the past. . . . Where subcontractors were used in the past to handle peak loads, they are now being used more as an integral part of the manufacturing process" (Pullin 1986, 90). Moreover, "[a]s subcontractors increasingly use high-tech manufacturing methods, they are demanding a more formal role in the production process. . . . Subcontractors are insisting that in return [for their high-tech manufacturing] they must be integrated more fully into the firms they serve, providing a real manufacturing function, and not just being telephoned on Monday and told to drill holes in 100,000 sheets of steel by Friday" (Ince 1986, 53).

For Italy, Murray (1983, 84) says that out-sourcing in the Bologna engineering industry ". . . has gone from a contingency solution of special problems to a more structured system. Initially [in the early 1970s], flexibility was found in putting-out to artisan workshops to get around rigidity in the factory. Now [after the late 1970s] it is the whole system, factory production and putting out, that works to give flexibility."

form of diversification. Uncertainty, on the other hand, is not calculable and, therefore, not insurable.

During the first few decades of the postwar period, firms tended to diversify in order to reduce their exposure to risk. But with the events of the 1970s (oil shocks, the breakup of the Bretton Woods system, the emergence of newly industrializing countries, and so forth), the resulting volatility of world markets had more elements of genuine uncertainty than "mere" risk. Hence, diversification was no longer the strategy of choice; building defensible positions was (Carlsson 1989a). This involved "flexible specialization": specializing in a particular business area (trying to build up unique competence not easily acquired by competitors) but hedging it with an increased ability to respond to new pressures, foreseen or unforeseen. This is accomplished by an intensified watchfulness for threats and opportunities, actual or potential, and by building up flexibility to respond when necessary. Obviously, the greater one's competence, the greater the probability of identifying threats and opportunities and taking timely and appropriate action. Conversely, the more diversified the firm, the less likely it is to possess unique competence in each business unit.

While networking may be seen as a way for firms to deal with uncertainty and to achieve flexibility by changing their relationships with external units (increasing their monitoring ability, sharing know-how, and freeing up resources), firms must also find ways to respond internally. Under the pressure of uncertainty, enterprises are intensifying the search for greater flexibility (Kanawaty et al. 1989, 294). A typical response of engineering firms has been to strive to increase their operational flexibility (the ability to change sequencing, scheduling, and the like on short notice) as well as tactical flexibility (ability to change the rate of production, product mix, and product design in the medium term) by investing in computerized, flexibly automated technologies.[13] The main component of these technologies is NCMTs.

In large plants, the adoption of NCMTs is being driven by the ability of these machines to reduce the cost of manufacturing both complex products (products with complex cutting shapes, a large number of machining operations, and so on) and a closely related family of products. Numerically controlled machine tools are advantageous in the manufacturing of complex products because they can control rapidly and accurately the movements of cutting tools and/or work pieces. (Manual controls can be more flexible and economic for batch manufacturing of simple products.) However, the fixed costs associated with complex products are often high. For example, the design costs of a complex part may be so high that a large amount of *cumula-*

---

13. See Carlsson 1989b for further discussion of various types of flexibility.

tive output is necessary for cost effectiveness, even if the equipment used in its manufacture is highly flexible. Although set-up time for NCMTs is short (due to the use of software), initial programming and debugging of programs may take considerable time, especially for the machining of complex parts.

For these reasons, complex NCMTs and other types of flexible automation equipment may be beneficial only when a large number of parts sharing the fixed costs of design and programming are manufactured in small batches. The manufacture of many complex parts is typical of many large-scale plants, such as those manufacturing aircraft, construction machinery, and engines and turbines. It is not surprising, therefore, that these plants were the early adopters of NCMTs.

But when the Japanese introduced microcomputer-based numerical controllers in the mid-1970s, two important things happened. First, the programmability, and therefore flexibility, of NCMTs increased dramatically. This helped all potential users, large and small. Second, cheaper and more flexible numerical controllers, in combination with other changes, led to the mass production of NCMTs, resulting in dramatically reduced prices. This, in turn, opened up a vast new market, namely, small- and medium-sized metalworking plants. Suddenly, automation came within reach of small producers for the first time. Previously, they had a choice between highly sophisticated, productive, and expensive NCMTs on the one hand and much less expensive, manually operated, conventional machine tools on the other. Thus, automation was often difficult to justify in small plants. This is why we observe that automation occurred initially almost exclusively in large plants. For them, the choice was not between automation and no automation, but, rather, between mechanized systems (e.g., transfer machines) and flexible automation in the form of NCMTs. In other words, the new Japanese NCMTs represented a change in kind for small plants, but only a change in degree for large plants. Hence the dramatic increases in the number of NCMTs in small plants relative to large plants I mentioned previously.

With automation now affordable to small as well as large plants, the former could compete with the latter for business in complex products. Such business had been outside the domain of the small firms. At the same time, the tendency toward specialization on the part of large firms was strengthened; they now found it more advantageous to subcontract or out-source components to smaller plants and firms.

Product Differentiation

Another factor changing the division of labor between large and small plants is the increased demand for product differentiation. By increasing the use of modular design (each product or part consisting of a number of modules, and each module being available with a variety of features), it is possible to achieve a final product of almost infinite variety. Flexible automation makes it possible to serve the needs of heterogeneous customers while spreading the design costs over a large output. The manufacturer then has the option of producing everything in-house or subcontracting or out-sourcing all or some of the components. The recent tendency has been for the original manufacturer to focus on certain key components, while subcontracting or out-sourcing others. In the former case, the subcontractor may very well have an on-line electronic exchange of information (specifications, drawings, and so on) with the contractor, permitting use of designs already made by the original contractor, quick and cheap changes in design, and the establishment of just-in-time delivery systems. Such an arrangement allows increased specialization for both original manufacturers and their suppliers, making it possible for all parties involved to exploit the economies of scale.

Recent developments in the automobile industry illustrate this phenomenon nicely. According to Kaplinsky (1988, 456), flexibility in production allowed the automobile producers to offer an increasing range of alternatives to customers. For example, when the Toyota Corolla was first introduced, it was available only as a sedan. Today it is available in five body styles (sedan, hatchback, hardtop, van, and coupe); when the various options are put together, there are more than 10,000 potential variations. The new flexible technology allows Toyota to produce all of these variations in a single plant; the existence of 10,000 plants, each producing a different type of car, is not required.

It is noteworthy that the increase in the number of variants came around 1980, just when the "new" NCMTs made their breakthrough. In the U.S. automobile industry, for example, the number of models offered by U.S. manufacturers fell during the 1970s (from 375 in 1970 to 247 in 1979), but it increased during the 1980s (to 313 in 1986). Similarly, the number of models sold by Japanese auto manufacturers increased from 46 in 1980 to 74 in 1985 (Carlsson 1989a, 34). This proliferation has continued.

A New Division of Labor between Large and Small Plants

What we observe, then, is a whole set of mutually reinforcing changes in the organization of manufacturing: large plants moving away from mass production and into batch production; increased specialization, causing large plants to shrink and allowing small manufacturers to shift toward higher volumes of production; subcontracting, out-sourcing, and networking, involving a new division of labor between large and small firms and between suppliers and customers.

In the 1980s, small plants appear to have prospered more than large plants under these new arrangements. Given their rapid accumulation of new NCMTs, it would not be surprising if the productivity gains of small plants were found to be greater than those of large plants. As Kelley and Brooks (1990) among others have shown, high labor cost is one of the most important factors governing the adoption of flexible automation. While systematic studies are lacking, anecdotal evidence abounds. For example, the installation of a flexible manufacturing system (FMS) formed by 43 NC machines in the Yamazaki Machinery plant reduced the labor requirement from 195 to 39 (Usui 1984; see also Jaikumar 1986).

Evidence of the type of change in the division of labor suggested here is provided in another study (Carlsson and Taymaz 1991): 44 manufacturing industries were grouped into two main categories—"final products" and "parts and components" industries. It was found that the final products industries had significantly higher concentration and coverage ratios in 1972 than did parts and components industries.[14] Between 1972 and 1982, the average concentration ratio declined in both groups, but the decline in parts and components was much greater. This means that production shifted from the largest to smaller plants in both groups of industries. The average coverage ratio for parts and components industries increased substantially. In other words, the proportion of parts and components produced by parts and components industries grew rapidly. Moreover, the average change in employment was negative in the final products industries but positive in the parts and components industries. The number of firms and establishments increased more in the parts and components industries than in the final products industries. This pattern of change generally supports the hypothesis advanced earlier.

To what extent is this story, based mainly on U.S. data, representative of other industrial countries, particularly those in the European Community?

Table 1 shows that the density of flexible automation techniques in Europe is similar, on the whole, to that in the United States. The numbers of NCMTs, industrial robots, and flexible manufacturing systems (FMSs) per worker are about the same in the United States as in the European Community. The United States has a significant lead in the use of computer-aided design (CAD) equipment, while Japan and Sweden are ahead in the other technologies.

A study of changes in manufacturing and manufacturing technology in the United States and Sweden, currently being conducted by the author,

14. The coverage ratio refers to the proportion of the total output of a product produced by the industry in which the product is classified (as distinct from other industries that may also produce the same good).

TABLE 1.   Density of Flexible Automation Techniques in Various Countries

Country	NCMT* (1984)	Industrial Robots* (1989)	FMS** (1988)	CAD*** (1985)
France	NA	3.98	NA	2.89
W. Germany	11.38	5.84	19.2	2.62
Italy	NA	8.57	NA	0.31
Japan	22.40	43.50	31.7	0.72
Sweden	22.18	9.35	108.1	3.76
United Kingdom	10.51	2.87	43.7	3.17
United States	11.73	4.64	17.6	6.33

Sources: Data from Edquist and Jacobsson 1988, 104 for NCMTs; Karlsson 1991 and OECD 1989 for industrial robots; Ranta n.d. and OECD 1989 for FMSs; Åstebro 1991 for CAD.

Note: NA = not available.

*Number of units per thousand employees in engineering industries

**Number of units per million employees in engineering industries

***Number of units per thousand employees in manufacturing industries

supports the view that the U.S. experience is not unique. The technological positions of these two countries during the 1970s were obviously different, especially regarding the use of mass production techniques, but the driving forces behind subsequent changes have been largely those described here. While it was certainly true in an earlier era that much technological change originated in the United States, technological change in manufacturing is now quite global in origin and diffusion.

Some Further Considerations

Summing up the argument thus far, there is a shift of output and employment toward small businesses in most industrial countries, this shift being driven by technological change in combination with changes in the global economy. Resulting from these observed changes is a new form of industrial organization, namely, networks of small plants or firms clustered around particular large enterprises.

Before exploring this set of changes in the context of Project 1992, two further issues need to be discussed. First, the observations made here refer primarily to *physical production,* that is, to only part of the total operations of manufacturing firms. (In a recent study of large Swedish manufacturing firms, goods processing accounted for only slightly more than half [56.2 percent], with marketing and distribution [21.3 percent], administration [7.9 percent], R&D [5.2 percent], design, engineering, and documentation [4.6 percent], preproduction planning [3.5 percent], and other [1.2 percent] making up the balance [Eliasson 1989, 30].)

While the relative importance of goods processing is likely to vary among firms and industries, the point is that manufacturing firms are involved in a wide range of activities beyond physical production. In some industries, such as pharmaceuticals, physical production represents only a small fraction of total operations, while R&D constitutes a much more important activity and a larger proportion of total costs.[15] In other industries, marketing costs may be more important than physical production costs.

This makes the distinction between plants and firms all the more important. The nonprocessing activities tend to be associated with firms, while goods processing takes place in plants. Thus, the observed shift of economic activity from large to small plants does not necessarily imply a diminished importance of large firms or that economic activity has become less concentrated in a few organizations. However, recent evidence for the United Kingdom indicates that concentration in manufacturing industries has tended to decline since about 1970, reversing the previous trend; recall that APS began to decline about 1970 as well (Hughes 1990). Similar developments occurred in the United States. In fact, it is possible (although not likely, in view of the specialization argument above and the evidence on the development of business concentration in countries for which data are available) that large firms have acquired more small plants, thus increasing their share of total output. Certainly it is possible that firms have reduced the number of businesses in which they participate while, at the same time, they may have strengthened their position in each remaining business (see Jacquemin in this volume). At the very least, this issue warrants further research.

The second issue is whether or not the decentralizing forces now at work in goods processing might be reversed in the future. After all, from 1800 to 1950, the technological trend was clearly beneficial to large-scale operations and mass production (Carlsson 1984). Is it possible that the pendulum will swing back toward mass production and larger production units?

In my view, such a swing is possible but not likely in the foreseeable future. But this is just a guess. It is based on the judgment that such a reversal would require the driving forces described here (both technological and economic) to be supplanted by other forces—and such forces are nowhere to be found on the current horizon.

Implications for Europe—Issues for Further Research and Public Policy

What does all this mean in the context of Europe and Project 1992, and what are the implications for public policy?

---

15. The recent merger activity and R&D collaboration among the largest pharmaceutical firms suggest that risk considerations and scale economies are very much alive.

If it is true, as I have argued, that the shift toward small businesses is driven partially by technological change in the form of automation, it is useful to examine the European position with respect to flexible automation in somewhat greater detail. Table 1 demonstrates that the European countries are performing fairly well with regard to the *use* of flexible automation technologies. For example, the density of NCMTs in Germany and the United Kingdom is on a par with that in the United States; the density of industrial robots is greater in Germany and Belgium than in the United States; and the United Kingdom has an advanced position in both FMS and CAD.

What about the supply side? Tables 2 and 3 give data on the production of computer numerically controlled (CNC) lathes and machining centers in Japan, Europe, and the United States. These two are by far the most important types of NCMTs—not only because, together, they represent some 60 percent of the total market for NCMTs (Ehrnberg and Jacobsson 1991, 8) but also because they form the basis for FMSs. The dominance of the Japanese in the production of both of these types of machines is evident, as is the dramatic decline of the United States. Europe's position is in-between, with some market share gains in machining centers balancing some losses in CNC lathes. Overall, it seems as though Europe is holding its own in these important technologies.

The European position appears stronger if we examine the accumulated sales of multimachine FMSs through 1988. According to Ehrnberg and Jacobsson (1991), of the 627 such systems sold before 1989, 395 had been supplied by European firms (383 of the deliveries having been in Europe);

TABLE 2. Production of CNC Lathes in Japan, Europe, and the United States, 1975–88 (in number of units and percentage of total production)

Year	Japan Number	Percentage	Europe[a] Number	Percentage	United States Number	Percentage	Total Number
1975	1,359	30	1,535	34	1,640	36	4,534
1977	3,900	53	2,332	31	1,178	16	7,410
1979	8,065	58	3,505	25	2,354	17	13,924
1981	12,133	64	4,904	26	2,021	10	19,058
1983	10,020	65	4,106	27	1,203	8	15,329
1984	16,555	72	4,818	21	1,524	7	22,897
1985	19,804	74	5,564	21	1,420	5	26,788
1986	15,988	68	6,438	27	1,163	5	23,589
1987	15,241	69	5,271	24	1,626	7	22,138
1988	20,942	74	5,734	20	1,762	6	28,438

Source: Data from Ehrnberg and Jacobsson 1991.

[a] In 1975–84, includes West Germany, France, Italy, the U.K., and Sweden; in 1985 and 1986, Sweden is excluded and Spain is included; in 1987 and 1988, includes only West Germany, France, Italy, and the U.K.

164   Singular Europe

TABLE 3. Production of Machining Centers in Japan, Europe, and the United States, 1978, 1982, and 1986–88 (in number of units and percentage of total production)

Year	Japan Number	Japan Percentage	Europe Number	Europe Percentage	United States Number	United States Percentage	Total Number
1978	1,377	39	649[a]	18	1,486	42	3,512
1982	6,936	73	1,335[b]	14	1,265	13	9,536
1986[c]	10,882	70	3,784[d]	24	918	6	15,584
1987[c]	9,027	67	3,348[e]	25	1,036	8	13,411
1988[c]	11,474	69	3,997[e]	24	1,277	8	16,748

Source: Data from Ehrnberg and Jacobsson 1991.
[a] U.K., West Germany, and Italy; the U.K. data from 1979.
[b] U.K., West Germany, and Italy.
[c] Machining centers and transfer lines, numerically controlled.
[d] U.K., West Germany, Italy, France, and Spain.
[e] U.K., West Germany, Italy, and France.

Japanese manufacturers had supplied 154 systems (115 in Japan), U.S. companies 78 (68 in the United States). Thus, nearly two-thirds of the world's FMSs had been sold by European firms and a slightly larger share installed in Europe. It is also quite evident that, until now, the markets for complex products requiring close collaboration between supplier and customer are still primarily national. Until the product has become more standardized, it is simply too costly for suppliers to become involved with distant customers. Thus, having domestic, or at least nearby, suppliers of such products appears to be of fundamental strategic importance. However, there are signs that the systems have now become sufficiently mature that this is likely to change in the future. In other words, the market for FMSs may now be in the same position as that for NCMTs in the mid-1970s (Carlsson and Jacobsson 1991a; Ehrnberg and Jacobsson 1991).

A closer examination of the data shows, however, that, of the 16 European FMS suppliers, 10 are German, 4 Italian, and 2 Swedish. (For comparison, the number of suppliers is 5 in the United States and 12 in Japan.) To the extent that primarily domestic markets are served, it is likely that potential customers in countries without domestic suppliers will not have access, or at least not timely access, to the technology, with the likely result that they will fall behind technologically. Recent evidence suggests that, indeed, the German and Italian positions are being strengthened while other countries in Europe are lagging.

The implication here is that while Europe seems to have performed relatively well thus far in this area of technology, the experience in the last two decades may not be a good guide to what might happen in the next decade. Second, significant differences clearly exist among the European countries, and these differences are likely to become even sharper in the future. These are both matters of concern within Europe, to governments and enterprises alike, particularly as they relate to small businesses.

In terms of diffusion and implementation of new technology, a closely related issue is the presence and density of networks linking suppliers, leading users, research institutes, academic institutions, and government agencies— and of policies regarding flexible automation (and other) technologies. A recent study of Sweden (Carlsson and Jacobsson 1991b) suggests that such networks ("technological systems") have played a major role in explaining the high rate of automation in Swedish industry (see table 1). A wide diffusion of technology requires the involvement of small as well as large businesses. Carlsson and Jacobsson (1991a) show that while technically advanced users are necessary for the establishment and survival of technically competent domestic suppliers, such suppliers are essential in order for smaller and less advanced firms to be able to acquire and use complex new technology. Carlsson and Jacobsson (1991b) suggest that an appropriate role of public policy may thus be to facilitate the creation and smooth functioning of such technological systems, in addition to providing the means for training a sufficient number of engineers.

A similar issue concerns the nature of supplier-customer relations. These can help or hinder the diffusion of technology to smaller units. Braunerhjelm (1991) suggests that small, independent firms limited to arm's-length relationships with their customers face serious difficulties in keeping up with and acquiring new technology. In contrast, small- and medium-sized firms with closer working (or networking) relationships with their industrial customers are in a much better position, both technically and financially, to do so. A further problem is that, in small countries (particularly on the periphery of Europe), small firms easily become too dependent on a single domestic customer but have difficulty establishing similar relationships with large firms in other countries. Barriers created by language, as well as by cultural and geographic distance, are very much in existence, despite the progress that has been made toward European integration. These barriers are likely to remain long after 1992. Even large firms will have to act aggressively if they wish to establish close working relationships with small suppliers in other countries.

A further issue that arises in the European context is what kinds of international networking linkages exist, not only in terms of customer-supplier relationships but also in such areas as technology or information sharing and marketing. To the extent that such linkages are established exclusively among entities in the same country, they may breed conflicts, as customer firms try to integrate their activities at the European rather than the national level. Small suppliers may suffer particularly. It appears that not much research has been done on these issues, and it is even less clear what role, if any, public policy should play.

The European Community has several programs in effect for small business. Since 1983, with limited success, the European Commission has promoted innovation among small- and medium-sized firms (SMEs). Language barriers and lack of information about firms interested in collaboration are among the factors hampering the program (Housely 1987). An EC policy on SMEs was instituted in 1988 (European Communities 1988, 24–26).[16] Among other things, it promotes cooperation in training and research between firms in different member countries; EC loans and grants have also been made available to SMEs. Euro-Info Centers were established to help SMEs keep track of legislation and opportunities open to them. Numerous requests for partnership searches gave rise to another program, the Business Cooperation Network, which provides direct business-to-business contacts. It is the first network of its kind in Europe (Tigner 1988). Finally, the EC's rules of competition have been implemented in such a manner as to promote small businesses.

At this time, it is difficult to evaluate the effectiveness of these programs and policies; it is simply too early to tell. But it should be evident from the previous discussion that the shift toward small businesses started, both in Europe and elsewhere, long before these policies were in place. The forces at work are much more fundamental, universal, and pervasive than any policy can hope to be. Indeed, the networking and supplier-customer relationships indicated above as conducive to and perhaps even necessary for a healthy small business sector may raise serious challenges to antitrust policy as conventionally interpreted. Thus, we are left more with an agenda for further research—because these issues are simply not yet well understood—than with a set of policy recommendations.

REFERENCES

Acs, Z. J., and D. B. Audretsch, eds. 1990a. *The Economics of Small Firms: A European Challenge.* Dordrecht and Boston: Kluwer Academic Publishers.
Acs, Z. J., and D. B. Audretsch. 1990b. *Innovation and Small Firms.* Cambridge, Mass.: MIT Press.
Åstebro, T. 1991. "The International Diffusion of Computer Aided Design." In *Computer Integrated Manufacturing.* Vol. 3, *Models, Case Studies, and Forecasts of*

---

16. SMEs are defined by the European Commission as firms with fewer than 500 employees and less than ECU 75 million in fixed assets (European Communities 1988).

Diffusion, ed. R. U. Ayres, W. Haywood, and I. Tchijov. London: Chapman and Hall. Forthcoming.

Braunerhjelm, P. 1991."Svenska underleverantörer och småföretag i det nya Europa." Working Paper no. 303. Industrial Institute for Economic and Social Research, Stockholm.

Carlsson, B. 1984. "The Development and Use of Machine Tools in Historical Perspective." *Journal of Economic Behavior and Organization* 5:91–114.

Carlsson, B. 1989a. "The Evolution of Manufacturing Technology and Its Impact on Industrial Structure: An International Study." *Small Business Economics* 1:21–37.

Carlsson, B. 1989b. "Flexibility and the Theory of the Firm." *International Journal of Industrial Organization* 7:179–203.

Carlsson, B. 1989c. "Small-Scale Industry at a Crossroads: U.S. Machine Tools in Global Perspective." *Small Business Economics* 1:245–61.

Carlsson, B., and S. Jacobsson. 1991a. "What Makes the Automation Industry Strategic." *Economics of Innovation and New Technology* 1:257–69.

Carlsson, B., and S. Jacobsson. 1991b. "Technological Systems and Economic Performance: The Diffusion of Factory Automation in Sweden." In *Technology and Competitiveness: The Dynamics of Created Advantages,* ed. D. Foray and C. Freeman. Forthcoming.

Carlsson, B., and R. Stankiewicz. 1990. "On the Nature, Function and Composition of Technological Systems." *Journal of Evolutionary Economics* 1:93–118.

Carlsson, B., and E. Taymaz. 1991. "Flexible Technology and Industrial Structure in the U.S." Working Paper. Department of Economics, Case Western Reserve University.

Edquist, C., and S. Jacobsson. 1988. *Flexible Automation: The Global Diffusion of New Technology in the Engineering Industry.* Oxford: Basil Blackwell.

Ehrnberg, E., and S. Jacobsson. 1991. "Technological Discontinuities and Firm Strategy—The Cases of Machine Tools and Flexible Manufacturing Systems." Working Paper. Department of Industrial Management and Economics, Chalmers University of Technology.

Eliasson, G. 1989. "The Dynamics of Supply and Economic Growth." In *Industrial Dynamics: Technological, Organizational, and Structural Changes in Industries and Firms,* ed. B. Carlsson, 21–54. Dordrecht: Kluwer Academic Publishers.

European Communities. 1988. "EC Policy on Small and Medium-Sized Companies." *Europe,* no. 279 (September): 24–26.

Helper, S. 1987. "Supplier Relations and Technical Change: Theory and Application to the U.S. Auto Industry." Ph.D. diss., Department of Economics, Harvard University.

Helper, S. 1990. "An Exit-Voice Analysis of Supplier Relations." In *Socio-Economic Perspectives 1990,* ed. R. Coughlin, 355–72. New York: M. E. Sharpe.

Helper, S. 1991. "How Much Has Really Changed between U.S. Automakers and Their Suppliers?" *Sloan Management Review* 32:15–28.

Housely, J. 1987. "Cross-Border Links for Small Businesses." *European Trends* 2:46–49.

Hughes, A. 1990. "Industrial Concentration and the Small Business Sector in the

U.K.: The 1980s in Historical Perspective." Working Paper no. 5. Small Business Research Centre, University of Cambridge.

Imai, K. 1989. "Evolution of Japan's Corporate and Industrial Networks." In *Industrial Dynamics: Technological, Organizational, and Structural Changes in Industries and Firms*, ed. B. Carlsson, 123–55. Dordrecht: Kluwer Academic Publishers.

Ince, M. 1986. "Suppliers Seek More Integration." *Engineer,* August 21–28, 53.

Jacobsson, S. 1986. *Electronics and Industrial Policy: The Case of Computer Controlled Lathes.* London: Allen and Unwin.

Jaikumar, R. 1986. "Postindustrial Manufacturing." *Harvard Business Review* 64:69–76.

Kanawaty, G., A. Gladstone, J. Prokopenko, and G. Rodgers. 1989. "Adjustment at the Micro Level." *International Labour Review* 128:269–96.

Kaplinsky, R. 1988. "Restructuring the Capitalist Labour Process: Some Lessons from the Car Industry." *Cambridge Journal of Economics* 12:451–70.

Karlsson, J. 1991. *A Decade of Robotics.* Tyresö, Sweden: Mekanförbundets Förlag.

Keiei Joho Shuppan. 1988. *Japan's Small Businesses Today.* Tokyo: Keiei Joho Shuppan.

Kelley, M., and H. Brooks. 1990. "External Learning Opportunities and the Diffusion of Process Innovations to Small Firms: The Case of Programmable Automation." Working Paper no. 90-15. School of Urban and Public Affairs, Carnegie-Mellon University.

Knight, F. H. 1921. *Risk, Uncertainty and Profit.* New York: A. M. Kelly.

Kutscher, R. E., and V. A. Personick. 1988. "Deindustrialization and the Shift to Services." *Monthly Labor Review* 109, no. 6: 3–13.

Liberatore, M. J., and G. J. Titus. 1986. "The Use of Computer Controlled Tools by Small Machine Shops." *Journal of Small Business Management,* 24 (January): 55–62.

Loveman, G., and W. Sengenberger. 1991. "The Reemergence of Small-Scale Production: An International Comparison." *Small Business Economics* 3:1–37.

MITI. 1983. *White Paper on Small and Medium Enterprises in Japan, 1983.* Tokyo: Ministry of International Trade and Industry.

Murray, F. 1983. "The Decentralization of Production—The Decline of the Mass-collective Worker?" *Capital and Class,* no. 19: 74–99.

Nishiguchi, T. 1990. "Japanese Subcontracting: The Evolution towards Flexibility." D.Phil. thesis, Oxford University.

OECD. 1989. *Industrial Structure Statistics.* Paris: Organization for Economic Cooperation and Development.

Pullin, J. 1986. "Good, Bad—and Unavoidable." *Engineer,* August 21–28, 87–92.

Ranta, J. N.d. "Economics and Benefits of Flexible Manufacturing Systems: Conclusions for Practice." IIASA, Laxenburg, Austria. Mimeo.

Thurik, R. 1991. "Recent Developments in Firm Size Distribution and Economies of Scale in Dutch Manufacturing." Research Paper 9004. Research Institute for Small and Medium-Sized Business in the Netherlands.

Tigner, B. 1988. "Taking Care of the Little Guy." *International Management* 43:35–39.

U.S. Bureau of the Census. Various issues. *Census of Manufactures*. Washington, D.C.: U.S. Government Printing Office.

Usui, N. 1984. "Yamazaki's Showplace FMS." *American Machinist*, May, 96–97.

Banking in the EC after 1992

Gunter Dufey

The integration of financial markets represents an important dimension of Project 1992 (EC 92), laid out in the famous Commission White Paper of 1985. Through the subsequent adoption of the Single European Act of 1986, the endorsement of the Delors Report on Economic and Monetary Union in May, 1989, by the Council of Ministers, and a whole series of directives pertaining to banks, securities firms, and insurance companies, the stage has been set for the removal of barriers to free trade in financial services and for the acceptance of the rights of establishment of one member country's financial institutions in any other.

The focus of this chapter is relatively narrow. Of primary interest here are the consequences of EC 92 for the structure of the European banking industry; of secondary interest is its effects on markets for financial services. Indeed, under the heading of "Europe 1992: Financial Integration," there actually exist three dimensions that, while related, remain distinct.[1]

First, there is the objective of monetary and economic union, whose essential elements are a common European currency (generally referred to as the European Currency Unit, or ECU) and a European central bank with the power to print money.

Second, financial integration entails free flow of financial resources within the European Community. Specifically, it involves the removal of barriers to the free flow of financial assets from one member state to the next. That goal reflects more than theoretical concerns, for as recently as 1989, only four member states (Denmark, Germany, the Netherlands, and the United Kingdom) failed to restrict foreign exchange transactions and cross-border flows of capital in some way. The other eight member states practiced various forms of exchange and capital controls. It is true that, within a political

The author acknowledges Pheng-Lui Chng, who provided research assistance, and William James Adams, Michael Moffett, and an anonymous reviewer, who provided helpful comments.

1. They are "independent" to the extent that one can exist without the other; in this context, "related" means that they reinforce each other.

climate of worldwide liberalization and driven by specific EC initiatives, these eight countries had already begun a process (completed by 1991) to dismantle and abolish such restrictions. The notable exceptions were Greece and Portugal, which still maintain considerable regulatory obstacles to cross-border financial flows.[2] Apart from the "classical" exchange and capital controls, there remains, however, a whole host of tax practices that, in the absence of adequate coordination at the EC level, impede and distort cross-border capital flows.[3]

The third dimension of financial market integration pertains to the markets for financial services (commercial banking, securities underwriting and trading, and insurance). In considering this dimension, it is necessary to distinguish between financial *markets* and the financial *industry*. Two extreme situations illustrate this distinction. A set of markets can exhibit a very high degree of integration, in the sense that each financial enterprise supplies the full spectrum of services, even though, for a variety of reasons, each firm is local in geographic scope. Vice versa, service markets can be fragmented one from another by regulatory or cost factors, even though each firm supplies its service in a broad geographic area.[4] When reviewing the literature on financial services in the EC, this point is sometimes overlooked.

In this chapter, I consider both the evolving structure of markets for financial services, with emphasis on banking services in the EC, and the likely evolution of the banking industry.

Markets for Financial Services in the European Community

It is tempting to follow the conventional wisdom and characterize the EC's financial markets as fragmented. Admittedly, a widely cited study by Price Waterhouse, undertaken in connection with the Commission's evaluation of Project 1992,[5] found considerable price discrepancies in the retail and middle

---

2. For details see "The Liberalization of Capital Movements in the European Community," *Kredietbank Weekly Bulletin* 34 (September 25, 1987): 1–6. Also, the U.S. Department of the Treasury issues (periodically) a comprehensive "Report on Foreign Government Treatment of U.S. Commercial Banking and Securities Organizations."

3. The only de facto coordination is the adoption of the principle of the imputation tax for corporate profits. This attempt to integrate personal and corporate taxation has been adopted, in principle, by all EC member states, but in such a variety of versions that one cannot speak of integration. In any case, EC considerations were, at best, implicitly at work when member states adopted the principle of this "tax credit" system. See also the fourth section of this chapter.

4. The classic example is the market for automobiles in Europe, where the major suppliers market their models in virtually all member states. Prices of given models differ across national markets by amounts significantly exceeding transportation costs.

5. See Emerson et al. 1988, 105.

market for frequently used financial services (see table 1). The Cecchini Report concluded that, by reducing these differences and some of their sources, major savings could be realized by European consumers of financial services. Indeed, such savings and various related efficiency gains in the financial services sector were projected by the Commission to account for roughly one-third of all the gains expected from EC 92.[6]

These data and conclusions should not be accepted without qualification. First, most of the services studied are highly differentiated in nature. As a result, it is notoriously difficult to compare prices, even within a given country. Second, it is difficult to devise a fair sample of products for international price comparison. Finally, it is next to impossible to distinguish price reductions stemming from a general improvement in communications technology, global deregulation, and other factors from those attributable to specific EC initiatives.

Nevertheless, while one can easily take issue with the more ambitious conclusions of the report about the welfare effects of financial market integration, the fact remains that, for many retail customers and small businesses in Europe, cross-border alternatives are not readily available, especially if the United States serves as the standard of comparison.[7] Thus, significant parts of the market for financial services must be currently characterized as fragmented.

Before considering the causes of such fragmentation in detail, it is necessary to recognize that, at the other end of the market spectrum (financial services for large corporations, particularly those with operations in more than one European country; the major banks, securities brokers, and insurance companies; and various governments and international institutions), the process of market integration has increasingly become a reality. In fact, this process has been going on for some time. However, it must also be noted that market integration at the "wholesale" level does not have a uniquely European dimension; the process is simply the result of the globalization of financial markets in general. This phenomenon is based on improvements in data-processing and communications technology that compelled widespread liberalization of government policies. Notably, the globalization process included such non-EC countries as the United States, Japan, Australia, and Hong Kong, while it excluded such southern members of the European Community as Greece, Portugal, and Spain.

In this broader globalization process, the so-called Euromarkets have

---

6. Emerson et al. 1988, 98–110.

7. Even in the United States there appear to be some regional differences in the pricing of retail financial services. See, for example, the retail deposit rates and rates for home mortgages reported in the *Wall Street Journal*.

played a special role. Beginning in the early 1960s, banks began to accept time deposits in convertible currencies and fund loans in those currencies *outside* the country where the currency served as means of payment. At first this business was conducted almost exclusively in U.S. dollars, later in virtually all currencies that were convertible for nonresidents. Banks based in London pioneered the practice, hence the misleading "Euro" label. But the practice quickly spread to New York, Toronto, the Caribbean, and the Pacific Rim, where banks based in Tokyo, Hong Kong, and, especially, Singapore took up this kind of intermediation eagerly, often with the support of the local authorities.

Banks operating in the EC, other than those with branches or subsidiaries in Luxembourg and London, were handicapped by costly regulations, especially reserve requirements that did not exempt foreign currency deposits. In contrast, their large customers were unrestrained and quickly took advantage of this burgeoning market, acting as both borrowers and depositors at banks outside their home countries. Through innovative syndication techniques, the banks who made the market were able to intermediate large amounts of funds for sovereign and large corporate clients worldwide. In fact, they became so good at this technique that a large portion of the loans to less developed and Eastern Bloc countries that eventually became ailing wound up on the books of the very same banks active in the market for syndicated credits.[8]

A similar phenomenon could be observed in the markets for fixed income securities, where large, parallel markets for bonds and short-term paper emerged outside the country in whose currency the securities were denominated. This occurred as a result of (*a*) restraints on the access of foreign borrowers to national markets, and (*b*) the predilection of many investors to hold a portion of their savings outside of their domestic jurisdiction, either directly or through financial institutions. Investors from many countries sought to escape existing or future exchange controls, taxes, or, simply, political and economic turbulence. Over the years, this Eurobond market, including the segment that provides equity-related issues (convertibles and bonds with equity warrants attached), has consistently ranked among the top three or four national markets for new issues. But, as with the deposit market, the Eurobond (or, more correctly, the offshore bond) market had no particular link to EC efforts to integrate national markets. Indeed, it preceded them by many years.[9]

---

8. For more extensive analysis of these markets, see G. Dufey and T. Chung, "International Financial Markets: A Survey," in *Library of Investment Banking*, ed. Robert L. Kuhn (New York: Dow Jones-Irwin, 1990), 3–29; Arie L. Melnik and Steven E. Plaut, *The Short-Term Eurocredit Market*, Monograph Series in Finance and Economics, no. 1991–1, New York University Salomon Center, 1991.

9. As a matter of fact, the EC occasionally seems to attempt to regulate these markets, simply because they are concentrated within the Community (in London and Luxembourg). The

A similar story can be told of the trading and listing of corporate equity instruments abroad: markets have become quite integrated in that most major European corporations are listed on one or more exchanges in other countries —frequently on the exchange of another EC member state—and a number of major stocks are traded in significant volume *outside* their home market. For example, Europe's major screen-based market, SEAQ International, displays prices of 750 non-U.K. stocks, of which 200 (not all European) are traded actively in a market that is tailored to the needs of large, institutional investors.[10] Once again, however, there is no specifically EC aspect to this phenomenon; EC directives dealing with the organization of European securities markets had not been adopted as of late 1991.

Changes in the Regulatory Environment

In the previous section, I argued that European markets for financial services, especially at the "wholesale" level, are characterized by a considerable degree of integration. However, considerable fragmentation is present in retail services and in the so-called middle market (services used by small- and medium-sized business enterprises). Since the EC 92 initiatives should impinge most forcefully on the retail and middle markets, I will now focus on these particular market segments.

Assuming that price differences indicate market segmentation, it is important to recognize that segmentation can be caused by a number of different factors. Markets can be segmented by regulations that limit the access of particular financial enterprises to particular financial markets (on the basis, for example, of nationality).[11] Markets can also be differentiated, however, by consumer tastes and risk preferences. Finally, markets can exhibit large price differences on account of cost and risk variations among them. Of course, such cost differences are also based on regulatory conditions, but it is important to keep in mind that the particular regulations that matter here are rules pertaining to activities *within* a national market. The most important characteristic of such regulations is that they apply in a nondiscriminatory manner.

How then does EC 92 affect this situation? The new rules for financial services in general, and for banking in particular, reflect three basic principles.

---

proponents of control tend to forget the existence of alternative sites outside the EC and, therefore, outside its regulatory reach.

10. "Europe's Capital Markets: A Survey," *Economist*, December 16, 1989.

11. "Cross-border services" refers to the provision of services by a credit institution located in one member state to consumers in another member state without the establishment of a branch or subsidiary in the host country.

1. EC directives and recommendations[12] establish that cross-border trade in banking, securities, and insurance services must be *liberalized*. National laws and regulations to the contrary must be altered.
2. The EC 92 directives introduce a general license, known as a "European passport," for providers of goods and services. Thus, financial enterprises authorized to operate in one member state may establish themselves in all other member states as well.
3. While home-country authorization and supervision is fundamental, in a number of crucial areas, *minimum Community standards* will have to be followed by all financial enterprises operating in the EC.

While EC 92 applies these three principles to all economic activities (more or less), the application to banking and financial services is especially challenging and significant. Indeed, attempts to integrate national banking markets preceded EC 92 by many years. The First Banking Directive of 1977 provides a common legal definition of "credit institution."[13] This concept applies only to institutions that take deposits and grant credit. By implication, separate rules must be drawn up for the securities and insurance industries.

The First Banking Directive, issued when the EC was buffeted by the oil shocks of the 1970s, represented a rather modest program of harmonizing banking regulations. The essential thrust of the directive was to shift control of EC banking activities from the host to the home country of the parent institution.[14] While the First Banking Directive was a modest first step, it illustrates two characteristics of general importance in the banking field. First, its major tenet, "parental responsibility," cannot be considered an innovation of EC policy. The so-called Cook Committee, comprised of the central bank governors from the major economic powers of the free world and meeting under the auspices of the Bank for International Settlements (BIS), had already established the principle that the parent bank and its regulators should exercise primary responsibility for an institution's branches abroad. The Cook Committee's approach was binding on all the major countries, including those in the EC.

Second, the major effect of the directive was not so much on cross-border activities but on the *internal* organization and regulatory environment

---

12. Directives bind member states as to policy goals but leave the national governments free to choose the form of implementation. Recommendations are just that; they have no binding force. See Uwe H. Schneider, "The Harmonization of EC Banking Laws: The Euro-Passport to Profitability and International Competitiveness of Financial Institutions," *Law and Policy in International Business* 22 (1991): 273.

13. Schneider, "Harmonization," 268.

14. Jean Dermine, ed., *European Banking in the 1990s* (Oxford: Basil Blackwell, 1990), 21–22.

of national markets. In his capacity as a high-level Italian central bank official, a fellow contributor to this volume makes this point very well.

> In banking, the most important of these rules is the 1977 Directive,
> which has already brought about some of the most fundamental changes
> in Italian banking regulations since 1936—reopening, among other
> things, the possibility of founding new banks, which had been precluded
> in practice for many years.[15]

The First Banking Directive was overshadowed by the Second Banking
Directive, which came into force during 1988–89 as part of EC 92. In comparison with the first directive, the second employs a more comprehensive
concept of banking. Indeed, the list of activities mentioned in the directive
suggests that the EC Commission had turned toward the concept of universal
banking. The list of services compiled in the directive includes all the activities in which universal banks engage, with the notable exception of providing insurance services.[16]

The Second Banking Directive also introduced the concept of a "European passport." Once licensed in one country, a provider of financial services
is authorized not only to sell them across borders within the EC, but also to
operate local establishments in other EC markets. Thus, the Second Banking
Directive extends the general EC principle of the mutual recognition of technical standards to banking supervision.

The new directive was also not conducive to excessive segmentation of
markets. It established one set of principles for all kinds of credit institutions,
and that included traditional commercial banks, savings institutions, credit
unions, building societies, and a host of others. Again, this measure, like
others, had the effect of changing rules *within* member countries. Most EC
members segment financial markets among various credit institutions. However, reforms in national markets, prompted in part by the Second Banking
Directive, enlarged the scope of various financial institutions, making them
more alike and reducing the segmentation of EC markets along product lines.

The Second Banking Directive was followed by a large number of others
designed to establish certain minimum regulatory standards. The most important of these is the directive of February, 1989, establishing minimum
standards for capital adequacy. Once again, there was nothing uniquely European about this capital adequacy standard; it simply reflects (*a*) the minimal
capital ratios and (*b*) the measurement definitions on which regulators from

---

15. Tommaso Padoa-Schioppa, "Towards a European Banking Regulatory Framework,"
Banca d'Italia Economic Bulletin, no. 6 (February 1988): 49.

16. Dermine, *European Banking*, 23.

many countries agreed during their BIS meetings. Generally referred to as the Basle Agreement, this accord formed the basis for the so-called BIS capital adequacy requirements.

The Second Banking Directive, in its revised version, also contained an important message with respect to banking institutions based in countries *outside* the EC. It established that third-country banks operate under the same principles as EC banks, but, upon entry into an EC member state, they are subject to review by the Commission. One of the review criteria is *reciprocity*, the manner in which the third-country bank's home government treats the EC's financial institutions. The entry of banks from third countries is then subject to a final decision by the Council of Ministers upon the Commission's recommendation. Importantly, however, this review does not apply to third-country institutions that are already established in the EC through a subsidiary (not merely a branch). However, Commission review may be triggered by an ownership change, including nationalization.[17]

The period between 1986 and 1990 saw a large number of other directives and recommendations dealing with such issues as solvency ratios, public disclosure of annual accounts, concentration of large credits, and deposit guarantee schemes. These measures have reinforced the basic principles of EC 92 with respect to banking: there will be no Community-wide central authority; home country rule will prevail, subject to minimum EC standards.

These minimum standards are only that—a minimum; they do not preclude individual national authorities, either by legislation or by interpretation of existing rules, from imposing higher standards on their own banks. This creates the distinct possibility of reverse discrimination.[18] For example, some countries (e.g., Germany) do not recognize accounting provisions taken for lower market values on real estate, securities, and financial investments as being part of a bank's capital. However, BIS/EC guidelines regard such provisions as "second tier" capital. This divergence in definition of capital would force German banks to maintain relatively high capital ratios (as defined by the EC). German bankers claim that this puts them at a disadvantage in the marketplace.[19]

Another contentious issue pertains to variations among member states in the role of commercial banks in the securities business. On the Continent,

---

17. For details see Douglas Croham, *Reciprocity and the Unification of the European Banking Market*, Group of Thirty Occasional Papers 27 (New York and London: Group of Thirty, 1989).

18. Schneider, "Harmonization," 270.

19. Arguably, the market would reward these higher capital ratios with lower deposit rates, due to lower risk perceptions. Of course, such an advantage is offset when the risk obtaining in other banking systems is projected onto the industry at large (insurance principle), or onto the public taxpayers in the country concerned through expected central bank rescue operations.

universal banks play a significant role in the securities business; hence, the same capital supports both traditional commercial banking and securities activities (such as underwriting and trading). According to EC definitions, however, securities houses are not banks (credit institutions). Thus, they do not have to comply with the various EC requirements for commercial banks. This provision may give nonbank competitors of universal banks an advantage in securities activities. This advantage pertains to investment banks from countries where banks and securities firms are separated (the United Kingdom and possibly Italy). But then again, the securities companies do not qualify for the European passport, either.[20]

Remaining Obstacles

In the previous section, I showed that EC 92 leaves many uneven spots on the "level playing field" of competition—due both to the regulatory structure chosen and to the uneven progress (across financial service markets) toward achieving the project's goals. In addition, serious differences in costs and (perhaps) in consumer preferences will cause the divergence in prices (reflected in table 1) to persist. This will be true even if the regulatory program is a success in terms of providing at least potential access for external service providers, thereby increasing competition. While the detailed analysis of each product segment of banking markets is beyond the scope of this survey, a review of just one such service, housing finance, illustrates this contention nicely.

Housing Finance in the EC:

A Confusing Kaleidoscope

Financing the purchases of homes and condominiums represents a significant proportion of total financing activity in all EC member countries, with magnitudes ranging from 20 to 40 percent of all credit activities. A single market in mortgage financing lies, however, in the distant future. In part, this is due to the nature of the business. Since mortgage finance

---

20. As of mid-1991, there were still some significant gaps in the 1992 program for financial services. While a draft of the investment services directive was submitted to the Council in early 1989, it faces a number of obstacles, particularly differences among member states over the extent, if any, to permit the trading of securities outside of recognized exchanges.

On the insurance side, the life insurance directive faces particularly severe obstacles, making it unlikely to meet the deadline of January 1, 1993. Since life insurance and the securities business compete directly with banks for the intermediation of savings, this delay could introduce distortions in markets for financial services. This effect is of particular concern due to the institutionalization of this competition in terms of *Allfinanz* in Germany and *bancassurance* in France.

TABLE 1. European Prices for Financial Services (in percentage above or below the average of the lowest four national prices)

Standard Service	Belgium	West Germany	Spain	France	Italy	Luxembourg	Netherlands	Great Britain
Banking								
Consumer credit[a]	-41	136	39	105	NA	-26	31	121
Mortgages[b]	31	57	118	78	-4	NA	-6	-20
Foreign exchange drafts[c]	6	31	196	56	23	33	-46	16
Commercial loans[d]	-5	6	19	-7	9	6	43	46
Insurance								
Life insurance[e]	78	5	37	33	83	66	-9	-30
Home insurance[f]	-16	3	-4	39	81	57	17	90
Commercial fire and theft[g]	-9	43	24	153	245	-15	-1	27
Brokerage								
Private equity transactions[h]	36	7	65	-13	-3	7	114	123
Institutional equity transactions[i]	26	69	153	-5	47	68	26	-47

Note: NA = not available.

[a] Annual cost of consumer loan of ECU 5,090, excess interest rate over money market rates.
[b] Annual cost of home loan of ECU 25,000, excess interest rate over money market rates.
[c] Cost to a large commercial client of purchasing a commercial draft for ECU 30,000.
[d] Annual cost (including commissions and charges) to a medium-sized firm of a commercial loan of ECU 250,000.
[e] Average annual cost of term life insurance.
[f] Average annual cost of fire and theft coverage for house valued at ECU 70,000 and contents at ECU 28,000.
[g] Annual coverage for premises valued at ECU 390,000 and inventory at ECU 230,000.
[h] Commission costs of cash purchase of ECU 1,440.
[i] Commission costs of cash purchase of ECU 288,000.

is based on using property as security for the lender, such finance is closely tied to the relevant national legal system governing ownership rights on real estate. Further, since "housing" is an important consumption good, the market is often politicized and housing finance is frequently subsidized. However, individual countries have chosen very different ways to do this! For the same political reasons, consumer protection motives affect the national regulation of housing finance—again manifesting itself in different ways from country to country. For example:

1. Home owners' rights conflict with the rights of mortgage lenders to take control of property upon default.
2. The default event itself is defined differently in various markets.
3. Countries tend to have specialized institutions that offer mortgage financing and they endow them with special privileges designed to lower the cost and increase the availability of housing credit. Again, this is true for most EC countries but unfortunately not for all!
4. Some of these mortgage institutions (e.g., Crédit Foncier de France) are government owned, presumably lowering the cost of equity capital and, therefore, the cost of housing finance.
5. France, together with other countries, offers prospective home owners a wide variety of subsidized mortgage plans.
6. Regulations aimed at consumer protection vary widely. In some countries, like France, mortgage lenders must provide binding offers for 30 days during which the applicant has the option to accept or reject the loan offered.
7. In some European countries, but by no means all, fixed rate mortgages are repayable without penalty.
8. In some countries, fixed rate mortgages are virtually prescribed, in others mortgage terms are so short the rates are de facto variable, and in still others mortgage rates float with a composite of several market rates.
9. In some countries mortgage loans are tied only to the property per se, in others they are due when the borrower sells his home.

It should come as little surprise, then, that prices for mortgage loans differ widely. Cost factors alone account for substantial price discrepancies.[21]

Taxes represent another special cost and an obstacle to financial market integration. Again, it is necessary to distinguish between taxes levied only on

---

21. Adapted from BHF-Bank, *Wirtschaftsdienst*, no. 1632 (April 6, 1991), 1–4.

cross-border financial transactions and internal taxes imposed at different effective rates in different countries, causing the relative prices of given financial services to differ artificially from one country to the next. As it turns out, the latter are virtually impossible to change.

The EC has tried its hand at tax harmonization, particularly in the context of value-added taxes; but it has not been very successful. Even efforts limited to harmonizing withholding taxes on cross-border financial transactions have failed. However, an EC directive to eliminate withholding taxes on cross-border payments of interest and royalties between related corporate entities is expected to be issued in late 1991 or early 1992.[22] Further, a proposed EC loss directive would allow a parent company or other entity located in one member state to offset profits with losses in another member state.

While some of these initiatives will undoubtedly yield results, remaining differences abound. Particularly noteworthy are rules regarding enforcement of taxes on interest and dividend income received by individual investors. Some countries apply very high rates to certain categories of such income, others have relatively low, flat rates, irrespective of the taxpayer's other sources of income. Others again, notably Germany, require that interest be included in personal income, but since there is only haphazard enforcement, large proportions of total interest income escape taxation altogether.[23] In contrast, dividends received from domestic corporations are subject to a 30 percent withholding tax.

Even greater discrepancies can be found when one looks at the tax treatment of interest paid. The rules on deductibility differ vastly among member states in terms of who claims the deduction and how the loan is used. A detailed analysis is beyond the scope of this chapter; the crucial point, however, is that, since people in each member state have successfully adjusted to each system, the constituencies objecting to reform are very powerful and they have successfully stymied EC tax harmonization efforts.

Structural Change in the Banking Industry after 1992

The preceding review of the legislative changes associated with EC 92 has shown that the regulatory environment of European financial institutions is about to change significantly. While some obstacles remain,[24] there is no doubt that the entry of financial institutions into other markets of the EC has

---

22. Among the EC member states, rates of withholding taxes on interest vary from 0.0 to 48.4 percent.

23. In November, 1991, the German government proposed a 25 percent tax on domestic interest income with DM 5,000 (10,000) tax free allowances for single (married) taxpayers respectively. No consideration was to be given for taxes paid in other EC countries.

24. Schneider, "Harmonization," 272.

been significantly liberalized. However, it must be clearly recognized that legislative changes only enlarge the scope for and the ability of financial institutions to provide services on an EC-wide basis. To what extent it is strategically viable for an individual financial institution to actually use this freedom is quite a different matter.

The following part of this survey will begin with a review of the lessons learned from the performance of international banking activities in general. It will then examine the extent to which market integration requires the entry of new financial institutions and to what extent such entry can be effected by providing financial services across borders. Third, a scheme is introduced that incorporates a standard classification of markets for banking products in order to provide a framework for analyzing the preceding issue. Fourth, I shall analyze, in some detail, the market segments where cross-border trade is effective and those that require control of the delivery system. In a final major section, I analyze the special conditions in the banking market with respect to foreign market penetration, using a framework based on foreign direct investment (FDI) theory.

Before proceeding, it might be useful to disassemble the complex activities that hide under the term *international banking*. Following the literature,[25] there is, first, *traditional international banking* that comprises cross-border transactions (payments and credits received from or extended to customers in other countries). This process often involves the use of foreign correspondent banks with whom payment arrangements and credit lines are established in order to facilitate the information flow and the agency costs (these are considerable in transactions that involve different political, legal, and social environments).

Second, there are the intermediation activities in offshore centers. In the second section of this chapter, when describing the Euromarkets, I pointed out that, for largely regulatory reasons, a considerable proportion of total credit intermediation activities has been moved to foreign banking centers. Such activities are centered in Europe (London and Luxembourg) on account of the virtually unlimited freedom to do business there in currencies other than the domestic one and with nonresident customers.[26]

The third mode of international banking involves entry into foreign markets via creation of offices, agencies, branches, or subsidiaries. One specific issue here is the mode of new entry (creation of de novo establishments,

---

25. See Robert Z. Aliber, "International Banking: A Survey," *Journal of Money, Credit and Banking* 16, no. 4, pt. 2 (November 1983): 661–712; Gunter Dufey and Ian H. Giddy, *The International Money Market* (Englewood Cliffs, N.J.: Prentice-Hall, 1978), chap. 1.

26. Except, of course, the usual obligations under private contracts and criminal laws. Indeed, centers compete for business not only by their liberal regulations but by the quality of their regulatory climate.

acquisition of an existing local enterprise, or some form of cooperative venture). For reasons to be discussed subsequently, bankers and public policy-makers have dwelled upon de novo establishment. This is the mode of international banking most affected by EC 92.

It is unwise to discuss international banking in Europe without reviewing this activity in a broader context. After all, the world has acquired considerable experience with international banking. While limited by various entry barriers, there has been significant activity in this respect worldwide, nevertheless.[27]

Traditionally, most banks that venture abroad are following their clients. Originally, this motive was announced to put local competitors at ease and to overcome regulatory hurdles to access. Abstracting from the colonial experience, the history of international banking clearly shows that banks went abroad to follow trade or to serve their own emigrant populations. After World War II, an additional motive emerged: to follow the banks' corporate customers, whose foreign direct investment activities offered both the challenge of retaining traditional clients and the opportunity to provide such new financial services as foreign currency loans and international cash management services. This phenomenon affected U.S. banks first, then their European and Japanese counterparts.

However, it is clear that once a bank had established a presence in a foreign market (often after lengthy and sometimes acrimonious negotiations with local regulators regarding reciprocity), it quickly sought opportunities to serve unmet needs for financial services in the foreign market.[28] After thirty years of experience, one can say, by and large, that the efforts to profit from such opportunities have met with only modest success. The reason is simply that local market imperfections tended to disappear quickly when foreign competitors tried to take advantage of them. If they did exist because of regulatory discrepancies, the protests of the local banks quickly caused the regulations to change, usually toward more liberalization. Furthermore, local competitors quickly reasserted themselves and became much more efficient under the threat of an actual or potential onslaught of foreign competitors.[29]

Success or failure in international banking is not easily measured.[30] Most

27. See Sang-Rim Choi, Adrian E. Tschoegl, and Chwo-Ming Yu, "Banks and the World's Major Financial Centers, 1970–1980," *Weltwirtschaftliches Archiv* 122 (1986): 48–64.

28. Gunter Dufey and Adrian Tschoegl, "International Competition in the Services Industries: Institutional and Structural Characteristics of Financial Services—with Specific Reference to Banking," report prepared for the U.S. Congress Office of Technology Assessment, 1986.

29. For a case study, see Jack Lowenstein, "Foreigners Weather Aussie Onslaught," *Euromoney*, April, 1991, 39–42.

30. *International Competitiveness of U.S. Financial Firms: Products, Markets, and Conventional Performance Measures*, Staff Study, Federal Reserve Bank of New York, 1991.

**TABLE 2. Estimates of the
Proportion of Total Banking Assets
Held by Foreign Financial Institutions
at the End of 1987 (percentage of
total banking assets)**

Belgium[a]	46
Denmark	1
France	16
Germany	4
Greece	NA
Ireland	11
Italy	3
Luxembourg[b]	91
Netherlands	10
Portugal	3
Spain	11
United Kingdom[c]	60

Source: Hawawini and Rajendra, *Transformation of the European Financial Services Industry.*
Note: NA = not available.
[a] Figure includes activities of "coordination centers" (finance companies) of multinational corporations.
[b] Figure includes private banking activities for global customers.
[c] Figure includes international syndicated loans and Eurobonds.

banks recognize that, at first, their operations will not be profitable. Furthermore, the nature of bank accounting is such that it is difficult to allocate costs to parts of an integrated system with many intangible assets. Thus, it is next to impossible to measure precisely the marginal contributions of individual parts of a vast organization, especially those operating abroad. Last, but not least, international tax differences and regulatory discrepancies provide strong incentives for banks to allocate profits in ways that may minimize taxes and the cost of regulatory constraints, but distort a bad evaluation system even further. Nevertheless, banks recognize that it will take an investment to buy market share and, therefore, it is only after several years that the success or failure of foreign banks becomes clear.

One reasonable proxy for the success or failure of a foreign bank might be the market share it ultimately gains. Tables 2 and 3 show the market shares of foreign banks in several countries where such financial institutions have a reasonably long history. If we eliminate the United Kingdom and Luxembourg, where the figures reflect considerable nonresident business and other special factors, the data show that the market penetration by foreign banks has

TABLE 3. Commercial Lending and Assets of Domestic and Foreign Banks (in billions of dollars and percentages)

	1986			1987			1988			1989		
	Domestic	Foreign		Domestic	Foreign		Domestic	Foreign		Domestic	Foreign	
	Amount	Amount	Percentage	Amount	Amount	Percentage	Amount	Amount	Percentage	Amount	Amount	Percentage
United States												
Commercial loans (C&I)	392	104	21.0	389	126	24.5	406	150	27.0	424	166	28.1
Total assets	2,449	539	18.0	2,473	606	19.7	2,615	674	20.5	2,779	750	21.3
Japan												
Loans and discounts[a]	1,867	41	2.2	2,103	49	2.3	2,318	45	1.9	2,862	49	1.7
Total assets	2,939	82	2.7	3,315	94	2.7	3,671	95	2.5	4,716	95	2.0
Germany												
Commercial loans	1,001	18	3.0	1,022	18	1.7	1,075	20	1.8	1,152	21	2.9
Total assets	3,412	144	4.0	3,620	151	4.0	3,852	168	4.2	4,131	190	4.4
United Kingdom												
Commercial loans[b]	78	39	33.5	104	47	31.3	121	60	33.3	165	82	33.3
Total assets	213	352	62.3	219	353	61.7	248	385	60.8	314	455	59.2

Source: Howe et al., "Competitiveness in Commercial Lending Markets."

[a]Figures include banking account balances only (trust account balances are not included).

[b]Commercial lending in the United Kingdom is defined as sterling and nonsterling private sector advances.

been very modest.[31] Even in the United States, the frequently cited proportion of commercial and industrial loans (C&I) held by foreign banks is not representative of the activities of foreign banks in general. Not only do these loans reflect purchased loans, which were originated by U.S. banks and then sold off, but C&I loans are only a small proportion of total bank assets. As of December, 1988, for example, total U.S. bank assets were $2,430 billion, while C&I loans amounted to only 24.9 percent of that total.[32]

Careful students of the international banking scene recognize quickly that there are very few success stories in this business, especially when looking at operations in a foreign national market. There do seem to be some unique conditions in the banking industry, which will be addressed later; first, however, we must deal with an issue that is more directly relevant for EC 92. Following the recent literature on international trade in financial services,[33] the effects of liberalizing the activities of competitors in international financial markets depends greatly on the specific nature of the services concerned. Particularly, one must distinguish between (*a*) those that can be offered across borders and (*b*) those that require a physical presence near the location of the customer.

With respect to the first category, the competitive factors that influence the pattern of trade are primarily regulatory costs that determine the location of the producer. It must be noted in this context that the regulatory costs factor comprises not only the existence of costly regulations, but includes, at the same time, (*a*) the presence of a regulatory framework that improves the safety of the transactions and provides an appropriate technical infrastructure, (*b*) skilled personnel, (*c*) access for expatriate managers and specialists, and (*d*) competitive costs of maintaining such an expatriate community (which range from the magnitude of hardship compensation all the way to the tax treatment of the compensation packages). These factors are relevant for the competition among international financial centers.[34]

---

31. Even these numbers overstate the real market share since the books of a foreign bank in a local market tend to be filled with assets that are related to international activities, particularly corporations that do business with the home country of the bank. Further, special factors often affect the data. Belgium, for example, includes the activities of coordination centers that are essentially finance companies of multinationals who, due to tax incentives given, concentrate liquid assets in those institutions.

32. Data on U.S. commercial banks' loan portfolios can be obtained from the *Annual Statistical Digest, 1988* (Washington, D.C.: Board of Governors of the Federal Reserve System, 1989).

33. See Rachel McCulloch, "International Competition in Services," NBER Working Paper no. 2235, 1987; John D. Montgomery, "Market Segmentation and 1992: Toward a Theory of Trade in Financial Services," International Finance Discussion Paper no. 394, Board of Governors of the Federal Reserve System, 1991.

34. Yoon S. Park and Musa Essayyad, eds., *International Banking and Financial Centers* (Dordrecht: Kluwer Academic Publishers, 1989).

Alternatively, services are offered across borders if they are tied to a particular currency or to access to market segments in a national market. To use a European illustration, if a large German company wants to raise funds in the commercial paper market of France, it is obvious that French investment banks, who have the distribution capabilities in that particular market, will have a significant advantage in capturing this business.

Clearly, such considerations apply to those markets that are listed in the last two rows of figure 1. Large corporations and financial institutions have the ability to absorb the information costs that must be incurred in shopping across numerous markets for the most economic offer. Indeed, to the extent that the services are available in an international financial center, the shopping costs are often less than when prices and conditions of financial services must be compared across a number of different jurisdictions.[35]

Markets that provide services for high-net-worth individuals are also characterized by cross-border transactions. There is a long tradition in Europe of the upper middle class holding a portion of its savings in Switzerland, Luxembourg, or London.[36] Just like savers elsewhere, they are motivated by the historical experience of economic and political turmoil and, more recently, by actual or threatened exchange controls and high levels of personal taxation. They are attracted to these offshore centers by confidentiality assured by law or practice (London).

While each of these locations represents a unified jurisdiction, the nature of private banking servicing the offshore accounts of high-net-worth individuals clearly shows national segmentation. To illustrate: the banks in Luxembourg that attract German customers are not exactly the same as those that attract the bulk of French customers. By the same token, the services that attract investors from various countries tend to differ by currency as well as by instrument. For example, investors have a preference for instruments expressed in their home currency. Fixed income securities are particularly attractive to Germans, reflecting an investment pattern practiced at home; the French, in turn, like short-term money funds and equities. However, portfolios offshore are not quite as concentrated as they are in national markets; while German investors, for example, have (almost) all their funds in DM bonds and, to a much smaller extent, in shares or equity-based mutual funds, once they transfer their portfolios to Luxembourg the proportion of non-German assets in their portfolios increases. The same is true with respect to institutions: savers from Germany with accounts in Luxembourg have a strong

---

35. One little vignette: English has become the sole language of the international wholesale markets for financial services.

36. Jurisdictions such as the Channel Islands and Isle of Man are treated simply as parts of the London financial market in every respect but taxation.

Activity or Service \\ Market Segment	Credit-Related Activities	Transactions-Related Activities		Securities-Related Activities		Corporate Finance Activities
	Lending including Credit Cards	Deposits, Payments, F/X, Trade Finance & Processing Operations	Swaps & Derivative Products	Underwriting, including Securitization, Trading & Brokerage	Asset Management, Insurance Marketing, Mutual Funds	Financial Advisory Services, Merchant-Banking, Venture-Capital, Mergers and acquisitions Services
Retail/ consumers			N/A			N/A
High-net-worth individuals						
Middle market commercial						
Large corporations						
Financial institutions including correspondent banking						

Fig. 1. Matrix of Banking: products, services, and market segments. (Services are defined by technology, skills, and risks; market segments are defined by common demand factors, e.g., scale, risk, and approach.) N/A = not applicable.

preference for maintaining them in the Luxembourg subsidiaries of German banks. However, these financial institutions do not have a lock on such customers; some German investors will use locally based banks or even subsidiaries of banks from third countries.

This observation is important because it shows the extent to which banking markets are contestable. To assess this characteristic one must find answers to essentially three questions.

1. To what extent can competitors match others in terms of costs, brand loyalty, technology, reputation, and similar characteristics?
2. How will entrenched competitors react to a competitive move in terms of price and quality?
3. How costly is it to exit a market?

It is difficult to answer these questions definitively for banking as a whole. One can do a little better by looking at individual segments of the market differentiated by product and major customer.

The analysis offered in the Cecchini Report made clear that any advantages from European financial market integration would occur primarily in retail banking and in services for middle market customers (i.e., small- and medium-sized business firms). It is also clear that many of these services will require a delivery system that is close to the client.

Lending to consumers, small businesses, and the middle market represents a good example of the differentiated nature of the market for banking services. Consumer lending tends to be a matter of playing the law of large numbers. The creditworthiness of the individual is assessed on standard measures, and, in many banks, such credits are evaluated in an automated fashion according to "standard scores." On the other hand, middle market lending requires the availability of skilled credit officers who are intimately familiar with the applicant's market and financial condition. Such services cannot be provided from a distance. Indeed, it is easier to service retail markets with highly standardized products from a distance, provided it is possible to do so at a significant cost advantage.

The markets for consumer lending are characterized by very high volume, where the cost of entry represents a substantial barrier. To illustrate the underlying issue, will French consumers utilize credit cards from Belgian banks? Probably not. What is more likely is that new suppliers from the national market, such as automobile finance companies or professional associations, will use their marketing clout to offer these products on a franchised basis.

With respect to standard deposit and payment services, retail customers are motivated by convenience, error-free service, and, to a certain extent, cost. Research in many industrialized countries shows that consumers tend to resist changing banks because the effort required to change accounts is perceived to outweigh the benefits. For most retail customers, locational convenience is the major determinant of bank choice; a close relationship with individuals who work at a given bank office is secondary. This characteristic of the market obviously gives established competitors a very strong position, and the only way to contest the market is for a foreign bank to purchase an established competitor. This issue will be analyzed subsequently.

Middle market customers are more price sensitive, and, in general, it is the credit relationship that tends to dominate the deposit, payments, and other processing operations required. Familiarity and a relationship with the bank's account officer seems to be the dominant factor. Once again, this requires a strong and established presence in the market. Developing customer relationships must be viewed by any new competitor as a fixed cost to be evaluated on a present value basis.

To the extent that retail customers invest in securities, they have much to gain in efficiency and convenience by keeping their payment, savings, and brokerage accounts in the same financial institution. Unsurprisingly, therefore, where universal banking exists, as in Continental Europe, it is invariably true that the basic account relationship of the customer also captures whatever securities activity there may be.[37]

In the middle market, where customers tend to have multiple credit relationships already, they are willing to split their brokerage business from the credit relationship.[38] The access to a trusted and competent investment advisor is a major concern in this business; thus, even if the relationship happens to be within the same financial institution, the bank officer handling the investment activities tends to be a different person than the one who approves business loans. For that reason, the market here is more contestable.

In any case, the availability of an investment advisor who at least speaks the same language severely limits cross-border transactions, except for the most sophisticated investors (who work through offshore center accounts in any case). Institutional presence is essential, and that presence cannot be easily established. This lesson has been learned by U.S. brokerage houses that have tried to penetrate European middle markets. Overall, their market share is very small and they have gained a foothold only with respect to those countries and clients that were willing and able to trade such unique products as financial futures on foreign exchanges, where domestic equivalents were not available.

Mutual funds represent a particular challenge as they make securities investment feasible for individual retail investors. Here again, however, access to these retail investors can only be gained through a local delivery system. This is less true for middle market customers, where the market seems to be truly contestable, since the target clientele can be approached through advertisements in newspapers, magazines, or direct mail. This seems to be a market where the EC directive of October, 1989, on mutual funds can be expected to make a difference. This regulatory change is particularly relevant with respect to money market mutual funds in Germany, which so far have not been available. The change in regulations is also pertinent to the

---

37. It is not without reason that major brokerage houses in the United States consider the ability to offer a money market fund with checking account features as a major competitive tool to maintain customer loyalty; many of these money fund activities per se are of very marginal profitability for their sponsors.

38. To the extent that the securities holdings of owner-managers often serve as collateral for business loans there is, however, a strong linkage.

entry of U.K.-based equity funds into markets of other member states. Such funds have shown superior performance relative to their Continental competitors and will benefit from EC 92.

Some observers see modest inroads with respect to corporate finance activities in the middle market.[39] However, one can already see the beginning of an interesting phenomenon: even the threat of entry of foreign competitors causes domestic financial institutions to "gear up" and strengthen their own offerings of such services. Financial products, after all, are not patentable; and if and when foreign entrants show that there are profit opportunities in a particular market, local competitors freed from regulatory constraints by the impact of the various EC directives will quickly jump into the breach. This is a general point of considerable significance in any overall assessment of EC initiatives in markets for financial services.

These rough and sketchy examples suffice to show that meaningful conclusions about the virtues of particular modes of entering foreign banking markets presuppose analysis of financial service markets segmented by customer group as well as by product. Vice versa, general statements about "banking" are not very meaningful because they embody excessive aggregation of what are very different business lines. Nevertheless, it is safe to say that significant segments of financial markets can be penetrated only by acquiring an existing intermediary. While EC rules do not remove all barriers to transborder acquisitions in the banking industry,[40] they do reduce them considerably. Thus, since 1985, EC 92 has generated a wave of transborder mergers, acquisitions, and joint ventures in commerce and industry (see Jacquemin and also Jenny in this volume).[41]

In contrast to the nonfinancial sector, in banking and financial services, there have been relatively few large-scale mergers and acquisitions. Tables 4 and 5 document the relevant trends between 1986 and 1989. A cursory glance reveals that mergers, acquisitions, and joint ventures involving banks in the same EC country account for 55 percent of the total during 1985–89. Indeed, involvement from outside the EC occurred more frequently than foreign involvement from within the Community (123 transactions vs. 106).

In value terms, table 5 shows that most transactions involved less than ECU 5 billion (an ECU is worth approximately $1.40). Clearly, large-scale mergers and acquisitions are rare. The desire to obtain a foothold within the EC explains the activity of financial institutions based in third countries. So

---

39. "The Single European Market: Survey of the U.K. Financial Services Industry," *Bank of England Quarterly Bulletin* 29 (August 1989): 407–12.

40. Spain had outright restrictions on the entry of foreign banks; Italy, France, Spain, Greece, and Portugal required consent of the authorities to enter by acquisition.

41. For data, see the EC's annual reports on competition policy and *European Deal Review*.

TABLE 4. Number of Mergers, Acquisitions of Minority Holdings, and Joint Ventures in EC Banking

	National[a]			Community[b]			International[c]			Total			
	Merger[d]	Acquisition[e]	Joint Venture	Merger[d]	Acquisition[e]	Joint Venture	Merger[d]	Acquisition[e]	Joint Venture	Merger[d]	Acquisition[e]	Joint Venture	Grand Total
1988–89	51	32	11	16	20	6	16	11	7	83	62	24	169
1987–88	53	38	16	12	15	7	13	28	7	78	81	30	189
1986–87	22	11	18	3	9	5	10	13	1	35	33	24	92
1985–86	12	10	10	4	3	6	9	8	0	25	21	16	62

Source: Commission of the European Communities, Nineteenth Report on Competition Policy (Luxembourg: Office for Official Publications of the European Communities, 223–25. 1990).
[a] All firms from the same member state.
[b] Firms from different member states.
[c] Some firms from inside, others from outside, the EC; effects inside the EC.
[d] Includes acquisitions of majority holdings.
[e] Acquisitions of minority holdings.

TABLE 5. Number of Mergers and Acquisitions in EC Banking, Breakdown in Terms of Combined Sales of Participating Firms (in billions of ECUs)

Year	National[a]				Community[b]				International[c]				Total			
	>1	>2	>5	>10	>1	>2	>5	>10	>1	>2	>5	>10	>1	>2	>5	>10
1988–89	22	15	3	1	11	9	4	2	8	8	5	4	41	32	12	7
1987–88	19	14	7	4	10	10	8	4	7	5	4	2	36	29	19	10
1986–87	9	6	5	3	2	2	1	1	9	7	5	3	20	15	11	7

Source: Data from Commission of the European Communities, *Nineteenth Report on Competition Policy* (Luxembourg: Office for Official Publications of the European Communities, 1990), 215.

[a] All firms from the same member state.

[b] Firms from different member states.

[c] Some firms from inside, others from outside, the EC; effects inside the EC.

far unexplained, however, is why there has been so little transnational merger activity in the financial field overall.

It is true that some of the regulatory changes have yet to be implemented; after all, the starting date for Europe 1992 is January 1, 1993. However, the theory of foreign direct investment (FDI) provides good reasons to suspect that more fundamental factors are at work. Indeed, I shall argue that, when applied to the banking industry, FDI theory would not predict a wave of big mergers and acquisitions among the EC's financial enterprises.

Foreign Direct Investment and the Banking Industry

According to a basic tenet of FDI theory,[42] ownership and control of a foreign asset can be obtained only if the acquirer pays the present owners more than their reservation price. Since prices are established on the basis of expected net cash flows, discounted by the cost of capital, the foreign acquirer can justify paying more than the current market price only if (*a*) its cost of capital is lower, or (*b*) its expected net revenues are higher. While the existence of differences in the cost of capital for companies based in various countries is a matter of some disagreement, there is very little to support a belief in systematic cost-of-capital differences within the European Community, particularly now that measures to liberalize capital flows have been implemented in all member states that matter (financially speaking). Thus, any acquirer of a foreign bank must anticipate increased net cash flows.

When considering future net cash flows that a foreign acquirer can extract from a local company, FDI theory emphasizes the fact that the foreign acquirer incurs special costs of controlling and managing an operation in a foreign environment. These costs are particularly relevant with respect to banking.

While technology has had an important impact, no financial institution has managed to obtain a lasting technological advantage. All banks use equipment procured from a limited number of global suppliers. Beyond bricks and mortar and technology, banking is a people business. The management of highly skilled specialists and large numbers of clerical personnel requires considerable skill. Indeed, in domestic contexts, it is often those management skills that differentiate banks.[43] Managing a work force across borders and

---

42. For a good review of the FDI literature, see John H. Dunning, "The Eclectic Paradigm of International Production: A Restatement and Some Possible Extensions," *Journal of International Business Studies* 19 (Spring 1988): 1–31; Peter J. Buckley, "The Limits of Explanation: Testing the Internalization Theory of the Multinational Enterprise," *Journal of International Business Studies* 19 (Summer 1988): 181–93.

43. Jean M. Hiltrop, "Human Resource Management in European Banking: Challenges and Responses," *European Management Journal* 9 (March 1991): 36–42.

cultural environments is extremely difficult. Not only is it necessary to alter the old culture of the acquired enterprise (difficult to accomplish even in a domestic context, as many failed bank mergers attest), but to do so across borders is an elusive feat, indeed. The success stories are few and far between.[44]

To the extent that a bank can develop a competitive advantage, it relies largely on an internal management culture (methods of informal cooperation, decentralization, and control that motivate thousands of employees to act in manners consistent with corporate goals). In short, it is "management" that distinguishes successful from unsuccessful banks. This is exactly the area where transborder mergers of financial institutions, even those mergers involving institutions that have managed to develop a successful corporate culture in their home countries, have encountered their biggest problems.[45]

Combining the facts that (a) with respect to most banking products, profitability is difficult to defend from competition, while (b) the management, control, and integration costs are very high, leads to the conclusion that FDI strategies are unlikely to succeed. This is true especially in view of the fact that economies of scale in banking—unlike certain segments of manufacturing—have proved to be ephemeral and may even be negative for cross-border consolidations.

Having concluded that cross-border mergers will not occur frequently, for lack of sufficient economic incentive, the temptation is to argue for the status quo after 1992. This would overlook, however, another significant arena of change: under the threat of competition from the outside, and contemplating the upcoming dynamic changes in nonfinancial markets introduced by EC 92, European banks are most likely to use their new freedoms to strengthen their positions by consolidating through *intramarket* mergers and acquisitions. Such intramarket mergers are easier to manage and, most important, create value by reducing competition and allowing the achievement of economies of scale in such specific areas as data processing, number of branches, and corporate overhead. In terms of transborder mergers, we should expect small-scale, "beachhead" investment and, possibly, a few new intra-European joint ventures;[46] indeed, these phenomena may have already oc-

---

44. As a matter of fact, U.S.-based institutions seem to have been somewhat more successful at managing multicultural white collar work forces. See Gunter Dufey and Adrian Tschoegl, "International Competition," 170–71. For a review of recent trends, see Richard Philips, "Trouble Abroad for Banks," *Euromoney—Corporate Finance*, September, 1991, 23–26.

45. The few successes in international banking are typically institutions that went into less-developed countries, where their unique skills and capabilities were not challenged by local competitors and where they found a political environment that gave them protection from competitors from other developed countries. This is a typical case for colonial or quasi-colonial situations.

46. "European Banking Alliances: Let-Down," *Economist*, September 7, 1991.

curred. For the most part, however, the new wave of mergers is likely to involve intranational combinations.

Conclusions and Outlook for Banking after EC 1992

None of the trends I have outlined are new. They involve activities that financial institutions have already started to undertake in *anticipation* of the regulatory situation after January, 1993.[47]

The major impact of the EC 92 initiatives in the financial field is to achieve free trade in financial services within the EC. This will facilitate the unhindered flow of capital among member states if not throughout the world. In those (few) instances where access to local market opportunities necessitates a presence, EC competitors will find the level of legal barriers significantly lowered, although some obstacles will remain. However, since many of these remaining obstacles are subject to discretionary decisions by national governments, the "European passport" will have value, provided member states will comply with not only the letter but also the spirit of EC 92. A set of minimal common standards will have wide-ranging effects on bank supervision in the various member states.

It is noteworthy that only a few months before the beginning of an integrated market for financial services, regulatory changes have been implemented only with respect to banking (albeit for a list of banking services that is very comprehensive). However, for enterprises in the securities and insurance industries, the timetable of EC 92 has not been met. Thus, there will be transitory consequences, at least, on competition.[48] In light of the increasing competition among categories of financial enterprise, the resulting market distortions may prove far from trivial.

The regulatory changes will reinforce existing trends toward integration of the several product segments of financial markets. This phenomenon of globalization precedes EC 92 and exceeds the scope of the EC.

Looking at specific segments of banking, the wholesale market is already largely integrated on a global scale. However, retail markets for financial services are fragmented and probably will remain so for some time. This is due less to the lack of competition from abroad than to persistent cost differ-

---

47. These conclusions have been affirmed by country-specific studies; for examples, see Bernard Marois, "The Impact of European Financial Integration on the Strategies of French Banks," Discussion Paper, Hautes Etudes Commerciales, 1991.

48. This chapter has focused on the banking industry rather than on all financial services. For an excellent survey of the investment banking industry in Europe, see Ingo Walter and Roy C. Smith, "European Investment Banking: Structure, Transactions Flow and Regulation," in Dermine, *European Banking*, 105–47. For a comprehensive survey of the European insurance industry, see "Pieces on the Board: A Survey of European Insurance," *Economist*, February 24, 1990.

ences in various national markets. Access to distribution systems is required for almost all products, and experience shows that such access is difficult for foreigners to gain. Cooperative ventures have failed on account of coordination and agency problems. Large-scale, cross-border financial acquisitions cannot be expected either, due to the absence of economies of scale and to the substantial costs incurred in managing service organizations across borders.

These factors do not preclude limited integration of markets via so-called beachhead investments. This strategy has already been implemented by financial institutions from outside the EC, primarily by banks from the United States, Japan, and Switzerland. Where gaps in the market are perceived to exist, as in certain national markets in southern Europe, acquisition of local financial institutions will be tempting. Even these acquisitions will have modest outcomes, however, because liberalization of the regulatory environment in the host markets, prompted primarily by EC 92, will spur local competitors to become more efficient.

Such increases in efficiency can be gained through *within-market* consolidation. Indeed, it is consolidations of precisely this sort that will occasion the most noticeable changes in the structure of European banking. EC 92 will stimulate such consolidation through a combination of actual or perceived threats of foreign competition, liberalization of rules (especially antitrust rules), and political concerns about the international standing of domestic financial enterprises. If consolidation takes the form of mergers and acquisitions, limited economies of scale may be realized and, at the same time, the cost of managing disparate work forces across borders can be avoided.

A related phenomenon will particularly affect middle market banking. Restructuring, including cross-border mergers, in the *nonfinancial* sector will cause substantial changes to established client relationships by making many of those clients, who used to be captive, susceptible to initiatives from both foreign and large national competitors. Thus, even without a large-scale restructuring of the banking industry in Europe, it is safe to predict substantial changes in competition for most sectors of banking (except for the most basic, retail banking services) not so much because of changes in the financial service industry per se, but because of changes among their clientele.

While it is difficult to make a case for dramatic changes in the demand for financial services, changes in the structure of European industry will increase the demand for cross-border financial services within the EC. Undoubtedly, this will affect the nature and organization of European financial enterprises.

BIBLIOGRAPHY

Aliber, Robert Z. "International Banking: A Survey." *Journal of Money, Credit and Banking* 16, no. 4, pt. 2 (November 1983): 661–712.

Annual Statistical Digest, 1988. Washington, D.C.: Board of Governors of the Federal Reserve System, 1989.

"Banks Face Shakeout as Europe Prepares for Unified Market." *Wall Street Journal,* April 4, 1989.

Choi, Sang-Rim, Adrian E. Tschoegl, and Chwo-Ming Yu. "Banks and the World's Major Financial Centers, 1970–1980." *Weltwirtschaftliches Archiv* 122 (1986): 48–64.

Croham, Douglas. *Reciprocity and the Unification of the European Banking Market.* Group of Thirty Occasional Papers 27. New York and London: Group of Thirty, 1989.

Dermine, Jean, ed. *European Banking in the 1990s.* Oxford: Basil Blackwell, 1990.

Dufey, Gunter, and Ian H. Giddy. *The International Money Market.* Englewood Cliffs, N.J.: Prentice-Hall, 1978.

Dufey, Gunter, and Adrian Tschoegl. "International Competition in the Services Industries: Institutional and Structural Characteristics of Financial Services—with Specific Reference to Banking." Report prepared for the U.S. Congress Office of Technology Assessment, 1986.

Emerson, Michael, Michel Aujean, Michel Catinat, Philippe Goybet, and Alexis Jacquemin. *The Economics of 1992: The E.C. Commission's Assessment of the Economic Effects of Completing the Internal Market.* Oxford: Oxford University Press, 1988.

"Europe's Capital Markets: A Survey." *Economist,* December 16, 1989.

"European Banking Alliances: Let-Down." *Economist,* September 7, 1991.

"European Banking to 1992: Bracing for the Shakeout." *Business International Money Report,* February 15, 1988, 57–58.

Fair, Donald E., and Christian de Boissieu. *Financial Institutions in Europe under New Competitive Conditions.* Financial and Monetary Policy Studies 20. Dordrecht: Kluwer Academic Publishers, 1990.

Fair, Donald E., and F. Léonard de Juvigny. *Bank Management in a Changing Domestic and International Environment.* Financial and Monetary Policy Studies 6. The Hague: Martinus Nijhoff Publishers, 1982.

Fassbender, Heino, and Peter Wuffli. "European Banking after 1992." *McKinsey Quarterly* (Spring 1990): 129–50.

Giovannini, Alberto, and Colin Mayer, eds. *European Financial Integration.* Cambridge: Cambridge University Press, 1991.

Hanley, Thomas H., John D. Leonard, Carla A. d'Arista, and Dina I. Oddis. "European Bank Equity Conference: The Competitive Position of U.S. Multinational Banks in a Global Marketplace." Salomon Brothers Inc. Stock Research, 1987.

Hawawini, Gabriel, and Eric Rajendra. *The Transformation of the European Financial Services Industry: From Fragmentation to Integration.* Salomon Center Monograph Series in Finance and Economics, no. 1989–4. New York: New York University, 1989.

Hiltrop, Jean M. "Human Resource Management in European Banking: Challenges and Responses." *European Management Journal* 9 (March 1991): 36–42.

Howe, J. B. T., G. Budzeika, G. G. Riela, and P. R. Worthington. "Competitiveness in Commercial Lending Markets." In *International Competitiveness of U.S. Financial Firms.* Staff Study. New York: Federal Reserve Bank of New York, 1991.

Hufbauer, Gary C., ed. *Europe 1992: An American Perspective*. Washington, D.C.: Brookings Institution, 1991.

International Competitiveness of U.S. Financial Firms: Products, Markets, and Conventional Performance Measures. Staff Study. Federal Reserve Bank of New York, 1991.

Key, Sidney J. "Financial Integration in the European Community." International Financial Discussion Papers K-7, no. 349. Board of Governors of the Federal Reserve System, 1989.

Levich, Richard M. "The Euromarkets after 1992." Working Paper no. 3003. National Bureau of Economic Research, 1989.

"The Liberalization of Capital Movements in the European Community." *Kredietbank Weekly Bulletin* 34 (September 25, 1987): 1–6.

Lowenstein, Jack. "Foreigners Weather Aussie Onslaught." *Euromoney*, April, 1991, 39–42.

Marois, Bernard. "The Impact of European Financial Integration on the Strategies of French Banks." Discussion paper. Hautes Etudes Commerciales, 1991.

McCulloch, Rachel. "International Competition in Services." Working Paper no. 2235. National Bureau of Economic Research, 1987.

Melnik, Arie L., and Steven E. Plaut. *The Short-Term Eurocredit Market*. Salomon Center Monograph Series in Finance and Economics, no. 1991–1. New York: New York University, 1991.

Montgomery, John D. "Market Segmentation and 1992: Toward a Theory of Trade in Financial Services." International Finance Discussion Paper, no. 394. Board of Governors of the Federal Reserve System, 1991.

Phillips, B. J. "Gearing Up for the New Europe." *Institutional Investor*, July, 1988, 47–55.

Padoa-Schioppa, Tommaso. "Towards a European Banking Regulatory Framework." *Banca d'Italia Economic Bulletin* 6 (February 1988): 49–53.

Park, Yoon S., and Musa Essayyad, eds. *International Banking and Financial Centers*. Dordrecht: Kluwer Academic Publishers, 1989.

Philips, Richard. "Trouble Abroad for Banks." *Euromoney—Corporate Finance*, September, 1991, 23–26.

"Pieces on the Board: A Survey of European Insurance." *Economist*, February 24, 1990.

Quantock, Paul, ed. *Opportunities in European Financial Services: 1992 and Beyond*. New York: Wiley, 1990.

"Report on Foreign Government Treatment of U.S. Commercial Banking and Securities Organizations." U.S. Department of the Treasury, 1990.

Schinasi, Garry J. "European Integration, Exchange Rate Management, and Monetary Reform: A Review of the Major Issues." International Financial Discussion Papers K-7, no. 364. Board of Governors of the Federal Reserve System, 1989.

Schneider, Uwe H. "The Harmonization of EC Banking Laws: The Euro-Passport to Profitability and International Competitiveness of Financial Institutions." *Law and Policy in International Business* 22 (1991): 261–88.

"The Single European Market: Survey of the U.K. Financial Services Industry." *Bank of England Quarterly Bulletin* 29 (August 1989): 407–12.

Turro, John. "European Community: Commission Readies Vote on Proposed Interest and Royalty Directive; Loss Directive Not Considered Front-Burner Issue." *Tax Notes International*, June, 1991, 617–19.

Walter, Ingo, and Roy C. Smith. "European Investment Banking: Structure, Transactions Flow and Regulation." In *European Banking in the 1990s*, ed. Jean Dermine, 105–47. Oxford: Basil Blackwell, 1990.

Whitehead, David D. "Moving Toward 1992: A Common Financial Market for Europe?" *Economic Review* (Federal Reserve Bank of Atlanta), (November-December 1988): 42–49.

Telecommunications in Europe:
Law and Policy of the European Community
in a Key Industrial Sector

Reinhard Ellger

Not until the 1980s did the EC take a legal and policy interest in telecommunications.[1] Before then, the member states assumed primary responsibility for the sector. Most created legal monopolies for the supply of telecommunications networks, services, and terminal equipment.[2] In terms of legal identity, these monopolies took one of two forms: an agency of government or an enterprise owned wholly by the state. Initially, their special rights were justified in terms of government's need to control telecommunications for political, military, and administrative purposes.[3] Later, telecommunications monopolies were justified in economic terms: it was argued that telecommunications constituted a case of natural monopoly that required legal protection because it was otherwise unsustainable.[4] The natural monopoly argument was perhaps valid at a time when telecommunications consisted mainly of establishing and operating nationwide networks designed to supply simple universal services to the general public.

The technological developments of the last two decades changed telecommunications enormously, prompting questions about whether the tradi-

---

1. For a survey of the activities of the EC in the field of telecommunications, see the collection of materials contained in Ungerer, Berben, and Costello 1989.

2. A good review of the historical background of and current developments in Europe is provided by Foreman-Peck and Müller 1988.

3. Cf. Rolf Oberliesen, *Information, Daten und Signale: Geschichte Technischer Nachrichtenverarbeitung* (Reinbek: Rowohlt, 1982), 47–70. Also Peter Otto and Phillip Sonntag, *Wege in die Informationsgesellschaft: Steuerungsprobleme in Wirtschaft und Politik* (Munich: Deutscher Taschenbuch Verlag, 1985), 63f.

4. See, e.g., Faulhaber 1987, 106ff.; Meyer et al. 1980, 112ff.; Vickers and Yarrow 1985, 4ff.; Carl-Christian von Weizsäcker, "Wirtschaftspolitische Begründung und Abgrenzung des Fernmeldemonopols," in *Kommunikation ohne Monopole*, ed. Ernst-Joachim Mestmäcker (Baden-Baden: Nomos, 1980), 128–30; Monopolkommission, *Sondergutachten*, vol. 9, *Die Rolle der Deutschen Bundespost im Fernmeldewesen* (Baden-Baden: Nomos, 1981), 25f.

tional, monopolistic structure of the sector was still appropriate. These changes were manifold: the development of such new transmission media as fiber-optic cables and satellites led to doubts about the natural monopoly characteristics of networks and services.[5] The convergence of telecommunications and data processing required the redefinition of borders between the heavily regulated, mainly noncompetitive telecommunications sector and the highly competitive, unregulated data-processing sector. Finally, the digitization of information processing and transmission blurred the formerly clear-cut distinction between telecommunications and electronic media. Once the integrated services digital network (ISDN) is introduced, all telecommunications and media services will be provided through one physical network.

These three developments led to discussion and legislative action in such important industrialized countries as the United States, Japan, and the United Kingdom, resulting in the introduction of more competition in telecommunications markets.[6] This discussion is also taking place in the EC. Its member states are rapidly becoming information societies.[7] It is obvious that telecommunications technology, networks, and services affect the future development of the EC economy decisively. As a result, Community institutions, especially the Commission, recognized the need for a coordinated approach to the regulatory change and technological development in the European telecommunications sector.[8] Furthermore, the EC is taking the necessary steps under the Single European Act of 1986 to establish a single internal European market.[9] The internal market encompasses an area without economic frontiers in which the free movement of persons, goods, services, and capital is ensured.[10]

In 1986, the world market for information processing and communications was valued at ECU 500.0 billion. The world market for telecommunications facilities at that time totaled ECU 90.0 billion, of which the EC had a share of ECU 17.5 billion. Whereas 2 percent of the EC's gross domestic product (GDP) was derived from the telecommunications sector in 1984, it will reach an estimated 7 percent by the end of the century. Until then, ECU

---

5. Ellger and Witt 1990, 279–81.

6. See, e.g., Robert R. Bruce, Jeffrey P. Cunard, and Mark D. Director, *From Telecommunications to Electronic Services: A Global Spectrum of Definitions, Boundary Lines and Structures* (London: Butterworth, 1986), 31ff.; Neumann 1989.

7. An information society is characterized by the importance of processing, disseminating, and transmitting information, relative to the importance of traditional capital and raw materials, as factors of production.

8. Commission of the European Communities, *Towards a Dynamic European Economy: Green Paper on the Development of the Common Market for Telecommunications Services and Equipment*, COM(87) 290 final (Luxembourg: Office for Official Publications of the European Communities, 1987), 59ff. (hereafter cited as EC, *Green Paper*).

9. OJ No. L 169/1 (June 29, 1987).

10. Art. 8a, EEC treaty.

500 billion will be spent in the sector. By the year 2000, about two-thirds of Community GDP will stem from information-related activities, and 60 percent of all jobs will depend on telematics.[11] These huge investments in telecommunications will have an enormous impact on such key industrial areas as microelectronics, software, data processing, the supply of services in general, and electronic audio-visual media. In subsequent sections of this chapter, I shall try to explore how the EC is planning to meet the economic and technological challenges in the telecommunications sector, and to discuss the legal framework provided by the EEC treaty and secondary law.

The Dual Approach of the EC toward the Development of Telecommunications in Europe

The developments in telecommunications just described have raised two sets of questions for Community institutions in general and the Commission in particular. First, in light of the ongoing international discussion of deregulation, what mix of regulation and competition is appropriate for telecommunications? Second, what measures of industrial policy are needed to enable the European telecommunications and data-processing industries to compete successfully in the world market?

In the Commission's opinion, these two sets of questions require different answers. In the field of telecommunications, EC activities have consisted of, on the one hand, measures of industrial policy aiming at the competitiveness of European industries in the world market and, on the other, of *Ordnungspolitik* with a tendency to liberalize the (to date) highly regulated telecommunications markets in order to exploit the full technological and economic potential of telecommunications.[12]

Industrial Policy Approach

During the last eight to ten years, the EC has adopted and implemented a wide variety of industrial policy decisions and measures in the fields of telecommunications, microelectronics, data processing, and information services.

These measures have aimed at the development of a specific European element in these areas. Furthermore, they have pursued the goal of putting the European industry in a better position to compete with its U.S. and Japanese counterparts in the world market. In order to achieve this goal, appropriate market sizes have to be established for the European industry, which is accomplished through integration of EC markets for telecommunications and infor-

---

11. EC, *Green Paper*, intro., 2f.
12. For a more general discussion of these issues, see Jacquemin in this volume.

mation processing. An example may illustrate this need. Digitization has led to a dramatic increase in R&D costs within the telecommunications sector. The development of a large digital switching system currently costs approximately $1 billion, of which nearly 80 percent is spent on software. In the early 1970s, the development costs for such a system were less than $100 million, of which only 20 percent was spent on software. It is estimated that the amortization of the high development costs requires a world market share of 8 percent. However, no national market in the EC represents more than 6 percent of the world market. In comparison, the U.S. telecommunications market represents more than 35 percent, and the Japanese 11 percent, of the world market. A common market within the EC would make up more than 20 percent of the world market.[13]

A further goal of the EC's industrial policy in telecommunications is to ensure independence from third countries. The measures taken by the Community in this respect must be considered "precompetitive" in the sense that, through cooperation between enterprises and academic, scientific, and governmental institutions, the industrial and scientific potential in this field is strengthened and developed. For this purpose, the EC has adopted a large number of programs such as ESPRIT,[14] RACE,[15] STAR,[16] and TEDIS.[17] An important facet of the EC's industrial policy in this field is the measures taken to coordinate ISDN networks on the Community-wide level.[18] For instance, the European program for R&D in information technologies is designed to satisfy "the need for the constitution or consolidation of a specifically European industrial potential in the technologies concerned; whereas its beneficiaries must therefore be the undertakings, universities and research centres which are best suited to attain these objectives."[19]

The EC's industrial policy programs do not seek directly to foster com-

13. See Ungerer 1987, 20.
14. Council Decision no. 84/130/EEC of 28 February 1984 concerning a European programme for research and development in information technologies (ESPRIT), OJ No. L 67/54 (March 9, 1984).
15. Council Decision no. 88/28/EEC of 14 December 1987 on a Community programme in the field of telecommunications technologies—research and development in advanced communications technologies in Europe (RACE), OJ No. L 16/35 (January 21, 1988).
16. Council Regulation (EEC) no. 3300/86 of 27 October 1986 instituting a Community programme for the development of certain less-favoured regions of the Community by improving access to advanced telecommunications services (STAR programme), OJ No. L 305/1 (October 31, 1986).
17. Council Decision no. 87/499/EEC of 5 October 1987 introducing a communications network Community programme on trade electronic data interchange systems (TEDIS), OJ No. L 285/35 (October 8, 1987).
18. Council Recommendation no. 86/659/EEC of 22 December 1986 on the coordinated introduction of the Integrated Services Digital Network (ISDN) in the European Community, OJ No. L 382/36 (December 31, 1986).
19. Council Decision no. 84/130/EEC.

petition within the telecommunications markets of the Community but, rather, try to improve European competitiveness in the world market. This is to be achieved by subsidizing close cooperation between European enterprises, universities, and government agencies to develop the technological capacity of the European telecommunications industry.[20]

Liberalization Approach

The activities of the EC in telecommunications are not limited to industrial policy. At least as important are the attempts of the EC Commission to liberalize the markets for telecommunications goods and services by applying the pertinent rules of the EEC treaty (namely, those on the free movement of goods and services and the rules of competition).

The Commission's main policy statement with respect to future actions in telecommunications is the Green Paper on Telecommunications of June 30, 1987.[21] The Green Paper emphasizes the growing importance of services, relative to goods, in the European economies. Technological development in telecommunications and information processing has substantially contributed to the tradeability of many services that formerly either did not exist or could only be supplied locally.

Between 1960 and 1983, the share of market services in EC GDP rose from 36 to 43 percent and the share of nonmarket services rose from 11 to 15 percent, whereas the share of manufactured products declined from 33 percent to approximately 26 percent. The Commission forecasts that, by the year 2000, two-thirds of GDP in advanced countries will be derived from information-related activities.[22] With information becoming an increasingly vital ingredient of economic activities, telecommunications (as the main system for distributing information in society) is growing in strategic importance. The increasing demand for information and its processing generates new telecommunications services, which, unlike their traditional counterparts, are not universal, but rather of interest for special groups of users. The traditional regulatory system for telecommunications was shaped for services that were to be offered to every interested user in the territory of a state at uniform and reasonable rates and equal conditions (universal services).[23] The most obvious example of such a universal service is voice telephony. The traditional regulatory setting excluded competition in the telecommunications services markets and did not lead to economically efficient results with regard to new, enhanced telecommunications services. The maintenance of the traditional regulatory

20. See Hellmann 1991, points 73 and 74.
21. EC, *Green Paper*.
22. EC, *Green Paper*, 45.
23. Ellger and Witt 1990, 279.

system endangers the swift balancing of supply and demand in a sector critical to the future development of the service economy in the EC as a whole.

In implementing its Green Paper, the Commission announced ten guiding principles for future lawmaking in the telecommunications field. These principles clearly show the determination of the Commission to liberalize European telecommunications markets quite profoundly.   .

1. The Commission tolerates special or exclusive national rights with regard to provision and operation of telecommunications infrastructure.
2. Exclusive national rights are also permitted for a limited number of universal services, insofar as those rights can be justified as safeguarding an overriding general interest. In the Commission's view, only voice telephony may be offered by a monopoly. Exclusive rights in telecommunications are subject to regular review.
3. All other telecommunications services are to be provided on a competitive basis. The public telecommunications organizations in the member states are allowed to compete in service markets with the other providers.
4. Strict requirements are to be established regarding standards for the network infrastructure and for services provided by the telecommunications organization or any other dominant supplier in order to ensure Community-wide interoperability.
5. Express conditions are to be defined by EC directives for the general requirements imposed by dominant network operators on the providers of competitive services, including interconnection and access obligations, and uniform standards, frequencies, and pricing principles (Open Network Provision, or ONP).
6. Telecommunications terminal equipment may be provided freely within the EC subject to type approval. The Community aims at the mutual recognition of type approval between member states.
7. Regulatory and operational activities of governmental telecommunications agencies are to be separated.
8. Strict and continuous review is to be undertaken for the operational activities of the telecommunications agencies under Articles 85, 86, and 90 of the EEC treaty.
9. The competition rules of the treaty (Arts. 85 and 86) are to be applied to new providers of competitive services in order to protect emerging competitive markets for telecommunications services.
10. The common commercial policy (Art. 113 of the EEC treaty) is to apply fully to telecommunications relations with third countries.[24]

---

24. Commission of the European Communities, *Towards a Competitive Community-wide Telecommunications Market in 1992: Implementing the Green Paper on the Development of the*

In the next section, I shall describe how and to what extent the primary and secondary law of the EC are appropriate for bringing about more competition in telecommunications markets. In so doing, I take stock of the extent to which the goals in the Commission's Green Paper have been reached.

Application of the EEC Treaty and of the EEC's Secondary Law to the Telecommunications Sector

The EEC treaty aims at the establishment of a common market among its member states. In its final stage, it will form a single internal market covering the entire territory of the EC, allowing all buyers and suppliers of goods and services unrestricted and free access. Article 8a of the treaty, which was added by the Single European Act of 1986, requires the Community to take the necessary measures for the establishment of this internal market. In particular, regarding trade between member states, Article 3 of the EEC treaty requires elimination of customs duties, quantitative restrictions on imports and exports, and measures having equivalent effects. Furthermore, the Community has to work toward the abolition of obstacles to the movement of persons, goods, services, and capital between its members, the establishment of a system of undistorted competition, and the approximation of laws of the member states as far as necessary for the proper functioning of the common market.[25]

The Free Movement of Telecommunications Goods

Survey
Title 1 of part 2 of the treaty, which covers the free movement of goods within the common market, forms a core section of the treaty. To the extent that these provisions call for the establishment of a customs union and the gradual abolition of customs duties between the member states, their goals have, to a large extent, been achieved. Of greater practical importance are the rules contained in Articles 30 to 37 (elimination of quantitative restrictions on trade and of measures having equivalent effects). As I will show, these rules are pertinent for trade in telecommunications equipment.

Applicability of the Rules to Trade in
Telecommunications Equipment
The provision of telecommunications services requires the existence of a physical telecommunications network (consisting of coaxial cables, fiber-

---

Common Market for Telecommunications Services and Equipment, State of Discussions and Proposals by the Commission, COM(88) 48 final (Luxembourg: Office for Official Publications of the European Communities, 1988).

25. Arts. 3(f) and 3(h), EEC treaty.

optic cables, radio frequencies or satellite channels, switching facilities, and terminal equipment) for the exchange of messages between users. Therefore, it might be said that telecommunications involve a mixture of goods and services. Traditionally, at least some terminal equipment installed at the customer's premises was supplied by providers of services operating under exclusive rights. It has occasionally been argued that the rules on the free movement of goods were inapplicable to telecommunications equipment, because the provider of services offers a comprehensive telecommunications package that includes not only the service as such but also the necessary physical equipment. If this argument is accepted, then trade in telecommunications equipment would be governed by the treaty's rules on the free movement of services (Arts. 59 et seq.). The distinction between goods and services is important because the relevant provisions of the treaty make the free movement of goods, on the one hand, and the free movement of services, on the other, subject to different requirements.

The European Court of Justice (ECJ), in *Sacchi*, distinguishes clearly between goods and services.[26] *Sacchi* dealt with television broadcasts, including advertising spots. The Court stated that broadcasting is subject to the treaty's rules on the free movement of services, whereas the trade in all (physical) materials required for broadcasting purposes, such as soundtracks, films, and apparatus, is covered by the rules on the free movement of goods.[27]

The same holds true for terminal and other telecommunications equipment. Consequently, the rules on the free movement of goods are applicable to intra-Community trade in telecommunications equipment.

Adjustment of State Trading Monopolies under Article 37

Until very recently, in most member states of the EC, the state-owned telecommunications administrations (PTTs) that provide telecommunications services on a monopoly basis were granted more or less comprehensive exclusive rights to provide terminal equipment for the customers of telecommunications services. For instance, in Belgium, Denmark, Greece, Ireland, Italy, Luxembourg, the Netherlands, Portugal, and Spain, the first telephone set to be installed at the customer's premises had to be provided solely by the PTT.[28] In Denmark and the Netherlands, private branch exchanges were also supplied by the telecommunications monopolies. In several member states, exclusive rights existed with respect to mobile telephones (Belgium and the Netherlands), radio pagers (Belgium, Greece, Luxembourg, and the Netherlands),

---

26. Italy v. Commission, Case 155/73, 1974 ECR 409ff.
27. Italy v. Commission, Case 155/73, 1974 ECR 409, at 427, grounds 7–8.
28. EC, *Green Paper*, fig. 8.

modems (Ireland and Spain), and telex terminals (Denmark, Ireland, the Netherlands, and Portugal).[29]

The sole right of the PTTs to provide terminal equipment has two consequences: as far as such exclusive rights extend, the customer is barred from connecting to the network equipment that is not provided by the monopoly. The sole right thereby limits the customer's choice of terminal equipment. It also deprives suppliers in one member state from gaining direct access to customers in other member states.

According to Article 37, "Member States shall progressively adjust any State monopolies of a commercial character so as to ensure that when the transitional period has ended no discrimination regarding the conditions under which goods are procured and marketed exists between nationals of Member States."

The application of Article 37 requires that PTTs with exclusive rights to provide telecommunications terminal equipment be considered state trading monopolies. To be considered as a *state* trading monopoly, one must have been granted one's exclusive right by statute or ordinance of the relevant member state.[30] The exclusive rights of the European PTTs for the provision of telecommunications terminal equipment are in fact based on statutory laws of the member states, so this requirement is met.

More problematic is the question of whether PTTs are *trading* monopolies. The ECJ defines state trading monopolies as organizations that "have as their object transactions regarding a commercial product capable of being the subject of competition and trade between Member States and, secondly, play an effective role in such trade."[31]

The PTTs, acting under sole rights for the provision of terminal equipment, are not in a strict sense trading (import) monopolies.[32] They do not prevent suppliers in other member states from exporting such equipment to a member state where such a sole right exists. Furthermore, customers are not prevented from buying the foreign equipment. They are not allowed, however, to connect it to the network, removing all commercial incentive for them to acquire terminal equipment supplied from another member state.

The second sentence of Article 37 makes clear that the term *state trading monopoly* has to be interpreted broadly. The provisions of Article 37 are applicable to any institution "through which a Member State, in law or in fact, either directly or indirectly supervises, determines, or appreciably influences

---

29. EC, *Green Paper*, fig. 8.
30. See Matthies 1987b, point 9; Hochbaum 1991, point 20; Kapteyn and Verloren van Themaat 1989, 408.
31. Costa v. ENEL, Case 6/64, 1964 ECR 585, at 598.
32. Scherer 1985, 398.

imports or exports between Member States."[33] According to the ECJ, the application of Article 37 is not restricted to imports and exports of goods that are directly subject to the sole right. The provision covers all measures connected with the existence of such monopolies and affecting trade between member states.[34] By prohibiting the connection of terminal equipment not supplied by the PTT granted the sole right, the monopoly indirectly determines the imports of such equipment into the member state.

Article 37 obliges the member states to adjust the state trading monopolies so as to eliminate discrimination against suppliers from other member states. The provision does not expressly require the member states to eliminate or abolish the state trading monopolies.[35] In *Manghera*, which dealt with the Italian state monopoly on tobacco, the ECJ held that the only way to eliminate the discriminatory effects of import monopolies on exporters from other member states was to strike down the exclusive right to import.[36] The same holds true for exclusive rights for the provision and maintenance of telecommunications terminal equipment.

Thus, although the term *adjustment* in Article 37 might seem to allow preservation of state trading monopolies, it actually announces the impossibility of eliminating discrimination while keeping the exclusive right. In my view, the adjustment obligation requires the removal of all exclusive rights vested in state trading monopolies. Article 37, however, does not require the member states to dissolve these entities. After the abolition of the exclusive right, the entities may, of course, continue their commercial activity on a competitive basis.

After the expiration of the transitional period (December 31, 1969), Article 37 became directly applicable, so that EC citizens can rely on it in member state courts of law.[37]

Restrictions on Imports of Terminal Equipment within the Community and Article 30

Article 30 prohibits all quantitative restrictions and measures of equivalent effect on trade in goods between the member states. The notion of "measures

---

33. Art. 37(1) 2d sentence, EEC treaty.

34. Cinzano v. Hauptzollamt Saarbrücken, Case 13/70, 1970 ECR 1089, at 1095.

35. See Pubblico Ministero v. Manghera, Case 59/75, 1976 ECR 91; Hansen v. Hauptzollamt Flensburg, Case 91/78, 1979 ECR 935, at 952, ground 8; Commission v. Italy, Case 78/82, 1983 ECR 1955.

36. Pubblico Ministero v. Manghera, Case 59/75, 1976 ECR 91, at 121, ground 13; see also Mestmäcker 1974, 633.

37. Costa v. ENEL, Case 6/64, 1964 ECR 585, at 597–98; Pubblico Ministero v. Manghera, Case 59/75, 1976 ECR 91, at 101; Rewe-Zentrale des Lebensmittel-Grosshandels v. Hauptzollamt Landau/Pfalz, Case 45/75, 1976 ECR 181, at 196f.; Matthies 1987b, point 32.

of equivalent effect" was defined by the ECJ in *Dassonville*.[38] The term covers all trading rules of member states that are capable of hindering, directly or indirectly, actually or potentially, intra-Community trade.[39] This very broad definition was narrowed by the Court in *Cassis de Dijon*.[40] Under the *Cassis de Dijon* ruling, obstacles to the free movement of goods caused by disparities between national laws of the member states relating to the marketing of goods are acceptable under EC law insofar as these rules are necessary to satisfy mandatory requirements not being taken care of by Community harmonization of laws.[41] As examples of such mandatory requirements, the Court cited fiscal supervision, the protection of health, and the protection of consumers.

Moreover, Article 36 allows member states to restrict the free movement of goods on various explicit grounds, including public morality, public policy, or public security, and the protection of the health and life of persons, animals, or plants. However, given its role as provider of exceptions to the general principle of free movement, Article 36 must be interpreted narrowly.[42]

In the field of telecommunications equipment, the cited provisions of the treaty are relevant in two respects: first, the PTT monopolies for the provision and maintenance of terminal equipment form a structural obstacle to the free movement of goods; hence they qualify as measures of equivalent effect. Second, insofar as terminal equipment is not exclusively supplied by the member state's PTT, the approval procedures for the equipment are subject to scrutiny under Article 30.

As to the first point, the ECJ has held that monopolies in the marketing, supply, and maintenance of terminal equipment are incompatible with Article 30 of the EEC treaty because they bar free movement within the EC.[43] Furthermore, the Court feels that there is no guarantee that the undertaking with the exclusive rights will be capable of offering the whole spectrum of terminal equipment demanded by customers and that it will be able to inform customers about the qualities and the operation of such equipment.[44] Regardless of an exclusive right to supply terminal equipment to customers, such

---

38. Procureur du Roi v. Dassonville, Case 8/74, 1974 ECR 837.

39. Procureur du Roi v. Dassonville, Case 8/74, 1974 ECR 837, at 852, ground 5.

40. Rewe-Zentral v. Bundesmonopolverwaltung für Branntwein, Case 120/78, 1979 ECR 649.

41. Rewe-Zentral v. Bundesmonopolverwaltung für Branntwein, Case 120/78, 1979 ECR 649, at 662, ground 8.

42. Commission v. Italy, Case 7/68, 1968 ECR 633, at 644; Marimex v. Italian Finance Administration, Case 29/72, 1972 ECR 1309, at 1318; Commission v. Ireland, Case 113/80, 1981 ECR 1625, at 1637f.; Müller-Graff 1991, points 22ff.; Matthies 1987a, point 3.

43. French Republic v. Commission, Case C-202/88, ground 34, as summarized in *Europäische Zeitschrift für Wirtschaftsrecht* (1991): 347 (hereafter cited as EuZW).

44. French Republic v. Commission, Case C-202/88, ground 35, EuZW (1991): 347.

apparatus can only be marketed in each member state if it has received a type approval by the competent administration. The type approval procedure offers the member states an opportunity to discriminate against terminal equipment imported from other member states. The type approval provisions and their application in the legal systems of the member states may contravene Article 30 in several ways. On the one hand, the contents of such rules may violate Article 30. On the other hand, the approval provisions may be applied in a discriminatory manner or the approval authorities may apply disproportionately high standards as to type approval.[45]

In the type approval procedures, the competent authorities are not allowed to apply requirements that are disproportionate in relation to the purpose of the approval procedure.[46] The competent authorities in the member states are obliged to cooperate in easing border controls and avoiding unnecessary costs for controls.[47] If equipment has been tested and approved in one member state, authorities in another member state may violate Article 30 by requiring the same tests and examinations to be performed again in the importing country even though the test results from the exporting country are available to them. Regulations of domestic law in the member states regarding type approval of terminal equipment that have effects equivalent to quantitative restrictions on imports are only acceptable under EC law if they satisfy the requirements of Article 36 or if, in the absence of harmonization by EC law, they pursue objectives of general public interest and are applied indiscriminately to nationals of all member states. Article 30 is directly applicable, such that citizens in the member states may rely on it in the national courts of law.

Rather than stick to a case-by-case application of the relevant treaty provisions, the Commission has adopted directives to liberalize EC markets for terminal equipment and to harmonize type approval throughout the Community. As those directives have a far-reaching effect for the intra-Community trade in such equipment, they deserve some attention here.

Liberalization of the Markets for Telecommunications Terminal Equipment

National laws restricting the free movement of telecommunications terminal equipment are valid under EC law only to the extent that the interests they serve are justifiable under Community law and insofar as they have not been

---

45. Schulte-Braucks 1987, 97ff.
46. Cf. Commission v. France, Case 188/84, 1986 ECR 419, at 436, ground 16; and Commission v. United Kingdom, Case 124/81, 1983 ECR 203, at 236, ground 16.
47. Commission v. United Kingdom, Case 124/81, 1983 ECR 203, at 239, ground 30; de Peijper, Case 104/75, 1976 ECR 613, ground 27.

harmonized by secondary law of the EC in a manner taking account of those interests. On May 16, 1988, the Commission adopted its directive on telecommunications terminal equipment, acting under its jurisdiction pursuant to Article 90(3) of the EEC treaty.[48] The directive obliges the member states to abolish all special or exclusive rights for importing, marketing, or maintaining terminal equipment. It thereby liberalizes, to a very large extent, the EC's terminal equipment markets and contributes to the development of a single European market in such equipment. Article 90(1) prohibits member states from adopting, maintaining, or enforcing any measures contrary to the rules contained in the treaty, in particular the competition rules, with respect to public undertakings and undertakings to which member states have granted special or exclusive rights. Under Article 90(3), the Commission is charged with supervising the application of the other provisions in Article 90.

In its legal considerations, the Commission justified the adoption of the terminal equipment directive by stating that special and exclusive rights relating to telecommunications terminal equipment in the member states violate Articles 30, 37, and 86. Such rights are considered incompatible with Article 30, because, in practice, they restrict imports from other member states. Moreover, they are said to violate Article 37 of the EEC treaty in that they discriminate against suppliers from other member states. Finally, the Commission states that the terminal equipment monopolies in the member states violate Article 90(1) and Article 86 in conjunction with Article 3(f). They limit the supply and marketing of such equipment and restrict technical progress; since the spectrum of equipment they offer is necessarily limited, the PTTs narrow consumers' choices.[49]

The core provisions of the directive on telecommunications terminal equipment are its Articles 2 and 3. Article 1 obliges the member states to withdraw all special or exclusive rights with respect to terminal equipment that they have previously granted to undertakings. The notion of undertaking is defined in the directive as encompassing a public or private body to which a member state grants special or exclusive rights for importing, marketing, connection, bringing into service, and/or maintaining telecommunications terminal equipment.

Moreover, member states have to make sure that competing "economic operators have the right to import, market, connect, bring into service, and maintain terminal equipment."[50] This means that once the special or exclusive rights have been withdrawn, terminal equipment will be offered by a variety

---

48. Commission Directive no. 88/301/EEC of 16 May 1988 on competition in the markets for telecommunications terminal equipment, OJ No. L 131/73 (May 27, 1988).

49. Commission Directive no. 88/301/EEC, considerations 3, 5, and 13.

50. Commission Directive no. 88/301/EEC, Art. 3.

of suppliers on a competitive basis. To assist manufacturers in gaining access to the markets for terminal equipment, the directive requires that the physical characteristics of network termination points be published. The directive calls on the member states to ensure that users have access to the new public network termination points no later than December 31, 1988. The new public network termination points put users of the network in a position to connect compatible terminal equipment to the network. The member states also have to communicate to the EC Commission a list of all technical specifications and type approval procedures used in the context of terminal equipment, together with references to where these regulations have been published. Unpublished specifications and procedural rules have to be published.

Long-term maintenance contracts between the formerly monopolistic suppliers of equipment and their customers also curtail the chances for market access by newcomers. Therefore, Article 7 of the directive grants customers the right to terminate such contracts with a maximum notice to the PTTs of one year.

Traditionally, the PTTs had a dual function. On the one hand, they exercised regulatory powers with regard to prices and conditions of customer use of the network; on the other hand, they had operational, commercial functions by providing the network and telecommunications services. With regard to terminal equipment, they provided such equipment to the customers and, at the same time, were responsible for the type approval of the equipment. In a liberalized terminal equipment market, the PTTs compete with third-party suppliers. In such a situation, it is inappropriate for the PTTs to act both as competitors and as regulatory bodies for the type approval of terminal equipment. Consequently, the directive requires the member states to establish an authority for type approval that is independent of the market participants—especially of the market-dominant PTTs.

The latitude of the member states to restrict the importation, marketing, connection, and bringing into service of terminal equipment is very limited. The approval of equipment can, in the absence of EC harmonization of technical specifications, only be refused if the equipment does not comply with the so-called essential requirements as laid down in the Council directive on the recognition of type approval for telecommunications terminal equipment.[51] At present, these essential requirements are: network integrity, safety of use, safety of employees of public network operators, and interoperability (in justified cases).[52]

---

51. Council Directive no. 86/361/EEC of 24 July 1986 on the initial stage of the mutual recognition of type approval for telecommunications terminal equipment, OJ No. L 217/21 (August 5, 1986).

52. Council Directive no. 86/361/EEC, Art. 2(17).

Moreover, the member states are entitled to require the manufacturers and suppliers of terminal equipment to possess the necessary technical qualifications for connecting, bringing into service, and maintaining terminal equipment. However, these requirements have to be based on objective, non-discriminatory, and published criteria.

France and four other member states (Germany among them) challenged the directive before the ECJ. Among other issues, the plaintiffs contended that the Commission acted outside its lawmaking powers under Article 90(3) and assumed incorrectly that the member states violated Articles 30, 37, 59, and 86 of the treaty by granting and maintaining exclusive rights in terminal equipment markets.

The ECJ upheld most of the directive by recognizing that exclusive rights in the equipment market are incompatible with Article 30 of the EEC treaty. The Court noted that *exclusive* importing and marketing rights are capable of restricting intra-Community trade in telecommunications terminal equipment.[53] As far as the directive refers to *special* rights in its Articles 2 and 9, these passages were struck down, because the Commission, according to the Court, failed to show what kind of special rights are meant by the provisions of the directive and to what extent the special rights are incompatible with treaty rules.[54] The Court also nullified Article 7 of the directive, which grants customers a right to terminate long-term maintenance contracts.[55] The Court stated that Article 90(3) of the treaty does not empower the Commission to grant such a right of termination, because it only grants the Commission jurisdiction with regard to measures of member states; conduct of undertakings that is contrary to the competition rules can only be reprimanded by the Commission in decisions directed against the relevant undertakings pursuant to Articles 85 and 86 of the treaty. Finally, the Court stated that the Commission failed to establish that the member states had used their influence over state-owned PTTs to bring about long-term contracts. Nor did the Commission show that the member states had enacted regulations forcing the PTTs to conclude such contracts. The Court stressed, however, that nothing prevents the Commission from dealing with this problem by applying Article 86 of the treaty to the PTTs directly by way of a decision under Article 189 of the treaty.

Another point in the judgment seems remarkable. Not only does the terminal equipment directive concern trade in terminal equipment as such (which undoubtedly is subject to the provisions on free movement of goods) but it also obliges the member states to abolish the existing exclusive rights for

---

53. French Republic v. Commission, Case C-202/88, ground 39, EuZW (1991): 348.
54. French Republic v. Commission, Case C-202/88, grounds 45–47, EuZW (1991): 348.
55. French Republic v. Commission, Case C-202/88, grounds 53–57, EuZW (1991): 348.

connecting, bringing into service, and maintaining terminal equipment. These activities, as the Court correctly observes, should be considered not trade in goods but trade in services.[56] In its legal considerations, therefore, the Commission relies not only on Articles 30 and 37 (free movement of goods), but also on Articles 59 (free movement of services), 3(f) (undistorted competition), and 86 (abuse of dominant position).[57] The Court upholds the directive by arguing that exclusive rights for the importation, marketing, connection, bringing into service, and maintenance of terminal equipment are not compatible with Article 30.[58] In applying Article 30 to services, the Court's approach contradicts a long-standing line of judgments in which the Court had carefully drawn a clear-cut boundary between goods and services.[59] The decision blurs this distinction to some extent. As the terminal equipment directive opens up for competition an economic sector that previously was regulated by the member states, and as the relevant economic activities in this sector also encompass services, not only Article 30, but also Articles 59, 3(f), and 86 would have been the correct legal bases for the decision.

In conclusion, it can be said that, in upholding essential parts of the directive, the Court confirmed the power of the Commission to order the member states to remove the exclusive rights they have granted their PTTs in the telecommunications terminal equipment sector.

Community-wide Type Approval of Terminal Equipment
Abolition of the exclusive rights of state-owned PTTs does not automatically create a fair chance for newcomers to enter a national market. The remaining problem is the requirement of type approval of terminal equipment and the national procedures for granting it. If a supplier in one member state decides to market its products in other member states, it must secure type approval in each member state in which it wants to sell. Multiple type approval procedures cost the supplier time and money, and multiple type approval standards reduce the likelihood that a given piece of equipment will satisfy the requirements of all member states.

To remove these obstacles to the free movement of terminal equipment in the EC, the Council adopted directives aiming at the mutual recognition of national procedures for type approval, certification, and testing. It began with its directive of July 24, 1986, obliging the member states to recognize the results of conformity tests undertaken in connection with common

---

56. French Republic v. Commission, Case C-202/88, ground 42, EuZW (1991): 348.
57. Commission Directive no. 88/301/EEC, considerations 7, 12, and 13.
58. French Republic v. Commission, Case C-202/88, grounds 43–44, EuZW (1991): 348.
59. See, e.g., Italy v. Commission, Case 155/73, 1974 ECR 409, at 427, grounds 6–7; Elliniki Radiophonia Tileorasi Anonymi Etairia v. Dimotiki Etairia Pliroforisis and S. Kouvelas, Case C-260/89, grounds 13–14, *Europäisches Steuer- und Wirtschaftsrecht* (1991): 284ff.

conformity specifications for mass-produced telecommunications terminal equipment.[60] The common conformity specifications are used in all member states. These conformity specifications are drawn up by the CEPT[61] on request of the EC Commission in the form of NETs (normes européennes de télécommunications).

A further step toward the mutual recognition of type approvals was taken in the Council directive of April 29, 1991,[62] which repealed the directive of July 24, 1986, effective November 6, 1991. The new directive prohibits the member states from restricting the marketing, free movement, or use of terminal equipment complying with the requirements set forth in Article 4 of the directive, namely: safety of users and of network personnel; electromagnetic compatibility; protection of network integrity; efficient use of the radio frequency spectrum; suitability for establishing, modifying, holding, and clearing of connections and charging for connections; and interworking of terminal equipment via the public telecommunications network (in justified cases). The aim of the directive is to facilitate the Community-wide supply and use of terminal equipment by submitting that equipment to the type approval procedure in just one member state.

The suppliers of terminal equipment can opt for one of two procedures to have their equipment approved. One choice is the traditional type approval procedure performed by the competent national authority. The other is the so-called EC declaration of conformity. This approach is very close to a self-certification by the manufacturer and, as such, is a novelty in several member states. To ensure that equipment in fact conforms with the common technical standards and the essential requirements set out in the directive, the competent national authorities perform strict production and quality controls under the supervision of the EC. Nevertheless, this procedure saves time for the manufacturers when marketing a new product.[63]

If equipment is imported from a nonmember country, the test results and documentation of the foreign type approval authorities will be recognized in the EC only in the event that there is an agreement between the EC and the third country.

---

60. Council Directive no. 86/361/EEC.

61. CEPT (Conférence Européenne des Administrations des Postes et des Télécommunications) is an association of 26 European public postal and telecommunications organizations. The organization is active in the fields of harmonization of operational procedures, technical standardization, and cooperation among its members. For a detailed treatment of CEPT, see Claude Labarrère, *L'Europe des Postes et des Télécommunications* (Paris: Masson, 1985).

62. Council Directive no. 91/263/EEC of 29 April 1991 on the approximation of the laws of the Member States concerning telecommunications terminal equipment, including the mutual recognition of their conformity, OJ No. L 128/1 (May 23, 1991).

63. See Schulte-Braucks 1990, 675–76.

Procurement of Telecommunications Equipment
by the PTTs

Although the PTTs have lost a substantial number of their formerly exclusive rights, they continue to be the sole operators of the national networks and the exclusive providers of voice telephony service in most member states. The dominant position of the PTTs in networks and universal services has led to monopsony in the procurement of the equipment used for the establishment and maintenance of networks and the provision of services, including central office switching, transmission equipment, and terminal equipment.[64]

Strong "buy national" policies of the PTTs resulted in 80 to 90 percent of all telecommunications equipment being procured nationally.[65] Within each member state, a small number of domestic suppliers delivered the bulk of equipment required by the domestic PTT. According to the Cecchini Report, the economic loss to the EC attributable to "buy national" policies amounted to ECU 3.0 to 4.8 billion.[66] These policies were said to be motivated by concerns of national interest and industrial policy.[67]

According to the Council directive of September 17, 1990,[68] neither state-owned telecommunications undertakings nor telecommunications entities operating under special rights may discriminate between suppliers of telecommunications equipment. In the telecommunications sector, the directive applies to supply contracts valued at not less than ECU 600,000.[69] In the case of construction projects, the directive applies to contracts estimated to be worth at least ECU 5 million.[70]

The directive establishes three different procedures for procurement, namely, open, restricted, and negotiated.[71] In the case of open procedures, all interested suppliers may submit tenders. In restricted procedures, only those invited by the contracting entity may bid. Under the negotiated procedure, the contracting entity consults suppliers or contractors of its choice and negotiates the terms of the contract with one or more of them.

The contracting entity may choose among the three procedures, provided

---

64. See Amy Plantin and Dimitri Ypsilanti, "Trends in Trade in Telecom," *OECD Observer*, no. 171 (August/September 1991): 18.

65. Schulte-Braucks 1990, 673.

66. Paolo Cecchini, with Michel Catinat and Alexis Jacquemin, *The European Challenge, 1992: The Benefits of a Single Market* (Brookfield, Ver.: Gower, 1988), as cited by Schulte-Braucks 1990, 673.

67. See Plantin and Ypsilanti, "Trends in Trade in Telecom," 18.

68. Council Directive no. 90/531/EEC of 17 September 1990 on the procurement procedures of entities operating in the water, energy, transport, and telecommunications sectors, OJ No. L 297/1 (October 29, 1990).

69. Council Directive no. 90/531/EEC, Art. 12(1)(b).

70. Council Directive no. 90/531/EEC, Art. 12(1)(c).

71. Council Directive no. 90/531/EEC, Arts. 1(6) and 15.

that it has made a call for competition. The call for competition must contain the information needed by suppliers to submit their tenders and must be published in the *Official Journal of the European Communities*.

Suppliers from all member states are entitled to take part in the competition. The choice among them must be made strictly according to business criteria (that is, on the basis of completion date, quality, after-sales service, price, and so forth). The directive obliges the contracting entities to ensure that there is no discrimination between suppliers and to provide unsuccessful bidders with legal recourse.

Free Movement of Telecommunications Services and the Right of Establishment

Article 59 of the EEC treaty stipulates that "restrictions on freedom to provide services within the Community shall be progressively abolished during the transitional period in respect of nationals of Member States who are established in a State of the Community other than that of the person for whom the services are intended."

Telecommunications Services as Services

Article 60 of the treaty defines services as economic activities normally provided for remuneration, insofar as they are not covered by the treaty provisions on free movement of goods, capital, and persons. In *Sacchi*, the ECJ held that the transmission of television signals is subject to the treaty rules relating to services.[72] In their basic form, telecommunications services comprise the incorporeal transmission of signals by way of electromagnetic impulses, optical signals, or radio waves. In the case of enhanced telecommunications services, additional elements, such as storage or processing of messages, are part of the communications service. Telecommunications services are regularly provided for remuneration in that customers using a telecommunications service have to pay fees to the provider. These activities are, therefore, services within the meaning of Articles 59 and 60.

The application of Article 59 requires that the service is provided by a supplier in one member state to a national residing in another member state. With regard to telecommunications services, this requirement is met if a network itself crosses national borders (for instance, in the case of an international satellite network) or if a network in one member state is operated by an enterprise established in another member state. In the case of value-added services, such services might be offered to a customer in one member state by

---

72. Italy v. Commission, Case 155/73, 1974 ECR 409, at 427, ground 6.

a supplier residing in another member state using international lines rented from network operators in the source and destination countries.

Article 59 and Telecommunications Services Monopolies

In the past, the PTTs in all member states were granted comprehensive and exclusive rights for the provision of telecommunications services, whether basic or enhanced. Such rights continue to exist in all member states but one. In the United Kingdom, two undertakings, British Telecom and Mercury Communications, have been licensed to provide nationwide telecommunications networks.[73] To enable Mercury Communications to gain sufficient market share, the United Kingdom's regulatory authority decided to grant no further licenses until the end of 1990.[74] At the moment, the United Kingdom is home to heated discussion about whether other competitors should be allowed to enter the market. It can be expected that this market will be open for further competitors in the near future.

The exclusive rights of the PTTs to provide networks and such universal services as voice telephony prevent providers in other member states from entering such markets. Thus, legal monopoly impedes the free movement of services required by Article 59.[75]

Until recently, commentators have interpreted Article 59 as prohibiting only those restrictions on transborder movement that discriminate by nationality or place of establishment.[76] This narrow interpretation implies that exclusive rights do not violate Article 59 of the treaty: foreign and domestic applicants are treated equally inasmuch as neither group is allowed to engage in activities covered by the monopoly. Such an interpretation would limit the meaning of Article 59 to the principle of national treatment of providers from other member states. However, if both the wording and the purpose of Article 59 are taken into account, it becomes clear that a broader interpretation is required.

On its face, Article 59 is not limited to discriminatory restrictions; rather, it speaks of restrictions on the freedom to provide services in general.[77] The ECJ takes as a starting point the function of Article 59 as a prohibition of any discrimination based on nationality or place of establishment. Numerous deci-

---

73. See James Foreman-Peck and Dorothy Manning, "Telecommunications in the United Kingdom," in Foreman-Peck and Müller 1988, 259; Neumann 1989, 6.

74. Neumann 1989, 6.

75. Ellger and Witt 1990, 317.

76. See Ipsen 1972, 654; Hans Jarass, "EG-Recht und Nationales Rundfunkrecht, Zugleich ein Beitrag zur Reichweite der Dienstleistungsfreiheit," *Europarecht* 21 (January-March 1986): 85; Troberg 1991, point 4.

77. Randelzhofer 1988b, point 2; *Encyclopedia of European Community Law*, vol. 2, *European Community Treaties* (London: Sweet and Maxwell, 1987), note to Art. 59.

sions, however, show that the meaning of Article 59 is not limited to discrimination; the provision is directed against "all requirements imposed on the person providing the service by reason in particular of his nationality or of the fact that he does not habitually reside in the state where the service is provided which do not apply to persons established within the national territory or which may prevent or otherwise obstruct the activities of the person providing the service."[78]

An interpretation of Article 59 going beyond a mere prohibition of discrimination is supported by the wording of other provisions of the treaty, for instance, that of Article 52, which explicitly limits the article's scope of application to the issue of discrimination between nationals of member states. The fact that Article 59 does not contain such an explicit reference to discrimination leads to the conclusion that it aims at the removal of all restrictions on transborder services, not simply at the elimination of discriminatory restrictions.[79] To what end does this reasoning lead with regard to telecommunications services monopolies?

According to Article 37, member states must adjust their state trading monopolies; in fact, this means they must abolish the special rights vested in those monopolies. This provision, however, applies only to monopolies trading *goods*.[80] The lack of a provision comparable to Article 37 in the part of the treaty dealing with services, and the mention of undertakings with special rights in Article 90(1), are evidence that service monopolies are not per se incompatible with the treaty.[81]

Nevertheless, member states are not at complete liberty to grant special or exclusive rights. This follows from Article 3(f) of the treaty, which requires the Community to establish a system ensuring that competition in the common market is not distorted. The treaty intends the creation of a common market for services based on competition. The member states are obliged by Article 5 of the EEC treaty to take all appropriate measures to fulfill the obligations arising under the treaty. These obligations include the duty to refrain from measures that are incompatible with such basic principles as those expressed in Article 3(f). The power of the member states to grant special or exclusive rights to state-owned or private undertakings, therefore, has to be construed narrowly, because monopolies inevitably restrict the free

---

78. Van Binsbergen v. Bedrijfsvereniging Metaalnijverheid, Case 33/74, 1974 ECR 1299, at 1309, ground 10; also Coenen and Others v. Sociaal-Economische Raad, Case 39/75, 1975 ECR 1547, at 1555, ground 6.

79. Cf. Müller 1988, 129, 143; Beutler et al. 1987, 317; Randelzhofer 1988b, point 2; Troberg 1991, point 4.

80. See Italy v. Commission, Case 155/73, 1974 ECR 409, at 428, ground 10; Hochbaum 1991, point 22; Matthies 1987b, point 11.

81. Emmerich 1983, 219–20.

movement of services in the common market.[82] *Sacchi* offers guidance as to the permissibility of service monopolies within the EC.

In *Sacchi*, following Article 90(1), the ECJ generally recognized the right of member states to grant special or exclusive rights to provide services.[83] This right is not, however, without limits. According to the Court, the removal of a commercial activity from competition by a member state—in the instant case, television transmission—may be justified by considerations of public interest of a *noneconomic* nature.[84] In contrast, economic interests cannot be used to justify such a removal. The exclusion of economic interests as justifications for exclusive rights is the consequence of the treaty's commitment to a common market for services under a system of undistorted competition. Moreover, if a member state adopts restrictions on the free movement of services, it must apply them indiscriminately to all persons and undertakings, notwithstanding nationality or place of residence or establishment.

The exclusive rights granted to the European PTTs by the member states are based on a variety of considerations.

—establishment, operation, and maintenance of a nationwide, pervasive telecommunications network satisfying all the needs of private and commercial consumers;
—provision of certain telecommunications services, such as voice telephone transmission, to all interested persons;
—equal access to the universal service for all interested persons, irrespective of their geographical locations and costs of connection to the network;
—equal prices for all users of a given universal service, resulting in cross-subsidization of connections provided below cost by connections provided above cost;
—keeping the prices of universal services low enough to permit everyone to use them; and
—widespread availability of lifeline services.

Among telecommunications services, the EC Commission accepts only voice telephone transmission as capable of being provided by a monopoly without violating treaty rules.[85]

---

82. Ellger and Witt 1990, 318; Müller 1988, 145ff.

83. Italy v. Commission, Case 155/73, 1974 ECR 409, at 429, ground 14.

84. Italy v. Commission, Case 155/73, 1974 ECR 409, at 429, ground 14: "Nothing in the Treaty prevents Member States, for considerations of public interest, of a non-economic nature, from removing radio and television transmissions, including cable transmissions, from the field of competition by conferring on one or more establishments an exclusive right to conduct them."

85. EC, *Green Paper*, 67.

The ECJ has interpreted narrowly the authority of member states to restrict the free movement of services on the grounds of public interest of a noneconomic nature. As a yardstick, the Court uses a "less-restrictive-alternatives" test[86] that requires the restrictions to be "objectively justified"[87] and "not excessive in relation to the aim pursued."[88]

In light of these requirements, network monopolies seem to be compatible with Article 59 to the extent that they serve the objective of establishment, operation, and maintenance of pervasive, nationwide telecommunications networks. The establishment of modern, nationwide telecommunications networks requires vast investments and the grant of an exclusive right relating to the provision of a telecommunications network. This is accompanied by infrastructural duties for the undertaking operating the network. Moreover, the EC supports the coordinated, Community-wide development of an ISDN, which will also require large investments in the future.[89]

The result of the analysis is different, however, with regard to telecommunications services offered on the network. In its Green Paper on telecommunications, the Commission concluded that, with the exception of voice telephony, special rights to supply telecommunications services are unjustifiable under EC law.[90] The Commission tolerates exclusive rights to supply voice telephone service in order to ensure the financial viability of the network providers, given their infrastructural duties. At present, voice telephony is the most important service in telecommunications. It accounts for approximately 85 to 90 percent of the total revenue derived by European PTTs from the provision of telecommunications services.[91]

All other telecommunications services are to be provided on a competitive basis; the establishment and maintenance of special rights violate Article 59. Except in voice telephony, sole rights in telecommunications services restrict the free movement of services between member states and are not justifiable. The Commission is planning to conduct regular examinations of whether the justifications for the monopoly in voice telephony remain valid.[92]

However, there remain some doubts about whether exclusive rights in network operation and voice telephony are justifiable under the yardsticks provided by the treaty and the ECJ.

First, the financial viability of the European PTTs seems to be predomi-

---

86. Scherer 1988, 93.

87. Ministère Public v. van Wesemael, Joined Cases 110 and 111/78, 1979 ECR 35, at 52, ground 29.

88. Criminal Proceedings against Webb, Case 279/80, 1981 ECR 3305, at 3326, ground 20.

89. Cf. Council Recommendation no. 86/659/EEC.

90. EC, *Green Paper*, 64ff.

91. EC, *Green Paper*, 74.

92. EC, *Green Paper*, 65.

nantly an economic consideration, whereas the ECJ allows member states to remove commercial services from competition only when removal is justified by considerations of public interest of a *noneconomic* nature. Nevertheless, this argument can be deflated by hinting at the fact that the PTTs have to be sufficiently funded in order to perform their infrastructural duties.

Second, the application of the "less-restrictive-alternative" test might provide an argument against the exclusive right in voice telephony. The provision of a universal service such as voice telephony, with equal access for every user and a pricing structure that ignores the users' locations, requires cross-subsidization between groups of users. This results in prices above costs on long-distance calls (for example) and below-cost prices on local calls.

An alternative to the monopoly in these areas would be state subsidies paid directly to network operators and providers of voice telephony to compensate for the higher costs incurred in supplying remote areas with service. However, it is doubtful whether such a system of direct state subsidies would ultimately lead to more competition in voice telephony and constitute a substantially less restrictive alternative to exclusive rights.[93]

Prohibition of a Service through the Law of a Member State

If one member state prohibits the provision of a certain telecommunications service legally provided in another member state, suppliers in the latter member state are barred from offering this service in the former.

Such a restriction, which prohibits domestic and foreign providers alike from offering the service, still has to be measured against Article 59. In *Debauve*, which involved a ban on television advertising in Belgium, the ECJ developed (without express basis in the treaty) an exception to the principle of free movement of services. A restriction on free trade in services does not violate Article 59 if there is no EC harmonization of national laws and if the general interest justifies the restriction.[94]

However, such a restrictive rule has to be applicable to all service providers indiscriminately, irrespective of whether they are nationals of the re-

---

93. See Ellger and Witt 1990, 320.

94. Procureur du Roi v. Debauve, Case 52/79, 1980 ECR 833, at 856, ground 13: "In the absence of any approximation of national laws and taking into account the considerations of general interest underlying the restrictive rules in this area, the application of the laws in question cannot be regarded as a restriction upon freedom to provide services so long as those laws treat all such services identically whatever their origin or the nationality or place of establishment of the persons providing them." Cf. also Van Binsbergen v. Bedrijfsvereniging Metaalnijverheid, Case 33/74, 1974 ECR 1299, at 1309, grounds 10–12; Ministère Public v. van Wesemael, Joined Cases 110 and 111/78, 1979 ECR 35, at 52, ground 28.

stricting state or nationals of other member states. Furthermore, the burden of proof that such a prohibition is justified by the general interest lies with the restricting member state. Moreover, the member state has to show that the restriction is "objectively justified"[95] and "not excessive in relation to the aim pursued."[96]

With regard to telecommunications services, it is hard to see how a service could be prohibited without violating Article 59. A service provider operating from another member state—for example, offering a value-added service—has to be admitted to the network by the network operator in the member state if it pays the fees and does not damage the network.[97] Only in exceptional cases could one imagine that the prohibition of a service would serve the general interest. One example might be prohibition of the use of video text service for pornographic messages.

National Laws Discriminating against Service Providers from Other Member States

Under Article 59, a member state may not prevent suppliers located in other member states from offering their services within its territory, on grounds of nationality or place of establishment, if domestic suppliers are allowed to provide the service.[98] Such restrictions might consist of discrimination in access to and use of the domestic network, discrimination in the availability of leased lines (leased lines are particularly important for providers of value-added services), or discrimination in prices for access to the domestic network.

Exceptions to the Principle of Free Movement of Services

Article 66 of the treaty, together with Articles 55 and 56, excludes the application of Article 59 under certain conditions. Under Article 55, to which Article 66 refers, the rules on free movement of services do not apply to activities connected with the exercise of official authority. Traditionally, the European PTTs had a dual function. On the one hand, as integral parts of government administration, they performed such regulatory tasks as setting technical standards, conditions for access to the network, and issuing type approvals for

---

95. Ministère Public v. van Wesemael, Joined Cases 110 and 111/78, 1979 ECR 35, at 52, ground 29.

96. Criminal Proceedings against Webb, Case 279/80, 1981 ECR 3305, at 3326, ground 20.

97. See Schulte-Braucks 1986, 304–5; Schulte-Braucks 1987, 93.

98. On the function of Art. 59 as a prohibition of discriminatory restrictions on the free movement of services, see in general Troberg 1991, point 6.

terminal equipment. On the other hand, the PTTs served as operators of the public telecommunications network and providers of commercial telecommunications services. Such a provision of services is not connected inevitably to the exercise of public authority. Therefore, such a provision does not justify exemption of the telecommunications sector from the applicability of Article 59.[99]

According to Article 56, the rules on free movement of services are not to prejudice the applicability of provisions of national law providing special treatment for foreign nationals on grounds of public policy, public security, or public health. With regard to telecommunications services, this provision bears no practical importance. It is difficult to perceive a situation in which considerations of public policy, security, or health justify discriminatory treatment of foreign service providers.

Freedom of Establishment
Article 52 requires each member state to eliminate restrictions on the freedom of establishment by nationals of other member states.[100] The right of establishment is important to suppliers of telecommunications services because establishment of foreign subsidiaries might permit especially close contact with foreign customers. Article 52 grants nationals of other member states the right of national treatment, that is, they must be treated no worse than nationals of the host member state.

Liberalization of the Markets for
Telecommunications Services
The traditional, comprehensive telecommunications services monopolies granted by the member states to their respective PTTs are no longer justifiable under the EC treaty. However, as in the terminal equipment sector, the Commission did not rely on a case-by-case application of the treaty to force member states and their PTTs to relinquish their monopoly positions. Rather, using its lawmaking powers under Article 90(3), it adopted the directive of June 28, 1990, on competition in markets for telecommunications services.[101]

The core provision of the Commission directive is contained in its second article, which obliges the member states to abolish all special or exclusive rights for the supply of telecommunications services. The liberalization en-

---

99. Cf. Scherer 1988, 92.

100. On the right of establishment, see, generally, Rolf Wägenbaur, "Inhalt und Etappen der Niederlassungsfreiheit," EuZW (1991): 427ff.; Randelzhofer 1988a; Kapteyn and Verloren van Themaat 1989, 427ff.

101. Commission Directive no. 90/388/EEC of 28 June 1990 on competition in the markets for telecommunications services, OJ No. L 192/10 (July 24, 1990).

compasses all telecommunications services, whether basic or enhanced, with the exception of voice telephony. The member states may subject service providers in the competitive sector to licensing or declaration duties only to ensure compliance with the so-called essential requirements. The directive specifically and explicitly defines these requirements as: security of network operations; network integrity; interoperability, if required; and data protection (in justified cases).[102]

These requirements are the only permissible bases for licensing or declaration procedures in the member state. The conditions for licensing have to be objective, nondiscriminatory, and transparent so that applicants from all member states are treated equally.[103] The latitude of the member states to refuse access to the public telecommunications network is very limited; applications may be refused by the member states only if the applicant does not comply with the essential requirements set forth above. A potential supplier whose application is refused must be informed of the reasons for the refusal, and member states must also provide for appeals of such refusals.[104]

By July 1, 1991, member states were supposed to have divorced the regulatory from the commercial functions of the PTTs by establishing separate authorities for the issuance of operating licenses, the control of mandatory specifications, and the surveillance of usage conditions.[105] The member states were also required to notify the Commission by December 31, 1990, of all measures taken to comply with the obligation to abolish all special rights for the provision of telecommunications services. Some exceptions were made with regard to packet- and circuit-switched data services. Insofar as leased lines are used for data services, member states may prohibit the service providers from simple resale of leased line capacity to the public. Such a prohibition is only permissible, however, until December 31, 1992.[106] After that date, even the simple resale of leased line capacity will be allowed under EC law. The PTTs were thought to need that two-year period to harmonize their prices for switched services and leased lines. In the absence of harmonization, it was feared that the PTTs would suffer serious losses of revenue through the simple resale of leased line capacity. The PTTs use volume- and time-sensitive prices with regard to data services offered through the public switched network; but leased lines are usually priced on the basis of a flat-rate monthly charge. For heavy users, a leased line is often cheaper than switched

---

102. Commission Directive no. 90/388/EEC, Art. 1(1).
103. Commission Directive no. 90/388/EEC, Art. 3.
104. Commission Directive no. 90/388/EEC, Art. 2.
105. Commission Directive no. 90/388/EEC, Art. 7.
106. Commission Directive no. 90/388/EEC, Art. 3.

communications. Absent coordination of prices for switched service and leased circuits, unrestricted resale of leased line capacity would allow competitors to offer data transmission services at prices below those of the PTTs.

With regard to packet- or circuit-switched data services for the general public, the directive authorizes the member states, in their licensing or declaration procedures, to impose various requirements on potential providers of services. These requirements are: the essential requirements mentioned above; trade conditions of permanence, availability, and quality of service; and measures to safeguard the ability of the PTTs to perform legitimate tasks entrusted to them by the member states in connection with the general economic interest (tasks such as ensuring pervasive availability of data services).[107]

These three conditions aim at the protection of the public telecommunications organizations that provide switched data services as a task of general economic interest. To fulfill this task, the public telecommunications organizations are burdened with infrastructural duties, which might make it difficult for them to compete with the private service providers on an equal footing. If the proper discharge of infrastructural tasks is obstructed by competition, the member state may take measures to keep the public telecommunications organization in a position to fulfill them.

Member states that have granted their PTTs network monopolies must nevertheless ensure that access to the network is provided on an objective, nondiscriminatory, and transparent basis.[108] Independent providers of service must be allowed to obtain leased lines upon request within a reasonable period of time. Leased lines frequently form the technical basis for the provision of value-added services (for instance, data-bank services or data-processing services). The availability of such leased lines is, therefore, of great importance to service providers.

Existing restrictions on the processing of signals before transmission over the public network must also be eliminated. Moreover, the characteristics of technical interfaces, which independent providers of services must know in order to use the public network, have to be made transparent through publication.

The directive allows the PTTs to participate in the liberalized markets for telecommunications services and, hence, to compete with private providers. However, as network monopolists and suppliers of services, the PTTs are prohibited from abusing their dominant market positions. The network monopolist sets the prices and conditions for the use of the public network by competing providers. Thus, the network monopolist is in a position to squeeze its competitors by charging them high prices for network access

107. Commission Directive no. 90/388/EEC, Art. 3.
108. Commission Directive no. 90/388/EEC, Art. 4.

while charging low prices to their customers. Such behavior is facilitated by the network operator's opportunity to engage in cross-subsidization. As a result, it may constitute an abuse of dominant market position under Article 86 of the EEC treaty. Fair competition would have been better achieved by excluding the network operators and voice telephony monopolists altogether from markets for other telecommunications services. However, it is doubtful whether the treaty contains a legal basis for such a solution. A second-best solution would have been to require the network monopolists to compete in service markets only through separate affiliates. Such a solution would at least have ensured transparency of commercial and financial relations between the network monopolists and their subsidiaries in competitive service markets.[109]

Access to Public Telecommunications Networks for Independent Service Providers (Open Network Provision)

Just because the services directive obliges the member states to remove most special rights regarding the provision of telecommunications services does not mean that competing providers will be able to enter telecommunications markets easily. In a number of member states, newcomers continue to face obstacles to access to the public telecommunications networks. These obstacles include: differences across member states in technical interfaces or service elements and lack of harmonized network termination points; differences across member states in the conditions for the use of public networks and services; varying or discriminatory pricing practices; and time-consuming and costly licensing and approval procedures.[110]

To remove these obstacles, and to provide equal access to and use of public telecommunications networks, the Council adopted the directive of June 28, 1990, on open network provision.[111] The directive provides the basic principles for harmonizing the conditions governing access to and use of public networks and services. Complete harmonization will require further Community directives, tailored to individual services. Presently under discussion are rules for voice telephony, leased lines, ISDN, and packet-switched data services.[112]

109. Cf. Ellger and Witt 1990, 323.

110. Schulte-Braucks 1990, 675.

111. Council Directive no. 90/387/EEC of 28 June 1990 on the establishment of the internal market for telecommunications services through the implementation of open network provision, OJ No. L 192/1 (July 24, 1990).

112. See Commission of the European Communities, "Draft Analysis Report on the Application of ONP to Voice Telephony," May 30, 1991, Doc. ONPCOM 91–43; Commission of the European Communities, "Draft Proposal for a Council Directive on the Application of Open

Application of EC Competition Rules to Telecommunications Markets

General Remarks

One of the most important functions of the EC is to establish and protect a system of undistorted competition in the common market. The foundations of Community competition law appear in Articles 85 to 90 of the EEC treaty. Unlike its provisions on the free movement of goods and services, discussed previously, these provisions of the treaty apply to undertakings engaged in economic activity.[113]

Application of the competition rules to state-owned or state-controlled telecommunications organizations presupposes that these entities can be characterized as "undertakings." The term *undertaking* must be construed broadly: qualifying as undertakings are all persons (natural and legal) that engage in an economic activity as independent or complementary market actors, that is, all who are engaged in the exchange of goods and services.[114] Under this functional definition of the term, state-owned or state-controlled organizations may qualify as undertakings insofar as they engage in entrepreneurial activities.[115] Thus, the competition rules of the treaty cover the behavior of public (i.e., state-owned or state-controlled) as well as private undertakings.

The characterization of public telecommunications organizations as undertakings poses problems because these entities have traditionally possessed lawmaking powers (such as the power to regulate the prices and conditions of use of services provided by the organization). The rules adopted on the basis of these powers are part of public (administrative) law.

This problem arose in *British Telecom*,[116] a landmark ruling by the ECJ in the field of telecommunications. In this case, British Telecom, which at the

Network Provision to Leased Lines," October 8, 1990; Commission of the European Communities, "Analysis Report on the Application of ONP to ISDN," November 19, 1990, Doc. ONPCOM 90–23; Commission of the European Communities, "Proposal for a Council Recommendation on the Harmonized Provision of a Minimum Set of Packet-Switched Data Services in Accordance with Open Network Provision Principles," February 12, 1991.

113. The most recent, comprehensive, and detailed description of the EC's competition policy in the telecommunications sector is provided by the Commission Guidelines no. 91/C 233/02 for the application of the EC Competition Rules in the Telecommunications Sector, OJ No. C 233/2 (September 6, 1991). Although not legally binding, these guidelines indicate, for member states and market participants (be they public telecommunications organizations, private suppliers of services, or private suppliers of equipment), the Commission's interpretation of how the rules apply to this particular sector.

114. Hydrotherm v. Compact, Case 170/83, 1984 ECR 2999.

115. Koch 1990a, point 8; Mestmäcker 1974, 650.

116. Italy v. Commission, Case 41/83, 1985 ECR 873.

time was wholly owned by the state, restricted the use of its network by telex-forwarding agencies. The Court qualified British Telecom's behavior as part of its business activities, since it involved setting conditions and prices for using the network.[117] The regulations concerned exclusively the business relations between British Telecom and its customers. The Court noted, in this context, that neither the adoption nor the contents of the practices was influenced by the British Parliament.

Under *British Telecom*, the competition rules of the treaty apply not only when public undertakings use instruments of private law (e.g., contracts) in dealing with their customers, but also when they act under public law. This broad interpretation of Articles 86 and 90(1) implies that public undertakings, when pursuing economic aims, are subject to the competition rules whether they act through private or public law. Otherwise, such undertakings could determine for themselves whether or not they were covered by the competition rules.[118] Also subject to the competition rules are regulations concerning the conditions of use or the prices of public telecommunications networks that have been adopted by the legislative or the executive branch of a member state government. Article 90(1) of the treaty obliges member states not to enact or maintain any measure contrary to the competition rules with regard to public undertakings or undertakings to which they grant special rights. If the behavior of a public undertaking is induced by a member state, the member state itself is subject to the competition rules.

By using its lawmaking power under Article 90(3), the EC Commission has adopted directives liberalizing the markets for terminal equipment and telecommunications services.[119] These directives contain numerous provisions that oblige the member states to withdraw special or exclusive rights in these sectors and that regulate the conduct of the dominant public telecommunications organizations in order to enable competitors to enter the market under fair and nondiscriminatory conditions. The directives specify the degree to which the competition rules of the treaty apply to the telecommunications sector. At the same time, the competition rules, along with the rules on free movement of goods and services, form the legal basis of the directives. Even though the Commission and the Council have, in recent years, adopted an impressive body of secondary law covering the telecommunications sector in particular, the general provisions of the competition

---

117. Italy v. Commission, Case 41/83, 1985 ECR 873, at 885, grounds 18–19.

118. Reinhard Schulte-Braucks, "Das 'British Telecom'-Urteil: Eckstein für ein Europäisches Fernmelderecht?," *Wirtschaft und Wettbewerb* 36 (March 1986): 209–10; Schulte-Braucks 1986, 301.

119. Commission Directive no. 88/301/EEC; Commission Directive no. 90/388/EEC.

rules remain applicable. Let me, therefore, survey the competition rules as they affect telecommunications.

Article 86 and the Abuse of Market-Dominant Positions in the Telecommunications Sector

Article 86 prohibits any abuse of a dominant market position within the common market, provided that it affects trade between the member states.

The application of Article 86 presupposes that the conduct of a dominant undertaking is at issue. An undertaking is considered to be dominant if it is in "a position of economic strength . . . which enables it to prevent effective competition being maintained on the relevant market by giving it the power to behave to an appreciable extent independently of its competitors, customers and ultimately its consumers."[120] The European PTTs possess legally protected exclusive rights with regard to the establishment and operation of public telecommunications networks and the provision of voice telephone service. Their dominant positions follow from the absence of competitors in the markets covered by sole rights.[121] The lack of competition in these markets puts the PTTs in a position of economic strength, enabling them to act, to a large extent, independently of their customers and their consumers. The exclusive rights normally cover the entire territory of the relevant member state.[122]

Furthermore, the application of Article 86 requires the abuse of a dominant position through the conduct of an undertaking, or, via Article 90(1), through measures of member states relating to public undertakings or undertakings granted special rights.

The first question arising in this context is whether the competition rules of the treaty limit the latitude of the member states to remove economic activities from competition by granting special or exclusive rights to undertakings. A clear majority of legal writers argues that Articles 90(1) and 86 do not cover the *creation* of market-dominant positions. According to this view, the

---

120. Europemballage and Continental Can v. Commission, Case 6/72, 1973 ECR 215; United Brands v. Commission, Case 27/76, 1978 ECR 207, at 277, ground 65; Hoffmann-La Roche v. Commission, Case 85/76, 1979 ECR 461, at 520, ground 38; Müller 1988, 188; Koch 1990b, points 13 et seq.; Schröter 1991, points 58–59; Beutler et al. 1987, 343.

121. Italy v. Commission, Case 41/83, 1985 ECR 873, at 886, ground 22; British Leyland v. Commission, Case 226/84, 1986 ECR 3297, at 3299f.; Beutler et al. 1987, 343; Schröter 1991, point 55.

122. Art. 86 refers to an abuse of a market-dominant position within the common market or in a substantial part of it. Telecommunications monopolies usually cover the entire territory of a member state, and that may be enough to qualify as "a substantial part" of the common market. See Elliniki Radiophonia Tileorasi Anonymi Etairia v. Dimotiki Etairia Pliroforisis and S. Kouvelas, Case C-260/89, ground 31, as summarized in *Europäisches Steuer- und Wirtschaftsrecht* (1991): 284ff.

acquisition of a market-dominant position by an undertaking (e.g., through internal growth or the granting of exclusive rights by a member state) does not fall within the scope of Articles 86 and 90(1), because the application of these provisions presupposes a previously acquired dominant position and aims at the goal of protecting competitors, customers, and consumers against abusive conduct by the dominant undertaking.[123] Thus, it is argued that Articles 86 and 90(1) are designed to deal with situations in which the competitive market structure has already been weakened by the presence of a dominant enterprise.[124]

Moreover, it is contended that Article 90(1) indicates that the treaty explicitly recognizes the power of the member states to grant special rights to (public or private) undertakings.[125] Once these enterprises have reached a dominant position, their behavior is subject to the rules provided by Article 86.

So interpreted, the competition rules of the treaty leave member states free to withdraw economic activities from competition. They could determine for themselves the scope of the system of undistorted competition called for by Article 3(f) of the treaty.

Just because Article 90(1) does not prohibit member states from ever granting special rights does not mean, however, that the treaty leaves member states with unlimited power to grant such rights. Arguably, the basic principles of the treaty amount to inherent limits on the power of member states to grant exclusive rights. Such an interpretation of the treaty has very recently been confirmed by the ECJ.[126]

In Article 3(f), the treaty makes clear that the common market is to function on the basis of a system of undistorted competition. It is one of the most prominent tasks of the EC to establish such a system. Article 5 of the treaty requires member states to take all appropriate measures to ensure the fulfillment of treaty obligations. These provisions, together with Articles 86 and 90(1), form the inherent limits on the power of the member states to remove economic activities from competition by granting exclusive rights.

Article 3(f) requires the Community to establish a system of *undistorted* competition. Such a system would also seem to require safeguards against the *elimination* of competition.[127] Under Article 5, the member states are bound

123. Mestmäcker 1974, 348–49; Koch 1990b, point 1; Schröter 1991, point 20.

124. Hoffmann-La Roche v. Commission, Case 85/76, 1979 ECR 461, at 541, grounds 91ff.; Schröter 1991, point 20.

125. Costa v. ENEL, Case 6/64, 1964 ECR 585, at 598, with reference to Art. 37; Italy v. Commission, Case 155/73, 1974 ECR 409, at 429–30, ground 14, with reference to Art. 90(1); Emmerich 1983, 220.

126. French Republic v. Commission, Case C-202/88, EuZW (1991): 346, ground 22.

127. Commission Directive no. 90/388/EEC, consideration 16.

to refrain from all measures that are incompatible with such a basic principle as that expressed in Article 3(f).

On the other hand, Article 90(1) implies that member states are entitled (under certain circumstances) to remove an economic activity from competition by granting exclusive rights. To understand the limits placed by the EEC treaty on the power of the member states to establish or maintain monopolies, *Sacchi* provides useful guidance. According to *Sacchi*, nothing in the treaty prevents the member states from granting special or exclusive rights to undertakings if such an act is justified by a general interest of a noneconomic nature.[128] This seems to imply that the removal of an economic activity from competition may be incompatible with Articles 90(1) and 86 if the measure cannot be so justified.[129]

As I have mentioned, the establishment and operation of a nationwide, pervasive telecommunications network forms the basis for the provision of all telecommunications services. The establishment and maintenance of such a network is, therefore, in the general interest of the member states. Furthermore, the Commission has recognized that the exclusive right to provide voice telephone service, granted by the member states to PTTs, is justified by the fact that voice telephony is a universal service to be available to every user on reasonable and equal terms and, thus, constitutes a general interest of a noneconomic nature.[130] (After all, voice telephony is the most important conduit for emergency messages.)

Exclusive rights with regard to all other services are not justifiable under the *Sacchi* standard. Consequently, in its services directive, referring, inter alia, to Articles 90(1) and 86, the Commission ordered the member states to withdraw special rights for all telecommunications services other than voice telephony.

Special rights granted to PTTs with regard to telecommunications services tend to extend the dominant positions these organizations already possess. The following conduct of network monopolists is abusive and prohibited under Articles 86 and 90(1): prevention and restriction of access to the network by competing providers of services; restrictions on technological progress in telecommunication; and tying the sale of services subject to exclusive rights to purchase of additional services that are not connected with network utilization agreements.[131] Such conduct is incompatible with Articles 3(f) and 86 of the treaty. If the abusive behavior is caused by measures of the member

---

128. Italy v. Commission, Case 155/73, 1974 ECR 409, at 429, ground 14.
129. Cf. Müller 1988, 194.
130. Commission Directive no. 90/388/EEC, consideration 18; EC, *Green Paper*, 66.
131. Commission Directive no. 90/388/EEC, consideration 16.

states, then, according to Article 90(1), the states themselves are subject to the sanctions of Article 86.

British Telecom[132] offers an example of abusive behavior by a monopolistic network provider. In the United Kingdom, telex companies were engaged in the business of forwarding messages from a sender in one foreign country to a receiver in another (mainly the United States). The business flourished because it proved to be cheaper and faster for end users to have their messages forwarded to the United States via Great Britain than to use the direct transmission path provided by their domestic PTT. The U.K. telex-forwarding companies did not use telex lines to transmit the messages, but rather they used telephone circuits for data transfer. The agencies made use of the low overseas tariffs from Great Britain to the United States and high tariffs for direct connections between the countries where the users were located and the United States.

Due to such arbitrage, the continental PTTs suffered losses. Upon their request, BT adopted regulations prohibiting the international business of the forwarders.

The EC Commission concluded that this prohibition constituted an abuse of a dominant position and ordered BT to allow the forwarders to continue their business.[133] Italy then challenged the Commission's decision before the ECJ. The Court confirmed the Commission's order, observing that Italy had shown no evidence that the forwarders used international leased lines (which are rented out on a flat-rate basis and cheaper than switched connections), so that there was no abusive behavior on behalf of the telex companies. In the Court's view, the forwarders' use of modern technological means constituted technical progress, which has to be regarded as being in the general interest. The obstruction of such technical progress was viewed as an abuse of a dominant position by BT and, as such, a violation of Article 86.[134]

BT based its behavior on the telegraph regulations of the ITU (International Telecommunication Union) and on recommendations of the CCITT (Comité Consultatif International Télégraphique et Téléphonique), a committee of the ITU. The relevant provisions in these instruments were aimed at the prevention of arbitrage. It could be expected that the ECJ would take a position on the relationship between the EC competition rules and international telecommunications agreements concluded within ITU. However, the

---

132. Italy v. Commission, Case 41/83, 1985 ECR 873.

133. British Telecommunications, Commission Decision no. 82/861/EEC of 10 December 1982 relating to a proceeding under Art. 86 of the EEC Treaty, OJ No. L 360/36 (December 21, 1982).

134. Italy v. Commission, Case 41/83, 1985 ECR 873, at 887, ground 26.

Court avoided this intricate question by interpreting the ITU and CCITT rules to mean that they were not aimed at the exclusion of competition altogether, but, rather, served the purpose of preventing abusive practices in competition.[135] As the conduct of the telex companies was not abusive, it did not violate ITU and CCITT rules as interpreted by the Court. Through this (obviously incorrect) interpretation, the Court avoided taking a clear position on conflict between the EEC treaty and the International Telecommunication Treaty.

The Commission, however, in its guidelines on application of the competition rules to the telecommunications sector, takes the position that the rules apply to those regulations and recommendations of the ITU and CCITT that cover international telecommunications.[136] The guidelines give other examples of what the Commission would consider abusive conduct by dominant telecommunications enterprises.[137] One such example is the creation of an artificial scarcity in international leased lines. Another example is discriminatory treatment of competitors with regard to network access, conditions of use, and price. Still another would be to cross-subsidize competitively offered services with revenue gained in the monopoly sector. A final example is predatory pricing to hinder market access for newcomers or to force established competitors to leave the market.[138]

Restrictions of Competition in Markets for
Telecommunications Services through Agreements
or Concerted Practices of Undertakings
Competition in telecommunications markets is threatened not only by the presence of monopolistic network providers,[139] but also through agreements or concerted practices between telecommunications enterprises. According to Article 85, "all agreements between undertakings, decisions by associations of undertakings and concerted practices which may affect trade between Member States and which have as their object or effect the prevention, restriction or distortion of competition within the common market" are prohibited as incompatible with the common market.

This provision is important with regard to the international system of cooperation between public telecommunications undertakings within the ITU

---

135. Italy v. Commission, Case 41/83, 1985 ECR 873, at 890, ground 42.

136. Commission Guidelines no. 91/C 233/02, nos. 139ff.

137. On the application of the EC's competition rules to telecommunications, see Commission Guidelines no. 91/C 233/02, nos. 84ff.

138. Cf. Commission Guidelines no. 91/C 233/02, nos. 102ff.

139. Italy v. Commission, Case 41/83, 1985 ECR 873; Commission Guidelines no. 91/C 233/02, nos. 83ff.

framework. Of particular concern is the system of splitting revenues from international telecommunications services.

The relevance of Article 85 to the telecommunications sector may be illustrated by the SWIFT-CEPT controversy.[140] SWIFT (Society for Worldwide Interbank Financial Telecommunication) provides a global telecommunications network for telecommunications traffic between its member banks. The network is operated on the basis of leased lines. SWIFT applied to the European PTTs for the provision of such lines. The PTTs, acting through CEPT (Conférence Européenne des Postes et des Télécommunications), were prepared to make leased lines available to SWIFT. However, they intended to depart from the traditional method of pricing leased circuits. Lines are normally leased on a flat-rate basis. The rate is considerably lower than the volume-sensitive prices paid for use of the public, switched networks. The members of CEPT, concerned with revenue losses caused by the operation of the private SWIFT network, intended to apply a volume-sensitive element, in addition to the flat rate, when pricing the lines leased to SWIFT. The EC Commission intervened, contending that the conduct of the PTTs, consisting of the concerted fixing of higher rates with regard to SWIFT, violated Articles 85 and 86. As the PTTs conceded and changed the proposed pricing system, the Commission did not make a formal decision in the matter.

Another example of how Article 85 is applied to this sector is the bilateral agreements between national PTTs, which are concluded within the framework of the International Telecommunication Convention, the International Telecommunication Regulations, and the CCITT recommendations. These cover the accounting system, the kinds and modes of operation of services, and the extent of traffic over the public networks.[141] The revenue derived from public international telecommunications services is divided between the PTTs on a cooperative basis. Typically, cost reductions, resulting from technological progress, do not result in decreased prices.

Therefore, the EC Commission recently launched a formal investigation under the competition rules, requesting that the EC's 15 telecommunications groups provide information on prices and costs in international telephone service. The investigation looks at both collection charges (raised from users) and accounting charges (transfers from the PTT that collects from the caller to the other PTTs that handle the call en route). The Commission took action in response to complaints voiced by U.S. telecommunications companies, alleging that the rates were unfairly high and that the present accounting system

---

140. Schulte-Braucks 1987, 88; Ramsey, "Europe Responds to the Challenge of the New Information Technologies: A Teleinformatics Strategy for the 1980s," *Cornell International Law Journal* 14 (Summer 1981): 279ff.

141. Commission Guidelines no. 91/C 233/02, no. 144.

unduly favors EC operators because they handle more incoming than outgoing traffic. The Commission intended to present some preliminary views on pricing of international calls by the end of 1991.[142]

Privatization of State-Owned Telecommunications Organizations under EC Law

In every member state but one, the PTT is a part of general government, a state-owned enterprise, or a state-controlled enterprise. The exception is the United Kingdom, where British Telecom, formerly a wholly state-owned undertaking, was privatized in 1984.

The privatization of a monopolistic, state-owned undertaking does not lead to more competition in a monopolized market as long as the sole rights vested in the public undertaking are not removed. The state-owned undertaking, operating under the grant of an exclusive right, is merely changed into a private monopoly.

The question of whether it is within the EC's powers to request the member states to privatize their public telecommunications undertakings is answered by Article 222 of the EEC treaty. According to Article 222, the treaty does not prejudice the choices of property ownership systems in the member states. It is, consequently, up to the member states to decide whether telecommunications markets are to be supplied by state-owned undertakings or by privatized entities.[143] Article 222 does not, however, prevent the application of other treaty provisions, especially the competition rules, to public undertakings.

Limits on the Application of Treaty Rules: Article 90(2)

Under certain circumstances, Article 90(2) of the treaty exempts particular undertakings from the application of treaty provisions. The provision reads: "Undertakings entrusted with the operation of services of general economic interest . . . shall be subject to the rules contained in this Treaty, in particular to the rules on competition, in so far as the application of such rules does not obstruct the performance, in law or in fact, of the particular tasks assigned to them." However, the second sentence of Article 90(2) provides that an exemption for such undertakings is not permissible if the development of trade in the EC is affected to an extent contrary to the interests of the Community.

---

142. Cf. Hill, "EC to Investigate Telephone Charges," *Financial Times*, July 5, 1991; "Verfahren der EG-Kommission: Kritische Beleuchtung der Telefongebühren," *Neue Zürcher Zeitung*, July 6, 1991.

143. EC, *Green Paper*, 71; Scherer 1988, 95.

PTTs are public undertakings whose objectives are to provide telecommunications services to the general public, namely, the establishment and operation of nationwide, pervasive telecommunications networks and the provision of voice telephony, a universal service. To this extent, these undertakings are entrusted by the member states with the provision of services of general economic interest. However, in order to justify an exemption from the application of treaty rules, it has to be shown that the performance of such tasks is, in law or in fact, obstructed by the application of treaty provisions. As Article 90(2) provides for an exception from the applicability of the treaty, it must be construed narrowly. Consequently, such undertakings are not exempt if the discharge of their tasks is merely made more burdensome, but not obstructed, by the application of the treaty rules.

As I have shown, the capacity of the public telecommunications organizations to fulfill their infrastructural tasks is very well maintained even if the treaty rules are applied to them. Therefore, there is no need to exempt these undertakings under Article 90(2) from the application of other provisions of the EEC treaty. The Commission, however, perceives situations in which it would exempt PTTs from the application of the competition rules under Article 90(2).[144]

The Separation of Power between Commission and Council: Article 90(3)

Article 90(3) requires the EC Commission to ensure that the provisions of Article 90 are properly applied. To reach this objective, the Commission is to address appropriate directives or decisions to the member states. The extent of this lawmaking power was at issue in a case before the ECJ discussed previously with regard to questions of substantive law.

The plaintiffs in this case also objected to the directive for procedural reasons. In their view, the Commission committed an abuse of procedure by adopting the directive under Article 90(3). The correct legal action would have been to institute lawsuits under Article 169 against those member states in which the structure of markets for telecommunications equipment was not compatible with the rules of the treaty.[145]

The Court did not accept this argument. Article 90(3) empowers the Commission to specify the obligations of the member states under Article 90(1). The directive on terminal equipment (like the services directive) determines the general obligations of the member states with regard to telecom-

---

144. Commission Directive no. 90/388/EEC, consideration 18; Commission Guidelines no. 91/C 233/02, nos. 21–22.

145. French Republic v. Commission, Case C-202/88, ground 16, EuZW (1991): 346.

munications undertakings to which they have granted special rights. The directive does not take into consideration the particular situations in the individual member states. Far from committing an abuse of procedure, the Commission used its power under Article 90(3) in a lawful manner.

The plaintiffs also argued that the Commission acted outside its lawmaking power under Article 90(3). Article 90(1) presupposes the existence of special rights. The maintenance of such rights, therefore, could not be regarded as a violation of Article 90(1). The Court refuted this argument by observing correctly that although Article 90(1) recognizes the existence of special rights, this does not mean that all special rights granted by the member states are necessarily compatible with the treaty.[146]

Finally, the plaintiffs alleged that the Council's powers granted under Articles 100a and 87 were violated in adopting the Commission directive under Article 90(3). The Council, in which the governments of the member states are represented, is not involved in the lawmaking process for Commission directives under Article 90(3). If directives are adopted under Articles 87 or 100a, the Council acts as the supreme legislative organ of the Community.

Article 100a concerns the adoption of measures for the approximation of laws relevant for the proper functioning of the common market. The approximation of laws of the member states was not the primary objective of the terminal equipment directive. Article 87 empowers the Council to adopt appropriate measures in order to give effect to the competition rules of Articles 85 and 86, which apply to all undertakings. Article 90(3), however, grants lawmaking capacity to the Commission with regard to measures of member states aimed at public undertakings or undertakings to which they have granted special rights. As the terminal equipment directive concerns measures of member states with respect to public undertakings, the Court held that the Commission acted within its lawmaking capacity under Article 90(3) and did not violate the jurisdiction of the Council under Article 87.[147]

The judgment of the Court confirming the lawmaking power of the Commission with regard to undertakings with exclusive rights in the telecommunications terminal equipment market bears an importance that goes beyond the telecommunications sector. It clears the way for the Commission to liberalize all markets in the member states presently characterized by the existence of legally protected monopolies, insofar as such monopolies cannot be justified under Community law. Examples include markets for the supply of water, gas, electricity, and transport.

---

146. French Republic v. Commission, Case C-202/88, ground 22, EuZW (1991): 346.
147. French Republic v. Commission, Case C-202/88, ground 27, EuZW (1991): 346.

Transposition of Secondary EC Law Relating to Telecommunications into the Legal Systems of the Member States: The German Example

The basic legal instruments used to liberalize telecommunications markets are the Commission's directives on terminal equipment and on services. These directives are addressed to all member states and must be transposed into their domestic law within specified periods. Normally, directives are not directly applicable, as they require transposition into the domestic law of the member states. However, in a situation where a member state does not comply with its obligation to transpose, a directive may become directly applicable if its provisions are unconditional and sufficiently precise.[148] Let us examine, by way of example, how German law has adopted the provisions of the two telecommunications directives.

On July 1, 1989, the act on the restructuring of the German Bundespost of June 8, 1989, came into force.[149] The act was framed in close cooperation with the EC institutions active in the field of telecommunications, providing for the splitting of Germany's PTT, Deutsche Bundespost, into three separate enterprises: postal services (Deutsche Bundespost Postdienst), banking services (Deutsche Bundespost Postbank), and telecommunications services (Deutsche Bundespost Telekom). The three are wholly state owned and responsible for the operational and entrepreneurial functions in the sectors of their activity, with the government minister responsible for regulatory tasks. Market structure in the telecommunications sector is essentially regulated by the telecommunications facilities act,[150] which also transposes the Commission's directives into German law.

Services

According to sections 1(1) and 1(2) of the telecommunications facilities act, the Federal Republic is the holder of the monopoly encompassing operation of telecommunications and wireless radio facilities. The Federal Republic delegates this monopoly to Deutsche Bundespost Telekom. Under section 1(4) of the act, everyone is entitled to provide telecommunications services by using

---

148. See Van Duyn v. Home Office, Case 41/74, 1974 ECR 1337, at 1349, ground 12; Kapteyn and Verloren van Themaat 1989, 340ff.; Eberhard Grabitz, "Artikel 189," points 60–64, in *Kommentar zum EWG-Vertrag*, ed. Eberhard Grabitz (Munich: Beck, 1989).

149. Gesetz zur Neustrukturierung des Post- und Fernmeldewesens der Deutschen Bundespost (Poststrukturgesetz) v. 8. Juni 1989, *Bundesgesetzblatt* (1989), I 1026.

150. Gesetz über Fernmeldeanlagen i.d.F. d.Bek. v. 3. Juli 1989, *Bundesgesetzblatt* (1989), I 1455.

leased lines or the public switched network run by Deutsche Bundespost Telekom. An exception, however, is made for voice telephone service. The right to provide voice telephony is held by the Federal Republic, and it, too, is delegated to Deutsche Bundespost Telekom.

Those who wish to offer competitive telecommunications services are not subject to a licensing requirement. They need only file a declaration with the minister for post and telecommunications. They must also notify the minister of changes to or termination of their activities. According to the telecommunications facilities act, Deutsche Bundespost Telekom is entitled to provide telecommunications services in competitive sectors.

Terminal Equipment

Type approval and licensing procedures for telecommunications terminal equipment are covered by section 2(a) of the telecommunications facilities act and by the regulation on the approval of telecommunications terminal equipment of March 22, 1991.[151] The market for telecommunications terminal equipment is fully liberalized, so that approved terminal equipment from a variety of suppliers may be connected to the network. Deutsche Bundespost Telekom is in the process of installing network termination points at customers' premises. The technical specifications for these network termination points have been published and are thus transparent, putting the manufacturers of such equipment in a position to produce equipment that fits the termination points.

By law, terminal equipment must be approved and licensed if it complies with the requirements contained in section 4 of the regulation on the approval of telecommunications terminal equipment. These requirements coincide (in part, literally) with those contained in the Commission's terminal equipment directive.

Approval tests and decisions are undertaken by the central bureau for approval in telecommunications, an authority attached to the ministry for post and telecommunications. This authority is, at least formally, independent of all equipment suppliers and service providers.

If the competent approval authority of another member state has confirmed that terminal equipment complies with the common technical specifications applicable throughout the Community, that confirmation is recognized by the German central bureau for approvals, and no further tests are required.

Section 2(a) of the telecommunications facilities act and the terminal

---

151. Verordnung über die Zulassung von Telekommunikationseinrichtungen v. 22. März 1991, *Bundesgesetzblatt* (1991), I 765.

equipment approval regulation transpose the provisions of the Commission directive on terminal equipment into German law.

Market Access for Foreign Suppliers of Telecommunications Equipment and Services: "Fortress Europe" in Telecommunications?

The EC's rules on the free movement of goods, services, persons, and capital are not applicable to trade with third countries. The basic treaty provision regarding external trade policy is Article 113. It announces a common commercial policy based on uniform principles regarding changes in tariff rates, conclusion of tariff and trade agreements, measures of liberalization, export policy, and measures to protect trade.

Since the end of the transitional period (December 31, 1969), the EC possesses exclusive power regarding trade policy toward third countries.[152] The member states, consequently, are barred from all lawmaking in the field—unless the Community has not made use of its powers therein. Potential conflicts between measures of the member states and subsequent Community measures are resolved by applying the principle of priority of EC law.[153] Once the EC has made use of its competence in foreign trade policy, the member states are barred from making their own laws in this field. The Community's competence covers trade in both goods and services.

In the field of telecommunications, the EC has not yet formulated a comprehensive foreign trade policy. However, the Commission's Green Paper on Telecommunications considers it an EC priority to develop principles for foreign trade in telecommunications services and equipment.[154] The Green Paper sets out the criteria determining the EC's position with regard to free trade in telecommunications services and equipment:

—the EC's interest in opening markets for telecommunications services and equipment in third countries;
—development of a common EC position on the regulation of services, for use in the negotiations on services during the Uruguay Round;
—examination of the effects of granting further market access to suppliers of services and equipment from third countries; and
—comparison of the effects of third-country access to EC markets with the potential for EC exports of telecommunications goods and services to the third country.[155]

152. Vedder 1986, point 1.
153. Vedder 1986, point 5.
154. EC, *Green Paper*, 157.
155. EC, *Green Paper*, 154.

Apart from being engaged in multilateral trade negotiations within GATT, the Commission is also discussing trade in telecommunications goods and services bilaterally with a number of third countries, including the United States and Japan.[156] The EC, however, has not yet concluded any binding international trade agreements, bilateral or multilateral, in the field of telecommunications.

Despite the absence of a clear and explicit common commercial policy for telecommunications, it can be said that liberalization of the sector within the Community bears advantages for suppliers located in third countries. The liberalization of formerly monopolized or, at least, highly regulated telecommunications markets improves access to these markets for third-country suppliers. A good example of this effect is provided by German telecommunications law. Under section 1(4) of the telecommunications facilities act,[157] "every person" is entitled to offer telecommunications services (except voice telephony) to the general public by using leased lines or the public, switched network. "Every person" as used in the act refers not simply to German nationals or EC citizens but also to providers from third countries.

With regard to the type approval of telecommunications terminal equipment, the procedure and the criteria for approval are the same for third-country suppliers as for German or EC applicants. A certain disadvantage exists for applicants from third countries as to the recognition of foreign test certifications through the German approval authority. Under section 15(8)(1) of the telecommunications equipment approval regulation,[158] the approval authority (by law) must recognize confirmations of conformity with common technical specifications issued by the approval authorities of other member states. Such an obligation does not exist with regard to testing procedures of third-country approval authorities. However, Article 10(5) of the Council directive of April 29, 1991, on the approximation of the laws of the member states concerning telecommunications terminal equipment, including the mutual recognition of their conformity,[159] provides for the recognition of documentation relating to the type approval of telecommunications terminal equipment made by third-country authorities, if an agreement between the EC and the respective country covers this issue.

Currently, providers from third countries are quite active in European telecommunications markets. Recently, the German ministry for post and telecommunications granted a license for the operation of a nationwide mobile telephone network to a consortium under the leadership of Mannesmann Mobilfunk GmbH. This consortium includes such non-EC companies as Pa-

156. EC, *Green Paper*, 161ff.
157. See n. 150, supra.
158. See n. 151, supra.
159. Council Directive no. 91/263/EEC.

cific Telesis. Through its Dutch subsidiary, Pacific Telesis holds 21 percent of Mannesmann Mobilfunk.[160] In the United Kingdom, the Bell operating companies have obtained nearly 90 percent of all cable franchises, allowing access to about 14 million households.[161] The U.S. trade balance with the EC in telecommunications equipment is positive.

All of this does not mean that the EC has no problems with third countries in telecommunications trade. Numerous complaints have been voiced in the United States that the EC, far from removing restrictions on imports of U.S. telecommunications goods and services, is erecting new barriers to trade.[162] The U.S. telecommunications industry is especially worried about being kept out of such European standard-setting organizations as CEN/CENELEC,[163] ETSI,[164] and CEPT.[165] It has requested an opportunity to provide input to the standard-setting procedures.[166] Such access will be a matter of negotiation between the United States and the European standard-setting organizations.

The most serious danger to free access to EC markets for telecommunications equipment and services is that the EC institutions will rely too heavily on the principle of reciprocity when deciding on the degree of market access.

Despite the problems now affecting trade in telecommunications goods and services, there is little need to fear a "Fortress Europe." Protectionism by the Community would be contrary to EC interests, as it would probably induce important third countries to bar the Community's telecommunications industry from access to their markets.

Summary and Outlook

Summing up, it may be said that application of the EEC treaty to the telecommunications sector has led to a substantial liberalization of markets for tele-

---

160. See Helmut Fangmann, Walter Scheurle, Michael Schwemmle, and Ewald Wehner, *Handbuch für Post und Telekommunikation: Poststrukturgesetz* (Cologne: Bund-Verlag, 1990), 390.

161. Lord Sharpe of Grimsdyke, "Privatization of Telecommunication," *Transnational Data and Communications Report* 14 (1991): 24.

162. See, e.g., United States Trade Representative, *1987 National Trade Estimate: Report on Foreign Trade Barriers* (Washington, D.C.: Office of the U.S. Trade Representative, 1987), 100–101.

163. Comité Européen de Normalisation (CEN); Comité Européen de Normalisation Electrotechnique (CENELEC).

164. ETSI: European Telecommunications Standards Institute.

165. French Republic v. Commission, Case C-202/88, grounds 53–57, EuZW (1991): 348.

166. See Dan R. Mastromarco, "The European Community Approach to Standardization: A Possible Mechanism for Improved Nonmember State Input," *North Carolina Journal of International Law and Commercial Regulation* 15 (Winter 1990): 47ff.

communications services and terminal equipment. The restructuring of these markets under the relevant secondary law of the EC, especially the directives on terminal equipment and on services, will contribute to the establishment of a single European telecommunications market. Sole rights for telecommunications services are only compatible with EC law insofar as they concern the operation of telecommunications networks and the supply of voice telephone service. The provision of these services at reasonable prices and on equal terms for all consumers is regarded as being in the general interest, thereby justifying a monopoly in these areas. However, the member states are free to liberalize their telecommunications markets further than is required by EC law. Thus, for example, the United Kingdom has liberalized beyond the level required by EC law.

The freedom to provide services, as guaranteed by Article 59 of the treaty, covers all other telecommunications services, whether basic or value-added in nature. They can be traded freely within the EC, and exclusive rights covering these services have to be abolished. Also, sole rights with regard to telecommunications terminal equipment have to be eliminated. Eventual achievement of the EC's open network provision will ensure equitable and nondiscriminatory access to and use of telecommunications networks for service providers on a Community-wide basis with harmonized requirements.

The liberalization of markets for telecommunications equipment and services has not reached its final stage. There are Commission proposals to open up markets that remain highly regulated (mobile radio and satellite communications are examples). In its recently published Green Paper on Satellite Communications, the Commission proposes such major changes for the provision of satellite telecommunications services as:

—full liberalization of the earth segment, including receive only and transmit/receive terminals;
—free access to space segment capacity on an equitable, nondiscriminatory, and cost-oriented basis;
—full commercial freedom to space segment providers, including direct marketing of satellite capacity to service providers and users (subject to licensing under and compliance with EC law); and
—harmonization measures necessary for the provision of Europe-wide satellite services.[167]

---

167. Commission of the European Communities, *Towards Europe-wide Systems and Services: Green Paper on a Common Approach in the Field of Satellite Communications in the European Community*, COM(90) 490 final (Luxembourg: Office for Official Publications of the European Communities, 1990), 121ff.

With regard to market access from third countries, no explicit and transparent commercial policy has emerged at the EC level. Nevertheless, a considerable degree of access to the European market has been reached. Although problems remain, there will be no "Fortress Europe" in telecommunications.

REFERENCES

Beutler, Bengt, Roland Bieber, Jörn Pipkorn, and Jochen Streil, eds. 1987. *Die Europäische Gemeinschaft: Rechtsordnung und Politik.* 3d ed. Baden-Baden: Nomos.
Ellger, Reinhard, and Detlev Witt. 1990. "International Free Trade in Telecommunications." In *Rules for Free International Trade in Services,* ed. Daniel Friedmann and Ernst-Joachim Mestmäcker, 275–339. Baden-Baden: Nomos.
Emmerich, Volker. 1983. "Nationale Postmonopole und Europäisches Gemeinschaftsrecht." *Europarecht* 18 (July-September): 216–26.
Faulhaber, Gerald R. 1987. *Telecommunications in Turmoil: Technology and Public Policy.* Cambridge, Mass.: Ballinger.
Foreman-Peck, James, and Jürgen Müller, eds. 1988. *European Telecommunications Organisations.* Baden-Baden: Nomos.
Hansen, Poul, ed. 1988. *Freedom of Data Flows and EEC Law.* Deventer: Kluwer Law and Taxation Publishers.
Hellmann, Rainer. 1991. "Gemeinsame Industriepolitik." In *Kommentar zum EWG-Vertrag.* 4th ed., ed. Hans von der Groeben, Jochen Thiesing, and Claus-Dieter Ehlermann, 4:6269–6325. Baden-Baden: Nomos.
Hochbaum, Ingfried F. 1991. "Artikel 37." In *Kommentar zum EWG-Vertrag.* 4th ed., ed. Hans von der Groeben, Jochen Thiesing, and Claus-Dieter Ehlermann, 1:548–610. Baden-Baden: Nomos.
Ipsen, Hans-Peter. 1972. *Europäisches Gemeinschaftsrecht.* Tübingen: Mohr.
Kapteyn, Paul J. G., and Pieter Verloren van Themaat. 1989. *Introduction to the Law of the European Communities after the Coming into Force of the Single Act.* 2d ed. Deventer: Kluwer Law and Taxation Publishers.
Koch, Norbert. 1990a. "Artikel 85." In *Kommentar zum EWG-Vertrag,* ed. Eberhard Grabitz. Munich: Beck.
Koch, Norbert. 1990b. "Artikel 86." In *Kommentar zum EWG-Vertrag,* ed. Eberhard Grabitz. Munich: Beck.
Matthies, Heinrich. 1987a. "Artikel 36." In *Kommentar zum EWG-Vertrag,* ed. Eberhard Grabitz. Munich: Beck.
Matthies, Heinrich. 1987b. "Artikel 37." In *Kommentar zum EWG-Vertrag,* ed. Eberhard Grabitz. Munich: Beck.
Mestmäcker, Ernst-Joachim. 1974. *Europäisches Wettbewerbsrecht.* Munich: Beck.
Mestmäcker, Ernst-Joachim, ed. 1987. *The Law and Economics of Transborder Telecommunications: A Symposium.* Baden-Baden: Nomos.
Meyer, John R., Robert W. Wilson, Alan Baughcum, Ellen Bartos, and Louis Caouette. 1980. *The Economics of Competition in the Telecommunications Industry.* Cambridge, Mass.: Oelgeschlager, Gunn, and Hein.

Müller, Joachim. 1988. *Dienstleistungsmonopole im System des EWG-V*. Baden-Baden: Nomos.

Müller-Graff, Peter-Christian. 1991. "Artikel 36." In *Kommentar zum EWG-Vertrag*. 4th ed., ed. Hans von der Groeben, Jochen Thiesing, and Claus-Dieter Ehlermann, 1:501–48. Baden-Baden: Nomos.

Neumann, Karl-Heinz. 1989. "Die Organisation der Telekommunikation in anderen grossen Industrieländern: Die Vereinigten Staaten von Amerika, Grossbritannien, Japan." In *Handbuch der Telekommunikation*, ed. Franz Arnold, vol. 2, sec. 11.3.20. Cologne: Verlagsgruppe Deutscher Wirtschaftsdienst.

Randelzhofer, Albrecht. 1988a. "Artikel 52." In *Kommentar zum EWG-Vertrag*, ed. Eberhard Grabitz. Munich: Beck.

Randelzhofer, Albrecht. 1988b. "Artikel 59." In *Kommentar zum EWG-Vertrag*, ed. Eberhard Grabitz. Munich: Beck.

Scherer, Joachim. 1985. *Telekommunikationsrecht und Telekommunikationspolitik*. Baden-Baden: Nomos.

Scherer, Joachim. 1988. "European Telecommunications Law: The Framework of the Treaty." In *Freedom of Data Flows and EEC Law*, ed. Poul Hansen, 85–106. Deventer: Kluwer Law and Taxation Publishers.

Scherer, Joachim, ed. 1987. *Nationale und Europäische Perspektiven der Telekommunikation*. Baden-Baden: Nomos.

Schröter, Helmuth. 1991. "Artikel 86." In *Kommentar zum EWG-Vertrag*. 4th ed., ed. Hans von der Groeben, Jochen Thiesing, and Claus-Dieter Ehlermann, 2:1783–1934. Baden-Baden: Nomos.

Schulte-Braucks, Reinhard. 1986. "Telecommunications and Freedom of Trade in Goods and Services under the EEC Treaty." In *The Law and Economics of Transborder Telecommunications*, ed. Ernst-Joachim Mestmäcker, 295–312. Baden-Baden: Nomos.

Schulte-Braucks, Reinhard. 1987. "Ordnungspolitische und Gemeinschaftsrechtliche Aspekte der Europäischen Telekommunikationspolitik." In *Nationale und Europäische Perspektiven der Telekommunikation*, ed. Joachim Scherer, 82–102. Baden-Baden: Nomos.

Schulte-Braucks, Reinhard. 1990. "Der Europäische Telekommunikationsmarkt: Gegenwärtige und Künftige Entwicklungen." *Computer und Recht* 6 (October 1990): 672–76.

Troberg, Peter. 1991. "Artikel 59." In *Kommentar zum EWG-Vertrag*. 4th ed., ed. Hans von der Groeben, Jochen Thiesing, and Claus-Dieter Ehlermann, 1:1053–71. Baden-Baden: Nomos.

Ungerer, Herbert. 1987. "Telematik: Das Ende der Nationalen Telekommunikationspolitik?" In *Nationale und Europäische Perspektiven der Telekommunikation*, ed. Joachim Scherer, 18–29. Baden-Baden: Nomos.

Ungerer, Herbert, C. Berben, and H. P. Costello, eds. 1989. *Telecommunications for Europe 1992: The CEC Sources*. Amsterdam: IOS.

Vedder, Christoph. 1986. "Artikel 113." In *Kommentar zum EWG-Vertrag*, ed. Eberhard Grabitz. Munich: Beck.

Vickers, John, and George Yarrow. 1985. *Privatization and the Natural Monopolies*. London: Public Policy Centre.

Prospects for Competitive Air Travel in Europe

Severin Borenstein

Though the Treaty of Rome provides for a common transport policy in the EC, its free-trade tenets have never really taken hold in the airline industry. The competition rules in the treaty were not even found to be applicable to the airline industry until a 1974 ruling by the European Court of Justice.[1] Since then, there has been slow progress in moving toward a more competitive and unified EC airline industry. Reports in 1984 and 1985 endorsed restrictions on the most anticompetitive practices of EC airlines, but stopped well short of U.S.-style deregulation.[2] European Council regulations passed in 1987 and 1990 have expanded application of Article 85 of the treaty to the airline industry and, thus, restricted some anticompetitive practices.[3] Nonetheless, the state of competition in the European airline industry is still far from the ideals embodied in Project 1992.

Project 1992 does not prescribe U.S.-style deregulation in air transport, but its presumption in favor of free-market competition and against government intervention implies oversight that more closely resembles the U.S. approach than the past policies in the EC. Historically, each member state has

The author thanks Jim Adams, two anonymous reviewers, and participants in the Europe after 1992 conference at the University of Michigan for useful discussions. Janet Netz, Rika Onishi, and Michael Schwarz provided excellent research assistance.

1. Commission v. France, Case 167/73, 1974 ECR 359.

2. See Commission of the European Communities 1984 and 1985.

3. Council Regulation (EEC) no. 3976/87 of 14 December 1987 on the application of Art. 85(3) of the treaty to certain categories of agreements and concerted practices in the air transport sector, OJ No. L 379/9 (December 31, 1987). Council Regulation (EEC) no. 3975/87 of 14 December 1987 laying down the procedure for the application of the rules of competition to undertakings in the air transport sector, OJ No. L 374/1 (December 31, 1987). Council Regulation (EEC) no. 2343/90 of 24 July 1990 on access for air carriers to scheduled intra-Community air service routes and on the sharing of passenger capacity between air carriers on scheduled air services between member states, OJ No. L 217/8 (August 11, 1990). Council Regulation (EEC) no. 2344/90 of 24 July 1990 amending regulation (EEC) no. 3976/87 on the application of Art. 85(3) of the treaty to certain categories of agreements and concerted practices in the air transport sector.

controlled its own domestic air travel and has negotiated bilateral agreements with other member states to regulate travel between them. But complete implementation of Project 1992 could be construed to imply (for instance) that Air France would be free to offer regularly scheduled service between Rome and Milan or that British Airways would have the right to set up a primary hub in Brussels. Such examples raise a number of issues regarding both the political feasibility and the economic desirability of European airline deregulation. Currently, the political questions are at the forefront, as government-owned airlines are threatened by carriers from other countries. The tension between economic sovereignty of individual countries and commitment to the principles of Project 1992 is made especially clear in this industry.

The Association of European Airlines (AEA) has expressed strong opposition to what it sees as attempts at U.S.-style deregulation.[4] The AEA and many other opponents of European airline competition argue that deregulation has not been successful in the United States. Individuals on both sides of the debate point out the differences between the U.S. experience and the circumstances in Europe: Higher population densities in Europe make airport expansion more difficult and make high-speed ground transportation more viable. Compatibility difficulties across countries make air traffic control (ATC) less responsive to changes than in the United States. The EC member states have more heterogeneous goals and much more autonomous authority than do the states of the United States. For instance, for national security and other reasons, most scheduled airlines in Europe are owned and subsidized by nation states.

Some concerns about the sustainability of airline competition in Europe do mirror those that were raised prior to U.S. deregulation and resurrected in the United States over the last few years. Not only are there now fewer competing airlines in the United States than shortly after deregulation, but each remaining successful carrier has established its own area of dominance at a hub airport. The airlines compete in carrying passengers who change planes at their hubs, but each carrier exercises substantial market power over the passengers who travel to or from the city in which its hub is located.[5] If a similar situation were to arise in Europe, the airlines that are already established at the centrally located European airports would be at a substantial advantage.

Airport capacity constraints, the most pressing concern about European airline deregulation, became a primary focus of U.S. airline policy only many years after deregulation. This problem has already arisen in Europe both

---

4. Association of European Airlines 1984.
5. See Borenstein 1989 and 1991; Hurdle et al. 1989; Levine 1987; U.S. Department of Transportation 1990; U.S. General Accounting Office 1990.

because population density is greater and because airport construction has not been pursued as aggressively. In Europe, however, the idea of rationing airport use with fees is better accepted.[6]

In this chapter, I investigate these and other issues in the liberalization or deregulation of the European airline industry. Because so much has been written on the successes of and difficulties with airline deregulation in the United States, I do not include a thorough review of that topic. I use previous analyses of the U.S. experience as a springboard to a study of the prospects for competition in European air travel.[7] I also do not attempt to forecast the economic benefits of European airline deregulation, though they could be substantial.[8] Rather, I study the factors that are most likely to impede movement toward a competitive airline market in the EC.

The second section gives a brief overview of the European airline industry and its regulation. The third section discusses the political barriers to competition among European airlines. In the fourth section, I focus on the institutional constraints, especially the shortage of airport capacity, that could lessen the gains from European airline deregulation. I discuss the constraints on airline competition that have appeared in the United States, and the potential for such difficulties arising in Europe, in the fifth section. Some final comments and conclusions comprise the sixth section.

The State of European Airline Competition

Serious consideration of reforming the European airline system dates from the early 1980s. Historically, air travel between EC countries has been controlled in much the same way as it is worldwide—through bilateral agreements between countries.[9] These agreements have generally specified the prices and amount of service that airlines from each country could provide on each designated route between the countries. In most cases, the airlines from each country have been allowed to provide 50 percent of the capacity on the route and, in most cases, the carriers from each country have been owned and operated by the governments. In order for a new fare or new type of service to be introduced between two countries, the approval of both governments has been necessary. One result of this double-approval approach is that no proposed fare would be allowed if either country's airline would be harmed by it.

Two airlines serving the same international route have usually been al-

6. McGowan and Seabright 1989.

7. For analyses of the U.S. experience, see Bailey, Graham, and Kaplan 1985; Borenstein 1992.

8. See McGowan and Seabright 1989 for an excellent analysis of this issue.

9. Commission of the European Communities 1979.

lowed (and often encouraged) to coordinate their pricing, scheduling, and capacity—arguably to maximize the efficient use of the flights and fares permitted. Such coordination could involve dividing city-pair routes so that only one of the airlines served each route, coordinating flight times and sharing revenues (usually within some limits) on routes served by more than one airline, limiting capacity increases to those agreed upon by both airlines, or agreeing to suppress competition from charter operations.[10]

The only service that most airlines have offered outside their home country has been flights to and from their country. "Fifth freedom" rights—an airline carrying passengers between two countries, neither of which is the airline's home country—have seldom been granted, and "cabotage"—the transport of passengers within a foreign (to the airline) country—has almost never been allowed.

Within each of the EC countries, scheduled air transport is even less competitive. Intracountry scheduled jet service has been provided by only one airline in many cases, usually a government-owned carrier. On routes with more than one airline, the carriers have coordinated schedules and routes so that no direct competition takes place. Fares have either been set directly or overseen by the government.

Table 1 lists the major airlines operating scheduled service within or between EC countries. The largest carriers, measured by revenue passenger-mile (RPM), are about half the size of American or United Airlines, about the same size as USAir in 1990. As in the United States, there are three major carriers in the EC. The smaller carriers, such as Sabena, are less than half the size of America West Airlines or Southwest Airlines. As in the United States, these small airlines are about one-tenth the size of the largest carriers.

The only significant source of competition in European air travel is the charter industry. Charter companies are privately owned and operate under less regulation than the scheduled carriers. They are limited mainly to serving tourists traveling to certain vacation destinations, mostly in Spain, Greece, and some resort islands. They are not permitted to operate scheduled service, have substantial restrictions on the method of sale and availability of refunds, and are forced to fly from less convenient airports and at less convenient times. Most charter air travel is sold as part of a vacation package that includes lodging and other services. The exception is the recent growth of the "seat-only" market, which now comprises about one-fourth of charter industry sales.[11] Still, there are few restrictions on the prices charter operators can charge, and multiple charter operators compete on many of the denser vaca-

---

10. National Consumer Council 1986 and Organization for Economic Cooperation and Development 1988.
    11. Gallacher 1989.

TABLE 1. Major Scheduled Airlines in the EC

Airline	Annual Revenue	Annual Revenue Passenger-Miles
Air France Group	10,466	36,287
Lufthansa	8,963	31,751
British Airways[a]	8,813	40,232
SAS Group	5,332	10,250
Alitalia	4,592	14,142
Iberia	3,695	13,743
KLM[a]	3,609	16,775
Aer Lingus[a]	1,236	2,861
Sabena[b]	1,065	4,201
Olympic Airways	941	4,825
TAP Air Portugal[b]	861	3,873
TAT	417	NA

Source: Data from *Airline Business*, September, 1991, 44–47.

Notes: Unless otherwise noted, all data are for year ending, December, 1990. Annual revenue is stated in millions of U.S. dollars; passenger-miles are stated in millions. NA = not available.

[a] Year ending, March, 1991.

[b] Year ending, December, 1989.

tion routes. In 1985, charter operations accounted for about 25 percent of international passenger trips within the EC and about 40 percent of passenger miles.[12] The largest charter operators in Europe, such as Virgin Atlantic or Sterling Airways, are about the same size (by revenue passenger-mile) as Aer Lingus or Sabena. No reliable data are available on the prices charged by charter operators, but there seems to be broad agreement in Europe that these companies are competitive with one another and that their prices are well below those of scheduled carriers on similar routes. In the United States, charter operations have accounted for less than 2 percent of passenger trips since deregulation of the airline industry. Just prior to U.S. deregulation, however, charters flourished because the Civil Aeronautics Board loosened the "travel package" and "group only" requirements on charters two years before it permitted the scheduled airlines to substantially lower their prices.[13]

Besides the important presence of the charter industry, the scheduled European airline market also faces competition from ground transportation, particularly trains. This is a much more important factor in Europe than in the United States, both because of the shorter average travel distances in Europe and because of the much more extensive intercity passenger railroad system. The average airline trip in Europe is about 600 miles, compared to over 900

12. Organization for Economic Cooperation and Development 1988.

13. Bailey, Graham, and Kaplan 1985.

miles for domestic travel in the United States.[14] Though U.S. travelers are more apt to use their cars for intercity trips than are Europeans, the much greater use of trains in Europe outweighs this effect, making ground transportation a more common alternative in Europe. In fact, the high-speed TGV trains in France have been estimated to deliver faster door-to-door trip times than does air travel for most trips under 200 miles. On routes where these trains compete with air transportation, air travel demand has been substantially depressed since the introduction of the high-speed trains.[15]

One of the first suggestions for change in EC air transport policy came in 1979–80, when the Commission began to investigate the compatibility of bilateral agreements and airline cooperation with Articles 85, 86, and 90 of the treaty. The memorandum that was finally adopted in 1984 established the foundation for applying the treaty to air transport. However, this foundation included giving the Commission the power to grant block exemptions for specific agreements on capacity sharing, revenue pooling, and fares.[16] In 1984, the EC issued a report that proposed greatly liberalizing the bilateral agreements between EC countries.[17] It argued that capacity sharing agreements should not guarantee the carrier from either country more than 45 percent of the traffic on a route, with an eventual reduction of this proportion to 25 percent. Similarly, the report suggested that, within a certain range, carriers should be allowed to cut prices without receiving formal approval from either country. After extensive debate and opposition from the largest European airlines, the member states agreed to many of these changes in December, 1987.[18]

Most of the significant changes proposed in this report were opposed by the AEA in a 1984 policy paper.[19] The AEA's arguments are disturbingly familiar, echoing statements made by many of the U.S. carriers in opposing U.S. deregulation. The paper expresses concern about maintaining an orderly market, using the U.S. airline industry as an example of what can happen if

---

14. Organization for Economic Cooperation and Development 1988; author's calculations from U.S. Department of Transportation "Origin and Destination Survey" for the second quarter, 1990.

15. Endres 1991; Reed 1990b.

16. Proposal for a Council regulation on the application of Art. 85(3) of the treaty to certain categories of agreements and concerted practices in the air transport sector, submitted by the Commission to the Council on March 20, 1984, OJ No. C 132/3 (July 9, 1984).

17. Commission of the European Communities 1984 and 1985.

18. Council Regulation (EEC) no. 3976/87 of 14 December 1987 on the application of Art. 85(3) of the treaty to certain categories of agreements and concerted practices in the air transport sector, OJ No. L 379/9 (December 31, 1987). Council Regulation (EEC) no. 3975/87 of 14 December 1987 laying down the procedure for the application of the rules of competition to undertakings in the air transport sector, OJ No. L 374/1 (December 31, 1987).

19. Association of European Airlines 1984.

order is not maintained. It argues that fares of every carrier on a route should be tied to the costs of all carriers in the market, not just the cost of the airline applying to offer a certain fare. It cautions that zones of flexibility in fare setting should be kept narrow. The AEA's reaction is particularly interesting because most of the U.S. airlines have since rejected these views and are now opponents of re-regulating the domestic U.S. airline industry.

In late 1989 and 1990, the EC further liberalized restrictions on the airline industry.[20] Given that these changes were finally adopted just two years before the scheduled completion of Project 1992, the new policy is probably as important for what it does not do as for the changes that it adopts. The new round of deregulation continued in the directions laid out in the 1984 study and the 1987 policy statement. It eliminated all capacity share restrictions by 1993 and instituted a "double-disapproval" system whereby a newly proposed intercountry fare is rejected only if both countries disapprove it. It did not agree to a full, open skies policy, which would permit any EC airline to fly any route. In fact, by explicitly moving to eliminate capacity share restrictions, it indirectly reinforced country distinctions, which would, by definition, be eliminated with cabotage and fifth freedom rights.

Political and Governmental Constraints on EC Airline Competition

The arguments that are made by member states in attempting to retard or halt EC airline deregulation are basically the same as those made by member states attempting to protect their other industries: (1) domestic production is in the national interest, particularly for security reasons; (2) the industry or firm is a source of national pride that generates benefits beyond the simple good or service produced; and (3) the industry has admittedly become sluggish and inefficient, but, with a brief period of protection, it will become competitive once again.[21]

Two aspects of the airline industry serve to bolster the opposition to open competition. First, in most cases, domestic travel within EC countries has never been provided by foreign airlines, at any price. There is no precedent for foreign firms in these markets, and many consumers are probably not

---

20. Council Regulation (EEC) no. 2343/90 of 24 July 1990 on access for air carriers to scheduled intra-Community air service routes and on the sharing of passenger capacity between air carriers on scheduled air services between member states, OJ No. L 217/8 (August 11, 1990). Council Regulation (EEC) no. 2344/90 of 24 July 1990 amending regulation (EEC) no. 3976/87 on the application of Art. 85(3) of the treaty to certain categories of agreements and concerted practices in the air transport sector, OJ No. L 217/15 (August 11, 1990).

21. This brief period always seems to begin at the time the statement is made, regardless of how many times it has been made previously.

aware that it is a serious option. Second, many countries and consumers still view air transport as a public utility. The idea of a foreign company operating a public utility within a country may be strange or even threatening. Related to this, of course, is the fact that most EC countries have airlines that are government owned or were so until their recent privatization.

State ownership of airlines or designation of flag carriers substantially compounds the difficulties of achieving open competition. Many editorials, newspaper articles, and even academic works cite the loss of pride that would result if the flag carrier of a country were forced to reduce or cease operations. The obvious alternative in many cases—subsidies from the home country—conflicts directly with Article 92 of the treaty.

The potential for home-country bias is heightened in the case of airlines because so much of the infrastructural support for the industry is publicly provided. Nearly all airports are controlled by national or local governments. Even where airport privatization has been completed, local governments play a substantial role in determining the expansion and use of airport facilities. Airport managers can play a very significant role in determining the commercial success of an airline's operations at the airport by influencing gate availability, the terms of gate leases, the rate of facility expansion, and the convenience of connections within the airport. In the United States, many airport managers have said that they are under considerable pressure to give special consideration to the airline that is locally dominant.[22] The pressure to aid home-country airlines, particularly incumbents with substantial local employment levels, is likely to be enormous. Yet, from the U.S. experience, it has become clear that ease of entry, especially by carriers with established operations elsewhere, is critical to obtaining the benefits of a competitive airline market.

Without a cross-national open-entry policy—one that would essentially eliminate the need for the word *cabotage* in the EC vocabulary—deregulation of the airline industry in Europe is sure to be a disappointment. Though some charter companies may prove able to enter certain routes with scheduled service, most are so small and their business so specialized that they would hardly be more prepared than a new, startup airline to compete with the larger and older scheduled airlines. The most likely potential entrants on any of the major European city-pair markets are scheduled carriers that currently serve both end points of the market from their own base city.[23] These will be foreign-country carriers in nearly all cases, particularly after the recent consolidation of airlines within France and the United Kingdom. An exclusion of

---

22. See Kilman 1987. This is due, in part, to the common U.S. method of financing airport expansion by selling bonds that are either guaranteed or are purchased by the local airline.

23. See Berry 1990 for evidence on the causation of new entry.

foreign-country airlines would dramatically reduce the potential for active competition.

Institutional Constraints on Airline Competition in the EC

The principal institutional constraint on the European airline industry is congested airports and air space. High land values around major European cities, along with environmental opposition to airport expansion, have limited the growth of airports. The shortage of airport capacity was apparent even prior to the liberalization of the last few years. Current estimates that demand could grow by 100 percent this decade with deregulation would, if true, lead to overcrowding much worse than is seen in the United States.[24]

Besides presenting a congestion problem, the shortage of airport capacity can also present a further stumbling block for competition. With very limited airport facilities, incumbent airlines have a much better opportunity to block entry by purchasing or leasing most of the gates at an airport. Even if there is an unregulated market for the facilities, an efficient or competitive allocation may fail to occur because it could be in the interest of one firm to buy up (and use less efficiently or not at all) the gates that would be necessary for a new entrant to be competitive on any routes.

In the United States, ownership or lease of existing facilities has fallen into fewer hands since deregulation.[25] Similarly, the markets for airport slots established at four U.S. airports have become increasingly concentrated since they were established in 1985.[26] The risk of these constraints interfering with competition seems to be greater in Europe than in the United States for three reasons. First, the shortage of facilities is currently much worse in Europe than it was in the United States prior to deregulation. Second, as shown in the next section, service at many of the large airports in Europe is already dominated by just one or two airlines, much more so than it was in the United States before deregulation. Third, the lessons from U.S. deregulation for airline marketing strategy are easily learned: airlines have much to gain by dominating an airport and excluding entry. These factors will interact with the marketing incentives and advantages from airport dominance that are discussed in the next section.

The problem of congestion also manifests itself in air traffic control

---

24. Reed 1990a.

25. U.S. General Accounting Office 1990.

26. See Borenstein 1988. A slot is the right to have a plane take off or land at the airport during a given interval. The U.S. airports that have slot markets are Kennedy and La Guardia in New York, National in Washington, D.C., and O'Hare in Chicago. At other U.S. airports, takeoffs and landings are allocated by queuing.

(ATC) delays and disputes. These are less likely to obstruct competition, because there does not seem to be any bias toward particular carriers in the availability of ATC communication. However, ATC problems will reduce the capacity of the system, create deadweight loss from delays, and limit the number of flights that can operate. The limit on flights could combine with natural economies of scale to reduce the number of competitors. Of greater concern is the possibility that governments could use the shortage of ATC capacity as an excuse to block entry, particularly in order to protect their own airlines. Theoretically, this shortage could be handled by setting a price on ATC services that clears the market with limited supply, but that solution would transfer all rents to the providers of ATC and would probably run into substantial political opposition. Of course, the long-run solution is to modernize and coordinate air traffic control in Europe. This could entail substantial cost for the EC, but it would produce even greater benefits.[27]

Market Constraints on Competition

The United States saw an impressive rise in airline competition in the early 1980s followed by a decline on many routes in the last few years.[28] Competition has declined most on nonstop routes to and from airports that serve as a hub for one airline. At the eight most-concentrated hub airports, prices average 19 percent above the national average.[29] The reasons for this single-airline dominance are discussed by Levine (1987) among others. Borenstein (1989 and 1991), Hurdle et al. (1989), and others have demonstrated the empirical connection between airport dominance and market power. Though some of the advantages of a dominant airline certainly flow from reputation and advertising economies, it is equally certain that some of the advantage is a result of the hub system itself and the marketing devices that U.S. airlines now use to reinforce their dominance advantages.

The decline of competition at the hubs is, in part, a natural outgrowth of the economies of scale associated with hub-and-spoke systems. In order to take advantage of these scale economies, an airline must run a large number of flights in and out of its hub airport. In many cases, the scale of operations necessary for one airline to support a hubbing system is also large enough to satisfy most of the demand for "local" travel to and from the hub airport. As a result, many airports receive extensive service from the airline that uses the airport as a hub and very little service from any other airline. Often, the only service offered by another airline is flights to its own hub airport. For instance, United serves Minneapolis/St. Paul, Northwest's primary hub, but only with flights to Denver and Chicago, United's two largest hubs.

---

27. Doganis 1989; Feldman 1990a; Reed 1989.
28. Borenstein 1992.
29. U.S. Department of Transportation 1990.

In recent years, U.S. airlines have created new marketing devices that augment these advantages. Frequent flyer programs (FFPs), for example, are recognized as inducing brand loyalty and are particularly beneficial to a dominant carrier in an area. If an airline serves the most routes and has the most flights from a city, then (1) the majority of a local resident's future flights are more likely to be on that airline than on any other, and (2) that airline is likely to serve a wider variety of "payoff" destinations from the city, destinations that are particularly attractive prizes to be awarded as FFP bonuses.

The importance of the former effect results from the nonlinearity of FFP payoff functions—the prize value per cashed-in mile increases with mileage—which encourages customers to accumulate all FFP mileage on as few airlines as possible. The latter effect might be seen as an artificial network economy. By making the FFP bonus a future trip on "any route we serve in the United States," the carrier creates an option on future travel that increases in value with the variety of destinations served by the airline from the FFP member's home airport. Both of these effects are magnified when the traveler who receives the FFP bonus does not bear the full money or time costs of adjusting travel plans to take advantage of the FFP, such as when the ticket is used by an employee whose time and ticket price are paid for by his or her employer.

The commission system used to remunerate travel agents exhibits many of the same properties and problems as FFPs. Travel Agent Commission Override Programs (TACOs) are contracts between an airline and a travel agent in which the airline agrees to increase the agent's commission rate, from 10 percent usually to somewhere between 12 percent and 18 percent, if the agent reaches certain sales goals. The goal may be a certain dollar-volume of sales (for example, the commission rate is raised from 10 percent to 14 percent if the agent sells more than $80,000 of travel on the airline in a month) or a certain share of the agent's business (for example, the commission rate is raised from 10 percent to 14 percent if more than 60 percent of the agent's air travel sales are with that airline). Thus, TACOs are essentially frequent-booker programs that, like FFPs, can be used most effectively by the dominant carrier at an airport for the purpose of biasing brand choice in travel purchases. Given the complexity of airline pricing and seat availability, it is simply unrealistic to think that such incentive schemes for travel agents would have no effect on their choice of airlines. The customer would find it very difficult to monitor his or her agent so closely that breaches of the agent's responsibility to the client could be detected with any confidence.[30]

---

30. TACOs seem to be quite effective in biasing the product choice of travel agents. Consider a 1988 survey of travel agents, in which 24 percent of the 702 responding said that their choice of carrier was "usually" affected by override payments, 27 percent said "sometimes," 13 percent said "rarely," and 35 percent said "never."

The most publicized strategic tool in the airline industry is probably the computer reservation system (CRS), which has been used in the past to bias the airline choice of travel agents and, thus, of consumers. In 1984, the U.S. Civil Aeronautics Board banned the most blatant display bias—the practice of an airline that owns a CRS listing its flights before those of other airlines—but subtle biases may remain. If so, they are likely to benefit the dominant airline in an area, because (other things being equal) travel agents are more likely to use the CRS owned by the locally dominant airline. The CRSs that have taken hold in Europe are structured in very much the same way as those in the United States, but they are jointly owned by many carriers. This probably lessens the likelihood that CRS bias could be used to the significant advantage of a single airline. Recent EC action under Article 85 has clarified the possibility of anticompetitive behavior involving CRSs.[31]

A CRS can help its owner to implement TACOs linking commission overrides to the share of airline bookings that a travel agent makes on a certain airline. TACOs of this sort require data on all of the agent's bookings. Such data would not be available to the airline—unless it owns the CRS used by the agent for ticketing. Joint ownership of the CRS does not impede its use for this purpose, and the EEC legislation on CRSs has not dealt with this issue.

In the past few years, concern in the United States has increased over the potential for use of CRS booking fees to discourage new entry into a market. If, for instance, most of the travel agents in a certain city use American's SABRE system, then a high fee charged to other airlines for tickets sold through SABRE is likely to discourage airlines from entering that city. In effect, American can raise the marginal cost of all other airlines selling tickets in the city by raising the booking fees charged to them.

Hub concentration and market power could be more or less of a problem in a deregulated EC airline market than they are in the United States. Geographically, the European market is less well suited to hub-and-spoke operations than is the U.S. market. Most scheduled air travel within Europe is on routes that are less than 900 miles, short enough that changing planes would usually increase travel time by at least 50 percent.[32] In the United States, only 21 percent of domestic passengers traveling less than 900 miles change planes, in contrast to 51 percent of those traveling more than 900 miles. If connections of less than 200 miles—short hops, most of which would be

31. Commission Regulation (EEC) no. 2672/88 of 26 July 1988 on the application of Art. 85(3) of the treaty to certain categories of agreements between undertakings relating to computer reservation systems for air transport services, OJ No. L 239/13 (August 30, 1988).
32. None of the significant airline markets within the EC is as long as a flight from San Francisco to Chicago, about 1,800 miles.

provided by rail service in Europe—are excluded, the proportions drop to 11 percent for trips under 900 miles and 42 percent for trips over 900 miles.[33]

In the United States, most medium and large airports have nonstop flights to other medium and large airports that are in the same region of the country. The 31 U.S. airports with more than one million enplanements per year, which include airports as small as Memphis and Baltimore, have nonstop service to most or all of the other medium and large airports that are within 900 miles. France, which is about 80 percent as large geographically as Texas, has 5 airports that are this size. Thus, no carrier is likely to be able to protect its dominated airport by capturing most of the intra-EC change-of-plane (or "feed") traffic, because such traffic will not be a very important factor in the economics of deregulated European airlines. Of course, some natural scale economies could flow to a dominant airline at an airport, even if that dominance arises only from service to local traffic.

Although intra-EC feed traffic is unlikely to be an important force, feed traffic from international flights outside the EC could be a critical factor. Currently, most EC countries permit nonstop service to non-EC countries to be provided only by carriers from the two countries on the route. Thus, Lufthansa gets nearly all of the U.S.-Germany traffic carried by EC airlines. Feed from such non-EC traffic could be an important factor that gives the home-country airlines an advantage in competing with other EC carriers.

Although CRS ownership in Europe is still in flux, it appears quite likely that, absent government restrictions, CRSs will eventually be owned by a few of the larger airlines. If this happens, the EC is likely to be faced with the same potential competition problems that have arisen in the United States. Similarly, the marketing devices used by U.S. airlines, FFPs and TACOs, are just beginning to take hold in Europe, but there is every indication that they will eventually be used as broadly as they have come to be used in the United States.

A dominant EC airline could employ the same marketing devices used by the major U.S. airlines—FFPs, TACOs, and CRSs. These programs can be implemented just as effectively in Europe if they are not legally restricted. The airport dominance advantage that these devices provide is not dependent on a hub-and-spoke operation. Many of the European airports already have a dominant carrier that is well situated to make use of these strategies. Table 2 shows the aircraft departure shares of the dominant airlines at the largest European airports. For comparison, table 3 shows the dominant carrier departure shares at some of the most concentrated large U.S. airports in 1979 and

---

33. These figures are calculated from the U.S. Department of Transportation's "Origin and Destination Survey" for the third quarter, 1989.

TABLE 2. Dominant Carrier Departure Shares at Major European Airports (in percentages)

City	Airline	Departure Share of All Airlines	Departure Share of EC Airlines
London			
Heathrow	British Airways	43	48
Gatwick	Air Europe	24	26
Total	British Airways	36	40
Paris			
De Gaulle	Air France Group	49	55
Orly	Air France Group	71	79
Total	Air France Group	63	56
Frankfurt	Lufthansa	62	72
Munich	Lufthansa	59	65
Madrid	Iberia	60	62
Amsterdam	KLM	30	32
Copenhagen	SAS	60	63
Rome	Alitalia	50	54

Source: Author's calculations from data in *Official Airline Guide*, Worldwide Edition, January 1, 1991.

1989. The departure shares at the European airports are fairly high even when all airlines at the airport are counted. When non-EC airlines are excluded from the totals (in order to parallel the domestic competition analysis for the United States), the numbers increase further. Each of the largest European airports has a dominant EC carrier, and the airport shares of these carriers are greater than the corresponding shares of U.S. carriers at major airports in 1979, just after deregulation. Thus, even if complete cabotage and fifth freedom rights were allowed within the EC—a system that would make intra-EC air travel legally equivalent to domestic U.S. travel—a carrier is positioned at each major airport to take advantage of the new freedom through airport dominance. In reality, complete freedom to enter any EC route is thought to be more likely around the year 2000 than in 1993.[34] In the meantime, the dominant airline at each EC airport, which is in every case a domestic airline, will be able to build further barriers to new competition from other EC countries.

The presence of charter operators, and the current division of traffic between charter and scheduled service, might offer some hope for competition. Charter operators generally have much lower overhead and much lower direct cost of operating aircraft. Accordingly, they might offer competition during the transition period, when fare restrictions are loosened but full

---

34. Reed 1988.

TABLE 3. Dominant Carrier Departure Shares at Major U.S. Airports (in percentages)

City	Airline	Departure Share 1979	Departure Share 1989
Chicago (O'Hare)	United	24	32
Dallas/Ft. Worth	Braniff/American	25	51
Atlanta	Delta	42	55
Denver	Frontier/United	23	45
St. Louis	TWA	33	83
Minneapolis	Northwest	30	77
Pittsburgh	USAir	59	85
Detroit	North Central/Northwest	24	63
Salt Lake City	Western/Delta	29	80
Charlotte	Eastern/USAir	45	93

Source: Data from U.S. Department of Transportation, *Secretary's Task Force on Competition in the U.S. Domestic Airline Industry: Industry and Route Structure* (Washington, D.C.: U.S. Government Printing Office, 1990), 1:200.

cabotage and fifth freedom rights have not yet been granted. The charter operators also derive some advantage from their experience in attracting and serving discretionary customers. Unfortunately, competition of this sort prevailed only briefly in the U.S. domestic market. Similar firms that entered high-density markets in the United States following deregulation cut prices to match their lower costs, but still had difficulty attracting the lucrative business traveler. Eventually, the major trunk airlines matched the low prices with restricted discounts that appealed to nonbusiness travelers, while maintaining greater frequency and higher service quality. By 1986, nearly all of the smaller, low-frills airlines had disappeared from the domestic scene.[35]

Because TACOs and FFPs seem to be among the principal causes of airport dominance in the United States, and because they have not yet taken hold in Europe on the same scale, the EC might do better to start deregulation from a more restricted approach in these areas. For instance, under Article 86 of the Treaty of Rome, FFP-like programs could be banned from use in intra-EC markets. A complete ban would put European airlines at a disadvantage in competing with U.S. and other airlines on international routes. Similarly, fixed commission rates could be imposed for all intra-European travel or,

---

35. These included Braniff, People Express, World Airways, and Air Florida, among many others. The notable exception is Southwest Airlines, which continues to thrive in selected markets, in part, by avoiding head-to-head competition with the major airlines.

somewhat less restrictively, each carrier could be required to pay the same flat rate to all agents with which it deals, though each airline would still be free to choose the rate it would pay.

Conclusion

Airline deregulation has not been a panacea in the United States and would not be a panacea in Europe, either. If competition is hindered by political forces or anticompetitive marketing practices, deregulation in Europe could result in increased prices and little new entry. Some of this has occurred in the United States, presenting an unfortunate model for European carriers in hindering competition. Yet the net effect of U.S. deregulation has still been quite positive. The potential social gains from U.S. deregulation were so large that even losses due to market power and inefficient airport capacity allocation have not reversed the overall impact. The potential gains from deregulation in Europe are probably even larger, because of the history of inefficient public ownership and the complete absence of competition on domestic routes. It is unclear whether the potential loss of competition under deregulation, due to anticompetitive practices by the carriers or continued government protection of local airlines, could completely offset the efficiency gains from increased productivity and flexible pricing.

McGowan and Seabright (1989) document many of the existing productive inefficiencies in European airlines, though they, too, recognize that perfect competition would not result from European airline deregulation. They also argue that, although contestability of airline markets has been rejected by numerous recent studies in the United States, the concept of "cost contestability" is still quite appealing. The idea is that airlines can quickly respond to new entry with price and quantity changes, but they cannot quickly change their cost structures. Thus, even if an incumbent's speed of response in prices and quantities might deter entry of a firm with similar costs, the potential entry of a much lower cost firm could still force an inefficient airline to cut costs in advance of that entry. The evidence on the application of cost contestability to the U.S. airline industry is mixed. Airlines have definitely moved to more efficient networks and fewer unproductive work rules since deregulation, but those changes occurred mostly in the first few years following deregulation. High-cost firms have survived with comparatively low productivity and most of the low-cost entrants have exited in the last five years.[36] As hub dominance has increased, the effectiveness of low-cost entrants in competing with locally dominant airlines has fallen and, presumably, so has their influence on airline costs.

---

36. Borenstein 1992.

Even the move to a truly competitive European airline industry would have its drawbacks. Increased productivity in a competitive market could mean decreased employment. The job (and firm) instability in a newly deregulated and competitive EC airline market would likely be greater than was seen in the United States, because most EC carriers are less efficient than U.S. airlines were before deregulation. In Europe, such upheaval is often cited as the principal result of U.S. airline deregulation. The temptation for governments to intervene, particularly where their own flag carriers are involved, might then prove irresistible.

Competition would certainly decrease stability in European airline markets. The potential consumer gains, however, are very large. The prospects for the implementation and maintenance of a competitive EC airline market are uncertain at best. Though the Commission is gradually moving in this direction legally, many barriers remain, both from member states and the behavior of the airlines themselves. The EC has many lessons that it can learn from the U.S. experience, particularly in the aggressive pursuit of competition policy.

European airlines can also learn from the history of deregulation in the United States. Unfortunately, it appears that they have already taken many lessons to heart. In the last four years, EC carriers have thrown themselves headlong into the merger and consolidation fray. Where carriers have not actually absorbed one another, they have tried to create joint operating agreements that would greatly reduce the likelihood of competition between them. British Airways has purchased British Caledonian; Air France has taken over UTA and Air Inter, its primary French competitors; and Air France also attempted to form a cooperative operating agreement with Lufthansa, but it fell apart under pressure from the EC. British Airways and KLM proposed to take substantial equity interests in Sabena and operate the airline cooperatively, but that, too, was scuttled by the EC.[37]

Thus far, the EC's efforts to block some mergers and negotiate concessions before allowing others is clearly inspired, in part, by what happened in the U.S. airline industry under the somnolent antitrust policies of the Reagan administration. Simply blocking mergers, however, is unlikely, by itself, to prevent the long-run decline of competition in the European airline industry. This has become apparent in the United States since 1989, when stricter antitrust enforcement has been evident, and at least six major airlines have filed for bankruptcy. European airlines are learning many other lessons from the technology and marketing devices used by U.S. airlines. These lessons could threaten the long-term survival of small- and medium-sized carriers. The EC is only beginning to think about how to cope with these factors while

---

37. Feldman 1990a and 1990b; Pilling 1991.

the European airlines are moving to take full advantage of the U.S. innovations. The ultimate effect of liberalization may depend on which group learns its lessons most quickly and thoroughly.

REFERENCES

Association of European Airlines. 1984. *EEC Air Transport Policy: AEA Views*. Brussels: AEA.

Bailey, Elizabeth E., David R. Graham, and Daniel P. Kaplan. 1985. *Deregulating the Airlines*. Cambridge, Mass.: MIT Press.

Berry, Steven. 1990. "Estimating a Model of Entry in the Airline Industry." Yale University. Photocopy.

Borenstein, Severin. 1988. "On the Efficiency of Competitive Markets for Operating Licenses." *Quarterly Journal of Economics* 103:357–85.

Borenstein, Severin. 1989. "Hubs and High Fares: Airport Dominance and Market Power in the U.S. Airline Industry." *Rand Journal of Economics* 20:344–65.

Borenstein, Severin. 1991. "The Dominant-Firm Advantage in Multi-Product Industries: Evidence from the U.S. Airlines." *Quarterly Journal of Economics* 106:1237–66.

Borenstein, Severin. 1992. "The Evolution of U.S. Airline Competition." *Journal of Economic Perspectives* 6. (Spring 1992): 45–73.

Commission of the European Communities. 1979. *Eighth Report on Competition Policy*. Luxembourg: Office for Official Publications of the European Communities.

Commission of the European Communities. 1984. *Progress Towards the Development of a Community Air Transport Policy*. Luxembourg: Office for Official Publications of the European Communities.

Commission of the European Communities. 1985. *EEC Air Transport Policy*. Luxembourg: Office for Official Publications of the European Communities.

Doganis, Rigas. 1989. "Capacity: Supplying the Demand." *Airline Business*, June, 82–86.

Endres, Glinter. 1991. "Tunnel Vision." *Interavia Aerospace Review*, February, 53.

Feldman, Joan M. 1990a. "Endgame in Europe Before It Starts." *Air Transport World*, April, 30–33.

Feldman, Joan M. 1990b. "The European Connections." *Air Transport World*, October, 44–51.

Feldman, Joan M. 1990c. "Liberalization Perhaps, but without Harmonization?" *Air Transport World*, February, 47–48.

Gallacher, Jacqueline. 1989. "Charting the Future." *Airline Business*, August, 48–50.

Hurdle, Gloria J., Richard L. Johnson, Andrew S. Joskow, Gregory J. Werden, and Michael A. Williams. 1989. "Concentration, Potential Entry, and Performance in the Airline Industry." *Journal of Industrial Economics* 38:119–39.

Kilman, Scott. 1987. "An Unexpected Result of Airline Decontrol is Return to Monopolies." *Wall Street Journal*, July 20.

Levine, Michael E. 1987. "Airline Competition in Deregulated Markets: Theory, Firm Strategy, and Public Policy." *Yale Journal on Regulation* 4:393–494.

McGowan, Francis, and Paul Seabright. 1989. "Deregulating European Airlines." *Economic Policy* 5:284–344.

National Consumer Council. 1986. *Air Transport and the Consumer: A Need For Change?* London: Her Majesty's Stationery Office.

Organization for Economic Cooperation and Development. 1988. *Deregulation and Airline Competition.* Paris: OECD.

Pilling, Mark. 1991. "Airlines Have New Fair Play Policeman." *Interavia Aerospace Review*, March, 11–13.

Reed, Arthur. 1988. "Will European Liberalisation Be Achieved by 1992?" *Air Transport World*, December, 82–84.

Reed, Arthur. 1989. "Europe: Threatening to Burst at the Seams." *Air Transport World*, September, 47–48.

Reed, Arthur. 1990a. "Aerial Gridlock in Europe?" *Air Transport World*, June, 29–30.

Reed, Arthur. 1990b. "HST: Threat or Alternative." *Air Transport World*, July, 42–44.

U.S. Department of Transportation. 1990. *Secretary's Task Force on Competition in the U.S. Domestic Airline Industry.* Washington, D.C.: U.S. Government Printing Office.

U.S. General Accounting Office. 1990. *Airline Competition: Industry Operating and Marketing Practices Limit Market Entry.* Washington, D.C.: U.S. Government Printing Office.

Part 3
Fortress Europe?

Introduction to Part 3

William James Adams

Many Americans care more about the EC's relations with the rest of the world than they do about its internal market. Some worry specifically that perfection of the internal market, without more, will prevent goods and services produced in the United States from competing on equal footing in one of the world's largest markets. Others worry more generally that the EC's focus on internal reforms will subvert the global liberalism of GATT.

The Community's agricultural policy gives rise to both types of fear.[1] Critics complain that tariffs (in the form of variable import levies) and (intentionally unreasonable) health requirements prevent American farmers from selling foodstuffs within the EC. Worse, the Community's penchant for disposing of surplus food outside its borders limits American sales in the rest of the world as well.[2] A source of bilateral friction for decades, the Common Agricultural Policy wounded, quasi-mortally, the Uruguay round of extensions to GATT.

Even in the agricultural context, viewed from the United States, it is easy to exaggerate the scale of fortress Europe. Nevertheless, commercial relationships between the United States and the EC are not devoid of real friction. This friction is described and analyzed by John Jackson.

Americans are not alone in their fear of exclusion from Europe. In most industries, Japanese enterprises have faced greater artificial obstacles to market-supply than have their American counterparts. The automobile case is

---

1. Other concerns mentioned frequently include the treatments of banking and television programming in the legislation of Project 1992. On banking, see Gunter Dufey's chapter in this volume. On television programming, see Council Directive no. 89/552/EEC of 3 October 1989 on the coordination of certain provisions laid down by law, regulation, or administrative action in member states concerning the pursuit of television broadcasting activities, OJ No. L 298/23 (October 17, 1989).

2. Agricultural surpluses occur because the EC will buy several foodstuffs from its farmers at prices well above those that would otherwise equate supply and demand. Rather than stock all surpluses indefinitely or release them on the internal market, the EC commits some to external uses.

273

particularly instructive. Even before the creation of the EC, some member states imposed strict quotas on imports from Japan. Following creation of the EC, the number of member states with such quotas actually increased. These national quotas remained in force despite implementation of a common external tariff on automobiles. Only in 1991 did the EC attempt to substitute Community for national control of trade in automobiles.

Gary Saxonhouse provides an economic analysis of trade between Japan and the EC. Rather than assume that protectionist intent achieves protectionist results, he explores the degree to which trade between the two areas can be explained by "natural" factors.

As the iron curtain rusted away, a third face appeared on fortress Europe: a face aimed at Eastern Europe. In the view of some, the EC's reluctance not only to admit Eastern European countries to the Community but even to admit their agricultural and textile products liberally might have jeopardized efforts to solidify democracy and launch economic progress in the volatile areas of the continent. John Steinbruner and Susan Woodward devote their chapter to relations between "The West" and Eastern Europe.

Jackson, Saxonhouse, Steinbruner, and Woodward view Europe through foreign lenses. In contrast, William Wallace provides a European perspective on Europe's role in world affairs. While recognizing the parochialisms that remain, he argues that Europe is developing a position of responsibility as well as strength in the community of nations.

The chapters in this section neither dispel nor confirm totally the existence of fortress Europe. Nevertheless, they do support, however tentatively, one conclusion: To the extent that the EC does protect itself artificially from outsiders, it does so to much greater effect on others than on Americans. Claims of protectionism in Europe fail to justify demands for protectionism in the United States.

The Changing International Context

William Wallace

In many respects, Western European integration is a child of the division of Germany and the cold war. The boundaries established by the developing confrontation between the United States and the Soviet Union defined its eastern limits. The conditions attached to Marshall Plan assistance gave impetus to economic integration—though American pressure failed to persuade Britain and the Scandinavians to join in the tighter political framework for integration that American policymakers preferred. French preoccupation with containing German economic recovery lay behind the Schuman Plan, which led to the establishment of the European Coal and Steel Community. French hopes that a divided Germany would not become too dominant a partner within an integrated Western European economy gave its government the confidence to negotiate the Treaties of Rome.[1]

For thirty years after the ratification of the Treaties of Rome, Western European integration developed within the broader political, security, and economic framework of an American-led "West": facing, across the fenced and fortified boundaries of Central Europe, the Soviet-led "East." The European Community enlarged from six members to twelve without taking in any of the European neutrals except Ireland: a historical anomaly whose neutrality was defined in relation to Great Britain rather than to any wider threat. The EC and its member states moved from the "Europessimism" of the late 1970s to the regained self-confidence of the late 1980s, after the implementation of the Single European Act and the initiation of the 1992 Program, without challenging the broader international framework that had given Western Europe stability and security and enabled its governments to avoid facing up to the awkward issues of foreign policy and defense.[2]

There had, of course, been a progressive shift in the balance of transatlantic relations since the 1950s, when the United States was, without ques-

---

1. For this history, see, for example, Alfred Grosser, *The Western Alliance: European-American Relations since 1945* (London: Macmillan, 1978).

2. William Wallace, *The Transformation of Western Europe* (London: Pinter for the Royal Institute of International Affairs, 1990).

tion, the dominant military and economic partner. Initiatives for deliberate change had come only from the United States; with the determined exception of France, Western European governments preferred gradual evolution to self-conscious redefinition. In 1962, President Kennedy had attempted to redefine European-American relations into an "Atlantic partnership": an initiative based on disappointed assumptions that Britain was about to join the EC and that France would remain a full member of NATO. Nixon and Kissinger launched the "Year of Europe" in April, 1973, in response to Britain's eventual accession, only to see their grand design run into the sands of a Middle East war and oil crisis. Since then, tentative steps toward Western European cooperation in foreign policy and defense, through the mechanisms of European Political Cooperation and Western European Union, have been a source of repeated transatlantic anxiety; as have the modernization of theater nuclear weapons, the implications for America's European allies of the Strategic Defense Initiative, the coordination of European and American *Ostpolitik*, and the management of arms control negotiations. The coordination of international monetary policy and negotiations over the rules of international trade have required active management, with the growing significance of Japan as an economic actor expanding transatlantic relations into a trilateral partnership. The containment of conflict over agriculture has been a constant problem. But the priority of maintaining Western cohesion in the face of the Soviet challenge, within Europe, in the Middle East, Asia, Latin America, and Africa, has given a sense of proportion to these disagreements among allies.

The 1992 Program was launched within this relatively stable global context. It aimed, through the creation of a fully integrated "domestic" market, to improve Western Europe's competitiveness vis-à-vis the United States and Japan; it did not, however, envisage any fundamental alteration of the transatlantic or trilateral political framework. Even so, the 1992 Program *would* have altered some aspects of transatlantic and trilateral relations. During the 1960s and 1970s, standards and rules governing international trade and commerce usually originated in the United States and then were adopted by (or imposed on) America's partners extraterritorially. By the 1980s, transpacific bargaining (for example on semiconductors) began between the United States and Japan; Project 1992 alone would have made it a matter for trilateral negotiation: the political weight of an organized European market would have imposed itself on companies and governments outside that market. The parallel drive to promote European competitiveness in high technology, through the family of programs that began with ESPRIT and through government support for such consortia as Airbus, was a more deliberate challenge to American dominance and the Japanese advance. Moves toward a single European currency present a long-term challenge, not fully appreciated on either side of the Atlantic, to the reserve position of the dollar. But the expectation remained that the postwar "transatlantic bargain," the Washington belief that Western Europeans had accepted a trade-off between America's provision of security and their allies' acceptance of a U.S.-led world economy, would hold.[3]

Between 1989 and 1991, however, external events *have* fundamentally altered the political and security framework within which the EC has developed. Europe after 1992 will be a *different* Europe—geographically, politically, economically, militarily—from the Western Europe that has been America's ally over the past forty years. And the United States, as it resumes the troop withdrawals that it halted when the immediacy of the Soviet threat became evident in 1946–47, will play a more peripheral role.

Old Europe and New Europe

The division of Germany, and of Europe, that marked the transition from World War II to the cold war was, in some ways, a solution to the insecurities that had bedeviled European politics for the previous 70 years: the threat that a united Germany, with the largest homogeneous population and the strongest economy in Europe, posed to its Western and Eastern neighbors; the ethnic tensions in the Balkans that had risen as the Ottoman empire declined; the unstable nations of Eastern Europe, without settled state structures or boundaries. The end of the division marks, in its turn, not simply a new era but also the reemergence of many of the unsettled conflicts that the cold war buried. Serbs and Croats, Slovaks and Czechs, have again taken up arguments suspended since the 1940s. Ukrainians and Belorussians whose territories were part of Poland between the wars, Lithuanians whose interwar boundaries differed from those they have inherited from the Soviet Union, Moldavians clamoring to rejoin Romania, Transylvanian Hungarians asserting rights within Romania, the Macedonian republic poking out of a disintegrating Yugoslavia to embarrass Bulgarians and Greeks who fought over its ownership with Serbs some 80 years ago: all represent actual or potential crises for the "powers" of Western Europe to manage, with the 1990s gloomily resembling the 1890s in the apparent impermeability of Eastern European problems to Western European solutions.[4]

The centrality of Germany and the weakness of the Russian empire—along with the equal fragility of the now-nostalgically-remembered Austro-Hungarian empire—were the keys to the European international order a century ago. In the very different circumstances that central and eastern Europe

---

3. Wallace, *Transformation*, chaps. 5 and 6, discusses this evolution in more detail.

4. Chris Cviic, *Remaking the Balkans* (London: Pinter for the Royal Institute of International Affairs, 1991), surveys the reemergence of these old tensions.

now face after their reemergence from the socialist bloc, similar concerns nevertheless underlie day-to-day policy.

Reunited Germany is a very different Germany from the Reich of 1871 to 1918: its population is smaller in relation to those of its neighbors, and its eastern frontiers are far to the west of Breslau, Posen, Königsberg, and Tilsit. Yet its 80 million population makes it, by a wide margin, still the largest state in Europe—raising problems for France, the United Kingdom, and Italy within the European Community, as they contemplate potential adjustments to the weights attached to votes in the EC Council of Ministers and to representation within the European Parliament, in which all four had been treated equally. Since the completion of rearmament at the beginning of the 1960s, the West German army had been the largest conventional military force within the Western alliance—carefully balanced by the presence of U.S., British, French, and Benelux troops on German soil in similar numbers. Incorporation of the former East German armed services into the German army is, however, being accompanied by substantial overall reductions; Germany's neighbors were complaining in 1991 about its government's reluctance to contemplate military operations outside Western Europe rather than reviving old fears of military aggression.

It is the weight of the German economy and its impact on its neighbors on all sides that causes most difficulty in managing the shifting patterns of European cooperation. The West German economy accounted for almost a quarter of the European Community's product throughout the 1980s. West Germany was the most important trading partner of *all* other members of the European Community except Ireland and of all EFTA members except Iceland; with most it had an almost structural trade surplus.[5] Incorporation of the five new Länder into the German economy has proved a source of immediate weakness—but also (potentially) of increased future strength. Germany's geographic position, the strength of its exporting industries, the long-term perspectives of its banks, all make it likely that economic recovery in Eastern Europe will pull the economies of those countries into close dependence on German markets, German industries, and German finance.

Here again the new carries echoes of the old. J. M. Keynes said of the pre-1914 European economy that "round Germany as a central support the rest of the European economic system grouped itself, and on the prosperity and enterprise of Germany the prosperity of the rest of the Continent mainly

---

5. On the economic and social centrality of Germany in Europe well before the events of 1989–91, see the chapters by Federico Romero, Roberto Aliboni, Per Wijkman, and Elke Thiel in William Wallace, ed., *The Dynamics of European Integration* (London: Pinter for the Royal Institute of International Affairs, 1990).

depended."[6] Bargaining within the European Community (during the run up to the Maastricht European Council of December, 1991) over monetary union, and over links between monetary union and more integrated and accountable European political institutions, has clearly reflected German awareness that the strength of its currency gives it the ability to extract political concessions from its partners, and unease in other capitals over the apparent choice between (1) accepting German linkage of German approval of, and cooperation in, a single currency to acceptance by others of the need for action on the democratic deficit, foreign policy, and defense, and (2) acquiescing in German dominance of a more loosely integrated European economy. The burden on the German economy of simultaneously providing financial assistance to the Soviet Union and its successor states (so as to speed the withdrawal of Red Army troops from its territory), subsidizing the transformation of the economy of the former East Germany, providing public and private finance to its other eastern neighbors, and contributing to defraying American expenditures on the war against Iraq had, it is true, led in the course of 1991 to a widening budget deficit and to inflation greater than had been experienced for many years. But the disproportion between these German subsidies and those of its partners only underlined the preponderance of the German economy within the Western Alliance in the aftermath of the cold war—and hardened the attitudes of German negotiators in EC and G7 bargaining.

The intermingled peoples of eastern Europe failed (during the revolts of 1848, the Napoleonic era, and the international system of the eighteenth century) to develop stable or coherent nation-states. Instability—and large-scale transfers of population—followed the emergence of the Balkan states from the Ottoman empire, and the post–World War I emergence of the Baltic and east-central states from the German, Austro-Hungarian, and Russian empires. Reincorporation into first a German, and then a Russian, imperium imposed renewed stability. The question for the member states of the European Community, as independence and instability again emerge, is how far—or for how long—a reluctant Western Europe can avoid imposing its own, hopefully more benign, imperium: through conditional association with the EC, through the prospect (and perhaps the early fulfillment) of full EC membership, through substantial subsidies in return for preferred policies, if necessary, even through the threat or use of military force in the event of prolonged local conflict. That is an entirely different agenda than that opened up by the 1992 Program, with a great many items that EC member states would prefer not to have had to address.

---

6. John Maynard Keynes, *The Economic Consequences of the Peace* (London: Macmillan, 1919), 15.

Western Europe's New Agenda

The speed and radical nature of change in Western Europe's political environment have already swept away the self-denying ordinance to which the EC had agreed: that no further applications for enlargement would be considered until the completion of the 1992 Program in January, 1993. During 1989 and 1990, with only the unwelcome Turkish application and the not-fully-considered Austrian application facing the Community, this was a tenable position. The negotiations with the EFTA member states to create an 18 or 19 member European Economic Area (EEA) had been proposed by Jacques Delors in January, 1989, as a means of providing these mostly neutral Western European states with an acceptable alternative to full EC membership.[7]

By the time the EEA negotiations were completed, in October, 1991, both sides had concluded that the agreement provided *not* an alternative to membership but a preliminary to the entry negotiations toward which, one by one, the EFTA members were moving. The Swedish government announced, in the summer of 1991, its intention to apply for full EC membership. The Finnish government appeared committed to follow in the spring or summer of 1992. The Norwegian and Icelandic governments were hesitating; but the Swiss, who only two years before had virtually excluded the possibility of eventual membership, were openly discussing the issue. The economic logic for membership was no stronger in 1991 than in 1989, although the process of negotiation had clarified how strong that logic was. What had changed was the political and security context, which made neutrality between the Eastern and Western "camps" no longer a relevant consideration or a bar to EC membership.[8]

If the prospect of the majority of EFTA members joining the EC seemed a distant one in the spring of 1989, the prospect of enlargement to the East appeared remote in the extreme. Member states of the EC, like their allies within the Atlantic Alliance, were committed to the principle of German unification—but none, not even the West German government, considered it to be attainable within the foreseeable future. The pace of events in 1990 carried the West German government and its partners along, faster than any wished to go. For the other countries of central and eastern Europe, direct incorporation into the EC was not an option; but it *was* an overriding objective to "rejoin the West," as President Havel has repeatedly put it. Here again, Western European policy has adapted, on an ad hoc basis, to expectations

---

7. Liechtenstein, a microstate that decided during the negotiations that it wished to be treated as a full and sovereign member of EFTA, represents the nineteenth "member."

8. Much of the background to these developments is provided in Helen Wallace, ed., *The Wider Western Europe: Reshaping the EC/EFTA Relationship* (London: Pinter for the Royal Institute of International Affairs, 1991).

and demands from the successor governments of the former COMECON—demands that have rarely been easy to satisfy and have sometimes been quite illusory.

During 1990, the governments of Poland, Czechoslovakia, and Hungary all declared their desire for full membership in the EC. Each of these had some sense of the difficulties and of the painful process of transition. But they were determined to press the pace; like the newly democratic governments of Spain, Portugal, and Greece fifteen years before, they saw acceptance into the European Community as at once the guarantee of democratic government, the surest path to sustained economic growth, and the symbol of regained status in the family of Western democracies.[9]

The Community's response (as of November, 1991) has so far been halting. The European Commission had only six "A" grade staff dealing with the whole of CMEA Eastern Europe in early 1989; economic relations with the CMEA states were limited. By mid-1991, the staff had expanded to more than 100, managing rapidly expanding programs of technical assistance and exchange, setting up missions in each of these countries, examining and reexamining the economic prospects and plans of their governments, and negotiating the first association agreements. The major member states have similarly scrambled to develop small-scale programs, while resisting suggestions of massive financial transfers on grounds both of their own constraints on public expenditure and of uncertainty about the recipient's ability to make good use of such assistance.

Negotiation of association agreements has proved a painful process, in which the pressure of domestic sausage producers and raspberry growers threatened to overwhelm wider political concerns. The products for which the former CMEA states were most anxious to gain free access to EC markets included beef, grain, dairy products, textiles, and iron and steel—the most sensitive sectors for EC member states. Western Europe, preoccupied by its own high levels of unemployment, halting growth rates, and fiscal constraints, has found it difficult to bridge the gap between political commitment and economic concessions: the sense of global crisis and domestic strength that enabled the U.S. government to launch the Marshall Plan in 1947 was absent, the political leadership more hesitant.

The opening to the East has also transformed the character—and the complexity—of a number of other issues already on the Community agenda. The physical dismantling of the iron curtain has given a new urgency to coordination of policies on migration and refugees; Romanian refugees have

9. See J. M. C. Rollo, ed., *The New Eastern Europe: Western Responses* (London: Pinter for the Royal Institute of International Affairs, 1990); John Pinder, *The European Community and Eastern Europe* (London: Pinter for the Royal Institute of International Affairs, 1991).

flooded into West Germany, Albanians have fought to be allowed to disembark in Italy, and the prospect of further flows from Yugoslavia and (above all) the former Soviet Union looms ominously on the horizon. Structural reform of the Common Agricultural Policy has been made both more unavoidable and more difficult. Agricultural production in the former East Germany will increase sharply as Western methods and Western prices become available; privatization and more efficient management in Poland, Hungary, and Czechoslovakia should lead to a more gradual rise in output. Nineteenth-century industrialization in Germany, Austria, and even northern Italy was fed from the surplus of these rich lands to the east. The potential for renewed surpluses is there, but the markets in the West cannot absorb them without substantial adjustment.

The future size and shape of the Community budget, the scale of financial transfers from richer to poorer states within the EC and from the EC as a whole to the former socialist states were becoming, in the course of 1991, highly contentious; with Spain and Portugal fearing that their economies would lose most from the opening to Eastern Europe (due to concessions on textiles and to diversion of private investment flows and Community development funds). Distribution of the burden of financial transfers to southern and eastern Europe was an issue in the EEA negotiations, the rich democracies of northern Europe accepting that they must contribute their share. During and after 1992, the issue of burden sharing will, therefore, loom large in budgetary negotiations within the EC, and in the EC's relations with its North American and Japanese partners—with the sharp difference from previous transatlantic bargaining over burden sharing that, in the 1990s, it will be the Europeans rather than the Americans who are the *demandeurs*.

Cooperation in defense and foreign policy was first forced onto Western Europe's agenda by the United States after the outbreak of the Korean War. The collapse, in 1953, of the proposals for a European Defense Community, the subsequent achievement of German rearmament within the looser framework of Western European Union, and the intransigence with which the French government under President de Gaulle posed the alternatives of European *or* Atlantic defense put off until the 1980s serious discussion of a Western European "pillar" within the Atlantic Alliance. "Political cooperation" in international diplomacy had been part of the Gaullist project for a *Europe des patries* alongside the EC; established as an intergovernmental process in 1970, the same clash of priorities between Atlantic and Western European made for extensive meetings with little effect for 20 years thereafter. The Kissinger-Nixon "Year of Europe" initiative in 1973 was intended, among other objectives, to ensure that the United States was assured a privileged relationship with European Political Cooperation, and that decisions could not be made that might adversely affect America's regional and global interests.[10]

The shift in American attitudes to the security of Eastern Europe between 1989 and 1991 therefore left Western European governments unprepared and confused. In the spring of 1991, American diplomats were still signaling that any discussions on closer defense cooperation in Western Europe would be unwelcome to Washington if they did not clearly assign a higher priority to the Atlantic Alliance. In August, 1991, the same American diplomats were telling their Western European counterparts that the conflict within Yugoslavia was a European problem for primarily European management. Uncertainty on both sides of the Atlantic about the long-term evolution of the Soviet Union, until after the failed coup of August, 1991, had discouraged any radical reconsideration of Western Europe's autonomous needs and objectives in foreign policy or defense. Dissolution of the USSR, and increasing signs of American preoccupation with other issues and other regions, made it clear to all member governments that these must now receive a far greater degree of attention—no longer as an arena for Franco-British shadow boxing, with the Americans and the Germans alternating as referees, but as a field in which new institutions will have to be constructed and new burdens shared.

The changes in the EC's external environment will oblige its members to redefine their global role and policies, and these will be discussed subsequently. Relevant here are the cumulative implications of the wider agenda for the EC's institutional structure. The 1992 Program, as originally envisaged, required a modest extension of majority voting and a limited increase in the set of policy areas within which the Community enjoys legal competence to act. The package appears in the Single European Act of 1986. The European Community structure required after 1992 will have to be strong enough to bear a much heavier weight of decision making, over highly sensitive areas of policy, with substantial financial implications, requiring higher standards of political accountability. It will also have to adapt to the arrival of additional members—perhaps, in the case of EFTA countries, as early as 1996–97. It was already recognized among all member states in October-November, 1991, that any modest package of institutional reforms that might be agreed at the Maastricht Summit in December, 1991, was unlikely to last as long as the previous SEA package. The prospect of enlargement, the demands of Eastern Europe, and the changing relationship with the United States will all compel a continuing process of institutional reform.

---

10. See William Wallace, "European Defence Cooperation: The Reopening Debate," *Survival* 26 (November-December 1984): 251–61; Wallace, "Political Cooperation: Integration through Intergovernmentalism," in *Policy-Making in the European Community*, 2d ed., ed. Helen Wallace, William Wallace, and Carole Webb (Chichester: Wiley, 1983), 373–402.

The European Community as an Emerging Global "Power"

When Henry Kissinger, in his "Year of Europe" speech, defined "Europe" as a regional power and the United States as a global power, he was asserting America's preferred relationship as well as criticizing Europe's reluctance to follow America's lead.[11] As a civilian power, Europe necessarily played a secondary role to the United States, its security provider and alliance leader. The shifting balance of global economic weight during the 1980s and the declining sense of threat from the East had modified this relationship without fundamentally altering its character. In GATT's Uruguay Round, the American negotiators continued to assume that they should define the terms for bargaining, while the Europeans (and Japanese) should respond. The Europeans then responded in fact as would a regional grouping defending its own interests rather than as a major global player concerned for the international economy as a whole.

As it moves toward the last stages of the 1992 Program, the EC already exports to and imports from third countries more than does either the United States or Japan. The likely addition of the small but wealthy countries of EFTA will strengthen still further its economic coherence and its weight in the international economy. It will be an economic grouping with a population and a GNP substantially larger than those of the United States. Moves toward a single European currency will effectively be moves toward a multicurrency international reserve system. To the extent that the ECU becomes a global reserve currency, alongside the dollar, closer cooperation and consultation will be required between European central bankers and their counterparts in Washington and Tokyo. Trilateral management of international economic relations as it evolved in the 1970s was a modification of America's postwar leadership role, rather than a shift to a fully balanced grouping. Diminution of America's political and military leadership role after the end of the cold war, and the persistence of external U.S. deficits, will force the EC and its member states to take a more active part in defining the terms of international economic relations and force the United States to accept the EC as a powerful and no longer politically compliant partner.

Reluctantly, hesitantly, the European Community is thus having greatness thrust upon it. The U.S. proposal in 1989 that the European Commission should take the OECD lead in analyzing the economies of, and in developing plans for assistance to, the socialist states was a first clear signal of the intended transfer of responsibilities for Eastern Europe across the Atlantic.

---

11. The "Year of Europe" is discussed in William Wallace, "Issue Linkage among Atlantic Governments," *International Affairs* 52 (April 1976): 163–69.

The U.S. demands for military burden sharing outside Europe during the 1990–91 Persian Gulf crisis exposed Western European incapacity—and raised acute questions about how far U.S. and European objectives in relations with the countries of the Middle East necessarily coincide, and how an EC that no longer has to accept American cold war priorities as overriding should best pursue its distinctive interests. Political instability in the countries of the southern Mediterranean and south of the Sahara, no longer a matter for Soviet-American rivalry in the search for clients, has become a matter for primarily European concern—partly because it is already clear that conflict and misgovernment to the south leads to a rising flow of refugees northward to Europe, with all the domestic complications that brings in its train.

American and European observers of the EC during 1991 will have skeptically observed an EC unable to assume the responsibilities placed upon it by outside countries. They may not, however, have observed the change of tone in discussions within national parliaments and press columns, as national governments appreciate the willingness of the American administration and Congress to transfer responsibilities and consider the implications for national policy of the transformed international context. Weak confederations have a tendency to look inward and neglect the interests of third countries. Instability around its borders, refugees from countries to its east and south clamoring for entry, and adjustment to America's gradual redefinition of its role and responsibilities in the European region will not allow the EC and its member states the luxury of such neglect.

The infant United States developed its institutions and economy for an extended period as a regional power, benefiting from the global role and responsibilities that Britain shouldered. The infant European Community has benefited, in turn, from three-and-a-half decades of American global leadership, which has extended into an active security and political role within the European region. Cut off from its former hinterland in central and eastern Europe, contained within the broader institutional structures of NATO and the OECD, its members have been able to concentrate attention on their own internal accomplishments. The 1992 Program fitted within that focus, its implications for Europe's major trading partners scarcely examined during its formative stages.

External developments, however, carry their own logic. The end of the cold war foreshadows the end of the "Atlantic world," as North Americans and Western Europeans understood it in the rhetoric of Eisenhower and Kennedy and their successors. It foreshadows the end of "Western Europe," as it has already destroyed the geographic and mental construct of "Eastern Europe." A wider European Community, with heavy responsibilities for assistance to its eastern neighbors, with intensive relations with the United States and Japan over global economic management, and responding to conflict and instability within the European region, will become a very different Community than the economic entity that was negotiated in 1956–57 by the governments of the six original participants. In spite of all the hesitations and confusions of its member states, it is likely to prove a stronger Community, too, than that which the designers of the Single European Act and the 1992 Program would have dared to imagine only a few years before.

United States Policy toward Eastern Europe

John D. Steinbruner and Susan L. Woodward

The remarkable sequence of political revolutions that swept through Eastern Europe in 1989 has radical implications for U.S. foreign policy—much more so than was immediately realized or has yet been implemented. The events document profound changes in the conditions of security. The long-perceived threat of a large-scale ground invasion of Central Europe by Soviet-led forces has disappeared as a practical matter, and the unmanaged disintegration of the Soviet military establishment has become a more compelling source of concern. As a consequence, the traditional policies of nuclear deterrence and containment embodied in an organized alliance confrontation are no longer the appropriate means of organizing international security. Deterrence and containment will undoubtedly continue to exist as by-products of maintaining Western military establishments, but the primary means of shaping the Soviet and Eastern European military postures is dictated by circumstance to become more positive in character. Confrontation is giving way to cooperative engagement as the predominant means of security policy.

Similarly, the revolutions in Eastern Europe produced a fundamental shift in economic conditions. After decades, even centuries, of frustrating and ineffective efforts to connect their economies to the more prosperous ones in Western Europe, the Eastern European societies are now making truly desperate efforts to do so, committing themselves to major transformations of their economic structures and political systems for the primary purpose of qualifying for inclusion in the European Community (EC). The disintegrating Soviet government, once an overpowering restraint on this inclination, has now joined it in a decisive policy shift that was the single most important trigger for the events of 1989. The prevailing pattern of Western economic policies

The research assistance of Andrew Portocarrero, Adrianne Goins, and Alf Hunter is gratefully acknowledged. The events covered in this chapter occurred while the former Soviet Union and Yugoslavia were in the process of dissolution. As a result, we have referred to each in various ways at various points in the chapter. On the other hand, in the interest of economy, we systematically refer to the Czech and Slovak Federal Republic by its old name of Czechoslovakia.

designed to isolate the Soviet Union and to detach Eastern Europe from Soviet influence is no longer appropriate or viable.

These developments alter the fundamentals of foreign policy with a forcefulness that cannot be ignored or deflected. With the withdrawal of Soviet ground forces from forward positions and the validation of Western technical competence provided by the Persian Gulf War, U.S. and NATO forces do not face any realistic prospect of direct challenge on their home territory without an inherently visible process of threatening development that would have to be measured in years if not decades. The Western allies have won the long battle for strategic position but now encounter the transforming effects of that fact. They will face strong internal fiscal pressures to align the size, technical configuration, and operational practices of their military forces with the dramatically reduced threat of deliberate aggression.

In doing so, they will have to acknowledge long subordinated threats of a very different character. However it is politically managed, the Soviet military establishment will probably retain nuclear weapons deployments capable of annihilating Western societies at long range. The routine daily management of those deployments requires sophisticated technical support, robust physical security, and strict operational control to assure that there is no accidental or unauthorized detonation of even a single weapon, no breach of physical custody, and no compromise of design principles.[1] Moreover, the operational handling of these forces in circumstances of perceived crisis will remain a major concern even if underlying political intentions are not. Though the use of those forces to initiate a projection of power will not be feasible, they will be configured for retaliation and, like the American nuclear arsenal, for extremely rapid reaction to any significant attack. The fact that two large establishments are primed to react to each other so rapidly and with such enormously devastating effect creates the possibility of an unintended catastrophe of monumental proportions. The probability of an uncontrollable interaction of these forces is believed to be very low, but that assertion cannot be proved and the probability cannot be measured exactly. With the burden of deterrence obviously diminishing, the inherent safety of nuclear weapons operations is emerging as the more compelling security problem, and the basic measures for responding to that problem involve cooperative regulation of the two establishments.[2]

At the same time, it is increasingly apparent that the more probable

---

1. See Kurt M. Campbell, Ashton B. Carter, Steven E. Miller, and Charles A. Zraket, *Soviet Nuclear Fission: Control of the Nuclear Arsenal in a Disintegrating Soviet Union*, CSIA Studies in International Security, Center for Science and International Affairs, John F. Kennedy School of Government (Cambridge, Mass.: Harvard University, 1991).

2. Bruce Blair and John D. Steinbruner, *The Effects of Warning on Strategic Stability* (Washington, D.C.: Brookings Institution, 1991).

security threats do not arise directly from the Soviet or Eastern European military organizations themselves but, rather, from the potential for violent disorder within their own societies. The revolutions of 1989 decisively rejected communist governments that had been imposed by force, but they did not and could not create democratic replacements nearly as decisively. The intricate network of attitudes, laws, traditions, and institutions that keeps national consensus and partisan competition in functional balance in the Western democracies is weakly developed throughout the former Soviet bloc, where separate ethnic identities are an even more severe problem. Moreover, while learning to forge policy by workable consensus rather than by authoritarian control, the political systems in these areas are forced to contend with an endemic economic austerity that sharply constrains the time-honored formula of offering benefits to everyone. Allocating economic sacrifice by majority vote is an art that no political system can claim to have mastered.

The predictable, short-term consequences of stabilization and economic reform—high unemployment, declines in living standards, and radical shifts in the structure of economic opportunity—will make it difficult to reach orderly, coherent political decisions. Surging nationalist sentiment and traditional ethnic antagonism will compound the difficulty. Under these conditions, spontaneous civil violence is possible on a scale sufficient to pose significant threats to regional security. Preventing it seems likely to replace resistance to deliberate aggression as a primary focus of Western security policies.

If viewed from a detached, Olympian perspective, the situation generates some strong presumptions about the eventual course of policy. It is not reasonable to expect economic and political reform to succeed in Eastern Europe or the Soviet successor states without significant international engagement. Nor is it realistic to neglect that necessary engagement because of detached skepticism about the ultimate outcome. Both general international interests and U.S. interests are too strong to justify replacing traditional antagonism with a passive attitude. Under the pressure of events, assertive, positive engagement will ultimately emerge as the primary principle of policy.

To anyone immersed in immediate politics, however, these presumptions are not readily detectable; indeed they are defied by prevailing sentiment. Domestic priorities are everywhere in the ascendancy, and strong national identity appears to be prevailing over broad international perspective. In the United States, political courting of angry middle-class voters has inflamed long-smoldering resentment over burden-sharing in defense and restrictive practices in trade among traditional allies. Spirited assertions of narrowly defined national interests have become popular. Corresponding sentiments have been expressed in Europe, particularly in France. A sense of rising economic potential and historic cultural dignity has generated appeals for independent European initiatives on matters of security and international economic policy—implicitly an expression of political rivalry with the United States (see William Wallace in this volume). On both sides of the Atlantic, there are strong emotional inclinations for going it alone. The imperative for positive engagement in Eastern Europe is not prominently articulated or widely discussed. There is virtually no evidence of any strong inclination to give it a full political mandate in a dramatic shift of policy analogous to the often-cited Marshall Plan.

Indefinite self-absorption is not feasible, however, for the United States or for the EC. The transformation in Eastern Europe is too momentous an event. The security and economic imperatives emerging from it are too powerful to be deflected by popular emotions. In the inevitable collision between unavoidable, longer term interest and immediate sentiment, political attitudes will necessarily be altered. One can reasonably guess that principles of cooperative security and of assertive economic integration will probably evolve into a major reformulation of U.S. policy but that the formative episodes will be particular: negotiating force reductions; providing debt relief and capital market access; liberalizing trade; establishing physical connections; and responding to the political claims of nationalist and human rights organizations. To see the emerging pattern, it is important to examine its several major pieces. The whole will probably be conceptualized, if ever, relatively late in the process.

Cooperative Security

Dissolution of the Warsaw Treaty Organization and political disintegration of the Soviet Union have already effectively ended any serious possibility of theater-scale warfare on short notice between ground forces in Central Europe. Though the new military configuration has only been partially defined, it is apparent that the residual deployments of the largest military establishments will be separated by thousands of kilometers and many interposed states. The calculated potential of these establishments might remain substantial, but they will not be able to assault each other without elaborate, time-consuming preparations that would include politically sensational violations of sovereign territory. For NATO members and for the redoubt of the Soviet military establishment in its home republics, this new circumstance provides substantial relief from the threats they have traditionally conceived and from the military burden they adopted in response. For the states positioned in the middle, however, this protective separation is not possible. Whether the threat be that of conventional aggression or the more diffuse consequences of disintegration, they are not in a position to guarantee the physical security of their territory without some appeal to the international community.

In many informal ways, the exposed states in Central Europe have expressed a desire to formalize a Western guarantee of their security, but a practical means of doing so has yet to be defined. No variant of the problems they might encounter would be resolved by joining NATO or any other security arrangement exclusively based in Western Europe. A residual Soviet military establishment still capable of posing a direct threat to these states would be unnecessarily provoked by an extension, to its borders, of a coalition from which it was excluded. A Soviet establishment subject to serious internal disintegration could not be stabilized by confrontational methods. The overriding logic for the Central European states, therefore, is to seek an inclusive arrangement that fundamentally unites the successor states of the Soviet Union and the Western powers in a common enterprise designed to guarantee the defense of national territory but to preclude offensive operations beyond it. That is the basic purpose of cooperative security.

Policy Design

The major objective of cooperative security is to prevent aggression by denying the means for carrying it out. It differs in that regard from the traditional idea of collective security, which refers to mechanisms for organizing international resistance to aggression once it has become an imminent threat or has actually occurred. Cooperative security is in the realm of preventive medicine, while collective security corresponds to emergency treatment.

Prevention in this case is to be accomplished by regulating the size, technical configuration, and operational practices of deployed military forces. Their overall capacities should be restricted (by mutual agreement) to enhance the performance of missions clearly associated with the defense of national territory and to inhibit the projection of power beyond it. It is acknowledged that this ideal probably cannot be categorically and unambiguously achieved, but it certainly is possible, in principle, to make the major establishments correspond with this criterion more closely than they now do.

There are several basic methods of approximating cooperative security requirements, and it is presumed that an effective arrangement would utilize all of them. The first is to set ceilings on the size of forces, making the aggregate firepower available to contiguous states as nearly equal as possible. A successful offensive against an equally competent opponent has traditionally required a substantial margin of advantage in firepower at the point of attack, and eliminating that advantage has been a primary means of establishing defensive force configurations. This equalization, calculated between the historical alliances, was the principal focus of the Treaty on Conventional Armed Forces in Europe (CFE) signed in the fall of 1990.

Unfortunately, however, basic firepower equalization between individual

292   Singular Europe

TABLE 1. Eastern European and Soviet Ground Force Balances after CFE

Country	Defensive Brigades[a] Possible before CFE[b]	Defensive Brigades Possible after CFE	Defensive Ground Perimeter (kilometers)[c]	Kilometers per Brigade after CFE
Bulgaria	50	37	1,363	37
Czechoslovakia	77	32	1,750	55
Hungary	29	23	1,250	53
Poland	55	39	1,950	50
Romania	71	35	1,838	53
Soviet Union	443	323	4,263	13

Source: Paul B. Stares and John D. Steinbruner, "Cooperative Security in the New Europe," paper presented at the conference on "The New Germany and the New Europe," Rottach-Egern, Germany, 1991.

[a] A defensive brigade has 40 tanks, 43 artillery pieces, and 60 armored combat vehicles (including spares), reflective of the weapons ratios to be found in Eastern European and Soviet armies after CFE is implemented.

[b] Includes the number of defensive brigades that can be formed from pre-CFE forces plus defensive brigade equivalents composed of the residual weapons.

[c] Considers a relatively smooth-lined military perimeter for defense of national borders (within the Atlantic To The Urals [ATTU] region, and excluding coastlines), rather than the often-twisting borders themselves.

states in Europe is not a feasible criterion, given the large differences in the size of the states and in their historical patterns of military development. In particular, as long as it remains integrated, the size of the residual Soviet establishment will probably be larger than those of the states on its European borders, as reflected in tables 1 and 2.

In order to adjust to this unavoidable fact, ceilings on the size and aggregate firepower of deployed forces must be supplemented by rules regulating the density of deployments (the ratio of force size to the perimeter of national territory to be defended), the concentration of forces at any given point, the rate of movement (the number of units that are allowed to be relocated in a given period of time), and the transparency of deployment plans and exercise activities. These rules can be designed to prevent an immediately threatening offensive concentration by one state against another even in in-

TABLE 2. Comparison of Soviet Forces with Bordering Eastern European States after CFE

	Soviet Union	Czechoslovakia	Hungary	Poland	Romania
Tanks	7,800	1,435	835	1,730	1,375
Artillery	7,400	1,150	840	1,610	1,475
Armored combat vehicles	15,500	2,050	1,700	2,150	2,100

Source: Same as table 1.

stances where their overall capabilities are substantially different. Under such an arrangement, the Soviet successor states, for example, could not mobilize an offensive concentration against any of the Eastern European states without ostentatiously violating the rules. A fully developed cooperative security arrangement would provide for a countermobilization by all the other members of the cooperative agreement if one state were to violate the rules. The purpose of this would be to assemble an equal, blocking force at the point of potential attack.

By fixing the number and location of ground force units and by monitoring their movement, agreements of this sort would substantially relieve the Eastern European states of any immediate fear of invasion but would have to be supplemented by somewhat more demanding rules for regulating tactical air operations and technical investment in order to form a comprehensive security arrangement. Given the ability of tactical air units to concentrate attack at any chosen point even while operating from dispersed remote locations, and given their potential effectiveness in preemptive operations, more continuous and more penetrating international monitoring of those operations is necessary to confer the same degree of reassurance. A practical means of doing this that enjoys some historical precedent is to manage military air traffic in Central Europe through internationalized institutions. This was being done by the two alliances in their respective areas before German reunification ended the legal basis for it. Those historical arrangements could be extended and combined to form a common European organization. Since air traffic control and the coded transponders on aircraft that provide the technical basis for it are vital ingredients of any tactical air operation, internationalized management is a potentially powerful means of providing general reassurance.

Similarly, internationalized licensing of weapons sales and monitoring of trade in sensitive technology offer a potentially powerful means of providing reassurance about the process of technical investment. Weapons sales have historically been an assertively national area of policy with a strong element of economic competition mixed into security calculations. Trade in technology relevant to military applications has been regulated through an informal Western consortium, the Coordinating Committee for Multilateral Export Controls (COCOM), whose main purpose has historically been to deny or retard access of the Soviet Union and Eastern European states to this technology. In response to the collapse of the Warsaw Pact and to the general corrosion of restrictive licensing efforts by international market conditions, the members of COCOM have recently liberalized their regulations, but they are still operating to impose technical restrictions on a strategic enemy. A cooperative security arrangement would replace these policies with ones that would define internationally agreed restrictions on weapons sales related to the appropriate size of defensively configured national forces and would facilitate trade in advanced technology under rules of end-use disclosure. For states cooperating with the international licensing of weapons sales, trade in sensitive technologies would be expedited as long as their application to legitimate commercial purposes could be verifiably determined.

Finally, a fully developed cooperative security arrangement would include provisions designed to improve the safety of strategic force operations. This would include a process for organizing, on an international basis, the implementation of the unilateral reductions of nuclear weapons announced by President Bush and President Gorbachev in the fall of 1991. These announcements affected approximately one-fourth of the total U.S. arsenal (estimated at about 18,000 warheads) and one-half of the Soviet arsenal (believed to total 27,000 warheads).[3] The process of identifying, protecting, storing, and ultimately dismantling the more than 17,000 warheads affected by these initiatives inherently requires several years of effort and provides a natural opportunity for internationalizing nuclear warhead management. The internal pressures on the Soviet military establishment are sufficiently severe that an internationalization of its provisions for physical custody and operational control may be a vital matter. Similarly, the Soviet warning system, whose assets are particularly affected by the dismemberment of the Union, may need international cooperation to assure its vital function of preventing any operational misjudgment under crisis conditions.

Formalization

The fundamental intention to base national security policies on cooperative methods and a partial outline of institutional mechanisms for doing so were proclaimed in the Charter of Paris issued by the Conference on Security and Cooperation in Europe (CSCE) heads of state in November, 1990.[4] The 34 political leaders jointly determined that "the era of confrontation and division in Europe has ended." They jointly declared that "henceforth our relations will be founded on respect and cooperation." They initiated annual meetings of foreign ministers constituted as a Council for the CSCE, a committee of senior officials and a secretariat to support its deliberations, and a Conflict Prevention Center to "assist the Council in reducing the risk of conflict" largely by effecting exchanges of information.

The vagueness of these provisions, however, and the well-known reluctance of the United States to vest CSCE with functions that might diminish the

---

3. See "Background Materials in the Bush-Gorbachev Arms Reduction Announcements," Arms Control Association, Washington, D.C., 1991.

4. See Commission on Security and Cooperation in Europe, *Charter of Paris for a New Europe* (Paris: CSCE, 1990).

significance of NATO suggest that the rhetorical intention has not yet been connected to the specific actions necessary to implement it. The meaningful practice of cooperative security requires the integration of the Eastern European states and the successor states of the Soviet Union not just into consultative bodies but, ultimately, also into international military command arrangements currently embodied solely in NATO. If that is to happen, obviously the purpose of those arrangements will have to be substantially redefined. Cooperative security also requires force reductions beyond those agreed upon in the CFE treaty and a much more extensive exchange of information, a prospect that was set forth in the Charter of Paris, but has not yet been reflected in the negotiating process.

The benefits to be achieved are probably sufficient to drive the cooperative security idea beyond the stage of rhetoric and beyond what the political revolutions in Eastern Europe automatically provided. With a fully developed arrangement, the large U.S. and Soviet military establishments would not only be better protected against the corrosive effects of the weapons proliferation process and the subtle dangers of strategic interaction, but could become substantially more efficient in their sustaining investments. U.S. forces and the annual expeditions required to support them could probably be reduced by half with a better overall result.[5] These prospects and the appeals from Eastern Europe for incorporation into some security order will weigh against the inertia of Western security conditions, and some substantially new arrangement seems likely to evolve.

Assertive Economic Integration

Appeals from Eastern Europe for economic reincorporation into what was called the "normal" relations of "Europe"—the banner of the 1989 revolutions —seemed, at first glance, a much simpler demand. No new institutions or economic order needed to be created, only a Western recognition that the political changes permitted full compliance with the terms of membership set out in the Treaty of Rome and that governments intended to do what was necessary to join the EC. But the division of Europe after World War II into separate economic as well as military alliances had defined the EC as well as Eastern Europe. To tear down the walls of economic segregation required reformulation of Western institutions and of the concept of Europe itself no less than it required Eastern reforms to achieve convertible currencies and free trade. And the potential for social and political disintegration under the economic hardships of the rapid road to market economies in the East, unless

---

5. William W. Kaufmann and John D. Steinbruner, *Decisions for Defense* (Washington, D.C.: Brookings Institution, 1991), 51–66.

foreign assistance was massive, also posed a new threat to Western security from breakdowns within civil orders that it could not ignore.

Neither Western Europe nor the United States was remotely prepared for this radical shift of intention and expectations. Although taking immediate advantage of the enormous propaganda victory of the collapse of communism in Europe, its leaders were slow to respond to the qualitatively new demands it raised for European integration, economic assistance, and collective policies toward trade, financial management, and defense. Project 1992 had been formulated and its practical steps actively engaged with essentially no consideration for its implications in Eastern Europe. A loose consensus in the West that the new commitment to democracy in the East must not be allowed to fail emerged rapidly at the level of political rhetoric, but, as a matter of economic practicality, these developments were distinctly inconvenient. Behind the embrace of Europe lay both economic institutions designed for isolation and extensive economic damage from decades of segregation. Even discussion of policies that might help to reverse the large differences in economic circumstance, apart from the question of EC membership, was viewed, in Europe, as a disruption of the schedule for EC 92 and, by its poorer members in southern Europe, as a real economic threat. Nor was the state of the Western economies so robust that visionary generosity would be easy to finance.

Given that no amount of political will could overcome the absence of conceptual preparation or the inherent difficulty of the problems posed, the West, in fact, temporized on critical details of policy toward Eastern Europe. The United States appeared to define the economic task as a "European" problem, while the EC seemed to shift responsibility further onto "frontline" Germany. The general rhetoric of encouragement and stern insistence on market orthodoxy was not matched by any change in the mental premises of postwar differentiation. National competition ensued over the form and amount of aid.

The pressure of Eastern events outpaced Western policy response, and, as in the past, it was security concerns that pushed toward greater engagement. Aid that weakened but in no way removed the policies of segregation flowed faster during 1991 in response to the threat of mass migration on German and Italian borders, civil war in Yugoslavia and its disruption of European transport and energy supply lines, and counterrevolution from demoted military and security establishments, particularly in the disintegrating Soviet Union. And the fact that Europe showed no willingness to respond to Eastern requests with a wholesale shift in policy on trade, debt relief, or foreign investment, or any dramatic political mandate for the region on the lines of the Marshall Plan, responding instead in pre-1989 terms of containment and political conditionality, belied its rhetorical insistence that this was a

European problem that could be addressed without involving the United States.

As European integration approached 1992, therefore, the status of the Eastern governments within Europe and with their electorates at home remained in limbo. Domestic reforms to create market economies and consolidate democratic regimes continued to depend on policies of economic coordination among the G7 economic powers, the evolution of the Atlantic Alliance in response to Soviet disintegration, and vacillation and competition within the EC over trade and aid. Statesmen in Poland, Hungary, Czechoslovakia, and Yugoslavia spoke more openly of disappointment with a still-fortress Europe that cared little for the magnitude of the changes they had initiated, and there seemed little appreciation that governments throughout the region continued to struggle with the economic difficulties and social forces that had led to revolution in 1989.

That political blow to communist regimes emerged directly from the increasing economic costs of segregation and the growing consensus during the 1980s, not only among informal oppositions and the articulate professional urban strata but even within ruling parties, that these costs could no longer be sustained. After 1975, declining shares of world trade, a worrisome shift in the composition of exports from higher to lower value-added goods, rising balance of payments deficits, and growing foreign debt revived the fortunes of those who viewed Western trade and economic liberalization as the key to growth.[6] A serious recession in 1982–84, triggered by Western banks reacting to the risk of Polish overindebtedness and labor unrest and to worsening East-West relations, forced governments with large foreign debt (Hungary, Poland, Romania, and Yugoslavia) to repay it with whatever domestic means they had available. Where debt was less of a problem (Bulgaria, Czechoslovakia, the German Democratic Republic, and even Albania), governments nonetheless focused their economic plans on removing the "foreign trade limitation" on growth.[7]

By 1985, the Council for Mutual Economic Assistance (CMEA) agreed to negotiate with GATT and the EC on tariff reductions,[8] and when, in November, 1987, Gorbachev declared the Soviet Union part of a "common

---

6. For the data to which all governments were responding, see the annual economic surveys by the United Nations Economic Commission for Europe.

7. Judith Varga-Suba, "The 'Foreign Trade Limitation' and Cyclical Growth," *Soviet and Eastern European Foreign Trade* 24, no. 3 (1988): 6–30.

8. See Leah A. Haus, *Globalizing the GATT: The Soviet Union's Successor States, Eastern Europe, and the International Trading System* (Washington, D.C.: Brookings Institution, 1992); Susan Senior Nello, "Some Recent Developments in EC-East European Economic Relations," *Journal of World Trade* 24, no. 1 (February 1990): 5–24.

European home" and its release of Eastern Europe (and thus the end of subsidized trade), the political limits on Hungarian and Polish reform disappeared. In this setting, EC 92 appeared, as had earlier stages of European integration, as an opportunity, but this time one from which exclusion would be increasingly costly. A kind of desperation took hold of many political leaders and opposition forces. Hungary and Poland entered negotiations on the pluralization required to enter Europe, while elsewhere citizens increasingly angry at recessionary austerity, sharp drops in living standards during the 1980s, and continuing political limits spilled massively into street demonstrations and over borders.

Political forces that had successfully opposed such an opening in the past and had interests in Eastern markets and politico-military bonds had gained in strength, however, from each rejection by the West of closer contacts with GATT or the EC, from each failure by the West to remove trade obstacles, from each Western trade recession, and from each Western military buildup. For the new democracies, as for the Soviet successor states, it was the principles of the EC that would prevent the resurgence of such forces. By removing the barriers to functional economic integration, irreversible changes that favor reform and remove the security threat would be laid; supranational economic and security cooperation would obviate military solutions in guaranteeing the borders and jurisdictions of cultural identities and national states.

Between mid-1989 and January, 1992, Western countries continued to resist the reconceptualization this argument required while they responded to the specific requests from the East for debt relief, capital market access, trade liberalization, infrastructural investment, and recognition of national claims to self-determination. Despite protectionist impulses, tough border controls, and antiforeigner sentiment in Western Europe, practical forces underlying the logic of integration began to have their effect in policies of cooperation, at least within the West and toward the central Europe three.

Debt Relief and Capital Market Access

The most urgent impulse for engagement in central and eastern Europe came from the burden of foreign debt carried over from the former regimes. All programs for economic reform were constrained by the policies necessary to repay this debt, to gain access to capital markets, and to secure foreign liquidity for critical imports. The fear that continuing austerities for such repayment would fuel popular discontent and undermine any possibility for a stable political transition preoccupied elected leaders. Nonetheless, the character of Western assistance only increased existing debt and created debtors of countries with little foreign debt in 1989. Although all Western creditors shared an interest in finding a satisfactory solution that did not bankrupt Eastern hopes for a stable market transition, they focused instead on the danger to existing arrangements, such as the negative effects on global capital markets of Eastern demand and on the global recession of German monetary contraction in response to the costs of unification, or assurances that Eastern Europe and the Soviet Union could guarantee debt repayment.[9] The issue of debt relief brought out national conflicts between public donors in Europe, Japan, and the United States. Meanwhile, commercial bankers threatened to close access to capital markets entirely; in the face of political uncertainty, they increased margins when they were willing to lend at all.

The focal tension for Eastern Europe was the vicious circle between debt and its limits on successful reform. Restrictions on foreign exchange delay critical modernization of existing firms, prevent the extension of export credits to maintain threatened trade links, and, in limiting Western sales, discourage foreign investors as well as domestic entrepreneurs. The policies of demand restriction and massive export promotion and draconian programs for stabilization and currency convertibility induce severe recessions, creating a climate of economic and political uncertainty that undermines public confidence and necessary stability. Credit restrictions, such as the "real" interest rate of 47 percent in Bulgaria in 1991, fall most heavily on new firms—small, private businesses and local investors—on which the hopes for privatization, economic recovery, and rapid turnarounds in standards of living are placed, while public sector firms must adjust to new markets and the withdrawal of government assistance far more rapidly and with higher unemployment than their economic viability would otherwise require. Severe wage restraints encourage labor unrest, competitive wage spirals, and political confrontations that fragile democratic governments cannot easily ignore, while banks and local governments find it difficult to enforce financial discipline when local production and employment fall drastically. The policies to repay debt also threaten popular commitment to marketization because of the hardship imposed.

As can be seen from table 3, debt levels in the first year of reform exceed, by substantial amounts, the safe limit (a debt level of 100 percent of exports and a debt-servicing ratio of 20 percent) necessary for economic growth to proceed. But the obstacles that debt poses have their source in the politics of the previous order. The worst case is the Polish debt of $45 billion in mid-1991, a figure comparable to the most severely indebted countries of Latin America. It resulted, however, from the failure of the development

---

9. Two efforts to calculate the effect of Eastern demands on capital markets are Susan M. Collins and Dani Rodrik, *Eastern Europe and the Soviet Union in the World Economy* (Washington, D.C.: Institute for International Economics, 1991); Congressional Budget Office, *How the Economic Transformations in Europe Will Affect the U.S. Economy* (Washington, D.C.: Congressional Budget Office, 1990).

TABLE 3.   Eastern European Debt in 1989 and 1990

	Total Debt[a]		Ratio of Net Debt to Exports[b]		Ratio of Debt to GDP[b]		Debt Service Ratio[b]	
	1989	1990	1989	1990	1989	1990	1989	1990
Bulgaria	10.7	11.1	234	327	—[c]	—[c]	24.3	—[d]
Czechoslovakia	7.9	8.1	75	80	—[c]	—[c]	—[c]	—[c]
Hungary	20.6	21.3	255	267	72.9	68.5	23.9	45.4
Poland	40.8	48.5	413	340	67.1	81.9	9.4	—[c]
Romania	0.7	1.2	−18	18	0.9	0.6	—[c]	—[c]
Yugoslavia	19.7	19.3	74	66	24.7	21.6	12.2	12.7

Sources: Data from World Bank, *World Debt Tables, 1990–91,* External Debt of Developing Countries, Supplement (Washington, D.C.: World Bank, 1991); United Nations Economic Commission for Europe, *Economic Survey of Europe in 1990–91* (New York: United Nations, 1991).
[a] Stated in billions of U.S. dollars.
[b] Stated in percentages.
[c] Data unavailable.
[d] Declared moratorium on all payments of principal and interest in March, 1990.

strategy of Communist party leader Edward Gierek to revive the economy with purchases of Western technology during the lending bonanza of the 1970s, and it grew by $20 billion in accrued interest alone after 1981 when the Polish government could not service its official obligations (it maintained payments on its commercial debt of $10 billion until November 1989)—due largely to the first stages of political revolution under Solidarity, the ensuing period of martial law, and the stiffened resolve of Western banks and the IMF against new Polish borrowing.

Apart from Poland, Western banks lent heavily and at relatively low margins to the rest of Eastern Europe after 1985 on the political assumption that communist regimes were better risks because they were politically stable, possessed authoritarian capacities to repay, had demonstrated their willingness to do so by the harsh domestic adjustment in 1982–84, and were protected for strategic reasons by a Soviet "umbrella" acting as final guarantor of any potential default. That calculus relieved the banks of normal incentives to scrutinize the economic viability of their investments, with the predictable result that the money lent did not generate an ability to repay. As a result, democratizing governments are now subject to a bitter irony. Harnessed to the burdens of repaying unproductive debt, they find that bank lending and foreign investment are in retreat because the fall of authoritarian governments has eliminated the *political* grounds on which the original lending was justified. Despite markedly different levels and compositions of debt between the countries of Eastern and Central Europe, Western capital markets still tend to view the region as a unit, assigning higher risk to Eastern Europe as a whole and acting to reduce their high exposures just when new capital is increasingly important to reform.

The Bulgarian case, finally, illustrates the great burden of external shocks to the region since 1985. As late as 1989, 60 percent of its trade was with the Soviet Union (and 80 percent within CMEA), and export production was configured for that market. Its attempts to cope with the unilateral economic withdrawal of the Soviet Union after 1985 (borrowing to finance hard currency imports and extending export credits to markets in developing countries) had brought its net debt from $1.60 billion in 1985 to $10.20 billion at the end of 1989. The global shocks of 1990 and 1991 were devastating: dollarization of CMEA trade, Soviet cutbacks in oil deliveries and inability to pay for contracted machinery, the effect of the Persian Gulf War on oil prices and Middle East trade (in which Iraq was the primary partner), and widespread default on the $2.35 billion credits to developing countries, despite a large devaluation of the lev, cut trade revenues equal to 15 percent of GDP in 1990. Although growth rates in 1988–89 were high, credit markets had already put up stiff resistance to new lending in 1989, and, by March, 1990, the Foreign Trade Bank had to suspend debt payments. Less favored by direct economic aid than Poland, Hungary, and Czechoslovakia, Bulgaria also remained hostage in trade liberalization (including Most Favored Nation status with the United States and the EC) to Western relations with the Soviet Union. Nonetheless, the agreement with the International Monetary Fund on January 30, 1991, reduced its initial request of $3.00 billion to $1.50 billion, according to observers, because the government had instigated discussions with creditors about possible debt forgiveness. Commercial banks await evidence on the IMF conditionality program, while the IMF and World Bank delay action waiting for the political situation to stabilize.[10]

The two countries with low debt, Romania and Czechoslovakia, achieved that status through an assertive independence that the new governments reject. Under the communists, the Czechoslovak government had been openly critical of its Polish counterpart for borrowing heavily in the 1970s and of the Hungarian and Yugoslav governments for their cycle, after 1975, of increasing debt, IMF conditionality programs, recession, and political discontent because they insisted on their long-standing policies of rescheduling and refinancing debt so as to retain open access to capital markets. After 1982, Romania under Ceausescu repaid its foreign debt entirely (in the name of

---

10. See "The International Trade and Financial Situation of Eastern Europe," in OECD, *Financial Market Trends* (Paris: OECD, 1990), 48–49; Marvin Jackson, "The Dangers of Procrastination in the Transition from Socialism to Capitalism," *Report on Eastern Europe* 2, no. 15 (April 12, 1991): 1–12; Deutsche Bank, *Rebuilding Eastern Europe* (Frankfurt am Main: Deutsche Bank Economics Department, 1991), 56–59.

national honor) and, in the process, bled the economy dry and reduced its population to primitive and inhumane conditions. But neither the Romanian nor the Czechoslovak path was a political option for their new governments, which sought foreign capital under conditions that do not favor easy servicing.

Eastern European appeals for help during 1990 secured individual gestures of humanitarian aid and technical assistance, as well as a French proposal for a European version of the World Bank to finance Eastern reconstruction. But the overall response remained one of caution, designed more to protect against risk than to address the regional problem or the lodestone of inherited debt. Although new leaders and their foreign economic advisors called for a new Marshall Plan, on the widespread conviction that immediate relief was critical to finance the first years of trade reorientation and to sustain democratic governments, no coherent strategy for aid had been advanced by 1992. Only in the spring of 1991 was there recognition of the need to coordinate the many outbursts of scattered aid through an international facility (assigned to the EC by the G7 powers). Imaginative debt relief packages have been proposed by Eastern economists, such as debt-for-equity swaps that would encourage privatization and give reassurances to entrepreneurs and savers making economic calculations that restrictive policies will lighten after a given period of demonstrated progress (e.g., five years). Concessionary grants, preferential loans, and debt relief for the costs of environmental cleanup and reorientation of energy systems (electrical, nuclear, and oil pipeline) to Western networks would benefit the rest of Europe as well. But the West chose, instead, to rely on the International Monetary Fund, with its structural adjustment loans, programmed conditionality, and access to World Bank infrastructural loans, as the prime response to debt.

All Western efforts to go beyond instinctive disengagement have generated internal disagreements. For example, recognizing the severity of the threat to Poland of its debt and wishing to reward the government for its radical stabilization program to achieve currency convertibility, the United States initiated a strategy of debt relief in the fall of 1990. But its request that others join in its write-off of 70 percent of Polish debt was not met with equanimity in the European Community. It caused outright opposition from Japan and the London Club of commercial banks and complex self-protective bargaining from the Paris Club.[11] French efforts to regain the initiative for

---

11. Of the Polish debt at the end of 1990, $35.0 billion was official and $10.0 billion was commercial bank loans. The U.S. share was $2.9 billion (although some argue it was closer to $4.0 billion) as of September, 1990; after hard bargaining and Polish agreement to resume interest payments, the Paris Club of official creditors agreed, in March, 1991, to reduce Poland's debt by 30 percent of its net present value over the following three years, followed by a further 20 percent reduction if the government holds to its IMF reform program after that. Although Polish debt is classified as disastrous, both Hungary and Bulgaria are high-debt countries, with Yugoslavia not

Europe, under its leadership, with the European Bank for Reconstruction and Development (EBRD), instead infused Atlantic quarrels into its formation. Its initial president, Jacques Attali, urged an outlay of $2.2 trillion[12] over twenty years to bring the two halves of Europe into line economically, while the United States and Britain imposed a limit of 40 percent on loans to the public sector in accord with their policy to promote the private sector. Tensions even arose between the United States and Germany over how much each was contributing to the reconstruction of the East German states, the Persian Gulf War, and Eastern European assistance, as each faced electoral backlash over taxes and domestic programs. Hedging on full engagement, donors designed aid around tests of "political commitment" to markets and democracy, independent of the level of debt or its cause, opening space for competition and patronage between them over which Eastern countries deserved greater favor or caution.

It is unlikely that these initial overtures will relieve the problem of debt. At first, Polish debt relief only obliged the government to resume debt payments, thus increasing its budgetary expenditures and net financial outflow.[13] The terms of debt reduction still had to be negotiated after April-May, 1991, with the United States, other official creditors, and commercial banks, with bilateral agreements differing according to the interests of each creditor. The severe constraints on domestic economic policy that remained were not likely to encourage new lending or foreign investment, and voters reacted angrily to the continuing privations of the IMF program in the presidential and parliamentary elections of 1990 and 1991. Debt relief has not been extended to Bulgaria, whose capacity to service its debt had meanwhile declined still further (Bulgaria had to suspend payments in March, 1990). Liberalization has removed border controls on the export of capital, with the consequence that the outflow of capital from Hungary during 1988–90 was some $3 billion and the transfer of profits abroad in 1990 was greater than the country's gain.[14] Reliance on IMF programs ignores the effects of external developments on the debt. These include the sharp decline in the dollar exchange rate

---

far behind. The Hungarian debt is owed largely to commercial banks, which makes debt relief less feasible. See the careful discussion of data in OECD, *Financial Market Trends*, 11–55.

12. Original capitalization of the EBRD, which was inaugurated April 15, 1991, and entered capital markets in the summer of 1991, was set at $12 billion.

13. To reopen talks with commercial banks in early May, 1991, the Polish government agreed to settle its interest arrears of almost $1 billion (on its total debt of $10 billion), beginning with a $100 million payment made the end of July, and the banks proposed exchanges of loans for concessional bonds (*Financial Times*, May 13, 1991). Japanese officials blocked a new loan of $500 million, already promised, as a result of the Paris Club agreement of April 19 (Martin Wolf, "Relief at Last from a Poisonous Legacy," *Financial Times*, May 3, 1991, sec. 3).

14. Tibor Palankai, *The European Community and Central European Integration: The Hungarian Case* (New York and Prague: Institute for East-West Security Studies, 1991), 4.

in 1989–90, affecting debt denominated in dollars but obligated largely in European currencies; continuing restrictions on Eastern exports in Western markets; loss of the important East German market after German unification; and collapse of Eastern and Southern markets.

The substantial amounts of transitional aid committed to Eastern Europe have involved much duplication. A large share has gone to the salaries and travel of Western advisors. The PHARE program of food and technical aid from the EC began with Poland and Hungary;[15] almost no aid or trade flowed to Bulgaria and Romania, and most resources to Yugoslavia (which has gone the farthest toward a real market economy) were stopped in September, 1991, as a sanction against its civil war. A large share involves nonconcessional loans that, like existing debt, must be repaid (largely within six years); a majority involves export credits tied to specific purchases in the crediting country. Even though these countries moved rapidly to allow full foreign ownership, profit repatriation, liberal tax havens, and minimal regulations on wages and jobs for foreign investors, financing of balance of payments and emergency energy and food needs has not been met by private banks and investors, who have retreated in the face of debt. Yet Western governments insist that only the banks (official and commercial) and private investors can supply capital and assess needs in the East. Thus, demand in the East grows for Western financial services, and profits accruing to Western financial institutions continue to flow out from East to West, but these same Western financial institutions remain reluctant to lend venture capital until institutions and politics stabilize. Net capital transfers were, in fact, *negative* during 1990: Eastern European countries paid out more than they received.[16]

Neither the creation of stable environments for investment, for managing political conflict, and for absorbing technical assistance and foreign investment, nor the removal of trade barriers in the West can occur overnight. If the result of "aid" is not simply another round of debilitating debt and net transfers to the West, then an innovative approach, capable of bridging the economic gap while obstacles to full integration are being removed, is essential.

Such an approach must directly acknowledge the unusual character of these transformations and, therefore, the inappropriateness of traditional remedies for debt. Financial institutions must be built, convertibility achieved,

---

15. The acronym stands for Poland/Hungary: Assistance to Economic Reconstruction, a program initiated at the meeting in July, 1989, designed by the EC Commission in September, and extended in April, 1990, to all countries in Eastern Europe.

16. Total direct investment in the three Central European countries during 1990–91 was only $1.5 billion, and the total of private lenders and investors during 1991 was "likely to be a net financial drain on the region" (Richard E. Feinberg, *Financial Assistance to Central Europe: How Real Is It?* [Washington, D.C.: Overseas Development Council, 1991], 11; *Financing Eastern Europe* [Washington, D.C.: Group of Thirty, 1991]).

infrastructural modernization begun, and trade barriers substantially liberalized in the West as well as the East before market signals can operate properly in these economies. Moreover, since these revolutions in economic and political systems must occur in a tightly compressed period of time, it is essential to provide programs of real debt relief in all cases without cutting all lines of credit in capital markets. Official investment must be provided until private capital markets relax and foreign investment begins to flow. Conditionalities must be devised that give Eastern populations and private investors some confidence that their austerity will be rewarded.

An end to political discrimination between countries within the region, pitting assumedly stronger and weaker countries against each other while favoring the stronger, is also essential to regional recovery, to the regional security and cuts in military budgets that are necessary to economic reform, and to the electoral balance of Western- and reform-oriented parties where great uncertainties in property and jobs give local and regional strength to those who represent the "good old days" and reversal. The legacy of a half-century of segregation is that private capital will not rush in until Eastern governments have provided the assurances and infrastructure that such capital demands—and until Western governments remove the obstacles they erected in the past.

Liberalizing Trade

The extraordinary efforts to redirect Eastern European economies and governments so as to achieve full integration with Western Europe and to endure the harsh austerity associated with reduction of the foreign debt presume that gains from trade and linkage will result. The commitment to free trade and to policies of export orientation in Eastern Europe resulted not only in applications to join the EC, but also in the rapid collapse of Eastern bloc trade and its confirmation with the dissolution of CMEA in the spring of 1991. Categories that justified discrimination in trade and aid by Western governments are no longer applicable. But it cannot be said that Western alliances—the EC, GATT, COCOM—or governmental systems of trade preferences and protections have gone as far in giving access to Western markets. The slowness of Western governments to accept the finality of changes in the East and remove former barriers is most dramatic in trade, where Eastern requests seemed to matter only insofar as they affected conflicts between the United States and the EC over agriculture in the Uruguay Round of GATT negotiations.

Even before the political events of 1989, Eastern countries had begun to eliminate their domestic foreign trade monopolies, to liberalize trade, and to adapt mutual trade to world market prices and currencies. Expectations of the gains from Western trade ran so high by 1990 that the pace of liberalization came to alarm even some of its friends. In the year following January, 1990, programs for full convertibility of their currencies were on track: Poland and Yugoslavia declared resident convertibility in January, 1990; Hungary and Czechoslovakia joined in 1991; and Romania and Bulgaria aimed at partial convertibility by the beginning of 1992. Realistic exchange rates (in most cases fixed, with periodic devaluation) are already policy.[17] IMF programs to support these moves govern policy in all seven countries (including Albania), and membership in the Council of Europe for the three Central European states was followed by their active and eventually coordinated negotiation of associate status in the EC, signed at the end of 1991. At the same time, this wrenching process of reorientation was taking place in a global economy in serious recession and a disruption of Middle Eastern trade and, for Eastern Europe, the very costly embargo on Iraq as a result of the Persian Gulf War.

The political price of this pace was already being felt in Poland by May, 1991, when government ministers were in open dispute over inflation and the damage to domestic employment of Balcerowicz's program. Meanwhile, the Hungarian government replaced the minister of finance in December, 1990, then the Central Bank director in December, 1991, to speed up the timetable of staged, gradual convertibility by 1994 for fear the West would lose interest beforehand. The acclaimed current account surpluses of 1990 in Hungary, Poland, and Yugoslavia were bought with negative growth (a decline in industrial output in Hungary of 4 to 6 percent, in Poland of 12 to 14 percent, and in Yugoslavia of 10 percent). The collapse of CMEA trade during 1991 reversed this brief success in trade while worsening the decline in industrial production in all countries to depression levels.[18] Substantial increases in poverty amid flagrant new wealth and the onslaught of serious unemployment caused by contractions at state firms forced to adjust within less than one production period pressed heavily on governments that all faced elections during 1991.

For all the hopes of long-run gains from trade in Eastern Europe, the current pattern of production and composition of exports could scarcely be less suited to the required reorientation. Their highest value-added products

---

17. There is much debate over appropriate exchange rate regimes for the transition. See John Williamson, *The Economic Opening of Eastern Europe* (Washington, D.C.: Institute for International Economics, 1991); Peter Bofinger, "Options for the Payments and Exchange Rate System in Eastern Europe," Discussion Paper no. 545 (London: Centre for Economic Policy Research, 1991).

18. For example, industrial production in Czechoslovakia fell 16.8 percent in the first six months of 1991 (compared to the same period in 1990), and 32.2 percent between June, 1990, and June, 1991 (*Foreign Broadcast Information Service*, July 22, 1991, 9). The average decline in industrial output for the region in 1991 was 20 percent, leading to a doubling of unemployment in the first nine months of 1991 and a quadrupling for the entire year (United Nations Economic Commission for Europe, *Economic Bulletin for Europe* 43 [November 1991], 1).

have been sold largely to the Soviet market (and hence according to Soviet specifications) or (with extensive export credits) to developing countries. Yet Soviet imports from Eastern Europe fell 10 percent during 1990 and another 10 percent in the first quarter of 1991. Between former CMEA members, trade contracted by 20 percent overall in 1990; in individual countries, however, the decline was much worse: the largest decline in exports was 42 percent (Romania), while the largest decline in imports was 35 percent (Poland). Former CMEA trade fell another 30 to 40 percent in the first six months of 1991. The worst case was Bulgaria: overall exports declined 58 percent (in dollar value) and imports declined 70 percent for the first eight months of 1991. After two years of decline in regional trade, Poland's terms of trade with former CMEA partners fell another 55 percent during the first five months of 1991.[19] The producers of these products are the large state factories that are slated for privatization—factories where industrial workers can still organize strikes against declining wages and potential unemployment. Most severely hit are Bulgarian firms,[20] but even Hungarian trade (which had shifted its composition between Eastern and Western markets the furthest prior to 1991)[21] suffered a loss of more than $2 billion in the first quarter of 1991 because of the Soviet inability to pay. Although Germany extended export credits to the former Soviet Union in order to let former East German firms down more slowly, IMF limits on government expenditures in Eastern Europe prevent its constituent countries from following the same policy. The drastic decline in Soviet trade in the first quarter of 1991 even caused foreign policy tensions,[22] with Poland accusing the Soviet Union of deliberate acts of sabotage.

The Eastern European comparative advantage in exports to Western markets is currently in those goods that are most restricted. More than 50 percent of Polish exports to the EC, for example, fall in the "sensitive" areas of textiles, coal, steel, and agricultural products. Processed foods and agri-

---

19. United Nations Economic Commission for Europe, *Economic Survey of Europe in 1990–91* (New York: United Nations, 1991), 74–75; "The Bulgarian Economy in 1990 and the First Half of 1991: Depression in the Balkans," *PlanEcon Report* 7 (October 10, 1991): 34–35; "Polish Foreign Trade in 1990 and the First Half of 1991," *PlanEcon Report* 7 (August 30, 1991): 30–31.

20. An attempt to estimate the economic consequences can be found in Andres Solimano, "Inflation and Growth in the Transition from Socialism: The Case of Bulgaria," PRE Working Paper no. 659 (Washington, D.C.: World Bank, 1991).

21. The OECD share of Hungarian exports was almost 55 percent by the end of 1990.

22. In the first two months, Poland paid $250 million for Soviet oil and received $20 million for its exports to the USSR, while it had expected a turnover of $1.5 billion each way; only two years earlier, 30 percent of all exports went to the Soviet Union, and Poland's exports to the Eastern market overall had fallen from 41 percent in 1988 to 25 percent in 1990 (Martin Wolf, "A Country That Is Open to World Trade," *Financial Times*, May 3, 1991).

cultural products would be prominent exports as well from Romania, Hungary, and Bulgaria if the Common Agricultural Policy of the EC permitted, while U.S. quotas on dairy products were a contentious issue for the Czechoslovak government throughout 1990–91. One of the most serious political issues in the second half of 1991, threatening political unrest in the fall and long-term damage to agricultural production as farmers stopped planting, was the overproduction of agricultural goods and declining farm incomes due to the collapse of external markets. Moreover, the obligatory reform of foreign trade policy under IMF programs forces governments to devalue when rising import costs and declining export receipts cut reserves and increase balance of payments deficits and domestic inflation. The result is to spread the burden beyond the specific regions and firms that have been undercut and enlarge the potential backlash against the speed of liberalization when equivalent speed is not forthcoming in the West.

Similar to their approach to foreign debt, Western governments reacted to Eastern trade difficulties as a need for short-term financing, the traditional remedy for market economies. To support currency convertibility, the IMF created billion-dollar stabilization funds on which Poland and Czechoslovakia could draw, and it provided credits to ease the higher costs of imported energy in Poland, Romania, Bulgaria, and Hungary. The EBRD offered its first loan to Hungary and the USSR ($500 million each) to restore mutual trade. Two-thirds of all official bilateral lending to the region in 1990–91 involved export credits.[23] Concerned about the political as well as economic consequences of the rapid collapse of CMEA and Eastern trade, Western authorities also sought an interim replacement short of integration with the West, such as a payments union or a free trade association for intraregional trade. Such recommendations were flatly rejected in the East, however, where governments and economists see them as an attempt to reisolate their economies. They argue that there are no obvious gains from trade between countries that have the same shortages and adjustment problems.[24] Membership in Western trade associations—EFTA, the Pentagonale,[25] and, above all, the EC—is their

23. In 1990, of $65 billion official bilateral debt to the USSR and Eastern Europe, $40 billion ($20 billion each to the USSR and to Eastern Europe) was official export credit agency financing; the new loans of $6–8 billion during 1990 are not expected to be extended and will probably drop in 1991 to $4 billion (Daniel L. Bond, *Trade or Aid?: Official Export Credit Agencies and the Economic Development of Eastern Europe and the Soviet Union* [New York: Institute for East-West Security Studies, 1991], 7–8).

24. For analyses of several proposals, see Williamson, *Economic Opening*, 32–35; the debate between John Hardt and Laszlo Csaba, *Transition* 2, no. 3 (1991): 1–4; the discussion in a research workshop on an Eastern European payments union held at the Centre for Economic Policy Research, London, as reported in the Centre's *Bulletin* 40 (August 1990): 15–18.

25. Based originally on a tourist and trade grouping (Alpe-Adria) between the Yugoslav republics of Slovenia and Croatia, Italy, and Austria, this was extended to include Hungary and

only interest. The primary issue, as one Hungarian official and leading expert on foreign trade expressed the regional perspective, was whether access to Western markets occurred "quickly enough to offset the shrinking of Eastern markets."[26]

But the path of trade itself is still guided by the spirit of former restrictions. The long-standing quarrel between the United States and the EC over the latter's quantitative import restrictions and the former's restrictive export controls has not been resolved despite the rhetoric of change. The EC continued to impose quantitative restrictions on imports and to subsidize producers in agriculture, coal, steel, and textiles. Eastern Europe suffered from the EC's aggressive enforcement of antidumping rules and pursuit of "voluntary" export restraint agreements. Despite Hungarian protests, the EC refused, until mid-April, 1991, to phase out trade barriers toward Eastern Europe; since the phase out can be reviewed after five years, the EC could still reverse course. The EC will take ten years to liberalize, and has maintained the uncertainty-promoting condition of a midterm review with respect to services, labor, and capital. Against Polish complaints that it has not reciprocated the Polish pace of import liberalization, the EC urges the Poles to reimpose tariffs and be less "naive."[27] Only the threat of a Soviet military coup in August, 1991, and belabored negotiations between the Central Europe troika and the EC over association agreements generated enough force to reduce some barriers to Eastern exports in late 1991; but even they did not prevent a last-minute French veto on beef (and a quieter Portuguese obstruction on textiles) from upsetting the September trade accord. Disputes over "domestic content" regulations for Hungarian automobiles held up associate membership for all three until the end of 1991. No arrangements were being contemplated for Romania, Bulgaria, Albania, or (the rump of) Yugoslavia. The December, 1991, vote at Maastricht actually raised fears in Central Europe that all would experience a new round of exclusion.

In the United States during 1991, all economies in the region remained classified officially as "nonmarket economies" subject to all the restrictions that classification entails. Most Favored Nation (MFN) status and the General System of Preferences had not been extended to Bulgaria, Romania, or Albania, pending congressional approval of changes in U.S.-Soviet relations; and MFN status to Hungary and Czechoslovakia is temporary, requiring an annual renewal that discourages foreign investors. Competition over technol-

---

Czechoslovakia in 1989. They agreed to admit Poland in July, 1991, making it a "hexagonale." It reformed again with the independence of Slovenia and Croatia in December, 1991.

26. Laszlo Csaba, adviser to the Hungarian minister of finance, paraphrased in Nicholas Denton, "Hungary Goes West with a New Urgency," *Financial Times*, May 2, 1991.

27. Wolf, "A Country That Is Open."

ogy trade with Japan, Germany, and France and a revival of congressional suspicion of Soviet behavior delayed reform of COCOM until the end of May, 1991. A new core list still embargos half of the previous items on the grounds of military significance, and the simplified procedures on sensitive goods for Poland, Hungary, and Czechoslovakia not only means continued bureaucratic discretion on import licensing, but also excludes Southeastern Europe on the argument that it is still too closely linked to the former Soviet Union. Uncertainty about the path of Soviet reform led the executive and leglislative branches of the American government to compete with each other to appear as the most steadfast protector of the national interest. As a result, more goods were subjected to review and rejected in practice (under COCOM), and new restrictions were introduced. The applications of U.S. businesses for Export-Import Bank credits to the region (including the USSR) in the first quarter of 1991 reached $850 million, but the congressionally imposed limit of $300 million was still in place and the bank was forbidden to operate at all in Romania and Bulgaria, pending presidential authorization and the waiver of the Jackson-Vanik amendment to the 1974 trade act (aimed at Soviet emigration). Where the Export-Import Bank has been engaged in allocating congressional appropriations under SEED I (Support for Eastern European Democracies Act), it grants short-term credits only, going strictly to public sector firms that are undergoing privatization and that also receive a governmental guarantee.[28] The bank's decision in 1990 to be more aggressive in assisting U.S. firms in Pacific trade excluded consideration of such activity in Eastern Europe, despite a clear competitive edge from European export credit agencies.

Ultimately, therefore, a policy of assertive economic engagement, responsive to the circumstances in Eastern Europe, will almost certainly require much more fundamental revisions of trade practices. Disagreements between the United States and Europe over trade restrictions and the COCOM list have not been sufficient to abandon their common purpose. If Eastern Europe is to be given market access that has serious practical consequence, the citadels that have been constructed around politically sensitive products in agriculture,

---

28. Where this is most apparent, in Poland, Foreign Trade Minister Ledworowski was understandably concerned that government extension of guarantees to the private sector set a dangerous precedent, but, without Polish government guarantees, the bank refused to reopen credit lines of $200 million in short-term credits and, through the Agency for International Development, of medium-term funds that may only go to the private sector. The contrast between its approach, amounting to a transfer of the risks of U.S. businesses in the private sector to *governments* in Eastern Europe, and that of Japan (which is to subsidize its own firms to reduce their risk) is stark indeed. So is the comparison to the decision of the Deutsche Bank to add Eastern European countries to its list of 59 countries at risk, for which it sets aside funds providing against 66 percent of its loans outstanding (*Financial Times*, March 28, 1991).

textiles, and steel will have to be breached. The regulation of militarily sensitive products will have to rely on a generalization of the end-use disclosure rule that has been specially developed for Poland, Czechoslovakia, and Hungary, rather than on the categorical denial that COCOM provisions still maintain.

Establishing Physical Connections

The most visible and costly legacy of the division of Europe is the separate systems of communication and their technological obsolescence in the East: Western insistence on the private sector in its aid programs and in its blueprints for Eastern European reforms overlooks the fact that, everywhere, infrastructural investment requires public financing, and that internal savings for such investments are severely lacking because of debt-constrained government budgets, unstable export earnings, market reforms, and conditionality programs that demand the retreat of public investment and government spending. The continuing barriers to the transfer of advanced technology ignore the fundamental precondition to any market economy of supporting infrastructure. This primary domestic obstacle in Eastern Europe to the shift in economic relations means that it must create services that do not exist, modernize telecommunications, reorient transport and communications networks westward, and modernize and clean up plant and transport that dangerously pollute. Telecommunications, in particular, is a "crisis sector."[29] Economic integration and political sustainability depend on connecting members of these populations with each other and with Western Europe, on reducing the costs of doing business in an environment that currently deters foreign investors, and on laying irreversible connections with the West.

It is often said that the dismal state of Eastern infrastructure is due to the underinvestment by communist governments in services—considered "nonproductive" by Marxian economists—and that the end of communist rule thus spells the end of this problem. But the extensive road, railroad, and urban public transport networks belie this argument. The crisis in infrastructure is explained better as a policy response to international conditions, just as its reduction now depends largely on the international environment. Governing parties sought to eliminate only those networks that brought market risks and foreign dependence, which they and their supporters blamed for the great economic and political instabilities of the period between the two world wars. Thus, they settled populations in territorially defined communities, replaced

---

29. See Timothy E. Nulty and Nikola Holcer, "Telecommunications: A Crisis Sector in Eastern Europe," *Transition* 2, no. 4 (1991): 1–3.

horizontal links of communication, finance, and political organization with hierarchical or communal links, and neglected the infrastructure required by spatially extensive markets.

The consequences were exacerbated and, in some cases, even necessitated, however, by the Western trade embargo on all goods of potential military application. The export control regime restricts access, above all, to telecommunications, computers, and advanced machine tools, and its structural consequences for Eastern economies were significant, as were the wasted expenditures on domestic research and development and the occasional subterfuge in trade needed to circumvent the official limits on technology transfer. In addition, the harsh restrictions (since 1979) needed to repay debt or increase capital accumulation for growth had the consequences of ever-greater cuts in government spending that were first directed at investment in physical infrastructure, social services, and capital construction.[30] By the mid-1980s, when the significance of the telecommunications revolution to economic growth was clear, the new economic plans of Central Europe gave priority in large-scale investment to closing the technology and capacity gap with the West; but continuing COCOM restrictions prevented their realization. When, in June, 1990, COCOM finally raised the possibility of de-control, the new Eastern European governments were slashing public expenditures to release resources for private investment, privatizing the public sector and services, and earmarking most of their hard currency earnings to repay foreign debt.

Current assessments of Eastern infrastructural needs focus on telecommunications and computers because these technologies play critical roles in finance and global trade. There is every economic reason (including the deteriorating environment), and no longer a security reason not, to introduce rapidly such advanced systems as cellular technology and fiber optics. Because the skill levels of this population in mathematics, computer sciences, and software development, and its general literacy, are unusually high, the rapid introduction of computer-based technologies will play to Eastern comparative advantage and reward those companies that invest in the region. The Polish strategy, to give priority to a mobile telephone system for businesses without waiting for the more expensive and time-consuming task of laying lines to satisfy household demand, illustrates the realism of leapfrogging to the newest technologies. So does the intention of all countries to replace analogue with digital technologies immediately.

Estimates of the capital needed to bring the Eastern European countries

---

30. See Peter Mihalyi, "Cycles or Shocks: East European Investments, 1950–1985," *Economics of Planning* 22, nos.1–2 (1988): 41–56.

up to the OECD norm in telecommunications alone by the end of the century vary.[31] The OECD puts the total at approximately $39.2 billion, but the Poles estimate they alone will need $12.0 to 15.0 billion. Czechoslovak plans for a digital overlay network require $2.0 to 3.0 billion. The Hungarians estimate $2.0 billion by 1995 plus another $3.0 billion by the year 2000, while the investment costs for the next three years, just to lay the basis for a digital-fiber optical network in Hungary, are budgeted at $1.4 billion (of which $350 million will come from foreign loans).[32] The World Bank estimates that network expansion will require $22.0 to 38.0 billion and rehabilitation of existing networks another $10.0 to 12.0 billion, making a total of $32.0 to 50.0 billion, or roughly 1.3 to 2 percent of total GNP. This implies an annual growth in infrastructure of 10 to 12 percent when GNP will optimistically grow at 2 to 2.5 percent.

Although rail and air transport are less backward (with the important exception of Bulgaria, where the only way to reduce the number of train wrecks in the late 1980s was to reduce train speeds to a crawl), the skyrocketing costs of imported energy during the 1980s led to a sharp decline in investments to retire older equipment and buy newer machinery. Moreover, environmental concerns are demanding a shift to electrification and new equipment as rapidly as possible. Proposals for consolidation of airlines have come forward, but massive investments in roads and railroads are needed. Hungary has completed its superhighway to Vienna, but European credits to Yugoslavia for its main artery of roads and railroads between Central Europe and the Middle East and Greece were held up, until war intervened, by negotiations between the EC and truckers over transit agreements. Elsewhere, where plans are not already in process, the extreme scarcity of public monies has led to bitter political battles (and accompanying delays) over priorities in constructing new roads, such as the quarrel that exacerbates national tensions in Czechoslovakia. Moreover, World Bank loans to Bulgaria (and Albania) await IMF approval, and the U.S. Export-Import Bank and Overseas Private Investment Corporation are prohibited from operating in Romania, Bulgaria, and Albania until Congress normalizes trade relations. Quarrels between countries over nuclear power plants and dams (Hungary and Czechoslovakia, Romania and Bulgaria, Austria and several countries), and the loss of half of all electricity supplies with the collapse of Soviet trade (without the capacity

---

31. See *OECD Observer*, no. 167 (December 1990/January 1991): 19–22; "Telecommunications Opportunities in Eastern Europe: The New Frontier" (Proceedings of a conference held at Palac Kultury, Prague, 1–4 October 1990); Nulty and Holcer, "Telecommunications."

32. Noteworthy are estimates for the former East German states of DM 60 billion, monies that have already been committed so that construction of one of the most advanced telecommunications sectors in the world is underway.

to utilize Western sources until operating systems are transformed), also demonstrate the urgent need for a regional solution to the problem of safe and reliable sources of energy. Here, too, Western action contradicted rhetoric.

The Western contribution to the development of physical infrastructure in Eastern Europe depends critically on two issues of policy—access to technology and public financing. Without revisions of traditional COCOM restrictions on technology considered to be militarily sensitive, the Eastern European economies cannot approach international standards in critical areas, most notably in telecommunications and computers. Without public international financing, the investment requirements of infrastructure development cannot be met. No amount of macroeconomic discipline, market reform, or definition of property rights can induce private investors to assume responsibility for general infrastructure that would benefit their competitors as much as themselves. General consideration of both topics was given prominent political impetus by the G7 summit meeting in Houston in 1990, and practical progress measured against the standards of the past has, in fact, been appreciable. Measured against the inherent requirements of successful economic integration, however, the Western response falls well short of that objective. The adjustments made so far to traditional policy reflect more the bureaucrat's cautious instinct to preserve existing policies against new conditions than they do the statesman's purposive shaping of the new conditions.

Adjustments to COCOM's controls on advanced technology exports proceeded along parallel paths beginning in early 1990. A U.S. presidential directive in January, 1990, mandated a special review and significant reduction of the list of items subject to COCOM control. That was inspired by a clear appreciation that the COCOM arrangement, which rested on political consensus rather than a formal international agreement, would not survive unless the scope of attempted control was more strictly limited. In the 1980s, ideological zealots in the United States, eager to impose sanctions on the Soviet Union, had expanded the list of controlled items to the outer limit of European tolerance. The events of 1989, particularly the rush toward German unification, made substantial retrenchment a political inevitability.

As a result of the U.S. initiative, the list of controlled items was cut by approximately one-third in June, 1990, and an exercise was also begun among COCOM members to develop an entirely new core list for the remaining items. That resulted, in May, 1991, in a list that was proclaimed to provide for an additional 50 percent reduction in the number of controlled items. The new core list significantly raised the technical thresholds for control in telecommunications and computers, thus allowing a freer flow of trade, but the top end of both markets remained proscribed. In particular, both the hardware and the software for the advanced digital switching technology that constitutes the core of modern telecommunications services remained subject to the general exceptions procedure that presumes denial of licenses to controlled countries. The main purpose of the revised core list, as with its predecessors, was to preserve multilateral trade discrimination against the Soviet Union on national security grounds. Former members of the Warsaw Treaty Organization were generally subject to the revised restrictions because of their historical involvement in Soviet military programs.

In addition to these multilateral adjustments, the United States also conducted a series of informal discussions with Poland, Czechoslovakia, and Hungary to work out special procedures for exempting them from the export restrictions that were still to be nominally imposed under COCOM rules. As a result of these discussions, all three countries established internal control arrangements designed to prevent any regulated items they received from being reexported and to assure that they are devoted exclusively to legitimate civilian uses. All three adopted regulations that allowed for U.S. inspection. In exchange for these actions, the United States arranged for a "favorable consideration" rule for these three countries, assuring that their applications for import licenses to restricted items would enjoy a presumption of approval and would be processed within 28 days—much more rapidly than under normal COCOM practice. These special arrangements give Poland, Czechoslovakia, and Hungary expedited access to all telecommunications technology after September 1, 1991 (with the exception of encryption equipment). That gives them the very important benefit of being able to invest in leading-edge telecommunications technologies rather than being forced to lag behind the world market. This benefit is being denied to the rest of Eastern Europe, however, and to the former Soviet Union. That continuing policy of denial seriously compromises economic integration.

International financing for infrastructural investment is not as formally regulated under prevailing Western policy, but it is similarly restricted. The mandate of the EBRD logically includes infrastructure investment, but with U.S. and British restrictions on all public lending to 40 percent of the bank's total (a total subscription of only $12 billion as of mid-1991), and loans being offered at near-market rates, the bank is, in practice, a very limited instrument. Although World Bank programs for telecommunications have committed $900 million between 1991 and 1994, the total direct and cofinancing loans forthcoming from international institutions amounts to just 40 to 50 percent of the estimated needs for foreign capital.

Under these conditions, both private foreign investment and government efforts to emphasize local manufacturing as a way to circumvent their limited hard currency reserves will be hampered by the slow growth that is projected for another 5 to 10 years (until the contractions of 1989–91 are overcome).[33] Governments have understandably chosen to invest first in projects that will generate their own hard currency, such as roads for tourism, and will depend largely on user fees for financing. But rising prices for utilities, telephones, and transport, at a time when prices on all consumer goods are rising rapidly, plus introduction of fees for such services as roads that had previously been free to use, have already generated substantial political discontent.

In economic assessments of infrastructure, it is easy to undervalue the political benefits of laying firmly and rapidly the physical means of global communication and integration. It was in response to the consequences of opening to the world market during the 1960s—to the unemployment, inequality, ethnic tensions, and political disorder that could recur—that governments in Czechoslovakia, Romania, and Yugoslavia attempted to disable antigovernment organizing by cutting lines of physical contact between citizens, both within the country and between countries in the region. In some cases, to inhibit the spread of alternative ideas and the organization of a political opposition, this included prohibitions against the private ownership of telephones and computers (in Romania, it was even illegal to possess an unregistered typewriter). But its consequences now are a brain drain of professionals who are cut off from essential information and contacts and a political environment that supports extremism and ethnic intolerance, because ethnic enclaves and particularistic loyalties are not undercut by geographic and social mobility.

In the present conditions, the one common link between reformers of all political camps in Eastern Europe is the commitment to the idea of integration and the model of the European Community. Although its appeal differs across political camps, this common ground may be the only basis for accommodating people on both sides of the most severe and intractable conflict in this region—that between internationalists and nationalists and, secondarily, that between the urban middle class and the rural and working classes—and thus for moderating the conditions that support authoritarian rule and usurpation. If, as in the past, the West invites participation only to close its doors again or insists on access to Eastern markets without granting comparable access to Western markets, the consequences in rising balance of payments deficits, unemployment, and declining budgets for poorer regions will bring forth popular pressure for nationalist retreat and protection. A policy of "wait and see" on the part of foreign investors and Western governments gives justification to those who would reimpose barriers to communication. In contrast,

33. See World Bank, "Economic Transformation in Eastern/Central Europe: Issues, Progress and Prospects," PRE Working Paper, Socialist Economies Unit (Washington, D.C.: World Bank, 1990).

a policy of institutionalizing informational and commercial links, and of promoting social exchanges, creates a powerful guarantee against political reversal.

Responding to Political Conflicts

Our argument for Western engagement in Eastern Europe met its first test in the Yugoslav civil war that began June 27, 1991—the first full-scale military confrontation on European soil since World War II. It met its second test in the collapse of the Soviet Union in a kindred explosion of ethnic antagonisms and demands for national sovereignty by the member republics after the attempted coup of August, 1991. It may also see duty during an anticipated Balkan conflagration and division of Czechoslovakia into separate states. The revival of nationalist politics, and virulent disregard for minority rights throughout the region, raised long-dormant questions about the integrity of international borders in Europe. Appeals for international support of the right to national self-determination and the collapse of authoritative institutions capable of managing old and new tensions between ethnic communities put the two principles of Western security and noninterference in the internal affairs of states in conflict. Without an active engagement on the part of the EC and the United States to incorporate the new democracies rapidly into cooperative arrangements that promise economic integration and national security, the postcommunist regimes in Eastern Europe will be extraordinarily vulnerable to major civil violence and political disintegration. This would present the EC, its member states, and the United States with demands to which they would have to respond and that would push, however reluctantly, toward active cooperation in attempts to resolve the new security threats and, in the process, toward reformulation of Western institutions as well.

The Yugoslav civil war demonstrated the inability of existing European institutions to prevent or moderate the dangers inherent in the new situation. The idea that the institutions of the CSCE, set in place after June, 1991, could address the range of likely conflicts in the region of Eastern and Central Europe, leaving the EC and NATO largely uncontested, fell victim immediately to the inadequacy of its size, to its consensual decision rules, and to the unwillingness of the United States and the USSR under Gorbachev to become actively involved. Although conflicts between EC states over the lack of a unified response to the Iraqi conflict of 1990–91 were said to force a recognition of the need for a common EC defense policy, it was the EC decision, with U.S. and Soviet acquiescence, to take the lead in attempting to negotiate the Yugoslav conflict that actually brought this home. Disagreements among Germany, Britain, France, and Spain, in particular, over the use of armed intervention, the proper response to demands for recognition of national sovereignty by Slovenia and Croatia, the use of economic sanctions, and the enforcement of an arms embargo revealed major conflicts of interest on questions of nationalism and defense. The failure of Lord Carrington's mission, the Hague Conference, and EC monitors to effect a cease fire and political negotiations, the persistent calls for U.S. or NATO involvement, and the resort to the peacekeeping and embargo mechanisms of the United Nations (at the urging of Britain and France, among others) demonstrated the consequences of delay (when the political situation was known to be deteriorating) and of giving low priority to developing the necessary mechanisms before they were needed. In reversing six months of opposition to the German proposal to gain leverage over the conflict by recognizing Croat and Slovene independence, the European Council appeared, at the very moment of its long-awaited meeting on economic and political union at Maastricht (on December 9–10, 1991), to concede primary influence in the region to Germany.

By avoiding the opportunity to build up CSCE institutions in response to the Yugoslav conflict, moreover, the West did nothing to prepare for its repetition elsewhere. It did nothing, that is, to help defuse potential conflicts between Czechs and Slovaks; Hungarians and Romanians (over Transylvania); Albania and Serbia (over Kosovo); Bulgaria, Greece, and Serbia (over Macedonia); and between and within republics of the former Soviet Union (over borders, security, territorial claims, and ethnic positions). When NATO temporized so long over the intense appeals of Central Europeans for greater guarantees of their security, they, too, began to abandon hope of CSCE assistance and to discuss regional security cooperation at the Višegrad Summit of February, 1991. International conventions and Western traditions did not offer much clarity on the region's conflicts between the principles of national self-determination, minority rights, and stable borders, whereas European- and international-level institutions seemed disinterested in both the massive arming of civilians in anticipatory self-defense and the lightning breakdown in the authority of Eastern military establishments.

There was also no major response to the threat of migration. In the first quarter of 1990 alone, 100,000 Romanians applied for emigrant visas (90,000 of which were approved). Between October, 1990, and April, 1991, 24,000 Albanians cascaded onto the eastern shores of Italy. Refugees from the Yugoslav civil war in neighboring countries, especially Hungary and Austria, numbered a half-million by the end of 1991. Illegal crossings on the Polish-German border by many claiming political asylum against ethnic discrimination in Eastern Europe (especially Romania) and the fear of a flood of migration from the former Soviet Union gave rise to bands of neo-Nazi skinheads attacking foreigners in Germany and to the victory of antiforeigner political parties in elections from Germany to France and Belgium during the fall of 1991. Although it also led to greater cooperation between the German and

Polish governments—cooperation that many heralded as the final end to World War II—German policy in the Yugoslav conflict appeared to do just the opposite.

The danger of nationalism and political instability arose directly from the new conditions. The economic consequences of the rapid programs for stabilization and privatization urged by Western advisors and creditors—unemployment, conspicuous wealth, desperate poverty, and the sale of housing, land, and factories to the highest bidder—encouraged ethnic suspicions and loyalties. Absent economic growth and stability, politicians substitute symbolic politics for democratic procedures and peaceful mediation, and they exploit old antagonisms and scapegoats to win votes. Because national identities frequently corresponded to regional economies, conflicts over economic policy, the pace of reform, and the unequal burden of industrial restructuring, unemployment, and tight monetary policy become national conflicts and demands for national autonomy. Where foreign economic support is tentative, politicians bolster their domestic political resources by diverting attention from economic sacrifices to national pride and by playing the role of protector to conationals in neighboring states.

Moreover, the speed of political change and the revolutionary extremism in rejecting anything associated with the former regimes opened the field to precommunist institutions that were not known for their tolerance—prewar political parties, the Catholic church, and nationalist movements. There was also a tendency for Westerners to confuse anticommunism with democracy and, thus, to ignore the neglect of minority rights, control of the media, and new forms of repression when they occurred under elected regimes. Domestic political pressures in Europe and the United States, exercised by émigré communities that acted as conduits for aid, arms, and diplomatic ties to the new governments in Eastern and Central Europe, reinforced this blindness. Nor does the return of xenophobic politics in Western Europe and the United States suggest that Western governments and advisers know how to ensure the tolerance, spirit of compromise, and institutional restraints necessary to democratic governance in situations of economic decline.

Western priority on strong central institutions that could guarantee foreign debt also was in conflict with the current of national autonomies and the need to create authority, not impose it. Its attempt to limit aid by differentiating between those (i.e., Poland, Hungary, and Czechoslovakia) deemed ready for more rapid incorporation and economic assistance and those where "political will" and "commitment to democratic change" appeared less steady, even though the marginal value of assistance to the poorer economies would clearly be greater, left Bulgaria, Romania, Yugoslavia, and Albania at a distinct disadvantage. But it also raised the price that Western governments would eventually pay to defend their own borders against internal wars that disrupt traffic in energy and goods, border conflicts, and migration. And the West's fluctuating commitment to trade access and Western membership, alongside the insistence on opening the Eastern economies to all forms of foreign investment and purchase, put Eastern leaders in the contradictory position of seeking to meet all conditions laid down by foreign capital while having to assert loudly their national independence for domestic consumption.

A policy of cooperative security applies not only to military security but also to the reduction of domestic conflicts that threaten civil order: by depriving those intent on civil war and nationalist conflict of the weapons of such antagonism, from strained government budgets to popular fears, and by putting in place a supportive environment for cooperation and democratic choice. The faster the pace of economic inclusion, and the shorter the period of severe austerity, the narrower will be the space for ethnic conflicts and reactionary politicians to gain hold of public opinion, for civil violence to escalate, for expenditures on armaments and internal security forces to rise, and for authoritarian rule to return. In place of withholding economic assistance, a punishment that worsens the very economic insecurities that give nationalist politicians their fuel, positive incentives from the outside to guarantee human rights and democratic procedures will be increasingly important as the political polarization of 1991 intensifies under the economic distress of global integration. The general belief that such guarantees and defused conflict will come best through membership in the European Community, substantial foreign investment, official aid quickly to convert military industries and build new infrastructures of connection, and an end to all political discrimination in trade and finance will continue to put pressure on the United States and EC alike for a more assertive response.

The European Community and World Trade: The Commercial Policy Dimension

John H. Jackson

The EC as Growing Federal State(?)

It is hard to visit Europe at this time without receiving the impression of enormous change, movement, and vitality. What appears to be occurring on that continent is no less than a multiforum, multidecade constitutional convention.[1] The metamorphosis of the European Community (EC) obviously has important implications for its external commercial policy, and, just as obviously, for the world's commercial trading system. It is not the purpose of this chapter to detail the intricate, interesting, and still evolving legal and constitutional institutions that channel and influence the EC's external commercial policy,[2] but a basic familiarity with those institutions is important in understanding their impact on the rest of the world.

In theory and current structure, the EC is an economic union: although sometimes described as a customs union, it is clearly broader than that. Yet from the outset it was clear that the founding fathers of the EC had in mind a much more profound goal. They saw economic union as one way to break the devastating pattern of war on the European continent, by establishing institutions that tied together different nations and cultures so as to provide incen-

---

1. See, e.g., European Parliament, Written Question no. 3046/90 by Elio Di Rupo to the Council: Role of the WEU within the European Political Union, January 28, 1991, OJ No. C 98/46 (April 15, 1991); "European Community: From the Atlantic to Where?" *Economist*, August 31, 1991, 44; European Parliament, Resolution on the Procedure for Consulting European Citizens on European Political Union, June 16, 1988, OJ No. C 187/231 (July 18, 1991); Emanuele Gazzo, "How to Meet the Challenge of Enlargement" (editorial), *Agence Europe*, no. 5568 (September 16–17, 1991), 1.

2. Eric Stein, "External Relations of the European Community: Structure and Process," in Collected Courses of the Academy of European Law, 13–83 (Florence: European University Institute, Fall 1991); Jürgen Schwarze, ed., *The External Relations of the European Community in Particular EC-US Relations* (Baden-Baden: Nomos, 1988); Henry G. Schermers, *Judicial Protection in the European Communities*, 4th ed. (Deventer: Kluwer, 1987).

tives to avoid war, and, indeed, to make war all but impossible. This clearly implied, at some stage, a political union as well as an economic union. What this further implies, however, is not so clear. There is much concern about the need to protect human rights, and some thought that the European Convention on Human Rights (with a broader European membership)[3] may suffice to provide this protection, even within EC matters, especially if the European Court of Justice (ECJ) is prepared to rely on or incorporate principles from that convention into the jurisprudence of the EC.[4] In addition, there is much discussion of the appropriate role of a European Parliament, a role that is currently evolving amid much discussion of the democratic deficit of EC institutions.[5]

The basic structures are reasonably well known and are described by other chapters in this volume.[6] What is remarkable is the development of several important principles of internal relationships that are analogous to constitutional principles in the United States. Three such principles can be mentioned: a legalistic sense of a written constitution, separation of powers, and judicial review. That these principles have developed in the EC is all the more remarkable because a number of the major member states do not embrace these principles in their own constitutions. Perhaps (as I have previously written),[7] a continental institutional structure must differ substantially from those of smaller, more homogeneous nation-states, especially those governed

---

3. The Council of Europe, created by statute in 1949, presently has 23 member states. See, Emanuel Decaux, "Conseil de l'Europe: Structures Politiques et Administratives," *Juris-Classeur Europe*, fascicule 6100 (Paris: Editions Techniques, 1989), at no. 33.

4. In Internationale Handelsgesellschaft v. Einfuhr und Vorratsstelle für Getreide und Futtermittel, Case 11/70, 1970 ECR 1125, the European Court of Justice held that "the protection of such rights, whilst inspired by the constitutional traditions common to Member States, must be ensured within the framework . . . and objectives of the Community." See P. S. R. F. Mathijsen, *A Guide to European Community Law*, 5th ed. (London: Sweet and Maxwell, 1990), 316–17. See also Liselotte Hauer v. Land Rheinland-Pfalz, Case 44/79, 1979 ECR 3727, and Hoechst v. Commission, Joined Cases 46/87 and 227/88, 1989 ECR 2859. Express reference to the European Convention for the Protection of Human Rights and Fundamental Freedoms is made in Rutili v. Minister for the Interior, Case 36/75, 1975 ECR 1219.

5. "European Parliament: Heal Thyself," *Economist*, April 13, 1991, 28–32; Andrew Hill, "Delors Warns on EC Union Proposals," *Financial Times*, April 18, 1991; "The Parliament Adopts a Resolution on the Need for Community Industrial Policy," *Agence Europe*, no. 5534 (July 13, 1990), 13–14; Jean-Victor Louis, "The European Economic Community and the Implementation of the GATT Tokyo Round Results," in *Implementing the Tokyo Round: National Constitutions and International Economic Rules*, ed. John H. Jackson, Jean-Victor Louis, and Mitsuo Matsushita (Ann Arbor, Mich.: University of Michigan Press, 1984), 31–34, 42–46 (hereafter cited as "European Community and Tokyo Round"); Emanuele Gazzo, "IGC on Political Union: Will the Real Questions Be Finally Raised?" (editorial), *Agence Europe*, no. 5537 (July 18, 1991), 1.

6. Joseph Weiler in this volume; Mathijsen, *Guide to European Community Law*, 15–110.

7. John H. Jackson, "United States-EEC Trade Relations: Constitutional Problems of Economic Interdependence," *Common Market Law Review* 16 (1979): 453.

from a single city—a city housing not only the major governmental institutions, but also most of the major economic and intellectual institutions.

The member states remain the sovereign entities, and some of them jealously guard their power and sovereignty, struggling against the creeping enlargement of EC powers resulting from the practice of the EC institutions, tacit acquiescence, and Court decisions. The phenomenon is not unlike what happened during certain periods of U.S. history.[8] In fact, there seem to be rather constant internal struggles for power, especially between the Commission and the Council, and between the Commission and the member states.[9] To an American, these struggles look familiarly analogous to struggles in the United States between the executive and legislative branches, and (at least earlier) between the federal government and the state governments. In both constitutional environments, external commercial policy has been one of the areas affected by these struggles, as I shall show in later sections of this chapter. It is often denied by member states that the EC has sovereignty, and clearly denied that the EC is a sovereign entity or nation-state. Of course, a key question for the future is to what extent the EC might become such.

Also analogous to the United States (from an American perspective) is the ECJ's judicial review. Developed through the evolution of its jurisprudence, the ECJ has effectively achieved the power to overrule legislation (regulations, directives, and decisions of the Commission and Council) on the grounds that it is not consistent with the "constitution" (the constituent treaties). Again, this is a judicial review power that does not exist in some of the member states, and it is remarkable that it has developed in the EC.

At least partly because of this judicial review, it is apparent to close observers of EC institutions and processes that a great amount of attention is paid to legal rules in this system. Perhaps this is not (yet?) so great as in the United States, but much effort is paid to establishing rule consistency and to predicting the reaction of the ECJ to various proposals.

The EC "Constitution" and EC External Commercial Policy

In the previous section, I noted the EC's constitutional institutions. Now I shall turn more specifically to the way these institutions shape external com-

---

8. See, e.g., Gerald Gunther, *Constitutional Law*, 11th ed. (Mineola, N.Y.: Foundation Press, 1985), 71–335.

9. Louis, "European Community and Tokyo Round," 21–76; Peter Riddell, "Thatcher Reaffirms Belief in National Sovereignty in EC," *Financial Times Weekend*, March 9–10, 1991; "The Balance of European Power," *Economist*, March 30, 1991, 28. See, also, the following cases before the ECJ (all titled Commission v. Council): Case 22/70, 1971 ECR 263; Case 51/87, 1988 ECR 5459; Case 131/87, 1991 1 CMLR 780; Case 242/87, 1989 ECR 1425; Case 275/87, 1989 ECR 259; and Case 11/88, 1989 ECR 3791.

mercial policy. Again, it is not my purpose to detail the many legal and political developments relevant to the EC's external relations, but a few broad points will assist in understanding some of the problems discussed in later sections.

Article 113 of the EEC treaty is the basis for EC power over external commercial relations of the member states.[10] It merits three remarks.

First, this article establishes that member states no longer have authority for unilateral actions on matters within Article 113 (unless some other exception in the EEC treaty can be found). In a sense, then, this is a delegation of authority over this subject from the member states to the EC institutions. This has great significance in a number of situations, including, of course, activity in GATT (discussed in the next section).[11]

Second, obviously, the definition of "common commercial policy" is extremely important. Whether a particular activity is within this definition can be highly significant for the allocation of power to the EC, although, as decades have advanced, other sources of power in the treaty have been relied upon for activities that sometimes seem similar or analogous to this.[12]

Third, as might be expected, practice and court decisions have established other sources of power for EC institutions in external commercial relations. As also might be suspected, questions of defining EC competence loom increasingly important (and sometimes controversial), as this competence effectively seems to expand through practice, foreign recognition, court decisions, treaty amendment, and possibly general public acceptance (and demands). So far, "common commercial policy" has not included "monetary policy," so that, in contrast to its GATT role, the EC as such does not play a role as representative in the Bretton Woods monetary institutions (the Interna-

---

10. Mathijsen, *Guide to European Community Law*, 280–320; Stein, "External Relations of the European Community," 27. Art. 113, EEC treaty reads as follows: Para. 1. After the transitional period has ended, the common commercial policy shall be based on uniform principles, particularly in regard to changes in tariff rates, the conclusion of tariff and trade agreements, the achievement of uniformity in measures of liberalization, export policy and measures to protect trade such as those to be taken in case of dumping or subsidies. Para. 2. The Commission shall submit proposals to the Council for implementing the common commercial policy. Para. 3. Where agreements with third countries need to be negotiated, the Commission shall make recommendations to the Council, which shall authorize the Commission to open the necessary negotiations. The Commission shall conduct these negotiations in consultation with a special committee appointed by the Council to assist the Commission in this task and within the framework of such directives as the Council may issue to it. Para. 4. In exercising the powers conferred upon it by this Article, the Council shall act by a qualified majority.

11. Louis, "European Community and Tokyo Round," 21–76; see also John H. Jackson, Jean-Victor Louis, and Mitsuo Matsushita, "National Constitutions and the International Economic System," in *Implementing the Tokyo Round*, ed. John H. Jackson, Jean-Victor Louis, and Mitsuo Matsushita (Ann Arbor, Mich.: University of Michigan Press, 1984), 201.

12. Stein, "External Relations of the European Community," 30–33, 35–61; Mathijsen, *Guide to European Community Law*, 163–287.

tional Monetary Fund and the World Bank). This could change following the intergovernmental conferences of 1991. Other questions of competence arose at the end of the Tokyo Round of GATT negotiations in 1979, such as whether the EC, as such, had competence over technical product standards or government procurement policy.[13] In the current Uruguay Round of negotiations, several new areas, namely trade in services and questions of intellectual property, raise similar questions of competence.

A very important part of this picture is the so-called treaty-making power of the EC. It is clear from the treaties and practice that the EC has international legal status to enter into agreements in its own right. For example, it has entered into agreements on commercial policy in the context of GATT without additional acceptances of the member states (although, of course, the member states exercise control over the use of this power through the Council).[14] It seems clear that such agreements are treaties under international law, imposing binding international law obligations on the EC (and all of its institutions, including the member states) and on the other parties to the agreements (such as the United States or Canada or Japan). There is a prescribed procedure for the EC to enter into such agreements, beginning with a Commission proposal to the Council for a mandate to open the negotiation, followed by supervision of the Commission's negotiators by the Council through a "113 Committee" of the Council (including member state representatives, receiving regular reports and approving or disapproving certain negotiating positions). When an agreement is finally drafted, the Commission proposes to the Council that the EC accept it, and if the Council approves by the necessary majority, then EC officials will "ratify" or indicate acceptance and the agreement will become final.[15]

One alternative to the procedure I have just described is the so-called mixed agreement. In some cases, the EC and its member states feel that it is appropriate, perhaps because of concern about how far EC competence reaches, to jointly enter into an international agreement—duly approved, signed, and ratified by the EC according to the procedures sketched above, but also approved and ratified by each of the member states through their own constitutional procedures (often requiring national parliamentary action).[16]

---

13. Louis, "European Community and Tokyo Round," 36–38.

14. Louis, "European Community and Tokyo Round," 21–76; see also Jackson, Louis, and Matsushita, "National Constitutions and the International Economic System," 201; "Protocols: 1964–67 Trade Conference," Contracting Parties to GATT, *Basic Instruments and Selected Documents*, 15th Supp. (April 1968), 4–36 (hereafter cited as GATT BISD); "Multilateral Trade Negotiations," GATT BISD, 26th Supp. (March 1980), 3–191, 201–22.

15. See, e.g., Louis, "European Community and Tokyo Round," 21–46; Stein, "External Relations of the European Community," 37–38; Mathijsen, *Guide to European Community Law*, 281.

16. Mathijsen, *Guide to European Community Law*, 283; Louis, "European Community and Tokyo Round," 24, 38–42, 46–48.

A very important development expanding EC competence came with decisions of the Court holding that EC institutions had the power to enter international agreements in any area that they had authority to regulate within the Community, and hinting at a more general "implied power" for Community institutions.[17]

The EC and GATT: Troubled Relationship?

Now I turn to several particular aspects of EC external commercial relationships, starting with the relationship with GATT, which is central in many ways.

GATT

From its beginning (in 1947), GATT included clauses designed to accommodate customs unions and free-trade areas. There is clear evidence that, as GATT was drafted, certain European leaders envisaged the possibility of a European economic union of some type, and wished to be sure that GATT obligations would not inhibit the formation of such a union. Thus, although one central feature of GATT is Most Favored Nation (MFN) treatment, which requires all GATT members to treat all other members equally, an important exception to this was built into Article 24 of GATT to allow members of a customs union (CU), free-trade area (FTA), or interim agreements leading to one of those to give preferred treatment to each other within certain limits.[18]

One requirement of GATT Article 24 is that "substantially all" the trade within the CU or FTA be free. Thus, the European Coal and Steel Community may not have met the requirements of GATT (although arguably it was an interim agreement, pending a broader union); but with the 1957 Treaty of Rome for a full customs union covering all products, it seems clear that the EC reasonably fulfilled the GATT criteria for an exception to MFN. The drafting of the EC treaties seemed to take GATT into account, and, indeed, language from a number of GATT clauses found its way into the EC treaties.[19]

It might therefore seem that the EC relationship with GATT would be entirely happy and relatively trouble free. It is probably fair to say that this has not been the case. A number of problems have arisen.

---

17. Stein, "External Relations of the European Community," 41–42. This, of course, is a field of study in its own right, of which a full discussion is beyond the scope of this paper.

18. John H. Jackson, *World Trade and the Law of GATT* (Indianapolis, Ind.: Bobbs-Merrill Company, 1969), 575–80.

19. Compare, e.g., GATT Art. 3 ("National Treatment on Internal Taxation and Regulation") with EEC treaty Art. 95, and GATT Art. 11 ("General Elimination of Quantitative Restrictions") with EEC treaty Arts. 30–32, 34, and 36.

Status of the EC and Its Agreements in GATT

The legal status of the EC in GATT is quite interesting. As indicated previously, the EEC treaty (Art. 113) clearly gives EC institutions competence over external commercial policy. It seems well agreed that this includes almost all of the subjects in the GATT agreement. Thus, the EC institutions exercise the principal representation role for the EC and its member states in GATT.

The theory of this representation is not entirely clear. It could be a theory of agency, whereby the treaty delegates to the EC, as agent, all of the commercial policy functions of the member states relative to GATT. All twelve of the member states are contracting parties of GATT, and thus are treaty bound by the obligations of GATT, but presumably they can delegate to an agent the authority to carry out the representation. Of course, the member states are still obligated under international law to comply with the norms of the GATT agreement. There seems to be some difference of opinion among EC scholars and officials about whether the agency theory is the correct one, or whether the EC, as a legal entity, has somehow succeeded to the privileges and rights of GATT membership.

One of the interesting facets of this is that the issue of sovereignty as such does not come up. GATT is one of the rare international organizations that can accept entities that are not sovereign states as members. GATT Article 26 specifies that, to be a contracting party, an entity need only be an "independent customs territory." From the beginning of GATT, there were colonial dependencies that could claim this status, although they did not have sovereign status. Today, Hong Kong is an example of an entity that has GATT contracting party status as an independent customs territory, but is not a sovereign nation. Taiwan is applying for such status.

It seems quite plausible, therefore, that the EC could assert that it is an "independent customs territory," and, thus, claim direct contracting party status in GATT. It has not done this, however, and it seems clear that the EC is not directly a contracting party in GATT (although some have argued that it is). Instead, the EC acts as the principal spokesman for the member states, as well as the EC institutions, at GATT meetings. There is an EC mission at GATT, with a chief of mission (rank of ambassador) and a substantial staff of officials and negotiators. The typical modus operandi is for the EC member states to meet (caucus) in advance of a GATT meeting and, along with the EC officials, establish a position that the EC representative will then take at the GATT meeting. At the GATT meeting itself, the member state representatives sit, mostly watching. In a few situations in GATT, a vote or treaty acceptance is required (a vote for a waiver, for instance), and, in such cases, the member states continue as contracting parties and thus indicate their vote or treaty acceptance to the GATT secretariat. They are obligated under the EC treaties to vote as instructed by the EC institutions (presumably after consensus agreement of the caucus). In this manner, therefore, the EC effectively has twelve votes. If the EC acceded itself as a contracting party, it could very well lose eleven votes, having only its own vote. On the other hand, it has been suggested that the financial contribution of the EC would then be measured by statistics that included only external trade to third countries, whereas now its financial contribution (generally based on its percentage of world trade) includes intra-EC trade.

The role of the member state representatives in GATT meetings has generated some interesting experiences. Insofar as a GATT meeting considers an issue that is not under the competence of the EC institutions (relating possibly to monetary policy or, conceivably, to certain service industry questions), arguably the member state representative still has the competence to speak for his country. But, with respect to commercial policy, the EC representative apparently takes the position that he is the exclusive spokesman in GATT.[20]

I previously said that the EC, as a customs union, seemed to fulfill the criteria specified in Article 24 of GATT for exemption from MFN, and this has largely been true. There has been some rumbling in GATT about one criterion under Article 24, namely, that when a customs union is formed, its common external trade barriers (tariffs) be "not on the whole higher than" was experienced by the rest of the world from the member states of this customs union prior to its formation. From time to time, questions have been raised about whether the EC had complied with this provision, but no specific measures ever came out of those questionings.[21]

More troublesome, however, has been the experience of several EC enlargements. The first enlargement, in 1973 (when the United Kingdom,

---

20. I have been told by persons who were present that several years ago, at a GATT council meeting, the EC representative spoke concerning a dispute between the EC and the United States. His statement reflected a prior bilateral negotiation between the EC and the United States. The French representative (it is said) did not completely like the EC representative's statement, and so he raised his card to be recognized to speak. At that point, the EC representative objected to the chairman of the council, arguing that member states had no right to speak on this issue (unless they had the permission of the EC representative). Needless to say, this put the chairman on the spot, and (it was reported) he consulted with the GATT director general, who also found the question awkward. After reflection, the director general and his staff apparently advised that the EC representative had correctly represented recent practice in GATT; the EC representative did have the sole right to speak on the issue concerned. I was told that, some weeks later, the representative from France apologized. This type of episode itself becomes part of the developing experience and evolution of the EC "constitution."

21. See GATT Art. 24(5)(a); "Treaties Establishing a European Economic Community and a European Atomic Energy Community," GATT BISD, 6th Supp. (March 1958), 68–109; "Customs Unions and Free-Trade Areas: Treaty Establishing the European Economic Community," GATT BISD, 7th Supp. (February 1959), 69–71; Jackson, *World Trade and the Law of GATT*, 610–18.

Denmark, and Ireland entered the EC), raised this issue of "not on the whole higher" to an important level. The United States in particular argued that the alignment of trade barriers of the acceding states to the common EC external barriers did not comply with GATT criteria. In addition, the GATT article provides that when acceding states raise tariffs on products for which they have "bound" a tariff in GATT (i.e., promised not to exceed an agreed maximum tariff level), those non-CU-member countries of GATT that are affected have the right to negotiate for "compensatory tariff reductions." The United States asked for such reductions particularly on the grounds that agricultural tariffs were raised despite bindings, entitling the United States to compensation. The same issue arose when Spain and Portugal acceded in 1986. This has been a festering controversy within GATT, particularly between the EC and the United States, and has not yet been completely resolved.[22]

Although the EC itself, and its basic treaty structure, may largely fulfill the provisions of GATT, substantial questions can be raised about some of the ancillary agreements on trade into which the EC has entered. Perhaps the most significant of these are the association agreements with EFTA (the European Free Trade Association) and the so-called Lomé agreements.

The EFTA was established in 1960 by a group of seven European countries that, at that time, did not wish to join the EC.[23] The EFTA is not a customs union, but a free-trade area. The EFTA agreement, however, largely omitted the agricultural sector from its rules. Thus, independent of the EC question, the EFTA agreement, it was argued, did not comply with Article 24 of GATT, which required "substantially all" barriers to be lifted. Again, GATT discussions of this dragged on without any definitive action.[24] In later

22. By the end of 1990, the United States threatened to impose 100 percent tariffs on some categories of EC agricultural products exported to the United States if the EC refused to extend the 1986 agreement requiring Spain and Portugal to import annually from the United States 2 million tons of corn and 300,000 tons of sorghum. In November, 1990, the United States initiated a proceeding under Sec. 301. By the end of December, the EC Commission proposed a 12 month extension of the agreement. See, e.g., "Highlights," *International Trade Reporter* 8, no. 1 (January 2, 1991): 1. This extension addresses the question of the "temporary character" of this agreement. According to the EC, such an extension exceeds the compensation to which the United States was entitled under GATT Art. 24(6) when Spain and Portugal acceded to the EC. "USTR Section 301 Committee Hears Testimony on Proposed Retaliation in Feedgrains Dispute," *International Trade Reporter* 7, no. 47 (November 28, 1990): 1797. "Customs Unions and Free-Trade Areas: Accession of Portugal and Spain to the European Communities—Report of the Working Party," GATT BISD, 35th Supp. (June 1989), 293–321.

23. The original seven members were Austria, Denmark, Norway, Portugal, Sweden, Switzerland, and the United Kingdom. Presently there are six members: Austria, Finland, Iceland, Norway, Sweden, and Switzerland.

24. Jackson, *World Trade and the Law of GATT*, 607–10; "Customs Unions and Free-Trade Areas: European Free Trade Association," GATT BISD, 9th Supp. (February 1961), 20–21, 70–87.

years, some of the EFTA countries joined the EC, and, both before and after that, the EC has had association agreements with members of EFTA, arguing that these, too, were free-trade agreements, although they continued to omit agricultural products from much of their discipline.

The Lomé agreement in force today is the fourth in a series of agreements between the EC and a number of third countries spread around the world (mostly in Africa, the Caribbean, and the Pacific; thus, the countries are called the "ACP countries"). Many of these countries were former colonies of EC member states, and thus the EC felt a special relationship with them. At the outset, the aim of the agreement was to provide a series of trade preferences between the EC and the ACP countries. There was no preference among the ACP countries themselves, but, initially, there were so-called reverse preferences by which ACP countries gave preference to EC products exported to them (as well as the EC preference given to the ACPs). Clearly, the whole structure was not one of a free-trade agreement, since the ACP countries maintained barriers among themselves. However, the EC lawyers cleverly argued that the structure of the arrangement was a *series* of free-trade agreements, each between the EC, on the one hand, and a single ACP country, on the other hand. They did not argue that it was a full FTA, but rather that each was an interim agreement tending toward an FTA, as permitted under Article 24 of GATT. There have been considerable questions about whether this really fulfilled the criteria of Article 24, and certain arguments have arisen between the United States and the EC.

Another dimension of the EC-GATT relationship relates back to the question, discussed earlier, of EC competence. While EC competence seems to be expanding,[25] its remaining ambiguities should be noted. Although (in the early 1970s) the EC criticized the U.S. constitutional system that divided authority over trade policy negotiations and implementation between the president and Congress, the irony was that, at the end of the Tokyo Round (1979), the U.S. process for approving the results worked smoothly while the EC had a major internal debate on whether member states must participate in the approval of the Tokyo Round treaties. In the end, a compromise decision was made for all treaties to be accepted by the EC and, in addition, to allow member states to also sign three of the dozen or so documents. It has been argued that the member state participation was a political gesture rather than a constitutional necessity.[26]

Similar difficulties may be faced at the end (if it ever occurs) of the Uruguay Round. There is no consensus about whether all the subjects of the Uruguay Round (for example, services or intellectual property) are suffi-

---

25. See note 20 above.
26. Louis, "European Community and Tokyo Round," 38–42.

ciently within EC competence to avoid the necessity of member state acceptance of some of the treaties.[27] The role of the European Parliament could also
be more significant at the end of this round.

EC Policies that Worry GATT

Almost from the inception of the EC, there has been developing concern that
the EC was maintaining a protectionist attitude toward trade from nonmember
countries. The first major GATT negotiation after the EEC treaty was the
Kennedy Round from 1962 to 1967. (The Dillon Round, 1960 to 1962, was
not that significant.) During the Kennedy Round, the EC's Common Agricultural Policy (CAP) emerged as an important issue. The European agricultural system even then appeared to be very protectionist, starkly limiting
the importation of competing agricultural goods. This was partly due to an
extensive price support system within the EC, protected by the variable levies
on imported agricultural goods. These border taxes (unlike traditional tariffs)
varied over time to ensure that external goods trading at world market prices
could not be sold in the EC at prices below those desired by the EC. This
aspect of CAP created two major legal problems within GATT. First, some of
the variable levies were applied to products for which individual member
states had bindings in the GATT. These bindings were either breached or
withdrawn, and, in those cases, GATT calls for compensatory measures. The
United States, in particular, demanded compensation, and has had off-and-on
desultory negotiations on such compensation for several decades. A second
problem was the mere fact that the variable levy varied. It was argued that
when a tariff varied, it no longer operated strictly as a tariff, but instead
became an "other measure," prohibited by Article 11 of GATT. Once again,
this is an argument that has never really been settled in GATT.[28]

Certain other measures taken by the EC have also raised considerable
GATT problems. For example, for a variety of historical reasons, some of the
EC member states (particularly France and Italy) have enforced quotas against
the importation of automobiles from Japan. It seems reasonably clear that
these quota provisions violate GATT, but they have nevertheless been toler-
ated; even today the Europeans, as they approach the 1992 deadline for a

---

27. Although it seems that the EC normally enjoys enough power under EEC Art. 113, it
could be argued that certain services, including financial services, may lie outside the intended
and habitual competence of the EC. See, Peter Gilsdorf, "Portée et Délimitation des Compétences
Communautaires en Matière de Politique Commerciale," *Revue du Marché Commun*, no. 326
(April 1989): 195; Jackson, Louis, and Matsushita, "National Constitutions and the International
Economic System," 201.

28. John H. Jackson and William J. Davey, *Legal Problems of International Economic
Relations*, 2d ed. (St. Paul, Minn.: West Publishing Company, 1986): 965–68.

single internal market, are struggling with a program to perpetuate, but hopefully phase down, the impact of the auto quotas.[29] It remains to be seen how successful this will be, and certainly the EC's protectionist measures against imported automobiles are among the most stringent in the industrial world.

Another problem that has been observed about the European Community has been its willingness, in one guise or another, to tolerate so-called voluntary restraint agreements (VRAs) on a variety of products. Many of these have been aimed at Japan, but a number of others have been concluded with other Asian and third world countries. Such VRAs have been an exceptionally difficult question for GATT generally, since they tend to escape the language of GATT legal norms, yet deeply undermine some of the basic principles and policy objectives of GATT.[30] These issues have been the subject of important discussions in past and present GATT negotiating rounds.[31]

Although other matters could be mentioned, I will conclude this section by noting the problem of antidumping duties applied by the European Community. GATT allows the use of antidumping duties in cases where there has been "injury" from the sale of goods into the EC at a price that is (arguably) less than that charged for the same goods in their home market. Yet, observers have noted that a great deal of manipulation can be used by importing governments to establish the margin of dumping and the fact of injury. It has been argued that the EC has been particularly adept at using the antidumping laws to restrain imports.[32] One result of this type of restraint has been the inducement of foreign manufacturers to build plants within the EC, so as to avoid the border restraint problem. This has been done by Japan for a number of

---

29. "EC to Set Rules on Japanese Cars," *New York Times*, April 29, 1991; Kenjiro Ishikawa, "Protectionist Plans for Europe's Single Market," *Economic Eye* (Autumn 1990): 26.

30. John H. Jackson, "Consistency of Export-Restraint Arrangements with the GATT," *World Economy* 11 (December 1988): 485–500; Michael Kostecki, "Export-Restraint Arrangements and Trade Liberalization," *World Economy* 10 (December 1987): 425; David Greenaway and Brian Hindley, *What Britain Pays for Voluntary Export Restraints*, Thames Essay no. 43 (London: Trade Policy Research Centre, 1985).

31. "Protocols: 1964–67 Trade Conference," GATT BISD, 15th Supp. (April 1968), 4–35; "Multilateral Trade Negotiations," GATT BISD, 26th Supp. (March 1980), 3–191, 201–22; Uruguay Round Draft Agreement on Safeguards, MTN.TNC/W/35 (Brussels: MTN, December 1990): 183. VRAs are often related to the notion of "grey area measures"; see "Statement by Ambassador Rubens Ricupero (Brazil) on Behalf of the Developing Countries, Trade Negotiations Committee," *News of the Uruguay Round of Multilateral Trade Negotiations*, NUR 049, August 6, 1991, 10; "Dunkel Assessment of Uruguay Round," *Inside US Trade*, Special Report (July 27, 1990): S3. On the Tokyo Round, see, GATT, "The Tokyo Round of Multilateral Trade Negotiations," II-Supplementary Report, chap. 5, Multilateral Safeguard System (Geneva: GATT, January 1980): 14; Jackson, "Consistency of Export Restraint Agreements with the GATT," 485–500.

32. John H. Jackson and Edwin A. Vermulst, *Antidumping Law and Practice: A Comparative Study* (Ann Arbor, Mich.: University of Michigan Press, 1989).

products, including automobiles and televisions. At this point, however, the EC became concerned that the parts that were imported were so substantial that the assembly within the EC was a "circumvention" of the antidumping orders. Such plants have been called "screwdriver plants," because they merely import parts and then a "screwdriver" is used to assemble them. To prevent this circumvention, the EC adopted, in 1987, a regulation that would treat the products of assembly plants within the EC as imports.

The Japanese brought a dispute procedure in GATT against the EC for this, and the GATT panel ruled that the EC's regulation was not consistent with its GATT obligations. The EC finally allowed the GATT council to approve this panel report, but the EC has not yet implemented it (it says it will at the end of the Uruguay Round).[33]

GATT Institutional Problems, Including Dispute Settlement

The institutional problems of GATT are well known. The GATT itself was never intended to be an organization, much less the principal organization for international trade regulation. Rather, an International Trade Organization (ITO) was negotiated in 1947–48 meetings. This charter would have established the principal international trade organization, but it never came into force because the U.S. Congress would not approve it. Thus, GATT, which was in force as a multilateral tariff-reducing agreement (approved by the U.S. president under advance authority delegated to him from the Congress),[34] gradually became the major international institution concerning trade in goods. Partly because of this unfortunate history, the GATT agreement is inadequate in terms of such institutional measures as dispute settlement, voting, amendment, and subordinate bodies. Yet GATT has effectively and imaginatively adapted and evolved to become the important institution that it is today. Nevertheless, there are a number of viewpoints about the need to restructure and improve GATT institutionally, so that it can better cope with the rapidly changing, interdependent world economic scene.[35]

The EC, on the other hand, has so far been generally skeptical of any moves to try to improve the GATT structure. Perhaps this was best demon-

---

33. Council Regulation no. 1761/81/EEC of June 22, 1987, OJ No. L 167/9 (June 26, 1987); GATT Panel Report, GATT Doc. L/665 (March 22, 1990), GATT BISD, 37th Supp. (June 1990), 132.

34. Jackson, *World Trade and the Law of GATT*, 35–57; John H. Jackson, *The World Trading System: Law and Policy of International Economic Relations* (Cambridge, Mass.: MIT Press, 1989).

35. John H. Jackson, *Restructuring the GATT System* (London: Royal Institute of International Affairs, 1990).

strated by the EC attitudes toward dispute settlement. There has long been a controversy within GATT as to whether its dispute settlement provisions (very sketchy in the GATT treaty, but evolving through practice) were merely to be a framework for negotiation of a "GATT or GABB,"[36] or were designed to be a "rule-oriented" system of diplomacy,[37] whereby a dispute procedure complete with a panel would reach a definitive legal conclusion as to whether a member country was fulfilling its GATT obligations. During certain periods (particularly in the 1960s), GATT used its dispute settlement process, but, in the 1970s, the United States began bringing a series of complaints, and soon the issue of the nature of the dispute settlement process was being hotly debated.

During the Tokyo Round of trade negotiations from 1973 to 1979, one of the most important issues was the improvement of the GATT dispute settlement process. The United States pushed for improvement (better procedures, better panelists, faster action, better reasoning in the panel reports) and was joined by most of the rest of the countries of GATT except the EC. The EC opposed improvements to the dispute settlement process and essentially blocked any such improvement for that negotiating round. One can surmise why the EC took this approach, but the EC then as now was concerned with its own constitutional development, and perhaps its negotiators felt that it was important to prevent, when feasible, external institutions such as GATT from interfering with some of the delicate internal compromises that were necessary for the strengthening and even survival of the EC as an institution.[38]

One of the very interesting developments during the Uruguay Round of negotiations (1986 to the present) was the substantial turnabout in the EC attitude toward GATT dispute settlement in particular, and toward the institutional strengthening of GATT in general. The EC has been among those urging substantial reform in GATT institutions and dispute settlement. Again, one can ask why this is the case. Perhaps such EC developments as the Single European Act and the progress toward its 1992 goals have given the EC the self-confidence and strength that enable it to begin to examine its relationships with the rest of the world in a somewhat different light. In addition, during the last few years, the United States has taken a number of unilateral actions that have directly applied restrictions on the trade of some of its trading partners

---

36. Robert E. Hudec, "GATT or GABB?," *Yale Law Journal* 80 (1971): 1299.

37. Jackson, *World Trading System*, chap. 4; John H. Jackson, "The Puzzle of GATT," *Journal of World Trade Law* 1 (March/April 1967): 131.

38. See, e.g., Ernst-Ulrich Petersmann, "Constitutionalism, Constitutional Law and European Integration" (Paper delivered at the Conference on EC 92 and Beyond: New Political Structure and Constitutional Problems of European Integration, University of St. Gallen, March 21–22, 1991); John H. Jackson, "United States-EEC Trade Relations: Constitutional Problems of Economic Interdependence," *Common Market Law Review* 16 (1979): 453.

(including the EC, Brazil, and Japan).[39] Some of these unilateral actions are associated with the U.S. statute known as Section 301. Europeans, among others, have been dismayed by some of these actions, and it is possible that they see a strengthened GATT dispute settlement process as operating as a constraint on these "irresponsible unilateral actions."[40]

It has been noted (especially by Americans) that the United States has generally taken the lead in promoting GATT negotiating rounds, often facing considerable footdragging or open opposition from the EC. Whether this attitude will also change is not known.

The Uruguay Round of GATT Trade Negotiations

A few words about the current state of the GATT Uruguay Round trade negotiations are necessary. This eighth major round of GATT negotiations, launched at Punta del Este, Uruguay, in September, 1986, continues today;[41] as this chapter was written, it was clear that these negotiations were in trouble. At the launch, the Punta Declaration manifested great ambition for the negotiations, with some major new areas to be discussed, including trade in services (as vast and important as all of the trade in goods covered by GATT), intellectual property, trade-related investment measures, and a number of items for remedying defects in the current GATT system. The most important initiatives of the latter variety involved trade in agricultural goods, subsidies, and dispute settlement.

Technically, as a matter of law, GATT applies to trade in agricultural goods just as much as it applies to trade in other goods, but, for a variety of historical reasons, agriculture has largely escaped the discipline of GATT.

39. "Semiconductor Market Tensions Diminishing, But Not Enough to Lift Sanctions, USTR Says," *International Trade Reporter* 5, no. 42 (October 26, 1988): 1428; "U.S. Commitment to Uruguay Round Perceived as Inconsistent with Policies, Report Finds," *International Trade Reporter* 6, no. 50 (December 20, 1989): 1646; "Hills Lifts $40 Million in Sanction after Brazil Pledges to Enact Patent Law," *International Trade Reporter* 7, no. 27 (July 4, 1990): 996; "Reagan Charging Patent Piracy, Imposes Sanctions on $39 Million of Brazilian Goods," *International Trade Reporter* 5, no. 42 (October 26, 1988): 1415.

40. See, e.g., Corrado Pirzio-Biroli, "A European View of the 1988 U.S. Trade Act and Section 301," in *Aggressive Unilateralism: America's 301 Trade Policy and the World Trading System*, ed. Jagdish Bhagwati and Hugh T. Patrick (Ann Arbor, Mich.: University of Michigan Press, 1990): 261–65; "Draft Final Act Embodying the Result of the Uruguay Round of Multilateral Trade Negotiations," GATT Doc. MTN.TNC/W/35 (November 26, 1990).

41. "Ministerial Declaration on the Uruguay Round," GATT BISD, 33rd Supp. (June 1987), 19–52; "Draft Final Act Embodying the Result of the Uruguay Round of Multilateral Trade Negotiations," GATT Doc. MTN.TNC/W/35 (November 26, 1990); Paula L. Green, "US-EC Trade Disputes Simmer as Talks Remain Stalled," *Journal of Commerce*, June 12, 1991; "GATT Launches Uruguay Round as Consensus Reached on Services, Agricultural Trade," *International Trade Reporter* 3, no. 38 (September 24, 1986): 1150.

The United States, as a major exporter of agricultural products, found this particularly troublesome, and tried in both the Kennedy Round (1962 to 1965) and the Tokyo Round (1973 to 1979) to address the matter and establish significant GATT discipline over the agricultural sector. In these endeavors, the United States (and other, similarly minded nations) has failed. Thus, once again in the Uruguay Round, the United States made it a high-priority matter to bring agriculture into GATT. Along with many other countries, it is also struggling to develop the new rules for trade in services and for intellectual property.

Much progress has been made on many of the 25 to 30 major issues being negotiated in the Uruguay Round, but as of March, 1992, little progress has been made in the agricultural sector. The original timetable for the Uruguay Round was to reach final negotiations by the latter half of 1990, culminating in a ministerial meeting in Brussels in December, 1990. This ministerial meeting occurred, and ended in failure, largely because of the agricultural question. On this issue, the EC role has been crucial. The EC leaders seem to recognize that CAP must be reformed for its own good. Many other members of GATT, particularly the Cairns group of agricultural exporting countries, feel that the reform is essential to their own trade.[42] The United States pushed hard, but the EC resisted just as hard, and thus the talks broke down at the end of 1990. It might be thought that agriculture once again could be sidestepped, so that the rest of the vast agenda of the negotiators might result in a decent or even substantial culmination of the round. Indeed, some may hope that that will still happen. However, there is an intricate connection between the agricultural subject and many of the other important subjects of the negotiation that makes that very difficult.

First of all, from the point of view of U.S. negotiators, it is hard to return once again to Congress with a package that does not seriously address the agricultural problem in GATT. Second, the United States (as well as other industrial countries) avidly wants substantial negotiating results in the areas of trade in services and intellectual property. It has achieved considerable success in the negotiation of a draft text on these subjects (more so for intellectual property than services, the latter being so complicated). However, for many of the developing countries, these two new subjects do not offer much in the

---

42. See, e.g., "Australian Trade Minister Presses Case for Reform in Agriculture Trade," *International Trade Reporter* 8, no. 40 (October 9, 1991): 1471. The members of the Cairns Group are: Argentina, Australia, Brazil, Canada, Chile, Colombia, Fiji, Hungary, Indonesia, Malaysia, New Zealand, the Philippines, Thailand, and Uruguay. "Australia Protests U.S. Budget Request Resulting in More EEC Wheat Subsidies," *International Trade Reporter* 8, no. 6 (February 6, 1991): 204; "Canada, Cairns GATT Proposals Criticized for Following U.S. Reform Plan Too Closely," *International Trade Reporter* 4, no. 42 (October 28, 1987): 1313.

form of concrete payoffs from the negotiation; yet their participation is key to adequate results on these subjects. Indeed, the developing countries are often the "payors" in these matters rather than the beneficiaries. Still, many of the countries are prepared to take on substantial obligations if they feel compensated by reciprocal advantages drawn from a substantial achievement in agriculture (as well as textiles and a few other areas). It is here that agriculture has been something of the linchpin of the whole negotiation, and, thus, some feel that, without a substantial result in agriculture, it will be impossible to achieve worthwhile results in services and intellectual property, and, therefore, the round fails. At that point, the negotiators (particularly those in the United States) worry about their ability to obtain legislative approval of the round results.

Thus, the general perception in the fall of 1991 was that the Uruguay Round was held hostage to the approach of the EC, which, in turn, is discussing extensive reforms of its agricultural policy but on a schedule that will not easily accommodate the Uruguay Round time table (which is deeply constrained by the U.S. statutory Fast Track procedure).[43]

The EC and the United States: Stormy Marriage

Early U.S. Views about the EC: Fond Approval

The original reaction of the United States to the European Community was highly favorable. In the general geopolitical context of the cold war, the United States saw this development as a way for both the defenses and the economies of Western Europe to be strengthened so as to offset the pressure of the military might to the east. The Trade Agreements Act of 1962, which established the U.S. domestic legal structure for the authority of U.S. participation in the Kennedy Round of GATT negotiations (the sixth major trade round), explicitly structured an "inducement" for the trade unification of Europe. This came in the form of a clause that allowed the United States to

---

43. "Uruguay Round Can Be Concluded in Five Months, EC Negotiators Say," *International Trade Reporter* 2, no. 39 (October 2, 1991): 1445; "GATT Talks Will Reach Decisive Phase in October and November, Dunkel Says," *International Trade Reporter* 8, no. 31 (July 31, 1991): 1148; Jackson and Davey, *Legal Problems of International Economic Relations*, 112, 151–55; "Senate and House Vote to Extend Fast Track for North American FTA, Uruguay Round Talks," *International Trade Reporter* 8, no. 22 (May 29, 1991): 802; Keith M. Rockwell, "Time for Delors to Take a Stand," *Journal of Commerce*, May 21, 1991; Richard Lawrence, "EC Standing Firm on Farm Trade Offer," *Journal of Commerce*, May 6, 1991; David Gardner, "A Slimmer Sacred Cow," *Financial Times*, January 24, 1991; "USTR Hills Opposes Setting Any New Deadline in GATT Talks until EC Moves on Agriculture," *International Trade Reporter* 8, no. 17 (April 24, 1991): 600.

negotiate deeper sets of tariff cuts in the context of the unified customs union
in Europe than would otherwise have been the case.[44]

In a number of other respects, the United States, in the earlier years, had
tended to favor the EC, even though some U.S. interests (particularly agriculture) became apprehensive about European trends and directions. Even in the
1970s, when the United States took several trade actions, it tended to do so in
a manner that tilted favorably toward Europe. For example, in the late 1970s,
the U.S. steel industry was pressing for antidumping and countervailing duty
actions against imports of steel and various steel products. This led the U.S.
administration to develop a "trigger price mechanism" (TPM) according to
which steel that entered the U.S. market below a certain trigger price benchmark would become subject to antidumping actions. In the implementation of
this TPM, it was generally recognized that there was a favorable bias toward
imports of steel from Europe as compared to those from Japan.[45]

In another case, an escape clause action regarding the importation of
motor cycles, the United States set up a quota system that had the appearance of
nondiscrimination, but effectively tilted the balance again in favor of Europe
and against Japan.[46] Thus, U.S. attitudes have largely favored the unification of
Europe into an economic (and, possibly, ultimately a federal) union.

However, as I have indicated, a number of U.S. interests, particularly in
agriculture and, later, in business, became increasingly apprehensive about
this U.S. tilt. Indeed, more and more complaints have been heard that the
United States had been giving away too much in trade negotiations with
Europe (a prominent view at the end of the Kennedy Round in 1967). Several
areas of EC endeavor were particularly worrisome to U.S. interests. For
example, the Europeans developed a set of "rules of origin" for determining
which products qualify for the favorable treatment associated with having
been produced inside the customs union or in a country with which the EC
maintains a free trade association agreement. Some such guidelines are necessary, but if the guidelines are very stringent (such as requiring 90 percent EC
content to be considered of EC origin), this will substantially inhibit imports
from such third countries as the United States.[47]

Furthermore, in order for a common market to succeed, there must be a

44. Trade Expansion Act of 1962; John W. Evans, *The Kennedy Round in American Trade
Policy: The Twilight of GATT?* (Cambridge: Harvard University Press, 1971).

45. Jackson and Davey, *Legal Problems of International Economic Relations*, 716–18; M.
C. E. J. Bronckers, *Selective Safeguard Measures in Multilateral Trade Relations: Issues of
Protectionism in GATT, European Community, and United States Law* (Deventer: Kluwer, 1985),
195–98.

46. Bronckers, *Selective Safeguard Measures*, 69 n. 61; "Action by the United States—
Heavyweight Motorcycles," GATT Doc. L/5493 (May 20, 1983).

47. Jackson and Davey, *Legal Problems of International Economic Relations*, 386–89.

certain harmonization of product standards so that economies of scale in production runs can be achieved without having to change product characteristics for each component of a fragmented market. Here again, there is a strong temptation for the industries within a customs union (or other trade area) to arrange the standards so as to make it more difficult for nonmember countries to export to the area. For example, if the Europeans generally use a metric system, whereas the United States uses some other measurements, a standard requiring the metric system would tend to disfavor the U.S. products. The United States worried about this, and one result of this worry was the consideration, during the Tokyo Round, of a "technical standards code" as part of that trade negotiation.[48]

The United States Turns Negative about Some EC Policies

One of the earlier major trade disputes between the United States and the EC resulted in what has been called the chicken war. The problem developed when, under CAP, the EC imposed new restraints on the importation of frozen chicken and turkey parts. This touched a sensitive nerve in U.S. agricultural circles, which had made considerable efforts to develop a market in Europe for the American product. The import restraints were quite clearly contrary to GATT obligations, which the EC treated as "withdrawn"; however, under GATT rules, this requires a compensatory reduction of other barriers.[49] The United States and the EC agreed that the EC owed compensation to the United States, but they could not agree on the amount. To break the stalemate, the then director general of GATT proposed an ad hoc panel to determine this amount (and no other issue). It did so, concluding that the amount of trade compensation owed to the United States was $25 million in equivalent trade, and this was followed by U.S. actions on certain products of export interest to member states of the Community, including small trucks (aimed at the German Volkswagen minibus, then quite popular) and cognac (aimed at France).[50]

---

48. Jackson and Davey, *Legal Problems of International Economic Relations*, 532–37; see also "The Parliament Adopts a Resolution on European Policy Concerning Standardization Certification and Testing," *Agence Europe*, no. 5534 (July 13, 1991): 14–15.

49. GATT Arts. 28 and 24(6); Jackson and Davey, *Legal Problems of International Economic Relations*, 355–56 and 407–8.

50. Due partly to the nature of its trade law, the United States raised tariffs on these products on an MFN basis. It simply chose products that were primarily shipped from the EC countries, so that, in theory, the reduction in trade *from Europe* would approximate the amount determined by the panel. Ironically, some years later, this higher tariff on the small trucks became an issue between the United States and Japan, but that is another story. See Jackson and Davey, *Legal Problems of International Economic Relations*, 355–56.

In the 1970s, the GATT nations began to gear up for the seventh major trade round, the Tokyo Round, and the United States pushed hard for developing a negotiation to discipline the use of subsidies when they affected products flowing in international trade. GATT had several clauses on this issue, but they were not very effective. One measure that the United States began to utilize extensively was the countervailing duty imposed unilaterally by the importing country to offset subsidies enjoyed by imported products. The United States was particularly concerned about subsidies on dairy products, and Congress provided (in the Trade Act of 1974, which established the framework for U.S. participation in the Tokyo Round) that countervailing duties would be mandatory in the United States except that, for a limited period of time (ending January 3, 1979), the United States could provide a waiver for foreign subsidizing actions to avoid countervailing them, provided certain criteria were met, including the satisfactory continuation of negotiations on rules regarding subsidies. An interesting situation occurred in 1978 and 1979 in this matter, because, in the fall of 1978, the negotiation was still not complete, while the deadline loomed close. The Europeans let the United States know that they would not tolerate countervailing duties on their exports of dairy products to the United States, saying, "We will not negotiate with a gun at our head." The U.S. negotiators tried to get Congress to extend the waiver in the last months of 1978, but, in something of a crisis situation, Congress adjourned in October without fixing this problem. Thus it was that, technically, before the Congress could reconvene in 1979, U.S. law mandated countervailing duties on subsidized imports, including dairy products from Europe.

The solution was intriguing. Officials in the United States recognized the force of the law but also noted that it would take "some time" for the administering department (at this time, the Treasury Department) to develop the case and establish the necessary administration to carry out the mandate. During that time, Congress would reconvene and be persuaded to extend the waiver, particularly in light of the fact that the trade negotiations were then virtually complete (spring of 1979). This is what happened, so a "dairy war" was avoided, and the Tokyo Round of agreements, including a subsidy code, were signed in April and implemented in the United States through legislation adopted in the summer of 1979.[51]

These are just two examples of the many that can be cited as U.S. interests became more and more concerned about growing EC protectionism. Issues that received attention in the United States included government pro-

---

51. Jackson, Louis, and Matsushita, "National Constitutions and the International Economic System," 155–58. Congress approved the Tokyo Round results by the overwhelming votes of 90 to 4 (Senate) and 395 to 7 (House).

curement practices, rules of origin (again), and harmonization of product standards (again). Needless to say, the EC also had its complaints against the United States. These complaints grew during the 1980s as the U.S. Congress became more assertive on questions of trade policy, partly from worries about the mounting trade deficit with such major partners as Japan, but also from worries about activities in Europe.[52]

The GATT Dispute Settlement Process between the EC and the United States

During the 1970s and 1980s, the dispute settlement process of GATT began to come into its own. Far more dispute procedures were initiated in GATT during these two decades than during any previous comparable period of GATT's history. As I have already mentioned, there was considerable concern about the efficiency and effectiveness of the GATT dispute settlement procedures, particularly in the 1970s and during the Tokyo Round. Despite the fact that the Tokyo Round resulted in no obvious substantial improvement in the legal procedures for dispute settlement, there were, nevertheless, some important changes, including additional GATT secretariat assistance that was designed to facilitate dispute settlement by bringing a measure of rigor and meaningful analysis to the process and by reducing the delays. The dispute settlement process in GATT has been largely dominated by the EC and the United States. Of 233 disputes between 1947 and 1986,[53] 125 (53 percent) included the United States as a party, and 68 (almost 30 percent) included the EC as a party. The number of cases between the United States and the EC was 35, or 15 percent of the total. Needless to say, these cases also tended to be the most difficult.[54]

The following examples (from the early 1980s) describe some of the difficult cases between the United States and the EC.

The Wheat Flour case involved a complaint by the U.S. that EC subsidies (as much as 75 percent) to aid exports of wheat flour to third markets (including Egypt) were a violation of the [subsidies] code and of the GATT rules regarding export subsidies. Export subsidy rules for agricultural products differ from those for manufactured or "non-primary" products. There seemed to be little doubt that the EC subsidies

---

52. See, e.g., Commission of the European Communities, *Report on United States Trade Barriers and Unfair Practices, 1991: Problems of Doing Business with the U.S.* (Brussels: Services of the Commission of the European Communities, 1991); and note 67, infra.

53. Jackson, *World Trading System*, 99.

54. See Jackson and Davey, *Legal Problems of International Economic Relations*, 332–59.

would have been violating the rules if manufactured products had been involved. But the rules are less absolute regarding agricultural products, requiring only that a subsidy not result in a nation "having more than an equitable share" of world export trade. The U.S. argued that the EC share of the world export market had increased from 29 percent to 75 percent over a relevant period and that the EC market share in a number of important and growing markets had increased, while U.S. export share of those markets had decreased. Yet the panel, partly influenced by special characteristics of the marketing of U.S. wheat flour, including aid under the U.S. PL 480 food aid program to assist developing countries, did not find that the EC had achieved "more than an equitable share." The panel refused to be guided in this case by an earlier export subsidy case in GATT history, also dealing with wheat flour, which might have been seen as a sort of "precedent" for some meaningful definition of "equitable share."

The Pasta case also involved a U.S. complaint against EC subsidies for exports (pasta), which in this case went to the U.S. market (particularly harming a U.S. regional pasta industry). The EC claimed that its subsidies to EC pasta makers for exporting were only such as were necessary to equalize the effective cost of the more expensive European durum wheat (which EC pasta makers presumably used) with the world market price for wheat. The EC price was higher because of its Common Agricultural Policy program of maintaining grain prices. For the pasta makers to be able to export, they needed to have inputs at prices equivalent to those of foreign competitors, so the EC provided a "cereals refund" to make up the difference. The EC claimed, therefore, that the subsidy was really one for wheat (and thus was governed by the rules for agriculture products). The panel, however, found both that the payments were made to the pasta makers for pasta exports and, more significantly, that pasta was not a primary or agricultural product, but was a processed good and therefore came under the rules for nonprimary products. In this case, the subsidies were forbidden by the code.[55]

55. Jackson, *World Trading System*, 101, 102; Jackson and Davey, *Legal Problems of International Economic Relations*, 732–44; "European Economic Community—Subsidies on Exports of Wheat Flour," report submitted March 21, 1983, GATT Doc. SCM/42, GATT BISD, 31st Supp. (June 1985), 201; 18 BNA ITEX 899–916 (1983); "European Economic Community—Subsidies on Export of Pasta," report submitted May 19, 1983, GATT Doc. SCM/43, GATT BISD, 31st Supp. (June 1985), 201; 8 BNA ITIM 468–77 (1983); "United States—Section 337 of the Tariff Act of 1930," report adopted November 7, 1989, Doc. L/6439, GATT BISD, 36th Supp. (June 1989), 345; "European Economic Community—Payments and Subsidies Paid to Processors and Producers of Oilseeds and Related Animal-Feed Proteins," report adopted January 25, 1990, Doc. L/6627, GATT BISD, 37th Supp. (June 1990), 86.

The "Fortress" Question

In the late 1980s, the United States became more and more concerned about the trends in European trade policy. This concern was also manifested by a number of other countries, particularly the Cairns group and many developing countries, as well as Japan (on Japan, see the chapter by Gary Saxonhouse in this volume). The worry persists today that the EC, as a vital and evolving institution, has become so engrossed with its internal evolution (and the constitutional decisions that it must make in that connection) that it does not seem to give much attention to its broader role in the world trading community. Furthermore, the structure of decision making within the EC arguably plays into the hands of special interest groups (rent seekers) that wish to embellish the restraints at the external border against imports from third countries, including the United States and a number of other GATT members. This decision-making problem may be part of the difficulty regarding the agricultural negotiations in the Uruguay Round.[56]

For its part, the EC denies that it is developing a fortress Europe and, in fact, points a finger at the United States itself for undertaking a number of protectionist measures, arguably more damaging than some of those found in Europe. Indeed, a certain amount of reciprocal name calling seems to be developing. The United States, by statute, is mandated to develop an annual trade barrier inventory, listing a number of trade barriers in many nations of the world that inhibit U.S. exports. Several years ago the EC began to develop its own counterlist. Following this, the Japanese have also come up with a list.[57]

The following are some of the ways in which the Europeans have (or are alleged to have) restricted imports.

1. Developing standards and harmonization techniques so as to inhibit imports.
2. Concluding the Lomé Agreements, giving preferences to European goods in Africa and elsewhere.

---

56. "Hills Expresses Concerns That European Community May Close Its Unified Market," *Inside U.S. Trade*, February 8, 1991, 8–9; "European Trade: Too Much Good Living," *Economist*, April 20, 1991, 69–70; "Brussels's Unreal Dominion: Fortress Europe Is Being Built, Brick by Insane Brick," *Economist*, May 4, 1991, 19–20; Keith M. Rockwell, "Negotiating Role Urged for EC Trade Ministers," *Journal of Commerce*, March 8, 1991; Renato Ruggiero, oral address at the Conference on Uruguay Round Negotiations: Crisis and Response (Royal Institute of International Affairs, London, March 7–8, 1991); Keith M. Rockwell, "Time for Delors to Take a Stand," *Journal of Commerce*, May 21, 1991.

57. Fair Trade Center, *Report on U.S. and EC Barriers* (Tokyo: Fair Trade Center, 1991); United States Trade Representative, *1991 National Trade Estimate: Report on Foreign Trade Barriers* (Washington, D.C.: Office of the U.S. Trade Representative, 1991); Commission of the European Communities, *Report on United States Trade Barriers and Unfair Practices, 1991.*

3. Devising government procurement rules that make it difficult or impossible for non-EC companies to bid on government contracts.
4. Agriculture and the CAP.
5. Rules of Origin.
6. Antidumping rules, and the techniques of measuring margins of dumping.
7. Voluntary restraint agreements of wide variety.

Many of these measures could also be complaints against the United States. The United States is obviously not free from comparable "fortress U.S." criticism, particularly as to a number of congressional measures. For example, with respect to imports of automobiles, steel, textiles, and high technology products (computers and semiconductors), the United States (like the EC) has adopted various measures to inhibit imports. Even in agriculture, the United States restricts imports (more in the case of dairy products and meat than in that of grains, of which the United States has been a strong net exporter).

Thus, the worry persists. Will the Community be more and more inward looking, or will it begin to assert a world leadership role on trade and economic policy matters? One of the strong arguments for conducting the Uruguay Round at this time was the contemporary effort of the EC to consolidate its internal market. It was thought that the GATT Uruguay Round would provide some opportunity for non-European countries to constrain otherwise allegedly protectionist impulses of the Europeans, so as to keep Project 1992 from being too fortress oriented. Thus, it is all the more unfortunate if the Uruguay Round results in failure. If the Uruguay Round evaporates as a restraint on the EC (as well as other countries, including the United States), what will then happen to the liberal trade policies that have been so prominently successful since 1947?

Conclusion

One broad and significant conclusion that can be gained from the history of the EC is that institutions do count. Despite a lot of literature and other expressions of opinion that international affairs and economic efficiency depend primarily on the ability and good will of key decisionmakers, the 35-year history of the European Community demonstrates clearly that institutional structures for conducting human affairs make a great deal of difference.

Another conclusion that can be made from examining the history of the EC is that when even a somewhat limited economic union is formed, as the union progresses and becomes more successful, it inevitably leads to a series of additional needs for coordinating economic decisions. For example, although trade is liberalized, that leads to questions of free movement of workers, transport policy, coordination of certain production sectors (such as agriculture or steel), problems of assisting adjustment, controlling state aids (subsidies), harmonizing product standards, and harmonizing taxation (indirect and direct), and this leads to deep matters of sovereign prerogative, including fiscal and interest rate policies, and even a common currency. In addition, it can be strongly questioned whether a purely economic union is viable without attention to a series of other, allegedly noneconomic matters, such as human rights, political coordination, and democratic institutions.

There are some important questions about the development of the EC itself, including whether it makes sense for it to continue to develop and enlarge to the point of as many as 440 million persons. At that point, does it become too much of a centralized control and regulatory system, causing considerable local tensions because local needs are not provided for? Or will the EC develop, through principles of subsidiarity, a satisfactory federalism that will recognize and accommodate the extraordinary amount of diversity of cultures and languages that is found within the European space.

Having said all that, I turn to the broader terrain of a world market. A key question about the EC is what role it will play on that world market. Will it be primarily regionally oriented, looking inward instead of to the broader world scene in such a way as to inhibit greater multilateralism in the world? If this occurs, will the world then turn (e.g., if the Uruguay Round is largely deemed a failure) toward a regional approach, with possibly three large regional blocks: the European Community, a North American free-trade area (perhaps extending to a Western Hemisphere FTA), and a Pacific basin region? What would this entail for world welfare? Clearly, this might damage world welfare and efficiency, and possibly lead to greater political tensions.[58]

Finally, we still must ask the question, what role will the EC play as a world political leader? In the light of the Persian Gulf War, many have commented on the renewing hegemony of the United States, the only world superpower of the moment. But the United States is clearly uneasy with such a role, and so is most of the rest of the world. Will the EC develop into a partner of the United States and, possibly, of one or two other power centers in the world, and will it do so in a way that permits cooperative protection of worldwide interests that include not only economic welfare but security and human rights as well?

---

58. "Far Eastern Economic Review," *Business Affairs*, July 25, 1991, 52–56.

Europe's Economic Relations with Japan

Gary R. Saxonhouse

In 1972, Zbigniew Brzezinski, who was later to become President Carter's national security adviser, wrote

> The emergence of the Common Market highlights the fact that increasingly the three economic pillars of possible global stability and cooperation are the United States, Japan, and Western Europe. Movement by stages towards a free trade area among these larger units . . . would make it easier to reduce the strains and imbalances that prevail in a more limited bilateral relationship. An international division of labor . . . could then more easily emerge permitting broader and more indirect exchanges of goods, services and products, reducing bilateral strains and imbalances. . . . In a bilateral U.S.-Japanese relationship, Japan will remain the weaker and hence a somewhat uneasy partner. In a wider cooperative framework of the developed nations Japan would be in the front rank of a global effort to reorder international political and economic relations. (Brzezinski 1972, 280–81)

At the time it was written, Brzezinski's outlook generated considerable attention. It was institutionalized in the nongovernmental Trilateral Commission, and it also played a role in helping to initiate the first Economic Summit among GATT members at Rambouillet (Hellman 1976). Trilateralism was an attempt to overcome, in the early 1970s, what was then a newly emerging impasse in U.S.-Japanese economic relations. It was at this time that Japan first began to run a large balance of payments surplus (as defined under the old Bretton Woods system) and a large current account surplus, both globally and particularly with the United States. While Japan's exports had been growing rapidly for decades, it was only in the early 1970s that the Japanese economy was both large enough and its technological base sufficiently sophisticated to pose a major problem for U.S. trade policy.[1] For the first time, the continued

---

1. Jorgenson and Nishimizu 1978 argued that, as early as 1973, Japan had outstripped the United States in the level of its technology. This finding served as a major intellectual prop for Ezra Vogel's best-selling *Japan as Number One* (1979).

rapid growth of the very large, export-oriented Japanese economy was seen to be imposing a faster pace of structural adjustment on its trading partners than many in the United States in particular thought was socially desirable.[2]

As Brzezinski suggested, there were many in both the United States and Japan who believed that the special security relationship between the United States and Japan and the weakness of Japanese ties with virtually all other major economies, particularly those in Europe, put an unhealthy burden on U.S.-Japanese economic relations. Harvard's Graham Allison, later an adviser to Secretary of Defense Caspar Weinberger, wrote that

> as an earnest of our commitment to consider Japan as an equal ally, the U.S. government should demonstrate respect by such steps as . . . insisting that our European allies stop discriminating against Japanese products. (Allison 1972, 45)

Special European barriers against Japanese products were seen as diverting Japanese exports from Europe to the relatively open U.S. market. While in 1970, 30.7 percent of Japanese exports found their way to the United States, only 15.0 percent of Japanese exports went to Western Europe (Nihon keizai kenkyu senta 1972).

With the perspective of two decades, while the Trilateral Commission remains exceedingly healthy, trilateralism's ambitions for international commercial policy have not been realized. In the late 1980s and early 1990s, Japanese exports have been still more heavily concentrated in the U.S. market than they were in the early 1970s.[3] As the U.S. market has become still more important for Japan, and as the role of Japanese imports in the U.S. economy has trebled between 1970 and 1990, U.S.-Japanese economic relations have increasingly been handled on an ad hoc, bilateral basis.[4]

Multilateral institutions, not to mention trilateral institutions, while never overly important in the postwar period in managing U.S.-Japanese economic relations, have become still less important in the last twenty years. For example, the Structural Impediment Initiative (SII) was a discussion of

---

2. While such a perception was widespread at the time, this does not necessarily mean it was an accurate appraisal of Japan's impact on the U.S. economy. Saxonhouse 1972 argued that, compared to the impact of technological and demographic change and macroeconomic fluctuation, the impact of Japanese competition on structural change in the United States was minor, at best, and very likely trivial.

3. In 1989, 33.9 percent of Japanese exports went to the United States (Tsushosangyosho 1991).

4. In 1970, imports from Japan were 0.55 percent of U.S. GNP (Nihon keizai kenkyu senta 1972); in 1990, imports from Japan were 1.70 percent of U.S. GNP (President's Council of Economic Advisers 1991).

the most fundamental character regarding the structure of the Japanese economy and the manner of its integration in the global economy. Nevertheless, this discussion was carried out exclusively on a bilateral basis between the United States and Japan. Japan's other trading partners, and the European Community, in particular, had no role at all in the negotiations (Saxonhouse 1991).

As Brzezinski observed, in the early 1970s, Japan was already a major force in the global economy. Japan's role in the global economy has more than doubled in the past 20 years.[5] To the extent that U.S. economic relations with Japan are increasingly handled bilaterally, multilateral institutions and processes as a whole are being undermined. From the beginning of the Bush administration until the nearly final breakdown of the Uruguay Round negotiations in December, 1990, far more attention was devoted by the most senior U.S. government officials to managing economic relations with Japan than was devoted to laying the basis for a successful conclusion to the most comprehensive and complex of multilateral trading negotiations. Indeed, the increasing confidence of many of the large, globally oriented U.S. corporations in the efficiency of such bilateral negotiations has gravely weakened domestic political support that is critical to congressional acceptance of whatever part is finally negotiated.

What is Europe's responsibility for the failure of trilateralism? Many in Europe would categorically reject the possibility of any such responsibility. Europe, it will be said, embraced trilateralism. The 15.0 percent share of Japanese exports that Europe took in 1970 had grown to 19.4 percent in 1989 (Tsushosangyosho 1991). Through 1990, Japan had direct investment in Europe of more than $55 billion, almost all of which had been committed since the early 1970s (Ministry of Finance Institute of Fiscal and Monetary Policy 1991). Indeed, the summer of 1991 saw two decades of increasingly high profile diplomatic interaction culminate in a joint declaration of common interests by Prime Minister Kaifu, representing Japan, and European Commission President Jacques Delors and Dutch Prime Minister Lubbers, both representing the European Community. This joint declaration aims to finally elevate the EC-Japanese trading relationship to the status of the relationship that both the EC and Japan maintain with the United States (Kojima 1991). The declaration promises regular ministerial meetings on a range of key issues, including international security, joint action on aid to developing countries, common efforts to reduce trade conflicts, and cooperation in science and technology.

---

5. In 1970, Japanese exports were 4.5 percent of global exports (Nihon keizai kenkyu senta 1972); by 1990, Japanese exports had grown to constitute 9.5 percent of global exports (Tsushosangyosho 1991).

While Europe is a somewhat more important market for Japan than was the case 20 years ago and while European-Japanese relations have far more priority and status than was the case 20 years ago, many find it difficult to believe that what is being witnessed in the 1990s is a movement toward the free-trade areas among the United States, Japan, and Western Europe that had been first envisioned by Brzezinski. Indeed, it is possible that, just as fear of the Soviet Union brought Western Europe to the Treaty of Rome in 1957, fear of Japan has brought Europe to EC 92 and the initiative for a single market. In this view, a great advantage of the initiative for a single market is that Europeans, who rightly or wrongly deeply distrust the Japanese, can continue the process of trade liberalization among themselves while holding non-European trading partners, but particularly the Japanese, at arm's length (Krugman 1991). If this is true, the substantive basis of Euro-Japanese relations is little changed over recent years.

It might be argued that if this is so, Japan has no one to blame but itself. While, with the exception of agriculture, Japan has removed most of its formal barriers against imported products, many allege that collusive arrangements by Japanese companies with the connivance of the Japanese government keep out virtually all imports for which a domestic substitute is available. Small wonder that, between the mid-1950s and late 1980s, the share of imported manufactures as a proportion of Japanese GNP stayed virtually constant, even as the share of imported manufactures in GNP trebled or quadrupled for every other major economy. Under such circumstances, it is argued that discrimination against Japanese imports is viewed as a provisional step taken to force a change in long-standing Japanese policies.[6] In this regard European practices may differ hardly at all from U.S. policies. Today, protective barriers such as voluntary restraint agreements (VRAs) restrict as much as 40 percent of all Japanese exports to the United States (Tsushosangyosho 1991).

Any real assessment of European, U.S., or Japanese culpability for the failure of trilateralism is highly complex. Such assessments are made particularly complex by the interdependence of barriers between markets. European discrimination against Japanese products surely improves the performance of U.S. firms relative to Japanese firms in the European market. The superior performance of U.S. firms in the European market relative to their performance in the Japanese market is then taken as prima facie evidence of Japanese discrimination against U.S. firms, which in turn is used as justification for U.S. discrimination against Japanese products.[7]

6. Typical statements in such a vein include Fallows 1989 and Johnson 1989. They find ready echoes in the continuing stream of statements by French Prime Minister Edith Cresson. For a contrary view, see Saxonhouse 1986 and 1989.

7. Congressman Richard Gephardt has regularly used U.S. performance in the European market as evidence that the Japanese compete unfairly in their home market (Nakajima 1991).

In the next section, the history of European discrimination against Japanese imports will be examined. Then an effort will be made to estimate the extent to which trilateral trade between Japan, the EC, and the United States has been distorted. Finally, the significance for the single market initiative and the future character of the global economy will be examined.

Japan, Europe, and GATT

While concern that Japanese economic progress might threaten U.S. prosperity is relatively new, European concern about Japanese economic might has remained quite real since at least the early 1930s, when Japan overturned 150 years of Lancashire dominance of global textile markets (Robertson 1990). It was not surprising, therefore, that Japan's admission as a contracting party to GATT in 1955 was highly controversial. Fourteen countries, including Belgium, France, the Netherlands, and the United Kingdom, that together accounted for 40 percent of Japan's exports to GATT members, invoked Article 35 (which allows member states to refuse to have their relations with another member state governed by GATT) against Japan (Hazumi and Ogura 1972). Among the major trading nations, only Canada, the Federal Republic of Germany, Italy, the Scandinavian countries, and the United States accepted Japan as a full member of GATT and gave it most favored nation status. Even among these countries, with the exception of the United States, all maintained hundreds of formal quantitative restrictions against particular Japanese products (Tsushosangyosho 1956). While the United States was alone in observing the letter of GATT in its relations with Japan, it was not above asking the Japanese government to voluntarily restrain the export of dozens of Japanese commodities (Komiya 1972).

Japan's experience during these years was unique. It is doubtful whether any other country has been subjected to the degree of discrimination within the GATT framework that Japan faced, particularly from its European trading partners. These restrictions on Japanese access to overseas markets were rarely a response to Japanese trade barriers. Rather, as Gardner Patterson noted a quarter-century ago, they reflected a fear of Japanese competition.

> Underlying these [fears] was the knowledge that Japan was a country with a large and talented population relative to its other factors of production, . . . that Japan just imports huge amounts of food and raw materials. . . . Japan was therefore seen as almost certain to be a particularly aggressive, international competitor in labor intensive manufactured goods. (Patterson 1966, 275)

In the years since 1955, the centerpiece of Japan's international diplomacy has always been to remove or mitigate discriminatory treatment of

Japanese exports. These efforts first began to bear fruit in 1963, when the United Kingdom ceased to apply Article 35 to Japan. Other European countries followed the United Kingdom's lead and, by 1972, among Western European countries, only Austria, Ireland, and Portugal still invoked Article 35 against Japan.

This did not mean, however, that most European countries had ceased discriminating against Japanese exports. Invariably, as a condition for ceasing Article 35 treatment of Japan, European countries were able to extract Japan's acquiescence to continued discrimination, both formal and informal, against its exports. Most European countries were only willing to cease applying Article 35 to Japan if Japan agreed not to use GATT proceedings even if these countries continued to discriminate against Japanese products (Shinkai 1972). In consequence, it is not surprising that, as late as the mid-1970s, member states of the European Community and the European Free Trade Association continued to maintain 108 special quantitative restrictions against Japanese products (Sazanami 1972). In addition to these formal restrictions, during these years European governments had also asked Japan to voluntarily restrict the export of more than 200 products (Komiya 1972).

Gerald Curzon and Victoria Curzon wrote in 1976 that, when Japanese wage levels approached European and North American levels, discrimination against Japan would cease. This has proven to be a poor prediction. While Japanese wage levels now exceed those of most European countries, discrimination against Japanese products continues. Many of the quantitative restrictions on Japanese products in place in the 1970s remain in force today or have been removed only during the past two years. Today, lack of reciprocity has replaced social dumping as the primary justification for discrimination against Japan.

Overlaying older restrictive practices, new protective measures have been taken in Europe against Japanese trade in the 1980s. Additional products, particularly in the electronics industry, have had their access to European markets curtailed. Some of this has come about as a result of specific restrictions, either formal or informal, against particular products by one or another European country. In other cases, access to the EC market as a whole has been curbed by the aggressive use of antidumping statutes. Attempts by the Japanese to mitigate the force of these restrictions by producing in Europe have been countered by new, onerous local content requirements.

Distortions in Trilateral Trade

In light of the preceding discussion, it is highly desirable to have some measure of the extent to which trade among the EC, Japan, and the United States is distorted by trade barriers. As my earlier discussion makes clear, such barriers can be of European, U.S., and/or Japanese origin. Whatever the barriers may be, it is clear that, except for selected agricultural commodities and some processed foods and foreign products, tariffs are now very low in all these markets and are unlikely to be a significant source of distortion for the pattern of trilateral trade (Saxonhouse and Stern 1989).

Measuring the impact of the nontariff barriers, however, can be difficult (Saxonhouse and Stern 1989). An obvious approach is to measure the price impact or quantity impact of such barriers against some barrier-free reference point. For price impact, for example, the prices of Japanese goods in the European market could be compared with prices of these same goods in some barrier-free market. While conceptually simple, such strictly comparable price data can be extremely difficult to obtain, even for a very limited number of products.[8] And as difficult as finding comparable price data might be, finding comparable quantity data is even more difficult.

In the absence of a natural reference point, some alternative, artificial benchmark needs to be constructed. This requires that a model of trade structure be elaborated. With such a model it is possible to make an estimate of what trade might be in the absence of special discriminatory barriers. These estimates can then be compared with the pattern of trade that does exist. The model that will be used to make such estimates can explain both cross-country and cross-commodity net and gross trade by making allowances for economies of scale and monopolistic competition.[9]

Assume that all manufactured goods are differentiated by country of origin. Given the same homothetic preferences usually assumed in empirical work making use of Heckscher-Ohlin-style trade models, each economy will consume identical proportions of each good.[10] This means that country j's export of good i to country k will be given by

$$X_{ik}^j = S_k Q_{ij} , \tag{1}$$

where $X_{ik}^j \equiv$ export of variety j of good i to country k, $Q_{ij} \equiv$ production of good i in country j, $\Pi_k \equiv \sum_i Q_{ik} \equiv$ GNP of country k,[11] $\Pi \equiv \sum_k \Pi_k \equiv$ global GNP, and $S_k \equiv \Pi_k / \Pi \equiv$ share of country k in global GNP.

---

8. Japan's Ministry of International Trade and Industry and the U.S. Department of Commerce have attempted to collect such data for more than 100 commodities in an effort to measure the impact of Japanese trade barriers on the access of U.S. and European goods to the Japanese market. To date, the effort has yielded only mixed results (Saxonhouse 1992).

9. The model presented here is an extension to bilateral trade of work presented in Saxonhouse 1989.

10. The use of Heckscher-Ohlin-style trade models is discussed in great detail in Leamer 1984.

11. The properties of Π, the GNP function, are described in more detail in Saxonhouse and Stern 1989.

$$S_k = \frac{\Pi_k}{\Pi} = \frac{\sum\limits_{s} W_{sk} L_{sk}}{\sum\limits_{i} \bar{Q}_i}, \tag{2}$$

where $L_{sk} \equiv$ endowment of factor of production s in economy k, $W_{sk} \equiv$ rental for factor of production s in economy k, and $\bar{Q}_i \equiv \sum\limits_{k} Q_{ik} \equiv$ global production of good i.

Following the approach taken in Heckscher-Ohlin analyses, if factor price equalization is assumed, then, by Hotelling's lemma, if Π_j is differentiated,[12]

$$Q_{ij} = \sum_{s=1}^{K} R_{is} L_{sj}, \tag{3}$$

where R_{is} is a function of parameters of Π_j and output prices, which are assumed to be constant.

Substituting equations 2 and 3 into equation 1, we get

$$X_{ik}^j = \sum_{s=1}^{K} \sum_{r=1}^{K} B_{isr} L_{sj} L_{rk}, \qquad i = 1, \ldots, N, \tag{4}$$

where B_{isr} are functions of Π_j and Π_k and where output prices will be constant under the assumptions already made. Equation 4 is a factor-endowment-based version of the gravity equation, which has been used for years as a framework for estimating bilateral trade relationships (Anderson 1979). Plausibly, it explains bilateral trade flows by the interaction between exporter and importer factor endowments. Alternatively, if equation 1 is first divided through by Π_k before equations 2 and 3 are substituted into it, we get export shares as a simple linear function of exporter factor endowments:

$$\frac{X_{ik}^j}{\Pi_k} = \sum_{s=1}^{K} B_{isr}^* L_{sj}, \qquad i = 1, \ldots, N. \tag{5}$$

---

12. The GNP function, Π, has been defined to allow for differentiated products and economies of scale. Following the approach taken by Helpman and Krugman 1985, this can be done by including optimal firm scale in Π_j. Provided optimal firm scale is small relative to market size, change in industry output can be achieved by changes in the number of firms in the industry. Firms are assumed to be identical. This means that at the industry level there will be constant returns to scale.

The structure embodied in equations 4 and 5 results from relaxing many of the strictest assumptions of the Heckscher-Ohlin model in order to incorporate hitherto neglected phenomena in a bilateral trade model. Still further relaxation is possible. For example, suppose that the assumption of strict factor price equalization across countries is dropped. Suppose, rather, that international trade equalizes factor prices only when factor units are normalized for differences in quality. For example, observed international differences in the compensation of ostensibly unskilled labor may be accounted for by differences in labor quality.[13] Instead of equations 4 and 5 we get

$$X_{ik}^j = \sum_{s=1}^{K} \sum_{r=1}^{K} B_{isr} a_{sj} a_{rk} L_{sj} L_{rk}, \qquad\qquad i = 1, \ldots, N, \qquad (4')$$

and

$$\frac{X_{ik}^j}{\Pi_k} = \sum_{s=1}^{K} B_{isr}^* a_{sj} L_{sj}, \qquad\qquad\qquad (5')$$

where $a_{sj} \equiv$ quality of factor s in country j.

Estimation Procedures

Equations 4 and 5' can be estimated for N commodity groups and J countries using cross-country data. For example, the term a_{sj} is not directly observable but can be estimated from equation 5'. Formally, the estimation of equation 5' with a_{sj} differing across countries and unknown is a multivariate, multiplicative errors-in-variable problem. Instrumental variable methods will allow consistent estimation of B_{isr}^*. For any given cross-country sectoral equation, a_{sj} will not be identified. In particular, for the specification adopted in equation 5', however, at any given time there are N cross-sections that contain the identical independent variables. This circumstance can be exploited to permit consistent estimation of a_{sj}.[14] Since the same error will recur in equation after

---

13. This was first pointed out by Leontief 1956 as a possible explanation for the empirical failure of the simple Heckscher-Ohlin model.

14. The approach taken here is analogous to the two-step "jackknife" procedure first proposed in Guilkey and Schmidt 1973. As an example of the approach taken here, let $a_{sj} = 1 + a'_{sj}$, assuming $E(a'_{sj}) = 0$. Using instrumental variable techniques in the presence of multiplicative errors allows consistent estimates of the B_{isr}^*. Using these estimates, for each economy, an $N(J - 1)X1$ vector (v_i) of the net trade residuals can be formed. Consistent estimates of the quality terms can be obtained from

$$(B_{isr}^* L_{sj})'(B_{isr}^* L_{sj})^{-1}(B_{isr}^* L_{sj})^1(v_i) .$$

TABLE 1. Country Sample for Empirical Work

Argentina	Malaysia
Australia	Mexico
Austria	Netherlands
Belgium	Nigeria
Brazil	Norway
Denmark	Philippines
Finland	Portugal
France	Singapore
Germany	South Korea
Greece	Spain
Honduras	Sri Lanka
India	Sweden
Indonesia	Switzerland
Ireland	Thailand
Israel	United Kingdom
Italy	United States
Japan	Yugoslavia

equation owing to the unobservable quality terms, it is possible to use this recurring error to obtain consistent estimates of the quality terms. These estimates of a_{sj} can then be used to adjust the factor endowment data in equations 4' and 5' to obtain more efficient estimates of B_{isr} and B_{isr}^*.[15]

Estimation of the Trade Model

Equations 4' and 5' are estimated with data taken from the 34 countries listed in table 1.[16] In addition, equations 4' and 5' are estimated for each of the 29 manufacturing sectors listed in table 2 for 1983. The six factor endowments used in this estimation include directly productive capital, labor, educational attainment, petroleum reserves, arable land, and transport resources.[17] The

---

15. Following Durbin 1954 and in common with two-stage least squares, the approach taken here uses synthetic instrumental variables. Factor endowments are ordered according to size, and rank is used as an instrument.

16. Since the factor endowment variables in equation 5' explain national development, there is no need to limit the sample used here to just the most advanced economies. In general, less-advanced economies impose more protection than the most-advanced economies. This development-related protection is explained by changes in the levels of the factor endowments. Typically, the higher the level of factor endowments, the less the protection.

17. Following the suggestion of Dixit and Norman 1980, transport costs are incorporated in the Heckscher-Ohlin framework by treating them as another factor of production. Transport costs are treated as proportional to the weighted average of country distance from potential trading partners. Countries are weighted in this calculation by their GNPs or GDPs. This particular approach allows the incorporation of transport costs within the bilateral Heckscher-Ohlin frame-

TABLE 2.   Trade Sectors in Sample

ISIC	Sector
311	Food manufacturing
312	Other food manufacturing
313	Beverage industries
314	Tobacco manufactures
321	Manufactures of textiles
322	Manufactures of wearing apparel except footwear
323	Manufactures of leather products except footwear and apparel
324	Manufactures of footwear except rubber or plastic
331	Manufactures of wood, wood and cork products, except furniture
332	Manufactures of furniture, fixtures, except primarily metal
341	Manufactures of paper and paper products
342	Printing, publishing, and allied industries
351	Manufactures of industrial chemicals
352	Manufactures of other chemical products
353	Petroleum refineries
354	Miscellaneous products of petroleum and coal
355	Rubber products
356	Plastic products not classified elsewhere
361	Pottery, china, and earthenware
362	Glass and glass products
369	Other nonmetallic mineral products
371	Iron and steel basic industries
372	Nonferrous metal basic industries
381	Fabricated metal products, except machinery and equipment
382	Manufactures of machinery except electrical
383	Electrical machinery, apparatus, appliances, and supplies
384	Transport equipment
385	Professional, scientific measuring, and control equipment
390	Other manufacturing industries

Heckscher-Ohlin equations 4' and 5' are assumed to hold up to an additive stochastic term.

Unlike the Heckscher-Ohlin net trade equations, the dependent variables in these bilateral equations will never be negative, but they will occasionally be zero. As most of the 29 equations to be estimated will contain some zero observations, equations 4' and 5' can be specified as a Tobit model.[18]

The results of estimating equation 4' using the a_s obtained from estimating equation 5' and excluding Japan from the sample are presented in tables 3

---

work without abandoning the possibility of factor price equalization up to some multiplicative constant.

18. The Tobit estimation methods used here for equations 4' and 5' are described in Greene 1981 and 1983, and Chung and Goldberger 1984.

TABLE 3.   The Estimation of $X^j_{ik} = \sum_{s=1}^{K} \sum_{r=1}^{K} B_{isr} a_{sj} a_{rk} L_{sj} L_{rk}$

ISIC	R^2	$F(35,957)$	ISIC	R^2	$F(35,957)$
311	.331	13.5**	354	.720	70.2**
312	.063	1.83**	355	.254	9.29**
313	.302	11.8**	356	.009	0.25
314	.389	17.4**	361	.174	5.75**
321	.220	7.7**	362	.323	13.0**
322	.515	29.0**	369	.266	9.89**
323	.505	27.8**	371	.511	28.5**
324	.592	39.6**	372	.538	31.8**
331	.174	5.75**	381	.336	13.8**
332	.283	10.8**	382	.454	22.7**
341	.605	41.8**	383	.161	5.24**
342	.544	32.6**	384	.195	6.61**
351	.491	26.3**	385	.197	5.87**
352	.017	0.472	390	.007	0.192
353	.891	223**			

** $\equiv$ significant at the .05 level, $F(35,957) = 1.43$.

and 4. In general, the results are interesting, occasionally surprising, but mostly plausible. For example, as noted in table 3, 26 out of 29 bilateral trade equations are statistically significant. These results mean it is possible to get a good explanation of the structure of bilateral trade when full advantage of the large degrees of freedom available is taken by including a large number of cross-country factor endowment interaction terms. Table 4 identifies the statistically significant role played by the interaction between exporter and importer factor endowments in explaining bilateral trade flows. The signs of these coefficients will reflect the degree of complementarity or substitutability between the various factors of production and their relative importance across sectors in the production processes.

Is Trilateral Trade Distorted?

The results presented in tables 3 and 4 are obtained by estimating equation 4' without using Japanese observations. Equation 4' has also been reestimated including Japan, but successively excluding U.S., French, German, U.K., and Italian observations. Using these estimated structures and successively varying Japanese, U.S., French, German, U.K., and Italian observations, tolerance intervals have been successively constructed for these countries' exports to many of their major trading partners. The constructed tolerance

TABLE 4. Number and Sign of Significant (.05) Coefficients on Factor Endowment Interaction Terms (B_{isr})

	CAPITAL$_{Exp}$		LABOR$_{Exp}$		EDUC$_{Exp}$		OIL$_{Exp}$		TRANS$_{Exp}$		LAND ARA$_{Exp}$	
	+	−	+	−	+	−	+	−	+	−	+	−
CAPITAL$_{Imp}$	6	15	11	9	10	5	12	7	8	5	14	7
LABOR$_{Imp}$	13	5	5	14	9	8	9	4	6	7	16	3
EDUC$_{Imp}$	15	3	12	10	7	11	10	6	6	3	9	6
OIL$_{Imp}$	8	7	8	3	11	6	3	13	4	7	7	10
TRANS$_{Imp}$	6	3	7	7	9	7	5	9	4	11	4	6
LAND ARA$_{Imp}$	11	4	17	5	11	4	6	11	5	6	7	12

Note: The rows index the factor endowments of importers. The columns index the factor endowments of exporters. The cells indicate how many significant coefficients of each sign are found for the associated interaction terms in the 29 estimated equations.

360   Singular Europe

TABLE 5. Extreme Observations on Japanese Exports

ISIC	Belgium	France	Italy	U.K.	Germany	Netherlands	U.S.
311	−1.61	−3.25**	−4.08**	−1.51	−2.78**	−1.68	−2.12
312	−1.48	−3.78**	−2.42	−1.23	−3.12**	−2.94**	−1.98
313	−2.41	−1.92	−0.98	−0.63	−1.15	−3.62**	−1.52
314	−3.15**	−1.63	−0.62	−0.51	−1.02	−0.06	0.23
321	−1.10	0.28	0.47	0.63	−1.02	−2.67**	−1.14
323	−0.63	−0.39	0.51	−0.68	0.45	0.23	−0.71
324	−3.23**	−0.41	−1.61	−1.23	−0.92	−0.14	0.23
331	−0.23	−3.85**	−1.06	−1.81	−2.96**	−0.42	0.13
332	−0.67	−2.12	−2.98**	−1.22	0.13	−0.98	2.63**
341	1.14	−1.60	−0.23	−1.34	−2.61**	−0.62	−1.01
351	−0.31	−0.34	−3.76**	−0.36	−1.63	−2.14	−0.26
352	−0.26	−0.91	−3.34**	−0.64	−0.61	−1.24	0.12
353	0.19	−0.83	−2.62**	−2.99**	−2.61**	−2.84**	−0.25
355	−0.43	−1.04	−2.84**	−0.28	−1.24	−1.69	2.91**
356	0.26	−0.67	−0.98	−0.61	−0.28	−0.93	0.03
361	0.34	0.29	−0.81	−0.94	0.45	0.61	2.98**
362	−0.14	−0.67	−0.03	−0.21	−0.18	0.40	−0.09
369	−0.79	0.98	−3.98**	−2.31	−0.64	−2.47	−0.93
371	0.27	−1.44	−1.93	−1.30	−1.58	−0.70	3.23**
372	−3.14**	−2.74**	−2.87**	0.60	−1.36	−2.81**	2.69**
381	−1.71	−2.23	−3.62**	−1.58	−1.58	−1.94	2.68**
383	−1.80	−1.46	−3.31**	−1.05	0.23	0.64	2.84**
384	−1.27	−2.84**	−4.32**	−1.52	−0.46	−0.98	2.23
385	−0.23	0.14	−0.63	−0.50	−0.14	0.01	−0.18
390	1.11	−0.28	0.44	−0.26	−0.71	0.98	−0.23

** ≡ actual value is outside tolerance interval, $T(.99, .99, .957) = 2.51$.

intervals indicate, with a probability of .99, that .99 of a univariate normal population will be found within the interval (Christ 1966). Observed exports are then compared with these tolerance intervals. Observations that fall outside these tolerance intervals are considered evidence of trade distortion. The test statistics for these comparisons are reported in tables 5 through 8.

The findings for Japanese exports to the European Community are striking when compared with Japanese exports to the United States. In some thirty instances, Japanese exports to the European Community appear lower than what might have been expected, given Japan's economic characteristics. In each of these cases, actual Japanese exports to the EC are below the lower limit of the tolerance interval. In no instance are Japanese exports to the EC above the upper limit of the tolerance interval. In sharp contrast, in no instance are actual Japanese exports to the United States below the lower limit of the tolerance interval. Indeed, in seven instances, Japanese exports are above the upper limit of the tolerance interval.

TABLE 6.   Extreme Observations on U.S. Exports

ISIC	Belgium	France	Italy	U.K.	Germany	Japan
311	−0.17	−0.95	−1.62	−0.23	−0.95	2.95**
312	−0.35	−0.25	−3.52**	−0.45	−1.66	3.62**
313	−1.22	−2.81**	−0.87	0.65	−0.54	1.54
314	0.74	−0.58	0.08	0.47	0.94	−2.71**
321	−0.06	0.51	−0.33	−1.27	0.55	0.92
323	0.61	0.88	−0.71	0.18	1.27	−4.15**
324	−1.02	−0.91	−0.62	1.85	−0.62	−2.91**
331	0.54	−0.75	−1.44	−0.80	0.69	−3.15**
332	0.57	0.62	−1.02	2.31	0.78	−0.62
341	0.71	−1.12	−0.25	−0.15	0.03	−2.75**
351	2.61**	3.15**	1.43	0.98	−0.66	3.60**
352	3.11**	−0.25	−0.74	−1.92	−1.28	3.62**
353	0.79	−0.61	−0.43	0.34	−0.18	2.74**
355	−1.62	0.96	−0.79	−1.85	−0.92	−1.78
356	0.77	−1.25	−0.67	0.95	−0.34	−1.51
361	−0.43	−1.70	−0.48	−0.09	−0.97	−1.98
362	1.52	−0.31	−0.51	0.62	0.28	−1.15
369	0.75	1.85	0.69	1.65	1.14	−0.52
371	−3.08**	−1.15	−4.15**	1.52	−2.15	0.50
372	1.44	−3.15**	−1.62	−2.93**	1.19	2.58**
381	1.27	−2.36	−3.85**	0.80	−3.11**	1.20
382	3.36**	0.21	0.67	3.14**	−4.08**	−3.61**
383	3.71**	1.84	1.59	1.17	−2.54**	1.09
384	−1.42	−0.99	−2.66**	−0.62	0.52	−1.78
385	2.62**	0.53	3.51**	2.74**	−0.41	−0.88
390	2.82**	0.71	0.25	1.12	2.77**	1.15

** ≡ actual value is outside tolerance interval, $T(.99, .99, .957) = 2.51$.

What about the exports of European countries to Japan? Remembering that the export performance of four European countries to the Japanese market is being evaluated, there are only 12 instances where actual European exports to Japan are below the lower limit of the tolerance interval. There are also 4 instances where European exports to Japan are actually above the upper limit of the tolerance interval. On net, Europe should be getting more goods into the Japanese market than it has been, but a mutual removal of all barriers, formal and informal, to trade in manufactured goods would probably lead to an increase in the European trade deficit with Japan.

These results also supply some limited evidence for the view that Euro-Japanese trade problems may be exacerbating U.S.-Japanese relations. Not only is Japan selling more in the U.S. market, the United States sells more in the European market than might otherwise be expected. At the same time, the United States is selling less to Japan than might be expected, given the

362   Singular Europe

TABLE 7. Extreme Observations on French and German Exports

	France		Germany	
ISIC	Japan	U.S.	Japan	U.S.
311	0.48	−1.56	0.38	1.12
312	−0.87	−1.81	0.53	−0.79
313	−0.07	−1.68	−0.04	−0.35
314	0.15	1.80	0.98	−1.48
321	−0.55	−0.59	−1.51	−1.12
323	−2.97**	0.62	−1.80	0.53
324	−3.55**	1.41	−2.66**	−0.61
331	−1.61	0.87	−3.14**	1.91
332	−0.91	0.68	0.23	0.92
341	−0.14	0.92	0.97	−0.71
351	−0.36	−0.21	3.15**	2.63**
352	0.91	0.59	3.62**	2.50
353	0.51	−0.91	0.66	−0.61
355	−0.53	0.85	0.48	−0.71
356	0.77	−1.57	0.98	−0.01
361	0.72	−2.14	−0.23	0.33
362	−0.07	0.94	−2.15	−1.89
369	0.54	0.71	−1.90	1.92
371	1.66	1.97	0.60	−0.77
372	1.74	−1.53	1.17	−3.74**
381	0.95	0.42	2.04	2.78**
383	−2.95**	2.63**	−1.37	0.95
384	−1.43	−0.75	−1.14	2.23
385	−1.59	0.68	2.77**	2.53**
390	−0.72	0.33	−1.21	0.87

** ≡ actual value is outside tolerance interval, $T(.99, .99, .957) = 2.51$.

structure of its comparative advantage. Consistent with the original premise of trilateralism, Euro-Japanese economic relations may well be increasing the bilateral trade deficit between the United States and Japan.

Europe 1992 and Japan: Quantitative Restraints, Antidumping Regulations, and Rules of Origin

In light of the evidence just presented, Japanese concern about EC policies that have distinctively discriminated against it in the past may well have considerable substance. Nonetheless, in the context of reworking European Community trade policy in preparation for 1992, quite significant actions have been taken to remove longstanding quantitative restrictions on Japanese im-

TABLE 8. Extreme Observations on U.K. and Italian Exports

	United Kingdom		Italy	
ISIC	Japan	U.S.	Japan	U.S.
311	0.33	−1.16	0.45	2.15
312	−0.54	−1.00	0.32	−0.45
313	−0.98	−1.51	−0.62	−0.75
314	0.06	−1.12	−0.15	−1.52
321	2.71**	1.50	0.77	−1.98
323	−0.81	0.74	−0.68	0.76
324	−0.92	1.71	−0.94	−0.15
331	−0.11	−1.23	0.92	0.34
332	−0.35	0.85	1.60	−1.77
341	−0.67	−0.13	−0.61	2.15
351	0.21	−3.15**	−1.95	2.74**
352	−0.98	−3.45**	−1.78	1.50
353	−0.59	−3.62**	−1.52	−1.63
355	0.32	−1.46	−3.78**	1.88
356	1.86	0.67	−1.97	−1.05
361	0.02	0.59	−2.37	3.62**
362	0.68	−3.41**	−3.18**	−0.21
369	0.16	−0.71	0.75	0.03
371	−1.32	−2.70**	−4.42**	2.52**
372	0.77	−1.25	−1.52	0.95
381	−0.15	−1.63	−2.86**	1.63
383	0.91	0.15	−3.14**	−0.24
384	−1.57	−1.88	−4.81**	1.14
385	−0.96	−0.95	−0.56	−0.81
390	−3.63**	0.06	−0.92	2.61**

** ≡ actual value is outside tolerance interval, $T(.99, .99, .957) = 2.51$.

ports. Indeed, many of the quantitative restraints against Japan, first imposed when it joined GATT, are finally being eliminated. Of the 150 quantitative restraints against Japan still imposed by member states in 1989, almost 100 have been eliminated in the past two years (Tsushosangyosho 1991). Given their 1950s origin and Japan's structural change since then, many of these quotas, such as Italy's quota on Japanese raw silk, have long since ceased to be binding. Other quotas that have been eliminated are not nearly so quaint. For example, the elimination of Portugal's quotas on Japanese machine tools and Japanese scientific equipment might be expected to result in more imports from Japan.

While older formal barriers, which have long been the target of Japanese economic diplomacy, are being eliminated, there is concern that new protective mechanisms have been developed to take their place. Most of this concern has been centered on the EC's use of its antidumping system to restrain exports from Japan and other Asian countries.

The hallmark of the EC's antidumping system has been its lack of transparency. Unlike U.S. practice, the EC can treat as confidential the antidumping data submissions of complaining parties, meaning that representatives of other interested parties may be denied access to the information used against them. Unlike the U.S. system, the EC system gives its administering agency (the Commission) considerable discretion in deciding antidumping cases. In practice, there is relatively little in the judicial review procedures of the European Court of Justice that limits this discretion. The Court has shown little interest in recent years in assessing the quality of the confidential information used by the Commission in making its determinations (Hindley 1988).

Quite apart from the traditional lack of transparency in the Commission's proceedings, amendments to the antidumping regulation have further inhibited Japanese access to the EC market. In particular, amendments were adopted in July, 1988, that codify previous Commission practice and require that the substantial marketing, advertising, distribution, and after sales services costs associated with the introduction of a product in a new market be reflected in any price calculation made in the Commission's antidumping proceedings (Vermulst 1987).

While changes in the EC's procedures have made it increasingly easy to use the antidumping system against Japanese competition, there has been increasing concern at the Commission about the effectiveness of this policy instrument. New amendments have been adopted to ensure that the desired impact is achieved. One amendment, also adopted in July, 1988, requires that any antidumping duty imposed be fully passed through to EC consumers. It also makes it much easier to initiate an investigation where it is alleged that this is not happening.

Of more concern to the Commission than the lack of full pass-through has been the increasing propensity of Japanese firms to avoid the antidumping duties levied on them by producing in Europe. In June, 1987, the EC amended its antidumping regulation so as to extend antidumping duties to foreign companies producing in Europe, if the company had been previously found to be dumping and EC content in production was less than 40 percent. This amendment allows the extension of antidumping penalties to parts imported for such production, even where no antidumping finding has been made for such parts (Lee and Herzstein 1989). This amendment has also allowed, for example, the extension of antidumping duties to imported goods produced by Japanese companies in the United States. In February, 1987, the EC imposed antidumping duties on photocopiers imported from a California plant owned by a Japanese company that had previously been charged with dumping in Europe photocopiers produced by the company in Japan.

As early as 1988, Japan complained to GATT about the anticircumvention amendments to the EC antidumping rules. In March, 1990, the GATT panel upheld Japan's complaint, finding that the EC's practices discriminated against foreign companies in Europe (Tsushosangyosho 1991). The EC has since allowed the GATT panel report to be adopted, but it has also deferred any change in its practices until the conclusion of the Uruguay Round.

Community-wide Quantitative Restraints for 1992

While the EC has worked to ensure that individual member states drop their restrictions on imports from Japan by 1993, in some important instances these individual restrictions are being replaced by Community-wide restraints. The most important example of this is in automobiles. Over the summer of 1991, the Commission and Japan agreed to a seven-year transition for removing restrictions on access to the European automobile market. The agreement assumes European demand for automobiles of 15.10 million units in 1999. It is forecast that 1.20 million units of this demand will be met by automobiles made in Japan. It is expected that an additional 1.23 million units will be supplied by Japanese-owned plants in Europe. The agreements also include country-specific export forecasts. It is expected that, in 1999, Japan will export 150,000 units to a 2.85 million unit French market, 138,000 to a 2.6 million unit Italian market, 79,000 to a 1.475 million unit Spanish market, 23,000 to a 275,000 unit Portuguese market, and 190,000 to a 2.7 million unit British market.

The agreement finally adopted allows for its continual revision as better information about future supply and demand becomes available. EC and Japanese officials are to meet twice a year to review rolling, three-year forecasts for the European market and to adjust import targets accordingly. How this adjustment will be made remains an issue. The Japanese earlier rejected a French proposal that would have given them a disproportionately small share of any increase in demand and would have required disproportionately large cuts in Japanese imports in the event of a downturn in demand.

The agreement explicitly states that there will be "no restrictions on Japanese investment or on the free circulation of its products in the Community." What is not spelled out is whether and by how much Japanese export targets will be cut by the agreement as Japanese transplant production increases over and above what is currently allowed in the 1999 projections. Before very long, this will be an issue of considerable substance because the future transplant production currently assumed in the agreement is well below what is expected by most informed observers. British trade officials project that Japanese transplants will build 1 million units in Britain and a total of 2 million units in the EC as a whole by 1999. Uncertainty about how this agreement will operate in practice may discourage future investment by Japanese automobile companies in Europe. This may happen at the same time that many member states and localities throughout Europe are encouraging further Japanese investment.

Reciprocal Access and the Joint Declaration

As Europe remakes its economic arrangements in the interest of creating a single, unified European market, increasing stress has been placed on allowing Japanese access to the market only insofar as reciprocal access is granted to European firms in Japan. While this issue has been framed most sharply for financial services, it underlies much more general concerns about the future of EC-Japanese relations. What reciprocal access might mean in the presence of substantial differences between economic institutions in the EC and Japan remains a matter of great controversy (Bhagwati 1991). The substantial publicity given the remarks on the character of the Japanese economy by French Prime Minister Edith Cresson underlines this concern.

Japanese diplomacy, while seeking to maintain and expand access for Japanese goods and investments in European markets, has also worked to broaden relationships with the EC. This is an effort to add a political and diplomatic dimension to what has been mostly an acrimonious trade dialogue. This effort has recently borne fruit with a joint declaration of common interests signed in July, 1991. As previously mentioned, the joint declaration aims to elevate EC-Japanese relations to the status of the relationships that both the EC and Japan maintain with the United States. Despite a 50 percent increase in the Japanese trade surplus with the EC to $18.5 billion during the first six months of 1991, there was no mention (in the declaration) of any need for reducing the imbalance in EC-Japanese trade flows. Rather, both sides note their "resolve for equitable access to their respective markets and removing obstacles, whether structural or other, impeding the expansion of trade and investment on the basis of comparable investment opportunities" (Kojima 1991).

Finale

The member states of the European Community have a long history of discrimination against Japanese products. Complicating U.S. economic relations, European trade policy certainly differs in degree, if not in kind, from U.S. trade policy toward Japan. While concerns about social dumping first motivated much of this discrimination, in recent years it has been sustained by the widely held belief that many unfair, if informal, barriers bar some European firms from participating in the Japanese market.

As Europe moves to create a unified internal market, the forms of discrimination against Japan are changing. While older quantitative restrictions maintained by individual states are being removed, the administration and increasingly broad application of Europe's antidumping regulations have posed special, new problems for Japanese firms seeking to take advantage of the unified European market. Both in the 1987 and 1989 amendments to its antidumping regulations and in the automobile agreement it recently negotiated with Japan, the EC, unlike the United States, has shown considerable interest in restricting the access not only of Japanese goods but also of Japanese investments.

REFERENCES

Allison, Graham. 1972. "American Foreign Policy and Japan." In *Discord in the Pacific*, ed. Henry Rosovsky, 7–46. Washington, D.C.: Columbia Books.

Anderson, James E. 1979. "A Theoretical Foundation for the Gravity Equations." *American Economic Review* 69:106–16.

Bhagwati, Jagdish. 1991. *The World Trading System at Risk*. Princeton: Princeton University Press.

Brzezinski, Zbigniew. 1972. "Japan's Global Engagement." *Foreign Affairs* 50:270–82.

Christ, Carl F. 1966. *Econometric Models and Methods*. New York: Wiley.

Chung, Ching-fan, and Arthur S. Goldberger. 1984. "Proportional Projections on Limited Dependent Variable Models." *Econometrica* 52:531–34.

Curzon, Gerald, and Victoria Curzon. 1976. "The Management of Trade Relations in the GATT." In *International Economic Relations in Western Countries*. London: Royal Institute of International Affairs.

Dixit, Avinash, and Victor Norman. 1980. *Theory of International Trade*. Cambridge: Cambridge University Press.

Durbin, James. 1954. "Errors in Variables." *Review of the International Statistical Institute* 22:23–32.

Fallows, James. 1989. "Containing Japan." *Atlantic Monthly*, May, 40–54.

Greene, William H. 1981. "On the Asymptotic Bias of the Ordinary Least Squares Estimation of the Tobit Model." *Econometrica* 49:505–13.

Greene, William H. 1983. "Estimation of Limited Dependent Variables by Ordinary Least Squares and Method of Moments." *Journal of Econometrics* 21:195–212.

Guilkey, D. K., and P. Schmidt. 1973. "Estimation of Seemingly Unrelated Regressions with Autoregressive Errors." *Journal of the American Statistical Association* 68:642–47.

Hazumi, Mitsuhiko, and Kazuo Ogura. 1972. "Tai-nichi sabetsu mondai no ippanteki heikei." In *Nihon no hikanzei boeki shoheki*, ed. Kiyoshi Kojima and Ryutaro Komiya. Tokyo: Nihon keizai shimbunsha.

Hellman, Donald C. 1976. "Toward a New Realism." In *China and Japan: A New Balance of Power*, ed. Donald C. Hellman, 1–17. Lexington, Mass.: D. C. Heath.

Helpman, Elhanan, and Paul R. Krugman. 1985. *Market Structure and Foreign Trade*. Cambridge, Mass.: MIT Press.

Hindley, Brian. 1988. "Dumping and the Far East Trade of the European Community." *World Economy* 11:445–64.

Johnson, Chalmers. 1989. "Their Behavior, Our Policy." *National Interest*, Fall, 17–24.

Jorgenson, Dale W., and Mieko Nishimizu. 1978. "U.S. and Japanese Economic Growth, 1952–1974: An International Comparison." *Economic Journal* 88:707–26.

Kojima, Akira. 1991. "Japan-EC Declaration Calls for Equitable Trade." *Nikkei Weekly*, July 27.

Komiya, Ryutaro. 1972. "Yushutsu jishu kisei." In *Nihon no hikanzei boeki shoheki*, ed. Kiyoshi Kojima and Ryutaro Komiya. Tokyo: Nihon keizai shimbunsha.

Krugman, Paul R. 1991. "The Move to Free Trade Zones." Photocopy.

Leamer, Edward E. 1984. *Sources of International Comparative Advantage*. Cambridge, Mass.: MIT Press.

Lee, William, and Robert Herzstein. 1989. "EC Dumping Law: A Growing Source of Trade Frictions." *1992: The External Impact of European Unification* (Washington, D.C.: Burraff Publications), 1 (July 28): 9–12.

Leontief, W. W. 1956. "Factor Proportions and the Structure of American Trade: Further Theoretical and Empirical Analysis." *Review of Economics and Statistics* 38:386–407.

Ministry of Finance Institute of Fiscal and Monetary Policy. 1991. *Financial Statistics of Japan*. Tokyo: Ministry of Finance.

Nakajima, A. 1991. "Proposed Restriction on Unilateral Retaliation Praised." *Nikkei Weekly*, December 28.

Nihon keizai kenkyu senta. 1972. *Sekai no no naka no nihon keizai*. Tokyo.

Patterson, Gardner. 1966. *Discrimination in International Trade: Policy Issues, 1945–1965*. Princeton: Princeton University Press.

President's Council of Economic Advisers. 1991. *Economic Report of the President 1991*. Washington, D.C.: U.S. Government Printing Office.

Robertson, Alex J. 1990. "Lancashire and the Rise of Japan, 1910–1937." *Business History* 32:87–105.

Saxonhouse, Gary R. 1972. "Employment, Imports, the Yen and the Dollar." In *Discord in the Pacific*, ed. Henry Rosovsky, 79–116. Washington, D.C.: Columbia Books.

Saxonhouse, Gary R. 1986. "Japan's Intractable Trade Surpluses in a New Era." *World Economy* 9:239–58.

Saxonhouse, Gary R. 1989. "Differentiated Products, Economies of Scale and Access to the Japanese Market." In *Trade Policies for International Competitiveness*, ed. Robert Feenstra, 145–74. Chicago: University of Chicago Press for the National Bureau of Economic Research.

Saxonhouse, Gary R. 1991. "Japan, SII and the International Harmonization of Domestic Economic Practices." *Michigan Journal of International Law* 12:450–69.

Saxonhouse, Gary R. 1992. "How Open is Japan: Comment." In *U.S. and Japan: Trade and Investment*, ed. Paul R. Krugman. Chicago: University of Chicago Press for the National Bureau of Economic Research.

Saxonhouse, Gary R., and Robert M. Stern. 1989. "An Analytical Survey of Formal and Informal Barriers to International Trade and Investment in the United States, Japan and Canada." In *Trade and Investment Relations among the United States, Canada, and Japan*, ed. Robert M. Stern, 293–353. Chicago: University of Chicago Press.

Sazanami, Yoko. 1972. "Kogyo seihin boeki ni tsuite no shiron." *Mita gakkai zasshi*, December.

Shinkai, Yoichi. 1972. "Wagakuni tsusho seisaku no kihon rinen." *Gendai keizai*, June.

Tsushosangyosho. 1956. *Nihon boeki no tenkai*. Tokyo: Shoko shupan.

Tsushosangyosho. 1991. *Tsusho hakusho heisei san-nen*. Tokyo.

Vermulst, Edwin A. 1987. *Antidumping Law and Practice in the United States and the European Communities: A Comparative Analysis*. Amsterdam: North-Holland.

Vogel, Ezra. 1979. *Japan as Number One: Lessons for the United States*. Cambridge, Mass.: Harvard University Press.

Zellner, Arnold. 1962. "An Efficient Method for Estimating Seemingly Unrelated Regressions and Tests for Aggregation Bias." *Journal of the American Statistical Association* 57:348–68.

Contributors

William James Adams is Arthur F. Thurnau Professor of Economics and Adjunct Professor of Law at the University of Michigan. The author of *Restructuring the French Economy: Government and the Rise of Market Competition since World War II* (1989) and the coeditor of *French Industrial Policy* (1986), he has been affiliated with Foreign Policy Studies at the Brookings Institution.

Severin Borenstein is Associate Professor of Economics at the University of California, Davis, where he also is Research Associate in both the Institute of Transportation Studies and the Institute of Governmental Affairs. Borenstein is Associate Director of the University of California Program on Workable Energy Regulation.

Bo Carlsson is William E. Umstattd Professor of Industrial Economics at Case Western Reserve University. He is currently directing a five-year, multidisciplinary research project on Sweden's technological system and future development potential.

Gunter Dufey is Professor of International Business and Finance at the University of Michigan Business School. His teaching and research interests comprise international financial markets and financial management in multinational corporations. He is currently on sabbatical leave in Tokyo at F.A.I.R., a research arm of the Japanese ministry of finance.

Dr. Reinhard Ellger is Research Fellow at the Max Planck Institute for Foreign and International Private Law, Hamburg. He has undertaken studies in the field of data protection in transborder data flows and international telecommunications law. Among his recent publications is *Der Datenschutz im grenzüberschreitenden Datenverkehr* (1990).

John H. Jackson is Hessel E. Yntema Professor of Law at the University of Michigan and former General Counsel to the U.S. Office of the Trade Representative. One of his latest books is *The World Trading System: Law and Policy of International Economic Relations* (1989).

Alexis Jacquemin is Professor of Economics at the Université Catholique de Louvain, and special adviser to the Forward Studies Unit of the President of the European Commission. The author of *The New Industrial Organization: Market Forces and Strategic Behavior* (1987), he is currently working on the driving factors shaping European socioeconomic development.

Frédéric Jenny is Professor of Economics at the Ecole Supérieure des Sciences Economiques et Commerciales (ESSEC) and General Counsel of France's Conseil de la Concurrence. He is the author of "French Competition Policy in Perspective," in *Competition Policy in Europe and North America* (1990).

Stephan Leibfried, sociologist and lawyer, is Professor of Social Policy and Social Administration at Bremen University's Center for Social Policy Research and a member of Special Research Unit 186 of the German National Science Foundation (DFG). His publications include "The United States and West German Welfare Systems: A Comparative Analysis," *Cornell International Law Journal* (1979).

Ernst-J. Mestmäcker is Professor of Law at the University of Hamburg, Director of the Max Planck Institute for Foreign and International Private Law, Hamburg, and erstwhile Chairman of Germany's Monopolkommission. The second edition of his *Kommentar zum Gesetz gegen Wettbewerbsbeschränkungen* (edited with Ulrich Immenga) was published in 1992.

Tommaso Padoa-Schioppa is Deputy Director General of the Banca d'Italia. The author of *Efficiency, Stability, and Equity: A Strategy for the Evolution of the Economic System of the European Community* (1989), he served as Secretary of the Delors Committee on Economic and Monetary Union (1989).

Gary R. Saxonhouse is Professor of Economics at the University of Michigan and Director of its Committee on Comparative and Historical Research on Market Economies (CCHROME). Saxonhouse has published widely on the structure and operation of the Japanese economy.

John D. Steinbruner is Director of Foreign Policy Studies, the Brookings Institution. He has most recently published (with William W. Kaufman) *Decisions for Defense: Prospects for a New Order* (1991).

William Wallace is Walter Hallstein Fellow in European Studies at St. Antony's College, Oxford. He is currently working on long-term trends in European integration, expanding on *The Transformation of Western Europe* (1990).

Joseph H. H. Weiler is Professor of Law at the University of Michigan and Director of the Academy of European Law at the European University Institute, Florence. He is currently a member of the Committee of Jurists that, at the request of the Institutional Affairs Committee of the European Parliament, is preparing a draft constitution for Europe.

Susan L. Woodward is Visiting Fellow in Foreign Policy Studies, the Brookings Institution. She is currently writing one book on the lessons of the Yugoslav civil war and another on the politics of the economic transitions in Eastern Europe.

Index

Abortion, 34
ACEC, 132
Acquisitions, 126, 142; banking, 192–93, 196, 197; and competition policy, 128, 129, 132, 136, 137. *See also* Joint ventures; Mergers
Act against Restraints of Competition, 83–84, 85
Adams, William James, 1–3, 7–10, 121–23, 137, 273–74
Adenauer, Konrad, 43, 44
Aer Lingus, 255
Aérospatiale, 94, 139
Africa, 276, 330, 343
African, Caribbean, and Pacific (ACP) countries, 330
Agriculture: and the changing international context, 276; and Euro-Japanese relations, 353; and GATT, 335–36, 337, 338, 344. *See also* Common Agricultural Policy (CAP)
Airbus, 276
Air France, 252, 255, 267
Airline industry, 251–69, 276. *See also* Air traffic control (ATC)
Air traffic control (ATC), 123, 252, 260
Albania, 139, 282; and democratic change, 319; and liberalizing trade, 306; refugees from, 318; and transport policy, 313; and the Yugoslav civil war, 318
Alenia, 94, 139
Alitalia, 255
Allison, Graham, 348
Alsatel v. Novasam, 80

Alsthom, 132
American Airlines, 254
America West Airlines, 254
Antidumping duties, 332–33, 338, 344, 352, 364–65
Antitrust policy. *See* Competition policy
Arms control, 276, 288; and cooperative security, 290–95; and weapons sales, 293, 294
Assent procedure, 14–15, 16
Association of European Airlines (AEA), 252, 256–57
Asylum policies, 40
Atlantic Alliance, 280, 282
Atlantic partnership, 275
AT&T (American Telephone and Telegraph Company), 94
Austria, 318; application of, for EC membership, 44; and banking in the EC, 173; and globalization, 173; industrialization in, 282; and Japan, 352
Austro-Hungarian empire, 277, 279
Automobile industry, 76, 273–74; and auto quotas, 331–32; and competition policy, 126, 131; and GATT, 339; and product differentiation, 159
Average plant size (APS) measures, 149–51, 152–56
Avions de Transport Régional (ATR), 139

Balkans, 277, 317
Baltic states, 279
Bank for International Settlements (BIS), 176, 178

DATE DUE

JUL 01 '92	
MAR 03 '94	
snap 3-9-94	
NOV 0 2 1994	
NOV ? ? 1994	
DEC 1 4 1994	
MAY 0 5 1999	

BRODART, INC.

Cat. No. 23-221